HUMAN-CENTERED *e*-BUSINESS

HUMAN-CENTERED *e*-BUSINESS

by

Rajiv Khosla
La Trobe University

Ernesto Damiani
Universita di Milano

William Grosky
University of Michigan

KLUWER ACADEMIC PUBLISHERS
Boston / Dordrecht / London

Distributors for North, Central and South America:
Kluwer Academic Publishers
101 Philip Drive
Assinippi Park
Norwell, Massachusetts 02061 USA
Telephone (781) 871-6600
Fax (781) 871-6528
E-Mail: < kluwer@wkap.com>

Distributors for all other countries:
Kluwer Academic Publishers Group
Post Office Box 322
3300 AH Dordrecht, THE NETHERLANDS
Telephone 31 78 6576 000
Fax 31 78 6576 254
E-Mail: < services@wkap.nl>

Electronic Services < http://www.wkap.nl>

Library of Congress Cataloging-in-Publication Data

Human-Centered e-Business
Rajiv Khosla, Ernesto Damiani and William Grosky
ISBN 1-4020-7442-5

Printed on acid-free paper.

Printed in United Kingdom by Biddles/IBT Global

TABLE OF CONTENTS

PREFACE

E-business has revolutionized the way organizations function today. From being just another channel a few years ago e-business has become a competitive necessity today. The Organization for Economic Cooperation and Development (OECD) predicts the size of e-Business to grow to US $ 1 trillion in 2003-5. This revolution or change in thinking can be traced along four dimensions. These are technology, competition, deregulation and customer expectations. The Internet technology has led to "death of distance", digitization of almost everything, and improvement in the information content of product and services. Along the competition dimension, customer orientation and service and global reach have become competitive imperatives. Deregulation of telecommunication industry and other industries, single currency zones and ever-changing business boundaries have further increased the potential for e-business. Finally, the changes along the first three dimensions have led to high customer sophistication and expectation. The demand for cost effective and convenient business solutions, high level of customization, and added customer value has led to change of focus from product-centric to customer-centric e-business systems. The customer-centric e-business systems are leading the development towards customer-centric market models as against product-centric market models , online data mining of users behavior, e-recruitment, customization of web sites, and interactive web-based applications. At another level, development of knowledge management systems represents customization, which is based on skill sets and tasks closely linked to the needs of the users or employees within an organization or wider communities

This book is about analysis, design and development of human-centered e-business systems, which cover applications in the above-mentioned areas. The applications employ a range of technologies including Internet, soft computing and intelligent agents. The book is relevant to practitioners with an information technology focus in business function areas like human resource management, marketing, banking and finance and cross-functional areas involving customer relationship management and enterprise resource planning. It is relevant to practitioners and researchers in information technology areas like e-business and e-commerce, knowledge management, human-centered systems, intelligent agents, soft computing, artificial intelligence, data mining, multimedia, and software engineering.

Human-centered e-business systems described in this book, among other aspects facilitate e-business analysis from a business professional's perspective and human-centered system design from a system development perspective. It does that by integrating research done in areas like e-business strategies and models, socio-technical information systems and work-oriented design, distributed and situated cognition in cognitive science, activity theory and psychological scales in psychology, semiotics in philosophy, problem solving ontologies and multi-agent systems in artificial intelligence, task based soft computing, component based software engineering, and information content based multimedia interfaces.

The book illustrates the benefits of the human-centered approach by describing work activity-centered e-business analysis of an intelligent e-sales recruitment application, integrating data mining technology with decision support model for profiling transaction behavior of internet banking customers, user-centered context dependent data organization using XML, user-centered decision support in knowledge management, optimizing the search process through human evaluation in an intelligent web-based interactive multimedia application. and multimedia-based user-centered interface design in medical diagnosis.

The book consists of three parts:

Part I: provides the motivation behind the book and introduces various e-business concepts and technologies. It then discusses the converging trends towards human-centeredness in e-business and other areas in information systems and computer science. This is followed by a detailed discussion on enabling theories in philosophy, cognitive science, psychology, and the work place, which contribute towards human-centered e-business system development. These converging trends and enabling theories are used as a foundation for developing a human-centered e-business system development framework and a Human-Centered Virtual Machine (HCVM).

Part II: describes applications of HCVM in areas like e-recruitment, customer relationship management and e-banking or Internet banking, e-commerce and knowledge management.

Part III: introduces the area of hypermedia information systems and hypermedia data modeling. It describes an application of intelligent soft computing agents based on human evaluation for a web-based identification of a missing person's clothing.

Part I is described through chapters 1, 2, 3, 4 and 5 respectively.

Chapter 1: outlines the impact of internet on organizations today and the converging trends towards human-centeredness in e-business and other related areas in information systems and computer science. It then describes the differences between a technology-centered approach and a human-centered approach to system development. The comparison is used to outline the criteria for human-centered systems development. The chapter also shows a correspondence between organizational levels and e-business architecture and applications described in the book.

Chapter 2: introduces the reader to various e-business concepts and technologies. The e-business concepts include types of e-business systems, e-business strategies and e-business models. The technologies described can be grouped under areas like Internet, intelligent systems, software engineering and multimedia.

Chapter 3: as the title suggests describes the converging trends towards human-centeredness in areas like e-business, intelligent systems, software engineering, multimedia data bases, enterprise modeling, data mining and human-computer interaction. The converging trends are followed by description of enabling theories for human-centered e-business system development in philosophy, cognitive science, psychology and workplace. The chapter ends with a discussion on these enabling theories and their contribution to the human-centered e-business framework developed in chapter 4.

Chapters 4 and 5: describe four components of the human-centered e-business system development framework at the conceptual and computational levels respectively. These four components are activity-centered e-business analysis, problem solving ontology, software transformation agent, and multimedia interpretation or multimedia based information presentation and interpretation. The four components are underpinned in human-centered criteria outlined in chapter 1, e-business strategies and e-business models described in chapter 2 and converging trends and enabling theories described in chapter 3.

At the computational level, a component based multi-layered Human-Centered Virtual Machine (HCVM) is realized through integration of activity-centered e-business analysis component, problem solving ontology component and the multimedia interpretation component with technology based models like, intelligent technology model, object-oriented model, agent model, distributed process model and XML/XTL (eXtensible Transformation Language) model. The five layers of the HCVM are used to development multi-agent e-business systems in chapters 6, 7, 8 and 9.

Part II is covered through chapters 6, 7, 8 and 9 respectively

Chapter 6: illustrates the application the activity-centered e-business analysis component, problem solving ontology component of the e-business system development framework described in an e-sales recruitment application. The chapter describes two intelligent models based on expert systems and adaptive clustering for on line behavior profiling, recruitment and benchmarking of sales and customer service personnel. .

Chapter 7: outlines various web-mining techniques employed for web content mining and web usage mining. It describes the application of HCVM in the customer relationship management area of Internet banking. It employs data mining techniques for profiling the transaction behavior of Internet banking customers, determining association between customer demographics and transaction behavior and several other useful associations.

Chapter 8: introduces the concept of context-dependent data management in human-centered e-commerce systems. It is followed by description of XML based context modeling and XML schema, and their integration with the client side context model based on HCVM. It includes a fuzzy agent based computation for flexible access to context information.

Chapter 9: outlines HCVM based human-centered multi-agent architecture for developing knowledge management systems with knowledge storing, knowledge indexing, knowledge sharing and decision support capabilities. It outlines components of a complex knowledge management system for knowledge sharing and decision support, which is aimed at a community of entrepreneurs, businessmen and government officials, enabling *Regional Innovation Leadership* (RIL).

Part III is described through chapters 10 and 11 respectively:

Chapter 10: discusses the basics of hypermedia information management. It examines the nature of multimedia data and the area of multimedia data modeling, followed by a discussion of content-based retrieval. The chapter outlines the need for bridging the semantic gap between the user and low level description of multimedia artifacts for multimedia applications. It covers several ways of modeling user semantics including relevance feedback and latent semantic indexing. HCVM based model of user semantics is also outlined.

Chapter 11: describes a user-centered Web based multimedia application for identifying a missing person's clothing before they went missing. The chapter is an illustration of relevance feedback humanization of soft computing agents like genetic algorithms, which optimize the search process based on human evaluation.

RAJIV KHOSLA
ERNESTO DAMIANI
WILLIAM GROSKY

ACKNOWLEDGEMENTS

The authors wish to acknowledge the support of several research students in Australia, Italy and the United States of America for completion of this work. The research students authors would like to acknowledge are Qiubang Li, Damian Francione, Damian Phillips, Petrus Usmanij Serena Nichetti, Giuliana Severgnini, Marco Degli Angeli and Mirco Polini.

The authors would also like to acknowledge the support provided by Victorian Partnership for Advanced Computing (VPAC), Melbourne, Australia for using their high performance computing facilities.

1 WHY HUMAN-CENTERED E-BUSINESS?

1.1 Introduction

In the last few years the Internet has had an enormous impact on businesses and consumers. Figure1.1 shows a comparison of adoption time of Internet as compared with other technologies like personal computer, radio and television. It has taken only four years for the number of Internet users to grow to 50 million compared to sixteen years for personal computer users and thirty-eight years for the radio. The brick-and-mortar companies have had to adapt not only with the pace of the technological change but also the disruptive affect of the Internet enabled e-commerce and e-business technologies. E-commerce and e-business have changed the way people live their lives and the way businesses operate. Many brick-and-mortar companies are still coming to terms with the pace of technological change and recognizing the true competitive advantage of e-business. However, given the technology-enabled nature of e-business, the e-business applications run a similar or higher risk than traditional business applications of being driven by technology-centeredness rather than human-centeredness or customer-centeredness. The stakes are higher than in traditional business applications because organizations embarking on e-commerce and e-business have been forced to look at ways to model customer or user's expectations from their businesses more explicitly as compared to the conventional business models in traditional commerce.

In this introductory chapter we firstly introduce the e-business and e-commerce concepts. We follow it with a brief overview of converging trends towards human-centeredness in a number of areas related to information technology including e-business, intelligent systems, software engineering, enterprise modeling and multimedia. In order to understand the meaning and implication of human-centeredness this chapter discusses the problems and issues with the technology-centered approach from a software development perspective and also in terms of the life cycle of technology-centered software products. We then outline the criteria for development of human-centered e-business systems. Finally, we show the correspondence between organizational levels and e-business architecture and applications described in this book

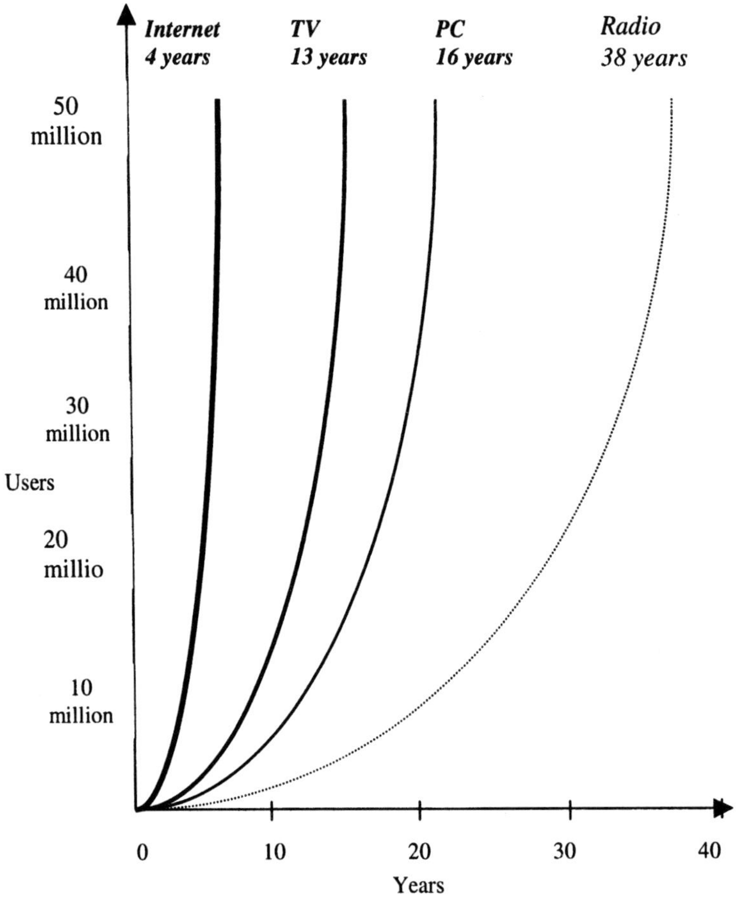

Figure 1.1: Comparison of Adoption Time of Internet with Other Technologies (adapted from Norris et. al. 2000)

1.2 e-Business and e-Commerce

Twenty-five years ago, most businesses often thought of telecommunications as telephone calls and paid little attentions to it. Today telecommunications has become a business necessity for business effectiveness and success. E-business and e-commerce are two recent business concepts, which cannot exist without telecommunications. E-business is the practice of performing and coordinating primary and secondary processes which add value to the internal value chain, supply chain and customer experience through extensive use of computer and communication technologies and computerized data.

Electronic Commerce (EC) is a part of e-business and can be broadly seen as the application of information technology and telecommunications to create trading networks where goods and services are sold and purchased, thus increasing the efficiency and the effectiveness of traditional commerce.

The Internet has introduced many new ways of trading, allowing interaction between groups that, due to limited resources or to remoteness, previously could not economically afford to trade with one another. These new ways of trading can be B2B (Business to Business), B2C (Business to Consumer), C2B (Consumer to Business), and C2C (Consumer to Consumer).

Whereas traditional commercial data interchange involved the movement of data from one computer to another, without user interaction, the new model for Web-based commerce introduced by the Internet is typically dependent on human intervention for EC transactions to take place.

Figure 1.2 shows the primary and secondary business activities in which e-business and e-commerce applications are being developed today.

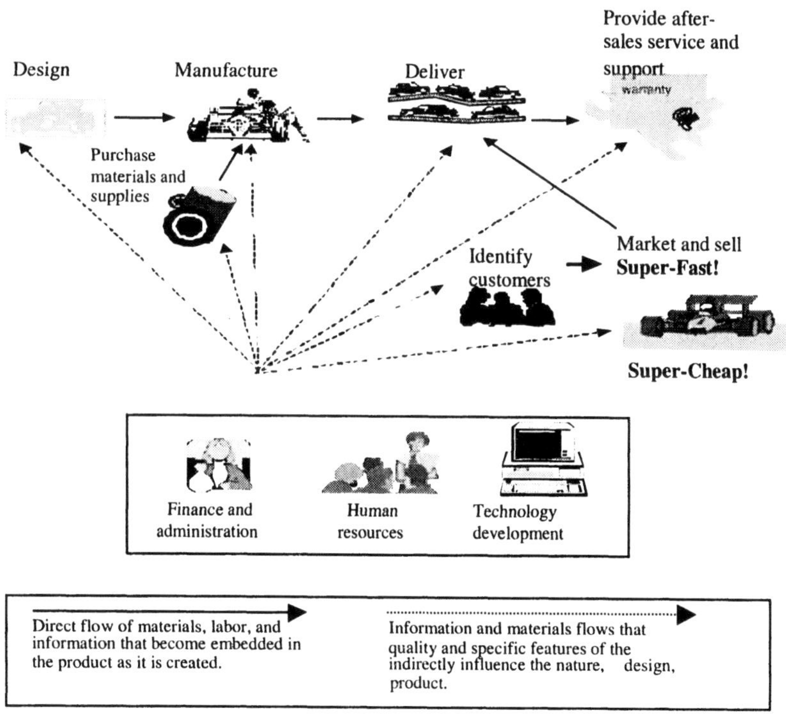

Figure 1.2: Primary and Secondary Business Activities

1.3 Converging Trends Towards Human-Centeredness

As can be seen from Figure 1.3, human-centeredness represents the latest stage of evolution of information technology. Figure 1.3 shows that human-centeredness has achieved different purposes or goals in different areas. For example, in e-business there has been a move towards user-centered market models from product-centered market models. Information technology is being used for customizing product and services and for achieving high level of customer satisfaction. In intelligent systems there have been efforts to humanize computational intelligence technologies (Takagi 2001, 2002) and develop technology independent practitioner-centered task-oriented architectures for construction of intelligent systems (Khosla et. al. 2000, 1997). The area of Human-Computer Interaction (HCI) has long being known for its emphasis

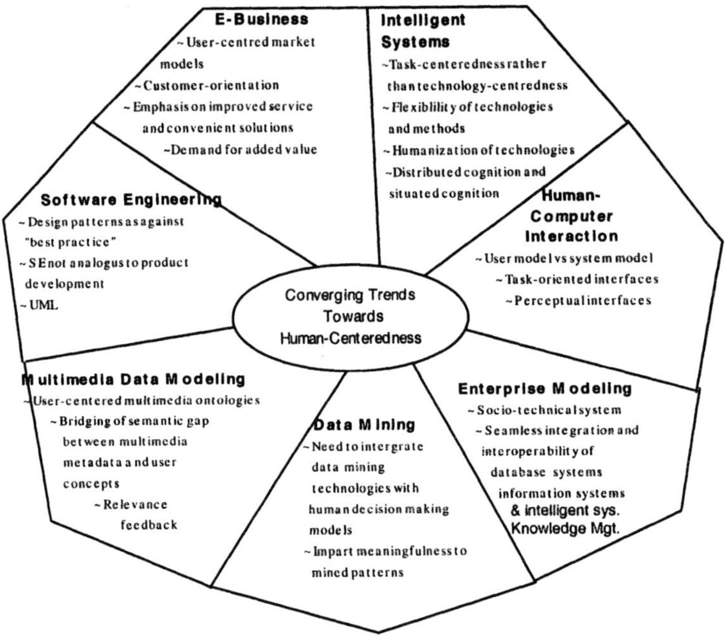

Figure 1.3: Converging Trends Towards Human-Centeredness

on human-centeredness. The HCI area has evolved from task-centered, perceptual and multimedia interfaces to sensory stimuli based interfaces. The area of software engineering has evolved from "best practice" concept to use of software design patterns employed successfully by practitioners in the field.

Further, today emphasis is on development of socio-technical information systems rather than purely technology-centered products. In areas like multimedia search, multimedia information retrieval the researchers are looking at ways to incorporate user-based semantics into the search process because of the interactive nature of the multimedia domain.

Finally, in order to impart meaningfulness to mined patterns from large databases and datawarehouses researchers are trying to integrate the data mining technology with decision making models of business managers. In the next section we look at the differences between technology-centered approach and human-centered approach from a software development perspective.

1.4 Technology-Centeredness vs Human-Centeredness

The technology-centered approach can be analyzed from a research perspective as well as from a marketing perspective. Most studies in computer science (and other science disciplines) can be seen as following technology-centered motto "Science Finds, Industry Applies and Man Conforms" (Chicago World Fair 1933). In other words, science invents new technologies, industry applies them for solving various problems and people or users are expected to comply with the nuances of the technology. This approach is also captured in Figure 1.4.

Thus in this technology–centered approach, technology is the prime driver in the system development process as shown in Figure 1.4. A technologist or a software developer armed with one or more technologies (e.g., object-oriented, neural network, etc.) models a software solution to a human problem.

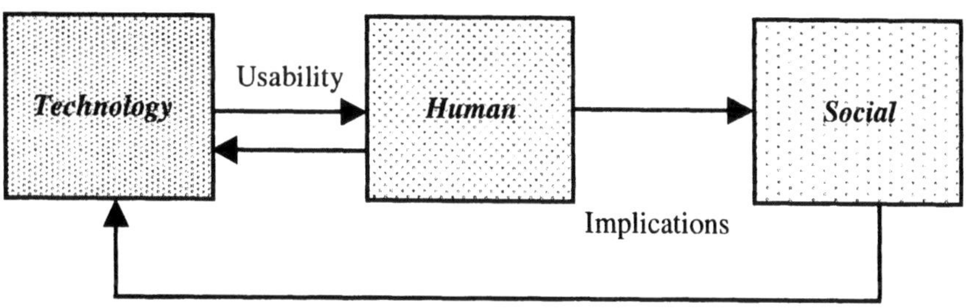

Figure 1.4: Technology-Centered Approach

The conceptualization of a problem domain in the technology-centered approach is largely based on system designer's perspective rather than the user's perspective (Figure 1.5). Once the technology-centered artifact is created it is connected to its users through user interfaces developed using usability engineering and human-computer interaction techniques. At this stage human-computer interaction and usability specialists play an active part in system interpretation. The technology-centered software system is handed over to the users who are provided with manuals (consisting of hundreds of pages) to get acquainted with its use. Over a period of time feedback from users (related to usability) and the social scientists (on social consequences of technology use) is employed to improve the future use of technology.

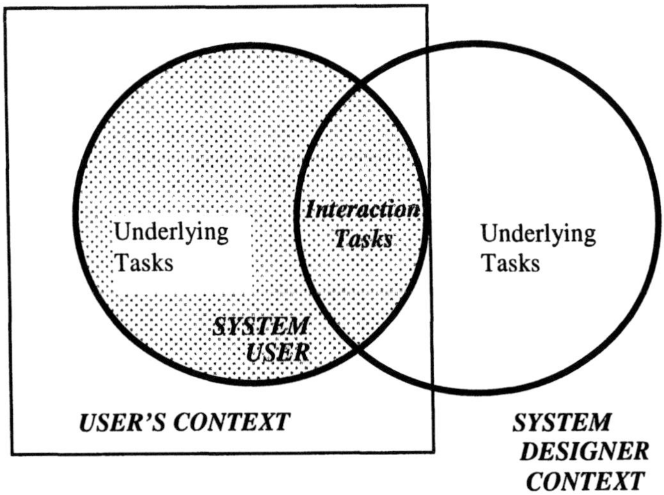

Figure 1.5: Context

Although the benefits of technology can by no means be underestimated, empirical studies on the impact of new technology on actual practitioner cognition and performance has revealed that new systems often have surprising consequences or even fail (Norman 1988; Sarter, Woods and Billings 1997). These surprising consequences and failures can be appreciated in the context that computerization/automation changes the nature of activity (and the tasks) in a field of practice, roles people play and strategies they employ to accomplish various tasks in that activity. The mismatch between the automated activity and how it was being done previously (i.e. before being automated) results in breakdowns in human-computer interaction (Norman 1988; Preece et al. 1997). These breakdowns occur at two levels, namely, the interaction level and the underlying task level. The interaction level determines the presentation efficiency of a computerized system. On the other hand, the underlying task level determines how involved the user is going to be with the system. As an analogy, the interaction level can be seen to represent a façade or the exterior features of a home. The underlying task level can be seen to represent the floor plan that determines the configuration and organization of various rooms (e.g., study, living, bedroom, etc.). The quality of the first one invites one into the home. The quality of the second one provides an immersive environment for one to live in.

The mismatch in these two levels manifests in different kinds of breakdowns in human-computer interaction. These include sheer complexity and bewilderment, cognitive overload, error and failure and others (Norman 1988). However more serious consequences can also result from the mismatch. Studies done of major accidents in power plants, aircraft and other complex systems (e.g. ambulance dispatch systems) found that 60 to 80 percent of accidents were blamed on operator error and incorrect actions by people (Perrow 1984; Preece et al 1997). Given the human limitations, the problem could have easily have lied with system modeling and design.

The remedial measures in most technology-centered systems are mainly applied at the interaction-level (through usability engineering and HCI methods) because the underlying technology and the system model are difficult to change once a software system has been developed.

As indicated in the introduction, the motivation for technology-centered approach also comes from the way the computer industry functions and markets itself. As Norman (1998) has put it

The computer industry is still in its rebellious adolescent stage. It is mature enough that its technology, functions and reliability should be taken for granted, but it still has a good deal of immaturity. It keeps trying to grow bigger, faster, and more powerful. The rest of us wish it would just quiet down and behave. Enough already. Grow up. Settle down and provide good, quiet, competent service without all the fuss and bother. Ah, but to make this change from youth to maturity is to cross the chasm between technological excitement of youth and the staid utility of maturity. It is a difficult chasm to bridge.

This chasm is shown in Figure 1.6. It represents the transition point in the technology life cycle of products in the computer industry. Figure 1.6 shows the transition of a product from a technology-centered infant to a human-centered adult. In early stages of the technology life cycle (left side of the curve in Figure 1.6), technology is used to fill basic unfilled technology needs of customers. For example, video-on demand, and learning-on demand are new technologies on the Internet and are in the early stages of their technology life cycle. Their customers generally are early adopters (innovators, technology enthusiasts and visionaries) who are ready to pay any price for the new technology. They have good technical abilities and are prepared to live with the idiosyncrasies of the new technology. Based on these early adopters, the computer industry labels the technology as a successful technology.

However, these early adopters who thrive on technological superiority, represent a small part of the potential marketplace. The majority of customers are late adopters and are represented on the right side of the chasm in Figure 1.6. These customers wait till the technology has established itself in the marketplace and has matured. This chasm or transition is reached once the basic technology needs have been satisfied. In this phase of the life cycle, the customers see the technology-based product as a commodity where user experience, cost and reliability dominate the buying decision. The technological aspects of the product are taken for granted and are no longer relevant.

Most of the time the technology-centered companies react to this change by loading their products with still more features or excess quality (represented by the shaded upper right hand part of the curve in Figure 1.6). Actually, what is required is a change in the product development philosophy that targets the human user rather than the technology. In other words, a more human-centered approach to product development is required. In this approach, technology is just one component that has to adapt to other system components. In the next section we outline the criteria for human-centered product development.

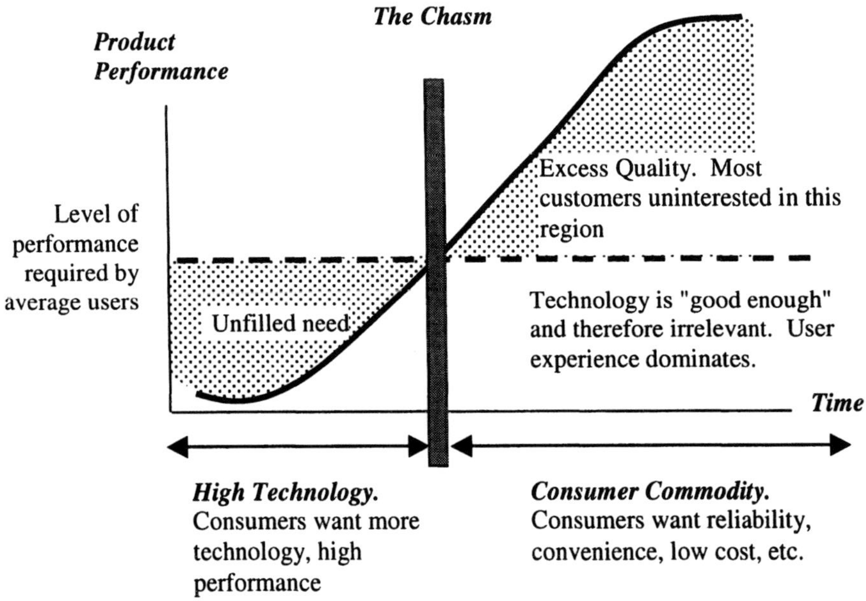

Figure 1.6: Technology Life Cycle of Products in Computer Industry (adapted from Norman (1998))

1.5 Human-Centered Approach

Human-centered development is about achieving synergy between the human and the machine. This synergism goes (as outlined in the preceding section) beyond human-computer interaction concepts, people in the loop philosophy and other interpretations given to human-centeredness. Although most systems are designed with some consideration of its human users, most are far from human-centered. The informal theme of the recently held NSF workshop on human-centered systems (1997) was people propose, science studies, and technology conforms. In other words, humans are the centerpiece of human-centered research and design (as shown in Figure 1.7). They are the prime drivers and technology is a primitive that is used -based on its conformity to the needs of people in a field of practice. The three criteria laid down in the workshop for human-centered system development are:

1. Human-Centered research and design is problem/need driven as against abstraction driven (although there is an overlap)
2. Human-Centered research and design is activity centered
3. Human-Centered research design is context bound.

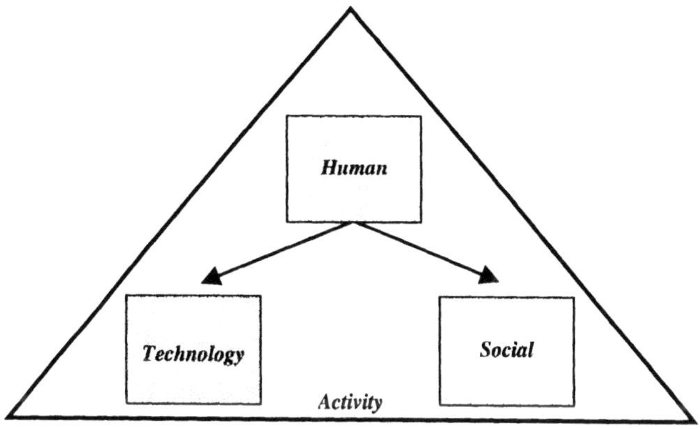

Figure 1.7: A Human-Centered Approach Leading to Successful Systems

The first criteria outlines a need for developing software systems that are modeled based on how people use various artifacts to solve problems in a field of practice. The modeling should include not only the normal or repetitive tasks but also exceptional and challenging situations. These exceptional and challenging situations can also be likened to breakdowns in problem solving. For example in the sales management area, a sales (or customer service) manager while recruiting new salespersons (customer service representatives) is faced with an exceptional situation of determining a benchmark for recruiting the new salespersons (customer service representatives). This benchmark should represent the type of salespersons who are successful in a their organization and culture. Another challenging situation is when they have to decide between two candidates who (as the sales manger perceives) are equally good for the job. On the other hand, a fresh sales recruit faces an exceptional situation when they are unable to understand or explain why a particular customer does not respond or "freezes up" during their interaction with them.

Further, this criteria also suggests that generic problem solving abstractions should be extracted from problem solving situations as people perceive and solve them, rather than employ abstract theories like graph theory or logic or other domain theories to solve problems in various fields.

The second criterion emphasizes system development based on practitioners or users goals and tasks rather than system designer's goals and tasks. In other words, this criteria emphasizes the need for maximizing the overlap between a user's model of the problem domain and a system's model of the domain. The focus is on how well the computer serves as an effective tool for accomplishing user's goals and tasks.

Finally, the third criterion emphasizes that human cognition, collaboration and performance is dependent upon context. It particularly looks at the representational context. That is, how the problem is represented influences the cognitive work needed to solve the problem (see Figure 1.8). Problem solving is distributed across external and internal representations. Software systems based only on internal representations or models of a problem domain are likely to put a higher cognitive load on their users as against systems that are based on external or perceptual representations. Other contexts that need to be taken into account are social/organizational context and task context (as outlined in the second criteria)

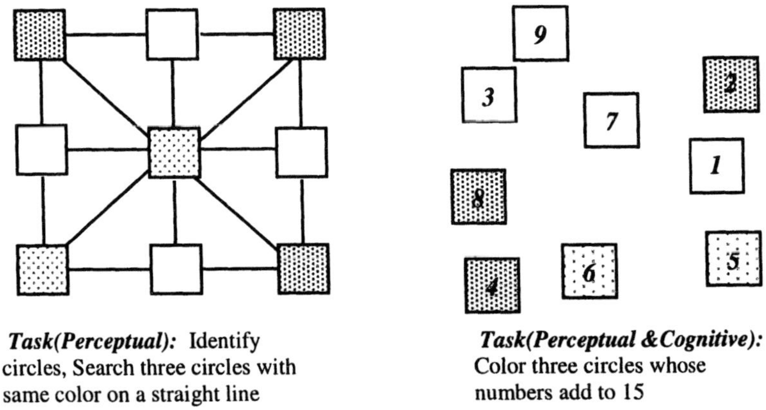

Figure 1.8: Two Representations of Tic-Tac-Toe

1.6 Organization Levels and e-Business

In this book we describe development of e-business system development architecture and e-business applications at the operational, knowledge, management and strategic levels of an organization as shown in Figure 1.9. The transaction based e-commerce at the operational level is described in chapter 8. Human-centered e-business framework and architecture at the knowledge level are described in chapter 4 and 5 respectively. E-Business decision support applications in e-sales recruitment, e-banking and multimedia (identifying clothing of missing persons on the web) are described in chapters 6, 7, 10 and 11 respectively. Finally, e-business strategies and models outlined in chapter 2, and knowledge management architecture described in chapter 9 are relevant for strategic decision making. The e-business architecture, and e-business applications are based on the three human-centered criteria outlined in this chapter and incorporate characteristics related to converging trends towards human-centeredness outlined in section 1.3 and described in detail in chapter 3

1.7 Summary

Human-centeredness has become a driving force in the evolution of information technology and e-business. This chapter outlines the converging trends towards

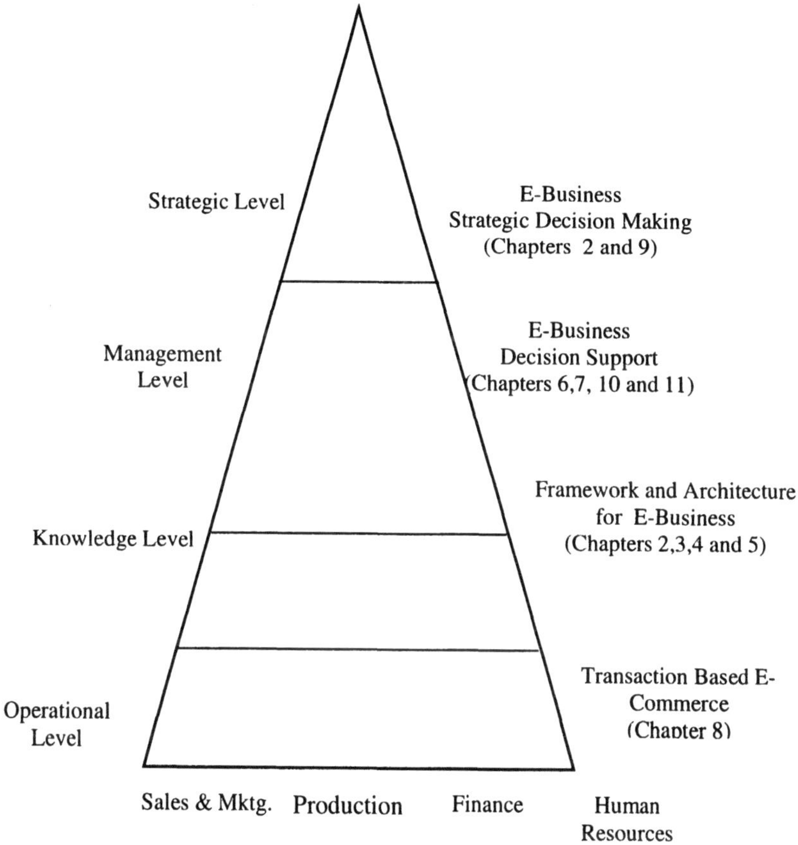

Figure 1.9: Organizational Levels and E-Business Applications

human-centeredness in a range of areas including e- business, intelligent systems, software engineering, multimedia, data mining, enterprise modeling and human-computer interaction. These trends have evolved not only because of social and psychological impact of information technology but also from a business perspective, the users and consumers today place high demands on information technology in terms of its convenience, cost, and customization. Since technology is the primary interface between a supplier and a consumer in an e-business environment, the need for human-centeredness is even greater. In order to understand the meaning and implication of human-centeredness this chapter discusses the problems and issues with the technology-centered approach from a software development perspective and also in terms of life cycle of technology-centered software products. It then outlines the criteria for a human-centered approach and human-centered systems. These criteria along with e-business strategies and e-business models described in the next chapter have been used as guidelines for developing the e-business human-centered system development framework and the human-centered virtual machine. Finally, in the context of human-centered e-business we outline the contributions made by the book at the operational, knowledge, management and strategic level of an organization.

References

Clancey W.J. (1989). "The Knowledge Level Reconsidered: Modeling How Systems Interact" in *Machine Learning* 4, pp 285-92.

Clancey, W.J. (1993) "Situated Action: A Neuropsychological Interpretation (Response to Vera and Simon)" in *Cognitive Science*, 17, 87-116.

Flanagan, J.,Huang, T et al. (1997). "Human-Centered Systems: Information, Interactivity, and Intelligence," *Final report NSF Workshop on Human-Centered Systems, February.*

Norman, D. A. (1993). Things That Make Us Smart. Reading: Addison-Wesley

Norman, D. A. (1988). The Psychology of Everyday Things. Basic Books: New York

Norman, D. A. (1998). *The Invisible Computer,* Massachusetts: MIT Press.

Norris, G. et. al., (2000), *E-Business and ERP: transforming the enterprise,* New York Chichester: John Wiley

NSF Workshop on *Human-Centered Systems, February 1997. Final report.*

Flanagan, J.,Huang, T et al. (1997). Human-Centered Systems: Information, Interactivity, and Intelligence.

Perrow, C., *Normal accidents: living with high-risk technologies.* 1984, NY: Basic Books.

Preece, J., et al (1997), *Human-Computer Interaction*, Massachusetts: Addison-Wesley Pub.

Sarter, N., Woods, D.D. and Billings, C. (1997), "Automation Surprises," in G. Slavendy, (ed.), *Handbook of Human Factors/Ergonomics*, second edition, Wiley,

Takagi, H.K.(2002) "Humanization of Computational Intelligence," Plenary Speech in IEEE world Congress On Computational Intelligence, Hawaii, May 2002.

Takagi, H.K. (2001) "Interactive Evolutionary Computation: Fusion of the Capabilities of EC Optimization and Human Evaluation," *Proceedings of the IEEE*, vol. 89, No. 9, September 2001, pp. 1275-96.

Zhang, J., Norman, D. A. (1994), "Distributed Cognitive Tasks", *Cognitive Science*, pp. 84-120

2 E-BUSINESS CONCEPTS AND TECHNOLOGIES

2.1 Introduction

The applications in this book employ a number of concepts and technologies associated with e-business. The e-business concepts include types of e-business systems, e-business strategies and e-business models. The technologies can be grouped under Internet and web technologies, intelligent technologies, web software engineering (Object-oriented and agents) technologies, and multimedia. E-business strategies and e-business models also provide the context in which e-business technologies are applied by organizations to gain competitive advantage. This chapter introduces the reader to these concepts and technologies.

2.2 e-Business Systems

E-Business is use of Internet technologies to Internetwork and empower business processes, electronic commerce, and enterprise communication and collaboration within a company and with its customers, suppliers, and other business stakeholders. Figure 2.1 shows the broad categories of e-business systems.

2.2.1 e-Commerce and Enterprise Communication and Collaboration Systems

E-commerce systems primarily involve buying and selling of products and services. Transaction processing and self-service systems fall into this category. Intelligent agents in the form of search agents, information brokers and information filters are used to support e-commerce systems. Enterprise communication and collaboration systems allow people to communicate, co-ordinate and co-operate together more effectively through the use of Internet tools such as e-mail (electronic communication tool), data conferencing (electronic conferencing tool) and project management (collaborative work management tools).

2.2.2 Decision Support Systems

Decision support systems provide managers and business professionals interactive information support for semi-structured and unstructured decisions. They enable managers to analyze business data from various perspectives. These perspectives may include what-if analysis, goal seeking analysis (e.g., to achieve a targeted profit of $2 million what volume of sales need to be made?) and optimization analysis. Decision support systems may involve use of several analytical models. These models could be based on intelligent, statistical and mathematical paradigms.

2.2.3 CRM and ERP Systems

In the context of e-business organizations have integrated front office (e.g., customer related) and back office (e.g., supplier related) business processes in order to develop customer-centric business strategies. As a result decision support systems today are designed as cross-functional systems as well as functional systems. Cross-functional enterprise systems allows organizations to achieve their e-business strategic goals, by using information technology to co-ordinate and share information across the various business functions such as manufacturing and supply, sales, marketing and after-sale service. This improves the business processes in terms of their efficiency and effectiveness. Enterprise Resource Planning (ERP) and Customer Relationship Management (CRM) are well known examples of cross-functional systems.

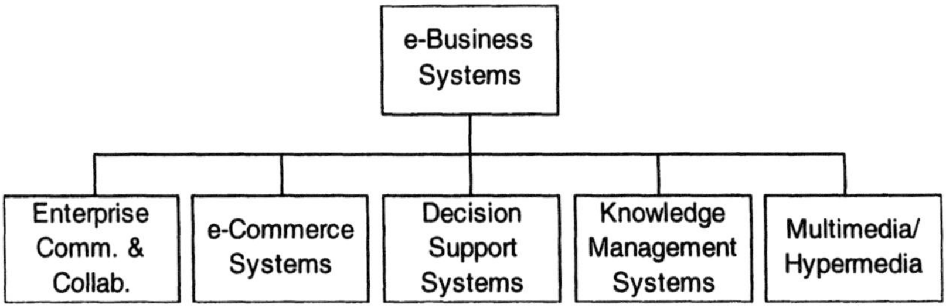

Figure 2.1: Broad Categories of e-Business Systems

ERP systems support the back office processes of an organization's activities mainly within the manufacturing, logistics, distribution, accounting, finance and human resource functions (O'Brien, 2002). For example a manufacturing company will use an ERP system to track "the status of sales, inventory, and invoicing as well as forecast raw material and human resource requirements" (O'Brien, 2002).

CRM systems facilitate customer service by providing software involved in the front line office activities in areas of sales, direct marketing fulfillment and customer service support. Advantages of such systems for example allow a business to mine customer buying behavior patterns and to identify such things as its best customers and those who are most profitable. Functional decision support systems, on the other hand, support traditional functions associated with marketing, human resource management, finance and accounting.

2.2.4 Knowledge Management Systems

Knowledge management systems are an emerging area in e-business. They exploit two types of organisational knowledge, namely, explicit knowledge (data, documents, procedures, reports and information stored in the computers) and tacit knowledge (organisational know-how and how-tos which reside with the employees) to develop knowledge based systems. As O'Brien (2002) has put it companies have to evolve into knowledge-creating companies or learning organisations *if* they want to achieve a lasting competitive advantage over their competitors. This organisational knowledge is disseminated throughout the organisation using enterprise portals and built into product and services. Researchers today are involved in developing suitable ontologies for structuring and indexing organisational knowledge. For example, a multinational like Siemens encourages its employees across the globe to use the company's enterprise portal, ShareNet for exchanging vital know-how in negotiating broadband network projects.

2.2.5 Multimedia Systems

Finally, websites today invariably store multimedia documents consisting of text, image, video and sound. . Multimedia systems are used for retrieval, decision making and reasoning in E-business applications. Unlike conventional database application multimedia systems involve a browsing component. Additionally, one needs to define ontologies based on user-centered concepts and cognitive processes rather than those based on low level media-centered data to bridge the semantic gap between the user and the system

2.3 e-Business Strategies

In the last five to seven years organizations have developed a range of e-business strategies. These strategies depend upon how far down the e-business path a particular organization has evolved. The evolutionary path can be broadly categorized under four e-business strategies (Norris et. al. 2000):

- Channel enhancement
- Value-Chain enhancement
- Industry Transformation
- Industry Convergence

2.3.1 Channel Enhancement

Most companies enter e-business to market, sell or buy products and services over the Internet. In so doing, they engage in e-commerce. The web is used as an enabler to enhance or supplement traditional channels of commerce. The Internet may be used to make sales, fulfil orders, procure raw materials and provide customer self-service.

The companies modify existing business processes and in some cases create new processes targeted at improving business performance. For example, a company may create a Business-to-Consumer (B2C) e-commerce website for its customers to receive sales quotations and place orders. This will lead to some modifications in the existing sales and billing business processes.

2.3.2 Value-Chain Integration

As the companies master the initial channel enhancement strategy through B2C and Business-to-Business (B2B) e-commerce, in order to enhance business value they explore opportunities to integrate customer and supplier operations. The channel enhancement strategy invariably does not involve integration of front and back office business processes. The front office business processes are customer related and may involve customer service, customer retention and loyalty programs, targeted marketing, and customer service and support. Most explore opportunity to use e-business to integrate customers and suppliers operations with their processes and systems (e.g., Wal mart POS). In this space, companies strive to use the Internet to implement e-customer relationship management (eCRM) and e-supply chain management (eSCM) capabilities. These allow companies to link their operations seamlessly with those of customer and suppliers. On the customer side, companies are creating personalized web sites and portals to simplify transacting business over the Internet and to capture information. On the supply side, companies are sharing design, planning and forecasting information with suppliers to increase the velocity of bi-directional information flow.

2.3.3 Industry Transformation

Internet, Intranet and extranet have opened new ways of achieving competitive advantage and adding to the bottom line. Companies who have advanced e-business capabilities are now undergoing an industry transformation process to leverage competitive strategies through traditional business model as well as through e-business capabilities. Thus companies may use the e-business infrastructure to offload non-core parts of their business and use the traditional model for competing on their core competencies. Or they may even use the e-business infrastructure to create new products and services and further enhance their competitiveness related to their core competencies. Thus in this stage of e-business evolution the line between companies becomes less and less pronounced

2.3.4 Convergence

Industry convergence is the coming together of companies from different industries to provide goods and services to consumers (e.g., 24-hrs delivery for orders placed on the Internet). The Internet enables these companies to easily partner in developing products and services geared toward providing customers a one-stop shop. In theory, convergence could occur without e-business.

2.4 e-Business Models

The e-business strategies described in section 2.3 can be realized using a range of e-business models. The e-business models described in this section have been adapted from the book authored by Peter Weill and Mike Vitale (2001) on e-business. The e-business models are listed in Table 2.1. These models are atomic e-business models that can be used in a stand-alone fashion or in combination of two or more models.

Table 2.1: e-Business Models (Weill and Vitale 2001)

• Direct to customer	• Shared infrastructure
• Content provider	• Value-net integrator
• Full service provider	• Virtual community
• Intermediary	• Whole of enterprise

2.4.1 Direct to Customer

The direct to customer model is shown in Figure 2.2. The ellipse or circle represents the firm of interest developing e-business capabilities. The hexagon represents the customer, supplier or business partner linked with the firm. The links between the entities represent the electronic relationship. It can be represented by a solid line or dashed line. If the link between the firm and customer is a solid line, the firm owns the relationship. If the link is a dashed line, either another firm or no firm owns the relationship. The electronic relationship between the two entities can be through the Internet or through other channels (e.g., call centers). The labeled arrows on the links show the flow of Product (P), Information (I), and money ($).

In the direct to customer model shown in Figure 2.2 the firm of interest owns the relationship or has the potential of owning the relationship. The firm of interest also owns the data and e-business transaction. For example, Compaq computers in Australia sell their products directly to their Internet customers and thus own the customer relationship, data and the e-business transaction. By owning customer relationship, data and transaction the firms can pass relevant information to their suppliers and improve their value chain, analyze customer data and customize their products.

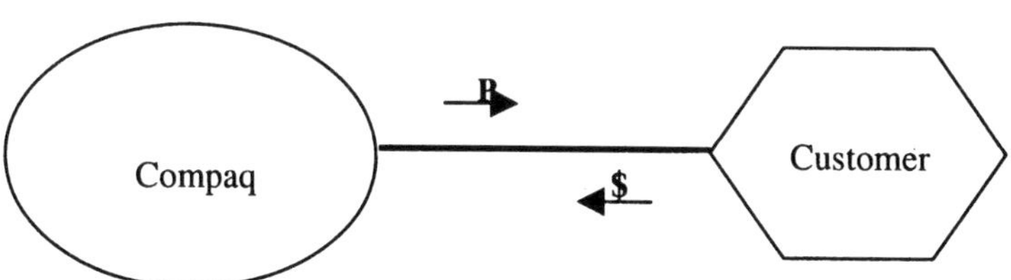

Figure 2.2: Direct to Customer Model

2.4.2 Content Provider

In contrast to the direct-to-customer model, the firm of interest in the content provider model shown in Figure 2.3 does not own the customer relationship. Thus the content provider e-business model directly conflicts with the direct to customer. As shown in Figure 2.3, the customer relationship, data and transaction is owned by an ally (shown as a rectangle) who has a better brand recognition (e.g., Saabre, CNN, Google) than the firm of interest (e.g., Accu weather). The firm of interest in this model owns the content, which represents one of their core competencies (e.g., Accu weather are well known experts in weather forecasting and meteorological information).

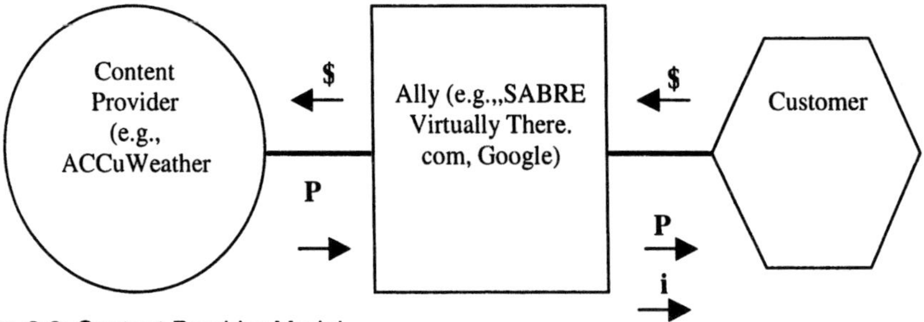

Figure 2.3: Content Provider Model

2.4.3 Full Service Provider

Companies in the insurance, banking and travel business areas are in the process of transiting from a traditional full (customer) service provider models to an e-business one. These companies are now providing a complete range of their core (as well as non-core) products and services through the Internet. The full service provider model shown in Figure 2.4 is an example of a banking and financial institution like ANZ bank providing a range of financial products and services to their customers. These products and services are produced by the bank or sourced from elsewhere (e.g., insurance products are sourced from an insurance company).

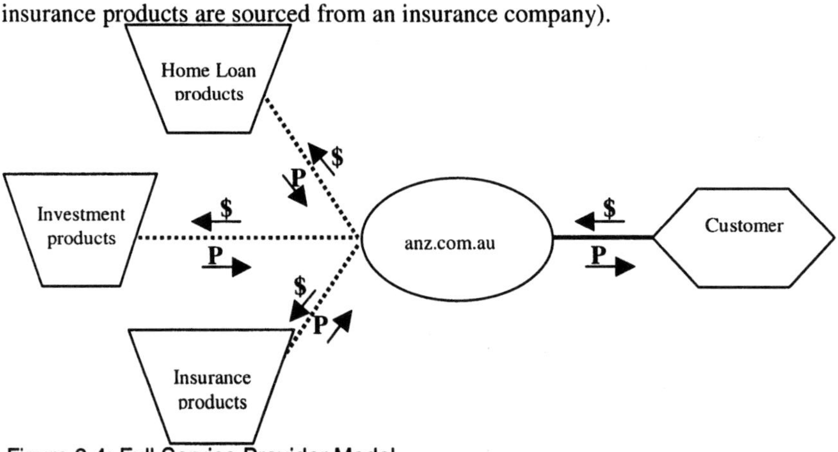

Figure 2.4: Full Service Provider Model

2.4.4 Intermediary

E-Businesses can also function as intermediaries between buyers and sellers. For example, e-brokers or shopping agents can be employed by buyers to locate providers of products and services, identify product specifications, establish price, complete sale and delivery. They can also be used to engage in surveillance of competitor activities on behalf of a company. In the intermediary model the customer relationship and data is owned by the intermediary and the transaction is owned by the company providing the product and service

2.4.5 Shared Infrastructure

The shared infrastructure model shown in Figure 2.5 reflects a business need to provide a generic service to customers along a particular dimension by companies who are otherwise competitors in the marketplace. This is especially true in the airline industry where airline reservation system (see Figure 2.5) is the shared infrastructure used by many airlines. The primary motivation for providing this service is low reservation cost for the collaborating airlines. As shown in Figure 2.5 the customer relationship in this model may be owned by an ally, namely a travel agent, and not service provider (virtuallythere.com) or any airline. The shared infrastructure firm however owns the data and the transaction.

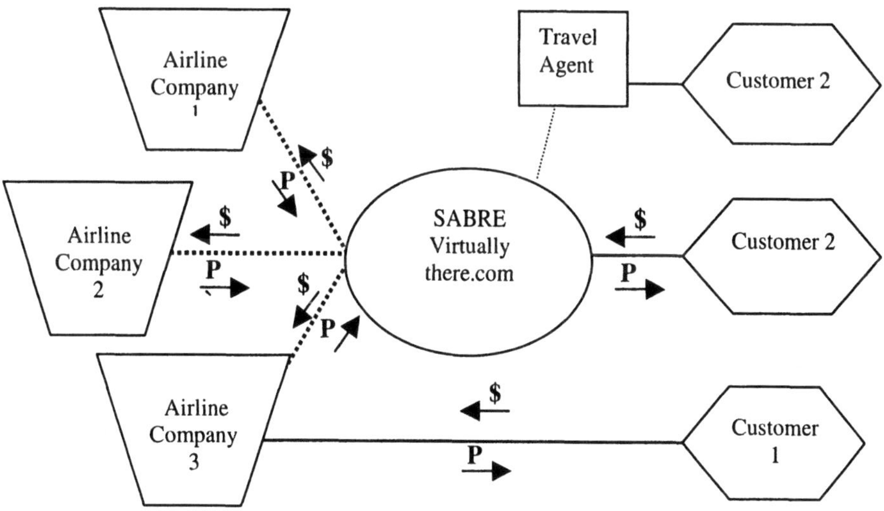

Figure 2.5: Shared Infrastructure Model

2.4.6 Value-Net Integrator

The Internet and the extranet have been important enablers in the value-chain integration of several firms. The value-net integrator model is a direct outcome of the integration of business process in the supply and selling chain respectively. One of the reasons stores like Wal Mart (Figure 2.6) are market leaders today is because they have reduced their inventory costs by directly connecting their customer related information systems with their suppliers. It allows them to share customer related data with their suppliers thus minimize inventory cost and improve customer service. In the value-net integrator model the firm strives to own the customer relationship, data and the transaction. However, it is possible that the primary customer relationship may be owned by an ally or by the supplier in some value-net integrator e-business models.

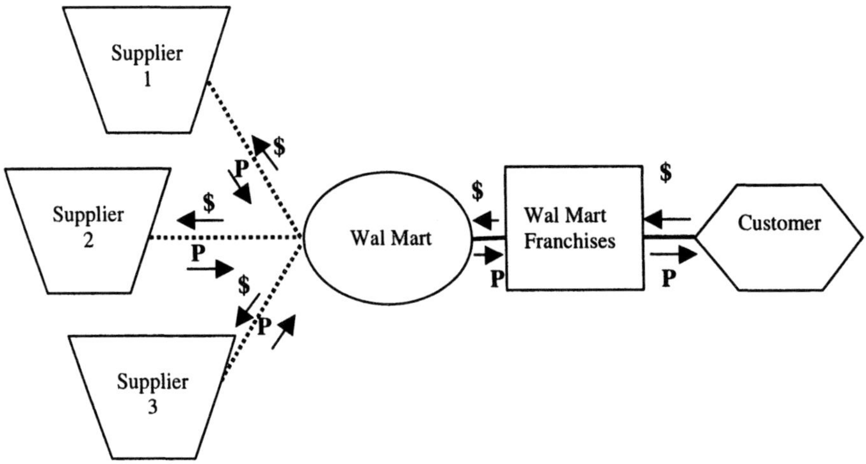

Figure 2.6: Value-Net Integrator Model

2.4.7 Virtual Community

The development of Internet chat rooms, discussion forums and bulletin boards have led to virtual communities of customer groups with common interest, suppliers, business partners and the firm. In the virtual community business model (Figure 2.7), the firm of interest is positioned between the members and suppliers of product and services.

The distinguishing feature of this model is that the members or customers are encouraged to communicate with each other directly through e-mail, chat rooms, bulletin boards and discussion forums.

As shown in Figure 2.7 the virtual community firm owns the customer relationship. However, the members and/or the suppliers may own the data and transaction.

2.4.8 Whole of Enterprise

The whole of enterprise model shown in Figure 2.8 is a recent development where the federal, state and local governments are developing e-business infrastructure to provide single point of contact to customers looking for information and services related filing tax returns, lifestyle events (e.g., registration of marriages, buying land and homes, etc.) and local community related events. The different business units shown in Figure 2.8 can represent government departments providing different

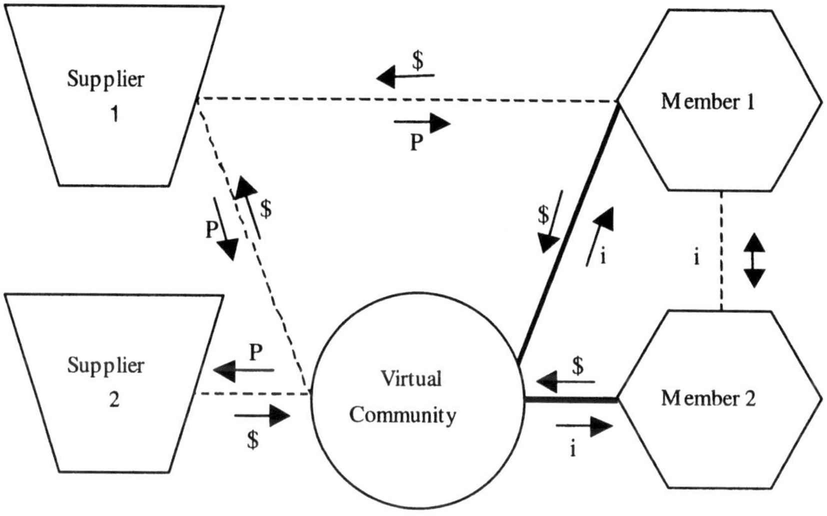

Figure 2.7: Virtual Community Model

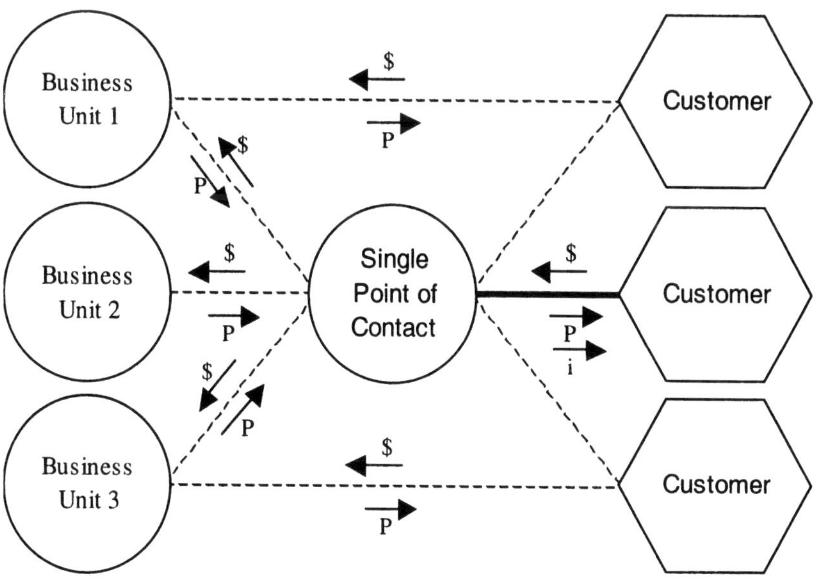

Figure 2.8: Whole of Enterprise Model

services. The single point of contact firm owns the customer relationship, data and transaction.

2.5 Internet and Web Technologies

Internet based is currently a driving force behind the evolution of many *Web-based technologies* such as HTTP, HTML, Java, CGI and others (Hamilton, 1997). However, in this section we focus only on concepts and technologies used in this book.

2.5.1 Internet, Intranet and Extranet

Intranet, extranet and Internet are part of the telecommunication network which enable development of e-business applications and e-business based competitive advantage in a global business environment. These telecommunication networks provide four strategic capabilities to businesses today (O'Brien 2002):

- Overcome geographic barriers
- Overcome time barriers
- Overcome cost barriers
- Overcome structural barriers

The Internet, Intranet and Extranet represent telecommunication networks at global, organisational and inter-organisational levels respectively. The Internet is a complex "network of networks" of computers. The World Wide Web (WWW) is a browsing application of the Internet. It is used to launch e-business and e-commerce applications on the Internet. Businesses use the Internet for collaboration among business partners, customer relationship management applications, cross-functional business applications, e-commerce, human resource and accounting applications, providing chat rooms and discussion forums for customers and others.

Intranet is an Internet-like network within organisations. Like the Internet it depends on the information technologies like, TCP/IP client/server networks, HTML Web publishing software, hardware and software such as Web browsers and server suites, network management and security programs (e.g., firewalls, encryption and passwords), and hypermedia databases. Intranet is used for developing enterprise-wide communication (e.g., voicemail, e-mail, and faxes) collaboration applications, employee web sites and knowledge management portals. An organisation's Intranet can also be accessed through the Intranets of customers, suppliers, and other business partners via Extranet links.

Extranets are network links that use Internet technologies to interconnect the Intranet of a business with the Intranets of its customers, suppliers, or other business partners (O'Brien 2002). Businesses use Extranets to establish direct private network links between themselves (e.g. a business and its suppliers), or create private secure Internet links between them called *virtual private networks*. That is, they allow businesses to develop strategic alliances with their suppliers, customers and other business partners.

2.5.2. The eXtensible Markup Language

The eXtensible Markup Language (XML) is a document mark-up *metalanguage* originally designed to enable the use of the *Standard Generalized Mark-up Language* (SGML) on the World Wide Web and later standardized by the World Wide Web Consortium (World Wide Web Consortium 1998). Today, a huge amount of information is made available in XML format, both on corporate Intranets and on the global Net. In this section, we shall give an outline of the main features of XML; the interested reader may refer to (Pardi 1999) for a comprehensive description of the language and its applications.

While HTML is defined by means of SGML (*Standard Generalized Mark-up Language*: ISO 8879), XML is a sophisticated subset of SGML, and is designed to describe the data using arbitrary tags. One of the goals of XML is to be suitable for the use on the Web; thus to provide a general mechanism for extending HTML. As its name implies, the *extensibility* is a key feature of XML; users or applications are free to declare and use their own tags and attributes. Therefore, XML mark-up ensures that both the logical structure and content of semantics-rich information is retained.

Other approaches, especially from academia, suggest that first order logic or special purpose formal languages such as KQML (Finin et al. 1994) would allow for more precise specification of content. While XML is currently becoming so widespread that it could be chosen based on this criterion alone, it should be noted that expressing semantics in syntax rather than in first-order logic leads to a simpler evaluation function while needing no agreement on an associated ontology. XML is widely accepted in the Web community now, and current applications of XML include *MathML* (Mathematical Mark-up Language) to describe mathematical notation, *CDF* (Channel Data Format) for push technologies, *OFX* (Open Financial Exchange) to describe financial transactions and *OSD* (Open Software Distribution) for the software distribution on the Net.

XML focuses on the description of information structure and content as distinct from its presentation. The data structure and its syntax are defined in a *Document Type Definition* (DTD) specification, which is a derivative from SGML and defines a series of tags and their constraints. In contrast to information structure, the presentation issues are addressed by *XSL* (*XML Style Language*) (Adler 1998), which is also a W3C standard for expressing how XML-based data should be rendered. XSL is based on *DSSSL* (*Document Style Semantics and Specification Language* ISO/IEC 10179) and interoperable with CSS (Cascading Style Sheet), which was originally a style definition language specific to HTML.

In addition to XML and XSL, XLL (*XML Linking Language*) (World Wide Web Consortium 1998) is a specification to define anchors and links within XML documents. Moreover, the *Extensible Forms Description Language* (XFDL) (Blair and Boyer 1999), developed by Tim Bray (Bray et al 1998), is an application of XML that allows organizations to move their paper-based forms systems to the Internet while maintaining the necessary attributes of paper-based transaction records. XFDL was designed for implementation in business-to-business electronic commerce and intra-organizational information transactions.

As such, XML has a great potential as an exchange format for general structured data and increases the productivity to author and maintain, together with style sheet and linking mechanism, while remaining the feature that HTML has provided.

XML documents can be classified into two categories: *well formed* and *valid*. An XML document is well formed if it obeys the syntax of XML (e.g., non-empty tags must be properly nested, each non-empty start tag must have the corresponding end tag). A well-formed document is valid if it conforms to a proper DTD. A DTD is a file (external, included directly in the XML document or both) that contains a formal definition of a particular type of XML documents. A DTD states what names can be used for element types, where they may occur, how each element relates to the others, and what attributes an element may have.

As shown in Figure 2.9, an XML DTD may include four kinds of declarations: element declarations, attribute list declarations, entity declarations, and notation declarations. Element declarations specify the names of elements and their content. Attribute declarations specify the attributes of each element, indicating their name, type, and default value. Attributes that must necessarily appear are said to be required (#REQUIRED). Entities allow for incorporating text and/or binary data into a document. There are two kinds of entities: internal entities are used to introduce special character in the document or as shorthand for some text frequently mentioned, external entities are external files containing either text or binary data. Notation declarations specify what to do with the binary entities.

```
<! --Sample DTD-->
<! ELEMENT DOCUMENT (HEAD?,INTRO, ALEAF*)>
<! ELEMENT INTRO (BT+)>
<! ELEMENT HEAD (LINK)>
<! ELEMENT ALEAF (BT, (%content)*)>
<! ELEMENT BT (PCDATA)>
<! ENTITY %content "(BT|FIGURE)">
<! ELEMENT LINK (EMPTY)>
<! ELEMENT FIGURE (FIGREF, FIGNUM)
<! ELEMENT FIGREF EMPTY>
<! ELEMENT FIGNUM (PCDATA)>
<! NOTATION tiff SYSTEM "viewer.exe">
<! NOTATION bmp SYSTEM "viewer.exe">
<! NOTATION eps SYSTEM "viewer.exe">
<! ATTLIST FIGREF
     SRC CDATA #REQUIRED
     TYPE NOTATION (tiff|bmp|eps) "tiff">
<!ATTLIST LINK
     REL CDATA  #REQUIRED
     HREF  CDATA #REQUIRED)
```

Figure 2.9. Sample XML DTD

The set of declarations defines the vocabulary that can be used in tagging a document. XML vocabularies can be *open* or *closed*, the former allowing for using additional tags beyond what is declared in the base DTD. When XML documents are shared between applications, an open vocabulary can be extended, with the receiving application determining how to interpret extended elements and attributes. Depending on the application, unrecognized extensions to a vocabulary can often be ignored. As far as links are concerned, there are two types of links: *simple links* (like the one used in Figure 2.11) which are similar to the HTML links, and *extended links*, which allow expressing relationships between more than two resources. In Figure 2.10 the LINK element is defined, the attributes of which allow for simple link definition. Elements and attributes declaration have associated the cardinality with which they can appear: character '*' indicates zero or more occurrences, character '+' indicates one or more occurrences, character '?' indicates zero or one occurrence, and no label indicates exactly one occurrence.

A sample valid document for the above DTD is shown in Figure 2.10.

```
    <? xml version="1.0">
    <! DOCTYPE DOCUMENT SYSTEM "http://127.0.0.1/document.dtd">
    <DOCUMENT>
    <HEAD> <LINK REL="0"
HREF="http://127.0.0.1/style.xsl"/></HEAD>
    <INTRO>
    <BT> This is a sample XML document </BT>
    </INTRO>
    <ALEAF>
    <BT> This is a leaf that contains a paragraph (this one)
    and a figure</BT>
    <FIGURE> <FIGREF SRC="image.tif"
TYPE="tiff"></FIGREF><FIGNUM>110.2<?FIGNUM></FIGURE>
    </ALEAF>
    </DOCUMENT>
```

Figure 2.10 Sample XML Document

It should be noted that the element LINK is used in Figure 2.10 to identify the XSL style sheet that contains presentation information for this document. Again as shown in Figure 2.11, declarations that form a standardized XML DTD are usually stored in separate files, which can be referenced, as an XML external subset through the Uniform Resource Locator that its author has assigned to a publicly available copy of the data. Alternatively, if public access is to be restricted, the document type definition can be stored as the internal subset within the document type definition sent with the message.

```
<!ENTITY % address SYSTEM "http://www.sample.org/XML/address.xml" >
<!ENTITY % items SYSTEM "http://www.sample.org/XML/items.xml">
<!ENTITY % data "(#PCDATA)">
<!ELEMENT order (deliverylocation, invoicing, order-no, item+) >
<!ELEMENT deliverylocation (address) >
<!ELEMENT invoicing (address) >
<!--Import standard address class-->
%address;
<!ELEMENT order-no %data; >
<!--Import standard item class-->
%items;
```

Figure 2.11. A DTD Fragment

Where DTD is based on classes of information shared by more than one message, each class of information can be defined in a separate file, known in XML as an external entity.
For example, an XML DTD could have the form shown in Figure 2.12.

DTD1

```
<!ELEMENT list-manuf
  (manufacurer+)>
<!ELEMENT manufacturer (mn-
  name,year,model+)>
<!ELEMENT mn-name #PCDATA>
<!ELEMENT year #PCDATA>
<!ELEMENT model
(mo-name,front-rating,side-
  rating,rank)>
<!ELEMENT mo-name #PCDATA>
<!ELEMENT front-rating #PCDATA>
<!ELEMENT side-rating #PCDATA>
<!ELEMENT rank #PCDATA>
```

DTD2

```
<!ELEMENT list-vehicles (vehicle+)>
<!ELEMENT vehicle(vendor,(make|reference),
model,year,color,option*,price?)>
<!ELEMENT vendor #PCDATA>
<!ELEMENT make #PCDATA>
<!ELEMENT reference EMPTY>
<!ATTLIST reference manufactured-by
  IDREF>
<!ELEMENT model #PCDATA>
<!ELEMENT year #PCDATA>
<!ELEMENT color #PCDATA>
<!ELEMENT option #PCDATA>
<!ATTLIST option opt PCDATA
  #REQUIRED>
<!ELEMENT price #PCDATA>
<!ELEMENT company (name,address)>
<!ATTLIST company id ID #REQUIRED>
<!ELEMENT name #PCDATA>
<!ELEMENT address #PCDATA>
```

Figure 2.12. Two DTDs about Cars

This DTD fragment defines two external and one internal parameter entity; moreover, it declares four locally defined elements and contains two parameter entity references (%address; and %items;) that call in the contents of the external entities at appropriate points in the definition. Both of the parameter entity references are preceded by explanatory comments.

Note that the source of each class of information is identified not in the call to the class itself (%address;) but within a formal definition of the data storage entities required to process the class definition references (the first two lines of the DTD). This technique allows files to be moved without having to change the main definitions of the DTD.

Of course, different applications may represent the same kind of information using completely different DTDs. As the focus on XML is shifting from document formatting to knowledge representation issues, this situation is becoming more and more common. As an example, we show two DTDs and two document fragments describing cars: in the former, the manufacturer company reports result data for the NHSC crash-safety test, in the latter auto dealers and brokers list their prices.

INSTANCE1

```
<list-manuf>
<manufacturer>
<mn-name>Mercury</mn-name>
<year>1998</year>
<model>
<mo-name>Sable LT</mo-name>
<front-rating>3.84</front-rating>
<side-rating>2.14</side-rating>
<rank>9</rank>
</model>
<model>
<mo-name>Sable LG</mo-name>
<front-rating>3.75</front-rating>
<side-rating>2.76</side-rating>
<rank>8</rank>
</model>
</manufacturer>
<manufacturer>
<mn-name>...</mn-name>
<year>1997</year>
<model>
<mo-name>...</mo-name>
<front-rating>3.05</front-rating>
<side-rating>2.00</side-rating>
<rank>11</rank>
</model>
</manufacturer>
</list-manuf>
```

INSTANCE2

```
<list-vehicle>
<vehicle>
<vendor>Scott Thomason</vendor>
<make>Mercury</make>
<model>Sable LT</model>
<year>1999</year>
<color>metallic blue</color>
<option opt="sunroof"/>
<option opt="M">A/C</option>
<price>26800</price>
</vehicle>
<vehicle>
<vendor>Scott Thomason</vendor>
<reference
 manufactured_by="C1"></reference>
<model>Sable LG</model>
<year>1999</year>
<color>metallic gray</color>
<option opt="SR">8</option>
<option opt="SF">ABS</option>
<price>27500</price>
</vehicle>
</list-vehicle>
<company id="C1">
<name>Mercury</name>
<address>Chicago</address>
</company>
```

Figure 2.13. Two XML documents

2.5.2.1 XML Namespaces

The above example should have highlighted the problem of compatibility between related DTDs at the level of tag and attribute names. Fortunately, XML provides *namespaces* (World Wide Web Consortium 1999), a simple and elegant mechanism for DTD extensibility. This technique leverages the Net's *Uniform Resource Identifier* (URI) namespace to allow arbitrary attributes and elements to be added to an existing XML vocabulary, and can be best illustrated through an example. Consider the following XML fragment:

```
<order orderno="33666">
    <vendor vendno="5573" />
    <part partno="4463" />
    <part partno="2930" />
</order>
```

This fragment indicates that vendor number 5573 is being ordered items 4463 and 2930; of course, for this document to be useful part numbers need to be shared between the vendor's and the customer's information system. Suppose now that the organization placing the order needs to annotate this message with additional information, adding an identifier that associates the order with a larger transaction. At first sight, simply adding an attribute as follows could make it:

```
<order orderno="33666" transid="12345">
<vendor vendno="5573" />
    <part partno="4463" />
    <part partno="2930" />
</order>
```

However, several problems arise, due to the fact that in general the application receiving the document at the vendor's site will have been developed independently from the sending application at the customer's site. If a closed vocabulary is used, the receiver may not recognize the additional elements/attributes added to the message.

Even if an open XML vocabulary is employed, the problem of *ambiguity* remains. This problem arises when both the sender and the receiver extend the vocabulary in the same way (e.g. adding independently two `transid` attributes with different semantics).

Namespaces were designed to relieve this problem, inasmuch as they allow attributes and elements to be scoped by a URI. The following XML fragment illustrates how XML namespaces can be used to unambiguously add the `transid` attribute to the order request:

```
<order orderno="33666"
       xmlns:acme="http://acme.org/trans/ns"
       acme:transid="55291" >
<vendor vendno="5573" />
    <part partno="4463" />
    <part partno="2930" />
</order>
```

This notation allows the vendor's application to detect that the `transid` attribute is scoped by the namespace http://acme.org/trans/ns and is not the same as the `transid` attribute used at its site (which would have a different namespace URI, e.g. `http://hop.org/trans/ns`). The following fragment illustrates how the request can be made completely unambiguous:

```
<order orderno="33666"
       xmlns:acme="http://acme.org/trans/ns"
       xmlns:hop ="http://hop.org/trans/ns "
        acme:transid="55291" >
         hop:transid="46722" >
<vendor vendno="5573" />
    <part partno="4463" />
    <part partno="2930" />
</order>
```

There are currently several initiatives to standardize domain-specific XML vocabularies, though it is unlikely that any of these standards will achieve 100 percent penetration in a particular application domain.

2.5.2.2. XML-based Agent Systems Development

XML, which was originally designed as a document standard for adding extensions to HTML, is becoming widely used as a means for autonomous agents to interoperate. As we have seen, the core XML specification is extremely simple as it only lays down the syntactic ground rules for forming valid XML messages. In other words, XML defines the minimal shared representation for data and message interchange needed to ensure that software agents can communicate. Moreover, XML neither mandates a type representation technique nor depends on a particular operating system, programming language, or hardware architecture. As long as two agents can exchange XML messages, they can potentially interoperate despite their differences.

Moreover, XML is easy to understand, author and process. Unlike binary-wire protocols like DCOM, CORBA/MASIF, or Aglets-Java/RMI, XML allows agents to easily create messages using standard string manipulation functions in the programming language of choice. The text-based nature of XML also makes it easier to debug and monitor distributed agent-based applications, as all agent-to-agent messages are readable to us when using a network debugging tool.

Due to the use of open vocabularies and namespaces, XML can support weakly typed communications. While strong typing has many benefits, it is extremely easy to build weakly typed systems using XML. This makes XML extremely adaptable to generic application frameworks, data-driven applications, and rapid development scenarios, such as disposable or transient Web-based applications. We shall elaborate on this subject in the following chapters.

2.6 Intelligent Technologies

Artificial Intelligence (or Hard Computing) and Computational Intelligence (or Soft Computing) technologies come under the umbrella of intelligent technologies. Some of the intelligent technologies are:

- Expert Systems
- Case Based Reasoning Systems
- Artificial Neural Networks
- Fuzzy Systems
- Genetic Algorithms
- Intelligent Fusion, Transformation and Combination

2.6.1. Expert Systems

Expert Systems handle a whole array of interesting tasks that require a great deal of specialized knowledge and these tasks can only be performed by experts who have accumulated the required knowledge. These specialized tasks are performed in a variety of areas including Diagnosis, Classification, Prediction, Scheduling and Decision Support (Hayes-Roth et al 1983). The various expert systems developed in these areas can be broadly grouped under four architectures.

- Rule Based Architecture
- Rule and Frame Based Architecture
- Model Based Architecture
- Blackboard Architecture

These four architectures use a number of symbolic knowledge representation formalisms developed in the last thirty years. Thus, before describing these architectures, the symbolic knowledge representations are briefly described.

2.6.1.1 Symbolic Knowledge Representation

Symbolic Artificial Intelligence (AI) has developed a rich set of representational formalisms that have enabled cognitive scientists to characterize human cognition. The symbolic representational power has in fact been seen for a long time as an advantage over the connectionist representations for human problem solving. The real reason according to Chandrasekaran (1990), for loss of interest in the perceptrons by Minsky and Papert (1969), was not due to limitations of the single layer perceptrons, but for the lack of powerful representational and representation manipulation tools. These AI knowledge representational formalisms are briefly overviewed.

Knowledge representation schemes have been used to represent the semantic content of natural language concepts, as well as to represent psychologically plausible memory models. These schemes facilitate representation of semantic and episodic memory.

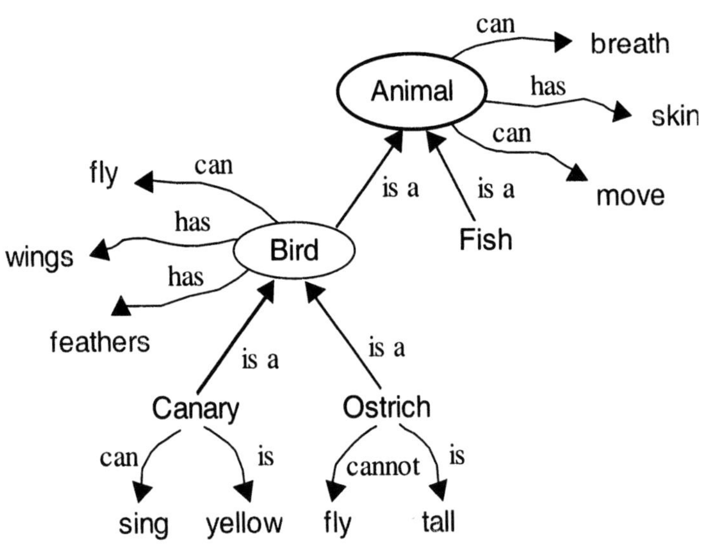

Figure 2.14. A Semantic Network

Human semantic memory is the memory of facts we know, arranged in some kind of hierarchical network (Quillian 1968; Kolodner 1984). For example, in a semantic memory "stool" may be defined as a type of "chair", in turn defined as an instance of "furniture". Properties and relations are handled within the overall hierarchical framework. Semantic networks are a means of representing semantic memory in which any concept (e.g. Bird in Figure 2.1) is represented by a set of properties, which in turn consists of pointers to other concepts as shown in Figure 2.14 (Quillian 1968). The properties are made up of attribute value pairs. Semantic networks also introduce property inheritance as a means to establish hierarchies and a form of default reasoning. Whereas, semantic nets provide a form of default reasoning, first order predicate calculus and production systems (Newell 1977) provide a means of deductive reasoning observed in humans. First order predicate calculus and production systems are both a representational and processing formalism. A predicate calculus expression like:

$$\forall X\ \exists Y\ (student(X)\ )\ AI\_subject(Y\ )\ \wedge\ likes(X;\ Y\ ))$$

provides a clear semantics for the symbols and expressions formed from objects and relations. It also provides a means for representing connectives, variables, and universal and existential quantifiers (like forall ($\forall$) and forsome ($\exists$)). The existential and universal quantifiers provide a powerful mechanism for generalization that is difficult to model in semantic networks.

Knowledge in production systems is represented as condition-action pairs called production rules (e.g., "if it has a long neck and brown blotches, infer that it is a giraffe").

If semantic memory encodes facts, then episodic memory encodes experience. An episode is a record of an experienced event like visiting a restaurant or a diagnostic consultation. Information in episodic memory is defined and organized in accordance with its intended uses in different situations or operations. Frames and scripts (Schank 1977; Minsky 1981) which are extensions of semantic networks are used to represent complex events (e.g., like going to a restaurant) in terms of structured units with specific slots (e.g., being seated, ordering), with possible default values (e.g., ordering from a menu), and with a range of possible values associated with any slot. These values are either given or computed with help of demons (procedures) installed in slots. Schank's (1972) earlier work in this direction on conceptual dependencies, involves the notion of representing different actions or verbs in terms of language independent primitives (e.g., object transfer, idea transfer). The idea was to be able to represent all the paraphrases of a single idea with the same representation (e.g., Mary gave the ball to John; John got the ball from Mary).

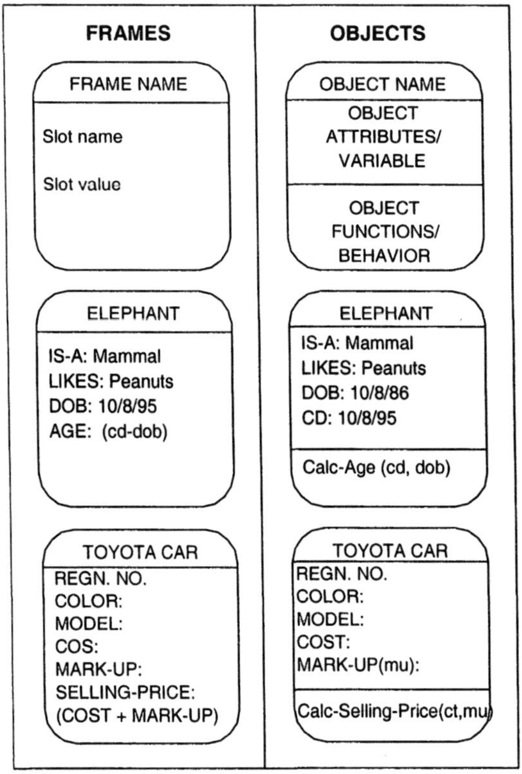

Figure 2.15. Frames and Objects

Object-Oriented representation, a recent knowledge representational formalism from research in artificial intelligent and software engineering has some similarities with frames as shown in Figure 2.15. It is a highly attractive idea, as it does both development from the theory of programming languages, and knowledge representation. The object-oriented representational formalism identifies the real-world objects relevant to a problem as humans do, the attributes of those objects, and the processing operations (methods) in which they participate. Some similarities with frame-based class hierarchies and various procedures (methods in objects) attached to the slots are evident. However, demons or procedures in frames are embedded in the slots, whereas in objects procedures or methods and attributes are represented separately. This delineation of methods from attributes provides them with strong encapsulation properties which makes them attractive from a software implementation viewpoint.

The four expert system architectures are now briefly described in the rest of this section.

The basic components of a rule-based expert system are shown in Figure 2.16. The knowledge base contains a set of production rules (that is, IF . . . THEN 8 rules). The IF part of the rule refers to the antecedent or condition part and the THEN part refers to the consequent or action part.

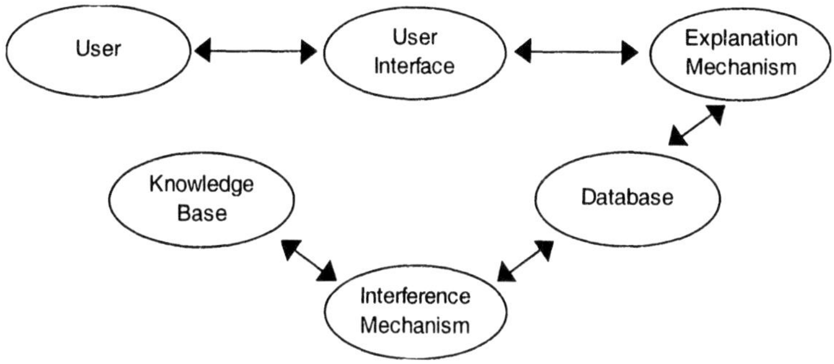

Figure 2.16. Components of a Rule Based Expert System

2.6.1.2. Rule Based Architecture

The database component is a repository for data required by the expert system to reach its conclusion/s based on the expertise contained in its knowledge base. That is, in certain types of expert systems, the knowledge base, though endowed with expertise, cannot function unless it can relate to a particular situation in the problem domain. For example, data on an applicant's present credit rating in a loan analysis expert system needs to be provided by the user to enable the expert system to transform the information contained in the knowledge base into advice. This information is stored in a database.

The inference mechanism in a rule based system compares the data in the database with the rules in the knowledge base and decides which rules in the knowledge base apply to the data. Two types of inference mechanisms are generally used in expert systems, namely, forward chaining (data driven) and backward chaining (goal driven). In forward chaining, if a rule is found whose antecedent matches the information in the database, the rule fires, that is, the rule's THEN part is asserted as the new fact in the database. In backward chaining on the other hand, the system forms a hypothesis that corresponds to the THEN part of a rule and then attempts to justify it by searching the data base or querying the user to establish the facts appearing in the IF part of the rule or rules. If successful, the hypothesis is established, otherwise another hypothesis is formed and the process is repeated. An important component of any expert system is the explanation mechanism. It uses a trace of rules fired to provide reasons for the decisions reached by the expert system.

The user of an expert system can be a novice user or an expert user depending upon the purpose of the expert system. That is, if the expert system is aimed at training operators in a control center or for education, it is meant for novice users, whereas if it is aimed at improving the quality of decision making in recruitment of salespersons, it is meant for an expert user. User characteristics determines to a large extent the type of explanation mechanism or I/O (Input/Output) interface required for a particular expert system. The user interface shown in Figure 2.16 permits the user to communicate with the system in a more natural way by permitting the use of simple selection menus or the use of a restricted language which is close to a natural language.

Many successful expert systems using the rule-based architecture have been built, including MYCIN, a system for diagnosing infectious diseases (Shortliffe 1976), XCON, a system developed for Digital Equipment Corp. for configuring computer systems (Kraft et al. 1984), and numerous others.

2.6.1.3. Rule and Frame (Object) Based Architecture

In contrast to rule base systems certain expert systems consists of both heuristic knowledge and relational knowledge. The relational knowledge describes explicit or implicit relationships among various objects/entities or events. Such knowledge is usually represented by semantic nets, frames or by objects. Figure 2.17 shows an object-oriented network for cars.

The is-a link is known as the inheritance or generalization-specialization link and is-a-*PART-OF* is known as the compositional or whole-part link. These two relational links give lot of expressive power to object-oriented representation. They help to express the hierarchies (classes) and aggregations existing in the domain. That is, VOLKSWAGEN and MAZDA 131 objects are of type SMALL CAR. Such hybrid systems use both deductive and default (inheritance) reasoning strategies for inferencing with knowledge.

Expert systems with hybrid architectures like CENTAUR (Aitkins 1983) - a system for diagnosing lung diseases use both deductive and default reasoning for inferencing with knowledge.

2.6.1.4. Model Based Architecture

The previous two architectures use heuristic or shallow knowledge in the form of rules. The model based architecture on the other hand, uses an additional deep model (derived from first principles) which gives them an understanding of the complete search space over which the heuristics operate. This makes two kinds of reasoning possible: a) the application of heuristic rules in a style similar to the classical expert systems; b) the generation and examination of a deeper search space following classical search techniques, beyond the range of heuristics.

Various models can be used to describe and reason about a technical system. These include anatomical models, geometric models, functional models and causal models (Steels 1989). Anatomical models focus on the various components and their

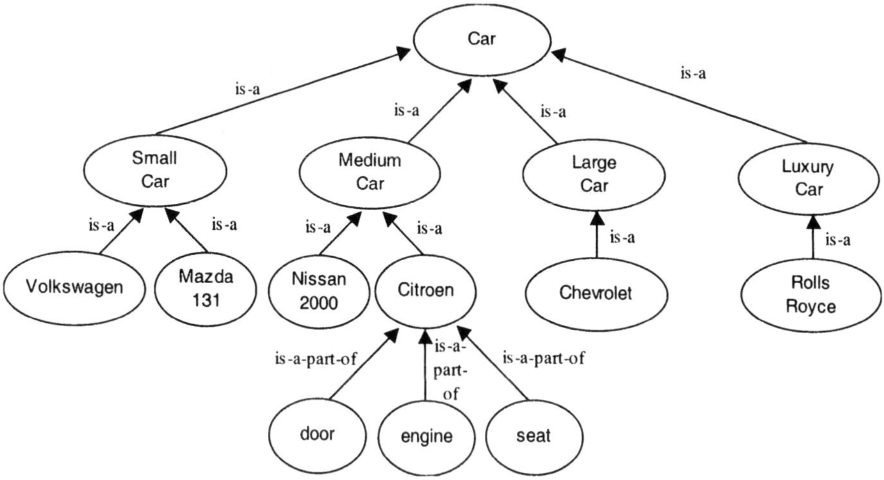

Figure 2.17. An Object-Oriented Network

part-whole relations whereas geometrical models focus on the general layout of the geometrical relations between components. Functional models predict the behavior of a device based on the functioning of its components. On the other hand, a causal model knows about the causal connections between various properties of the components but unlike a functional model does not know how each of the components actually works. Causal models represent an alternative, more abstract, view of a device which is particularly effective for diagnosis in cooperation with a functional model.

First generation expert systems are brittle, in the sense that as soon as situations occur which fall outside the scope of the heuristic rules, they are unable to function at all. In such a situation, second generation systems fall back on search that is not knowledge-driven and therefore potentially very inefficient. However, because these traditional search techniques can theoretically solve a wider class of problems, there is a gradual degradation of performance.

Model based reasoning strategies have been applied on various problems, e.g., XDE (Hamscher 1990), a system for diagnosing devices with heuristic structure and known component failure modes, HS-DAG (Ng 1991), a model based system for diagnosing multiple fault cases in continuous physical devices, DIAGNOSE (Wang and Dillon 1992), a system for diagnosing power system faults, etc.

2.6.1.5. Blackboard Architecture

Blackboard systems are a class of systems that can include all different representational and reasoning paradigms discussed in this section. They are composed of three functional components, namely, knowledge sources component, blackboard component, and control information component, respectively.

The knowledge sources component represents separate and independent sets of coded knowledge, each of which is a specialist in some limited area needed to solve a given subset of problems. The blackboard component, a globally accessible data structure, contains the current problem state and information needed by the knowledge sources (input data, partial solutions, control data, alternatives, final solutions). The knowledge sources make changes to the blackboard data that incrementally lead to a solution. The control information component may be contained within the knowledge sources, on the blackboard, or possibly in a separate module. The control knowledge monitors the changes to the blackboard and determines what the immediate focus of attention should be in solving the problem. HEARSAY-II (Erman et al 1980) and HEARSAY III (Balzer 1980; Erman et al 1981) -a speech understanding project at Stanford University is a well-known example of blackboard architecture.

2.6.1.6. Some Limitations of Expert System Architectures

Rule based expert systems suffer from several limitations. Among them is the limitation that they are too hard-wired to process incomplete and incorrect information. For this reason they are sometimes branded as 'sudden death' systems. This limits their application especially in the real-time systems where incomplete information, incorrect information, temporal reasoning, etc. are major system requirements. Further, knowledge acquisition in the form of extraction of rules from a domain expert is known to be a long and tedious process.

Model based systems overcome the major limitations of rule based systems. However, model based systems are slow as may involve exhaustive search. The 12 response time deteriorates further in systems that require temporal reasoning and consist of noisy data. Also, it may not be always possible to build one. Blackboard systems, which combine disparate knowledge sources, try to maximize the benefits of rule based and model-based systems. The major problem, however, with these systems lies in developing an effective communication medium between disparate knowledge sources. Further, given the use multiple knowledge sources it is not easy to keep track of the global state of the system.

Overall, these architectures have difficulty handling complex problems where the numbers of combinatorial possibilities are large and/or where the solution has a non-deterministic nature, and mathematical models do not exist. Artificial neural networks have been successfully used for these types of problems.

2.6.2.Case Based Reasoning Systems

In some domains (e.g. law), it is either not easy or possible to represent the knowledge using rules or objects. In these domains one may need to go back to records of individual cases that record primary user experience. Case based reasoning is a subset of the field of artificial intelligence that deals with storing past experiences or cases and retrieving relevant ones to aid in solving a current problem. In order to facilitate retrieval of the cases relevant to the current problem a method of indexing these cases must be designed. There are two main components of a case based reasoning system, namely, the case base where the cases are stored and the case based reasoner. The case based reasoner consists of two major parts:

- mechanism for relevant case retrieval
- mechanism for case adaptation.

Thus given a specification of the present case, the case based reasoning system searches through the database and retrieves cases that are closest to the current specification.

The case adapter notes the differences between the specification of the retrieved cases and the specification of the current case, and suggests alternatives to the retrieved cases so that the current situation is best met.

Case based reasoners can be used in open textured domains such as the law or design problems. They reduce the need for intensive knowledge acquisition and try to use past experiences directly.

2.6.3. Artificial Neural Networks

The research in artificial neural networks has been largely motivated by the studies on the function and operation of the human brain. It has assumed prominence because of the development of parallel computers and, as stated in the previous chapter, the less than satisfactory performance of symbolic AI systems in pattern recognition problems like speech and vision.

The word 'neural' or 'neuron' is derived from the neural system of the brain. The goal of neural computing is that by modeling the major features of the brain and its operation, we can produce computers that can exhibit many of the useful properties of the brain. The useful properties of brain include parallelism, high level of interconnection, self-organization, learning, distributed processing, fault tolerance and graceful degradation. Neural network computational models developed to realize these properties are broadly grouped under two categories, namely, supervised learning and unsupervised learning. In both types of learning a representative training data set of the problem domain is required. In supervised learning the training data set is composed of input and target output patterns. The target output pattern acts like an external "teacher" to the network in order to evaluate its behavior and direct its subsequent modifications. On the other hand in unsupervised learning the training data set is composed solely of input patterns. Hence, during learning no comparison with predetermined target responses can be performed to direct the network for its subsequent modifications. The network learns the underlying features of the input data and reflects them in its output. There are other categories like rote learning which are also used for categorization of neural networks.

Although, numerous neural network models have been developed in these categories, we will limit our discussion to following well known and popularly used ones.

- Perceptron (Supervised)
- Multilayer Perceptron (Supervised)
- Kohonen nets (Unsupervised)
- Radial Basis Function Nets (Unsupervised and Supervised).

Here again, before outlining the neural network architectures, the knowledge representation in neural networks is briefly overviewed.

2.6.3.1. Perceptron

The Perceptron was the first attempt to model the biological neuron shown in Figure 2.18. It dates back to 1943 and was developed by McCulloch and Pitts. Thus as a starting point, it is useful to understand the basic function of the biological neuron which in fact reflects the underlying mechanism of all neural models.

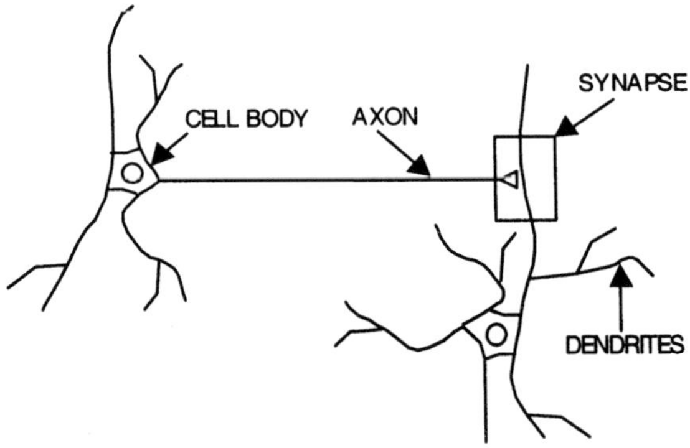

Figure 2.18. A Biological Neuron

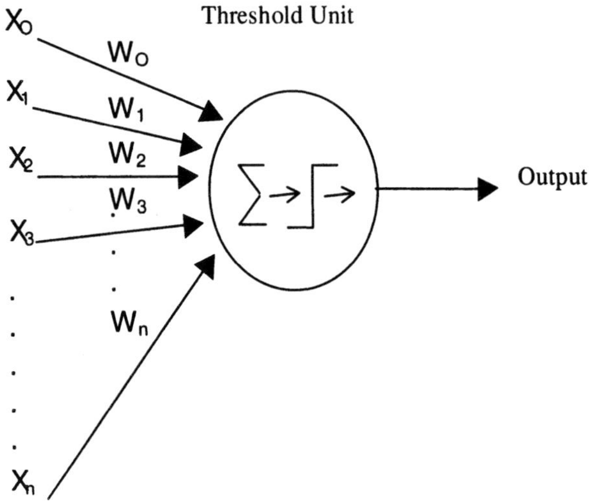

Figure 2.19. The Perceptron

The basic function of a biological neuron is to add up its inputs and produce an output if this sum is greater than some value, known as the threshold value. The inputs to the neuron arrive along the dendrites, which are connected to the outputs from other neurons by specialized junctions called synapses. These junctions alter the effectiveness with which the signal is transmitted. Some synapses are good junctions, and pass a large signal across, whilst others are very poor, and allow very little through. The cell body receives all these inputs, and fires if the total input exceeds the threshold value.

The perceptron shown in Figure 2.19 models the features of the biological neuron as follows:

a. The efficiency of the synapses at coupling the incoming signal into the cell body is modeled by having a weight associated with each input to the neuron. A more efficient synapse, which transmits more of the signal, has a correspondingly larger weight, whilst a weak synapse has a small weight.
b. The input to the neuron is determined by the weighted sum of its inputs

$$\sum_{i=0}^{n} w_i x_i$$

where x_i is the ith input to the neuron and w_i is its corresponding weight.

c. The output of the neuron, which is on (1) or off (0), is represented by a step or heaveside function. The effect of the threshold value is achieved by biasing the neuron with an extra input x0 which is always on (1). The equation describing the output can then be written as

$$y = fh[\sum_{i=0}^{n} w_i x_i]$$

The learning rule in perceptron is a variant on that proposed in 1949 by Donald Hebb, and is therefore called Hebbian learning. It can be summarized as follows:

1. set the weights and thresholds randomly
2. present an input
3. calculate the actual output by taking the thresholded value of the weighted sum of the inputs
4. alter the weights to reinforce correct decisions and discourage incorrect decisions, i.e. reduce the error.

This is the basic perceptron learning algorithm. Modifications to this algorithm have been proposed by the well known Widrow and Hoff's (1960) delta rule. They realized that it would be best to change the weights by a lot when the weighted sum is a long way from the desired value, whilst altering them only slightly when the weighted sum is close to that required. They proposed a learning rule known as the Widrow-Hoff delta rule, which calculates the difference between the weighted sum and the required output, and calls that the error. The learning algorithm basically remains the same except for step 4, which is replaced as follows:

4. Adapt weights - Widrow-Hoff delta rule

$$\Delta = d(t) - y(t)$$

$$w_i(t+1) = w_i(t) + \eta \Delta x_i(t)$$

$$d(t) = \begin{cases} 1, \text{ if input from class A} \\ 0, \text{ if input from class B} \end{cases}$$

where Δ is the error term, $d(t)$ is the desired response and $y(t)$ is the actual response of the system. Also $0 \leq \eta \leq$ is a positive gain function that controls the adaptation rate.

The delta rule uses the difference between the weighted sum and the required output to gradually adapt the weights for achieving the desired output value. This means that during the learning process, the output from the unit is not passed through the step function, although the actual classification is effected by the step function.

The perceptron learning rule or algorithm implemented on a single layer network, guarantees convergence to a solution whenever the problem to be solved is linearly separable. However, for the class of problems, which are not linearly separable, the algorithm does not converge. Minsky and Papert first demonstrated this in 1969 in their influential book, Perceptrons using the well-known XOR example. This in fact dealt a mortal blow to the area, and sent it into hibernation for the next seventeen years till the development of multilayer perceptrons (popularly known as 'backpropagation') by Rumelhart et al. (1986). If the McCulloch-Pitts neuron was the father of modern neural computing, then Rumelhart's multilayer perceptron is its child prodigy.

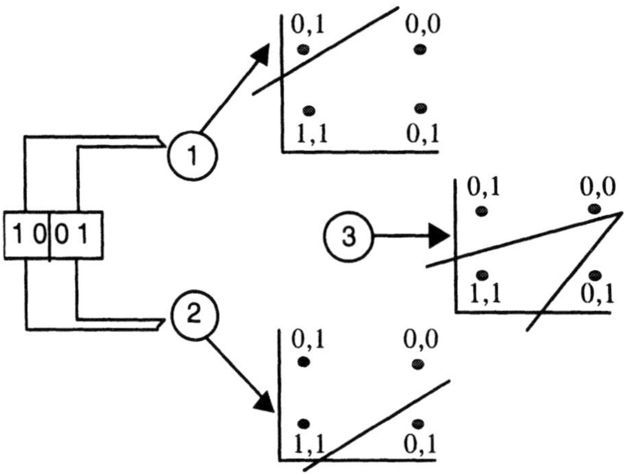

Figure 2.20. Combination of Perceptrons to Solve XOR Problem

2.6.3.2. Multilayer Perceptrons

An initial approach to solve problems that are not linearly separable problems was to use more than one perceptron, each set up to identify small, linearly separable sections of the outputs into another perceptron, then combining their outputs into another perceptron, which would produce a final indication of the class to which the input belongs. The problem with this approach is that the perceptrons in the second layer do not know which of the real inputs were on or not. They are only aware of the inputs from the first layer. Since learning involves strengthening the connections between active inputs and active units (Hebb 1949), it is impossible to strengthen the correct parts of the network, since the actual inputs are masked by the intermediate (first) layer. Further, the output of neuron being on (1) or off (0), gives no indication of the scale by which the weights need to be adjusted. This is also known as the credit assignment problem.

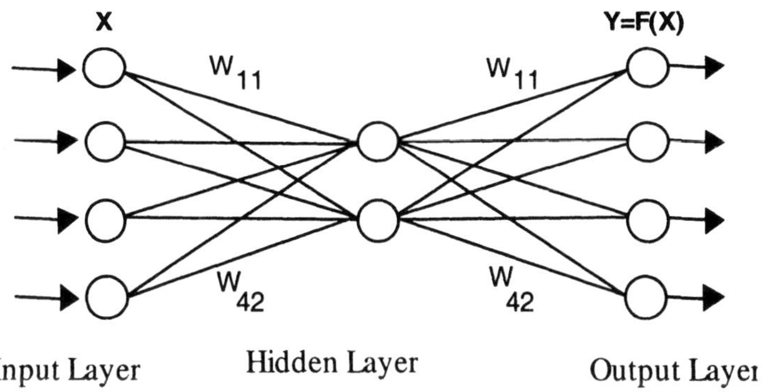

Figure 2.21. Multilayer Perceptron

In order to overcome this problem of linear inseparability and credit assignment, a new learning rule was developed by Rumelhart et al. (1986). They used a three layer multipreceptron model/network shown in Figure 2.21. The network has three layers; an input layer, an output layer, and a layer in between, the so-called hidden layer. Each unit in the hidden layer and the output layer is like a perceptron unit, except that the thresholding function is a non-linear sigmoidal function (shown in Figure 2.22),

$$f(net) = 1/(1+e^{-knet})$$

where k is a positive constant that controls the "spread" of the function. Large values of k squash the function until as $k \rightarrow \infty$ *f(net) → Heavside function.*

It is a continuously differentiable i.e. smooth everywhere and has a simple derivative. The output from the non-linear threshold sigmoid function is not 1 or 0 but lies in a range, although at the extremes it approximates the step function. The non-linear differentiable sigmoid function enables one to overcome the credit assignment problem by providing enough information about the output to the units in the earlier layers to allow them to adjust the weights in such a way as to enable convergence of the network to a desired solution state.

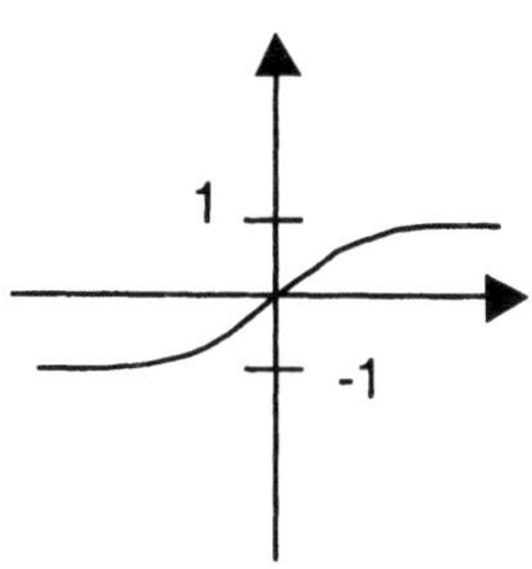

Figure 2.22. Sigmoidal Function

The learning rule, which enables the multilayer perceptron to learn complex non-linear problems, is called the generalized delta rule or the 'backpropagation' rule. In order to learn successfully, the value of the error function has to be continuously reduced for the actual output of the network to approach the desired output. The error surface is analogous to a valley or a deep well, and the bottom of the well corresponds to the point of minimum energy/error. This is achieved by adjusting the weights on the links between units in the direction of steepest downward descent (known as the gradient descent method). The generalized delta rule (McClelland, et al. 1986) does this by calculating the value of the error function for a particular input, and then back-propagating (hence the name) the error from one layer to the previous one. The error term delta for each hidden unit is used to alter the weight linkages in the three layer network to reinforce the correct decisions and discourage incorrect decisions, i.e. reduce the error.

The learning algorithm is as follows:

- Initialize weights and thresholds. Set all the weights and thresholds to small random values.
- Present input and target output patterns. Present input $X_p = x_0; x_1; x_2; ::::; x_n- 1$ and target output $T_p = t_o; t_1; ::::; t_{m}- _1$ where n is the number of input nodes and m is the number of output nodes. Set w_0 to be - theta, the bias and x_0 to be always 1. For classification, T_p is set to zero except for one element set to 1 that corresponds to the class that X_p is in.
- Calculate actual output. Each layer calculates

  $$y_{pj} = f[\sum_{i=0}^{n-1} w_{ij}x_i] = f(net_{pj}) = 1/(1+e^{-knet}{}_{pj})$$

  where w_{ij} represents weight from unit i to unit j, net_{pj} is the net input to unit j for pattern p, and y_{pj} is the sigmoidal output or activation corresponding to pattern p at unit j and is passed as input to the next layer (i.e. the output layer). The output layer outputs values o_{pj}, which is the actual output at unit j of pattern p.
- Calculate the error function E_p for all the patterns to be learnt

  $$E_p = 1{=}2[\sum_j (t_{pj} - o_{pj})^2]$$

  where t_{pj} is the target output at unit j of pattern p.
- Starting from the output layer, project the error backwards to each layer and compute the error term δ for each unit.

  For output units

  $$\delta_{pj} = ko_{pj}(1 - o_{pj})(t_{pj} - o_{pj})$$

  where δ_{pj} is an error term for pattern p on output unit j

  For hidden units

  $$\delta_{pj} = ko_{pj}(1 - o_{pj}\sum r\, \delta_{pr} w_{jr}$$

  where the sum is over the r units above unit j, and δ_{pj} is an error term for pattern p on unit j which is not an output unit.
- Adapt weights for output hidden units

  $$w_{ij}(t + 1) = w_{ij}(t) + \eta\, \delta_{pj} o_{pj}$$

  where w_{ij} represents the weights from unit i to unit j at time t and j is a gain term or the learning rate.

2.6.3.3. Radial Basis Function Net

The Radial Basis Function (RBF) net is a 3-layer feed-forward network consisting of an input layer, hidden layer and output layer as shown in Figure 2.23. The mapping of the input vectors to the hidden vectors is non-linear, whereas the mapping from hidden layer to output layer is linear. There are no weights associated with the connections from input layer to hidden layer. In the radial basis function net, the N activation functions g_j of the hidden units correspond to a set of radial basis functions that span the input space and map. Each function $g_j(\|x - c_j)\|)$ is centered about some point c_j of the input space and transforms the input vector x according to its Euclidean distance, denoted by $\| \|$, from the center c_j . Therefore the function g_j has its maximum value at c_j. It has further an associated receptive field that decreases with the distance between input and center and which could overlap that of the functions of the neighboring neurons of the hidden layer.

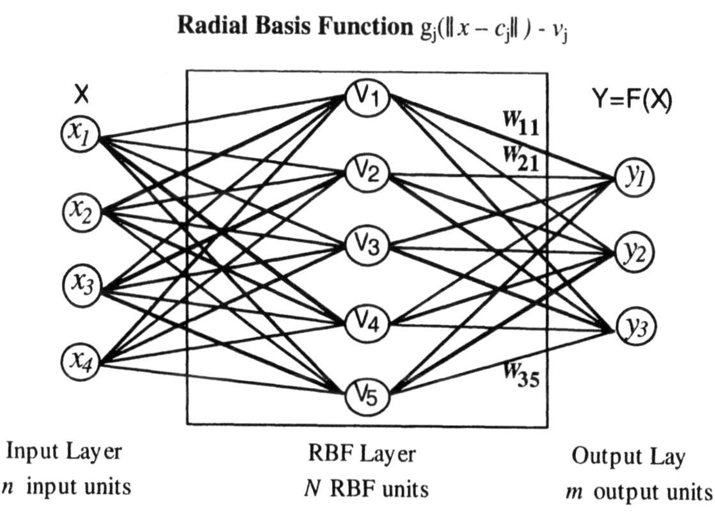

Figure 2.23. Radial Basis Function Net

The hidden units are fully connected to each output unit y_i with weights w_{ij}. The outputs y_i are thus linear combinations of the radial basis functions i.e.

$$y_i = \sum_{j=1}^{N} w_{ij} g_j(\|x - c_j\|)$$

One such set of radial basis functions that is frequently used are Gaussian Activation functions centered on the mean value c_j and with a receptive field whose size is proportional to the variances fixed for all units:

$$g_j(\|x - c_j\|) = exp(\|x - c_j\|^2/4\sigma^2)$$

where:

$\sigma = d = \sqrt{(2N)}$ with N number of (hidden) RBF units and d the maximum distance between the chosen centers.

One could use an unsupervised learning approach to determine the centers c_j and the width σ of the receptive fields, see Haykin (1994). One could then use the delta learning rule to determine the weights between the hidden units and the output units. Sincc thc first laycr can bc said to bc trained using an unsupervised approach and the second using a supervised approach one could consider such a net as a hybrid net. The RBF network is an important approximation tool because like spline functions it provides a quantifiable optimal solution to a multi-dimensional function approximation problem under certain regularization constraints concerning the smoothness of the class of approximating RBF functions.

The applications of multilayer perceptrons can be found in many areas including natural language processing (NETalk- Sejnowski and Rosenberg 1987), prediction (airlines seat booking, stock market predictions, bond rating, etc.) and fault diagnosis.

The use of neural networks is dependent upon availability of large amounts of data. In some cases, both input and output patterns are available or known, and we can use supervised learning techniques like backpropagation, whereas in other cases the output patterns are not known and the network has to independently learn the class structure of the input data. In such cases, unsupervised learning techniques characterized by Kohonen nets, and Adaptive Resonance Theory are used. The more commonly used Kohonen networks are described in the following section.

2.6.3.4. Kohonen Networks

Kohonen's self-organizing maps belong to a class of clustering algorithms, which employ a distance measuere for clustering data. They are characterized by a drive to model the self-organizing and adaptive learning features of the brain. It has been postulated that the brain uses spatial mapping to model complex data structures internally (Kohonen 1990). Much of the cerebral cortex is arranged as a two-dimensional plane of interconnected neurons but it is able to deal with concepts in much higher dimensions.

The implementations of Kohonen's algorithm are also predominantly two-dimensional. A typical network is shown in Figure 2.24. The network shown is a one-layer two-dimensional Kohonen network. The neurons are arranged on a flat grid rather than in layers as in a multilayer perceptron. All inputs connect to every node (neuron) in the network. Feedback is restricted to lateral interconnections to immediate neighboring nodes. Each of the nodes in the grid is itself an output node.

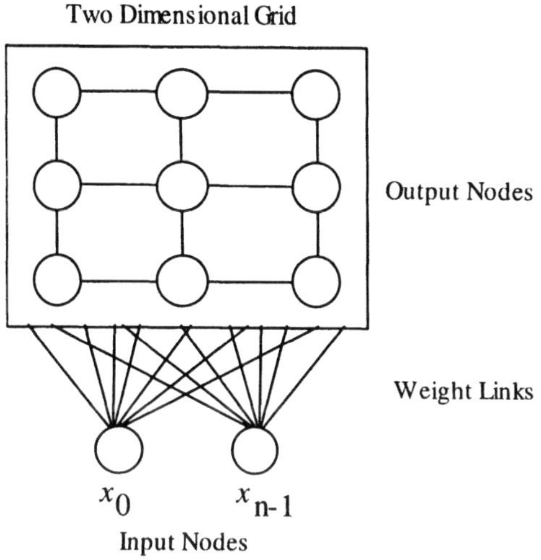

Figure 2.24. Kohonen's Self Organizing Feature Map

The learning algorithm organizes the nodes in the grid into local neighborhoods or clusters (shown in Figure 2.25) that act as feature classifiers on the input data. The biological justification for that is the cells physically close to the active cell have the strongest links. No training response is specified for any training input. In short, the learning involves finding the closest matching node to a training input and increasing the similarity of this node, and those in the neighboring proximity, to the input. The advantage of developing neighborhoods is that vectors that are close spatially to the training values will still be classified correctly even though the network has not seen them before, thus providing for generalization.

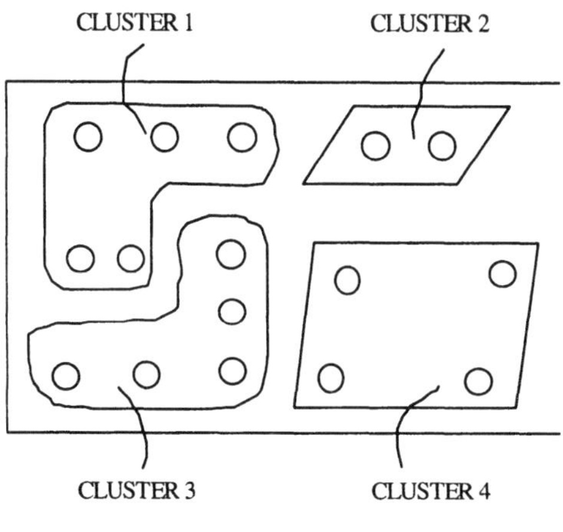

Figure 2.25. Kohonen Network Clusters

The learning algorithm is notionally simpler than the backpropagation algorithm as it does not involve any derivatives.

1. Initialize network

Define $w_{ij}(t)$ $(0 \leq i \leq n - 1)$ to be the weight from input i to node(unit) j. Initialize weights from the n inputs to the nodes to small random values. Set the initial radius of the neighborhood around *node j*, $Nj(0)$, to be large.

2. Present input

Present input $x_0(t); x_1(t); x_2(t); :::::; x_{n-1}(t)$, where $x_i(t)$ is the input to node i at time t.

3. Calculate distances

Compute the distance dj between the input and each output node j, given by

$$d_j = \Sigma_{l=}0(x_i(t) - w_{ij}(1))^2$$

4. Select minimum distance using the Euclidean distance measure

Designate the output node with minimum d_j to be j^*.

5. Update weights

Update weights for node j^* and its neighbors, defined by the neighborhood size $N_j{}^*(t)$. New Weights are

$$w_{ij}(t+1) = w_{ij}(t) + \eta(t)(x_i(t) - w_{ij}(t))$$

For j in $N_{j*}(t)$,hspace1cm $0 \leq i \leq n - 1$

The term $\eta(t)$ is a gain term $(0 < \eta(t) < 1)$ that decreases in time, so slowing the weight adaptation. The neighborhood $N_{j*}(t)$ decreases in size as time goes on, thus localizing the area of maximum activity.

6. Repeat steps 2 to 5.

The most well known application of self-organizing Kohonen networks is the Phonetic typewriter (Kohonen 1990) used for classification of phonemes in real time. Other applications include evaluating the dynamic security of power systems (Neibur et al. 1991).

2.6.4. Fuzzy Systems

Fuzzy systems provide a means of dealing with inexactness, imprecision as well as ambiguity in everyday life. In fuzzy systems relationships between imprecise concepts like "hot," "big," and "fat," "apply strong force," and "high angular velocity" are evaluated instead of mathematical equations. Although not the ultimate problem solver, fuzzy systems have been found useful in handling control or decision making problems not easily defined by practical mathematical models.

This section provides introduction to the reader on the following basic concepts used for construction of a fuzzy system:

- Fuzzy Sets
- Fuzzification of inputs
- Fuzzy Inferencing and Rule Evaluation
- Defuzzification of Fuzzy Outputs

2.6.4.1. Fuzzy Sets

Although fuzzy systems have become popular in the last decade, fuzzy set and fuzzy logic theories have been developed for more than 25 years. In 1965 Zadeh wrote the original paper formulating fuzzy set and fuzzy logic theory. The need for fuzzy sets has emerged from the problems in the classical set theory. In classical set theory, one can specify a set either by enumerating its elements or by specifying a function f(x) such that if it is true for x, then x is an element of the set S. The latter specification is based on two-valued logic. If f(x) is true, x is an element of the set, otherwise it is not. An example of such a set, S, is:

$S = x : weightofpersonx > 90kg$

Thus all persons with weight greater than 90 kg would belong to the set *S*. Such sets are referred to as crisp sets.

Let us consider the set of "fat" persons. It is clear that it is more difficult to define a function such that if it is true, then the person belongs to the set of fat people, otherwise s/he does not. The transition between a fat and not-fat person is more gradual. The membership function describing the relationship between weight and being fat is characterized by a function of the form given in Figure 2.26.

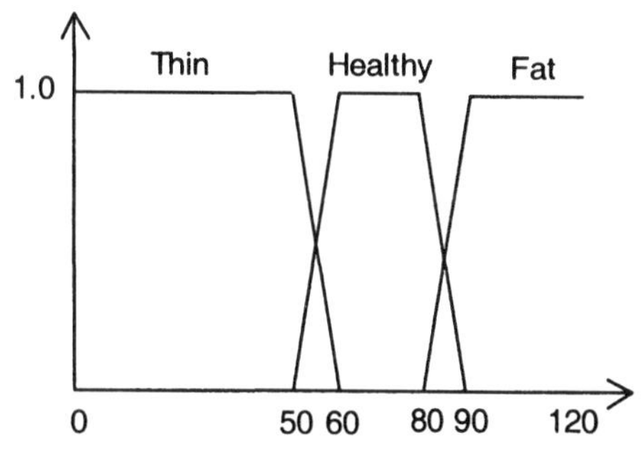

Figure 2.26. Fuzzy Membership Function

Such sets where the membership along the boundary is not clear-cut but progressively alters are called fuzzy sets. The membership function defines the degree of membership of the set x : x fat. Note this function varies from 0 (not a member) to 1 (definitely a member).

From the above, one can see that the truth value of a statement, *person X is fat*, varies from 0 to 1. Thus in fuzzy logic, the truth value can take any value in this range, noting that a value of 0 indicates that the statement is false and a value of 1 indicates that it is totally true. A value less than 1 but greater than 0 indicates that the statement is partially true. This contrasts with the situation in two-valued logic where the truth value can only be 0 (false) or 1 (true).

2.6.4.2. Fuzzification of Inputs

Each fuzzy system is associated with a set of inputs that can be described by linguistic terms like "high," "medium" and "small" called fuzzy sets. Fuzzification is the process of determining a value to represent an input's degree of membership in each of its fuzzy sets. The two steps involved in determination of fuzzy value are:

- membership functions
- computation of fuzzy value from the membership function

Membership functions are generally determined by the system designer or domain expert based on their intuition or experience. The process of defining the membership function primarily involves:

- **defining the Universe of Discourse (UoD):** UoD covers the entire range of input values of an input variable. For example, the UoD for an input variable Person Weight covers the weight range of 0 to 120 Kilograms
- **partitioning the UoD into different fuzzy sets:** A person's weight can be partitioned into three fuzzy sets and three ranges, i.e. 0-60, 50-90 and 80-120 respectively
- **labeling fuzzy sets with linguistic terms:** The three fuzzy sets 0-60, 50-90, and 80-120 can be linguistically labeled as "thin," "healthy" and "fat" respectively
- **allocating shape to each fuzzy set membership function:** Several different shapes are used to represent a fuzzy set. These include piecewise linear, triangle, bell shaped, trapezoidal (see Figure 2.26), and others. The shape is said to represent the fuzzy membership function of the fuzzy set.

Once the fuzzy membership function has been determined, the next step is to use it for computing the fuzzy value of a system input variable value. Figure 2.27 shows how the degree of membership or fuzzy value of a given system input variable X with value Z can be computed.

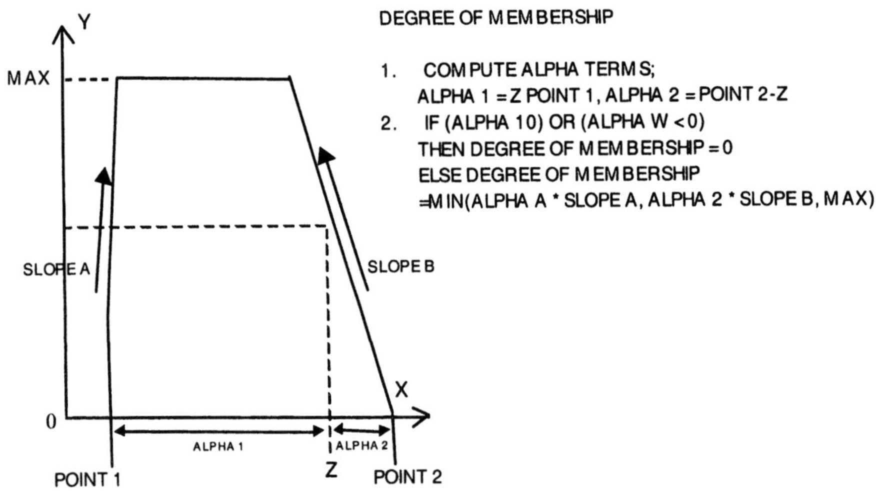

Figure 2.27. Fuzzification of Inputs

2.6.4.3. Fuzzy Inferencing and Rule Evaluation

In order to express relationships between imprecise concepts and model the system's behavior, a fuzzy system designer develops a set of fuzzy IF-THEN rules in consultation with the domain expert. The IF part of a fuzzy rule is known as the antecedent and the THEN part is known as the consequent. The antecedent or antecedents of a fuzzy rule contain the degrees of membership (fuzzy inputs) calculated during the fuzzification of inputs process. For example consider the Fuzzy Rule 1:

IF share_price_is_decreasing AND trading_volume_is heavy THEN market_order_ is_sell

Here, the two antecedents share_price_is_decreasing and trading_volume_is_heavy are the rule's fuzzy antecedents. Further share price and trading volume are fuzzy inputs with fuzzy sets "decreasing," "stable" and "increasing," and "light," "moderate" and "heavy" respectively.

The consequent of the fuzzy rule is represented by the THEN part which in this case is market_order_is_sell. Generally, more than one fuzzy rule has the same fuzzy output. For example, Fuzzy Rule 2 can be :

IF share_price_ is_decreasing AND trading_volume_is_moderate THEN market_order_is_sell.

In order to evaluate a fuzzy rule, rule strengths are computed based on the antecedent values and then assigned to a rule's fuzzy outputs. The antecedent values are computed based on the degree of membership of an input variable. For example, the fuzzy value of the antecedent share price is decreasing will correspond to the degree of membership of the "decreasing" fuzzy set of share price input variable. The most commonly used fuzzy inferencing method is the maxmin method. In this inferencing method minimum operation is applied making the rule strength equal to the least-true or weakest antecedent value.

For example, say, for share price of $50, and trading volume of 1000 contracts, the degree of membership values for fuzzy sets "decreasing," "heavy" and "moderate" are 0.7, 0.2, and 0.4 respectively. Rule strength of Fuzzy Rule 1 and 2 can be computed as follows:

Rule (firing) Strength of Fuzzy Rule 1 = min(0:7; 0:2) = 0:2
Rule (firing) Strength of Fuzzy Rule 2 = min(0:7; 0:4) = 0:4

The fuzzy output of selling shares is carried out to a degree reflected by the rule's strength. Since two rules apply to the same fuzzy output, the strongest rule strength is used in this case. This is done by applying the max operation as follows:

Market_order_is_sell = *max(min*(0:7; 0:2*); min*(0:7; 0:4)) = 0:4

2.6.4.4. Defuzzification of Outputs

Defuzzification is required to determine crisp values for fuzzy outputs or actions like *market_order_is_sell.* Another reason for defuzzification is to resolve conflict among competing outputs or action. For example, competing output market order is hold can also be triggered based with a rule strength of say, 0.6 on the share price of $50, and trading volume of 1000 contracts with a Fuzzy Rule 3:

IF share_price_is_stable AND trading_volume_is_small THEN market_order_is_hold

In order to resolve the conflict between competing outputs one of the common defuzzification techniques used is the center-of-gravity method.

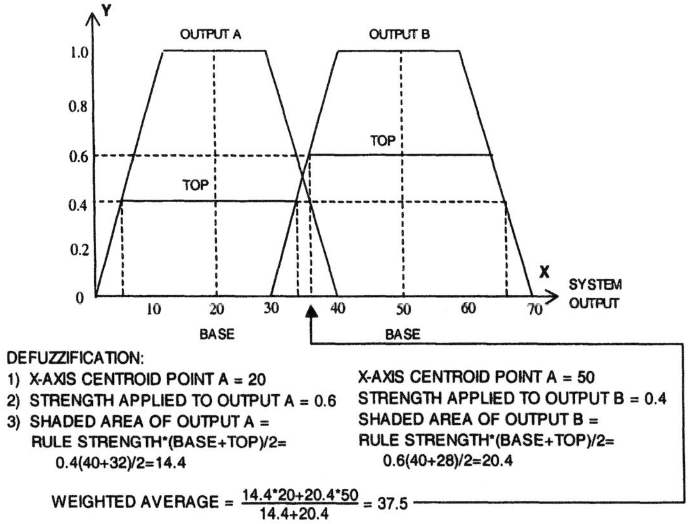

Figure 2.28. Defuzzification of Outputs

For a general case, the following steps as shown in Figure 2.28 are taken for defuzzification:

- determine the centroid point on the X-axis for each competing output membership function. In Figure 2.28 it is 20 and 50 for the competing outputs A and B respectively
- compute new output membership trapezoidal areas based on rule strengths of 0.6 and 0.4 for competing outputs A and B respectively as shown in Figure 2.28
- compute the defuzzified output by taking a weighted average of X-axis centroid points and the output membership areas (for rule strengths 0.6 and 0.4 respectively).

Fuzzy systems have been applied in a number of industrial control applications under the following conditions:

- When the system is highly nonlinear and mathematical models do not exist or are difficult to build.
- When parameters of the system change.
- Where sensor accuracy is a problem.
- Where the system may receive conflicting or uncertain input but must still make correct control decisions.

The satisfaction of these conditions provides number of advantages to systems modeled on fuzzy logic. These include increased efficiency of control cycles which may result in reduced power consumption or higher stability, requirement of less expensive and less accurate sensors because of the ability to model imprecision in sensor data, and ability to extract knowledge from an expert using everyday language. In spite of a number of advantages, fuzzy systems also suffer from some disadvantages. These include problems with learning of control process, tuning/optimization of membership functions, and optimization of rules. Genetic algorithms that are good at optimization problems are described in the next section.

2.6.5 Genetic Algorithms

Genetic Algorithms (GA's) were pioneered at the University of Michigan by John Holland and his associates (Goldberg 1989; Holland 1975; Jong 1988) . Genetic algorithms are stochastic algorithms whose search methods model the laws of natural selection and Darwinian evolution. Living organisms are problem solvers and evolution by natural selection selects good problem solvers and removes poor ones. The 'knowledge' that each organism gains, when trying to adapt to an ever changing environment, is reflected in the makeup of its chromosomes.

The GA maintains a **population** of strings. The strings symbolize solutions to a particular problem. New populations are iteratively created by the GA from the old populations by ranking the strings and interbreeding the fittest to create new strings. It is expected that new strings are nearer to the optimum solution to the problem. At each iteration (new **generation**), random new data may be added to a string in order to insure diversity over long periods and prevent stagnation.

"Survival of the fittest" is a notion used by GA's. As a measure of how well a particular candidate solution solves the problem we use a **'fitness function'** The concept of a fitness function is an instance of a more general AI concept, the objective function. The fitness function takes a string and assigns a relative fitness value to the string. It then selects the fittest string so that it can be used to create new and 'fitter' populations. The main purpose of the fitness function is to rank the strings by obtaining the strings fitness value.

The population can be thought of as a collection of interacting creatures. For example consider a species of rabbits (Michalewicz 1992). For each generation the faster, smarter rabbits live and breed to produce 'fitter' baby rabbits, while the slow, dumb rabbits tend to die off without breeding. Occasionally a mutation occurs, causing a diversification of the rabbit population. The ensuing generations will be faster, smarter rabbits.

2.6.5.1 Genetic Algorithms and Biology

All living organisms are made up of cells. Each cell contains strings of DNA **chromosomes** as shown in Figure 2.29. These act as building instructions for the organism and determine a range of hereditary aspects. GAs have string structures that are equivalent to chromosomes. A chromosome can be divided further into smaller units called **genes**. These are equivalent to the elements within a GA string. The location of a gene within a chromosome is called a **loci** (string position). A gene encodes a specific characteristic of the organism. (e.g., eye color). The value of a gene is called an **allele**. (e.g., blue eyes) and are analogous to the values stored in the GA string elements. The complete collection of genetic material in an organism is called the **genome**. **Genotype** refers to the particular set of genes in a genome.

In sexual reproduction, crossover takes place. A child's genetic material is a combination of the genetic material provided by the two parents. Some genes are inherited from the mother and the others are inherited from the father. Very rarely mutation (alteration of a gene) of the genetic material can occur. In nature the probability of mutation is very low since an enormous amount of mutations can destroy good genetic code.

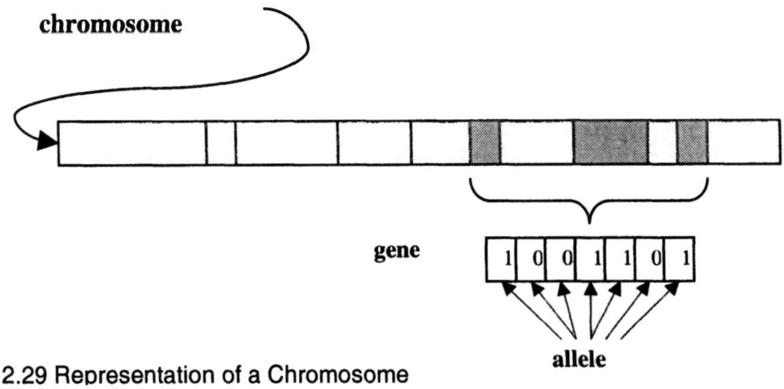

Figure 2.29 Representation of a Chromosome

2.6.5.2 Reproduction

Reproduction (also known as Selection) is based on reproduction in nature and survival of the fittest. The key idea is to give preference to better individuals, allowing them to pass on their genes to the next generation. For each generation, the reproduction operator chooses strings that are placed into a mating pool. The fitness function determines from the string's fitness value the likelihood that the string will be selected and copied for possible inclusion in the next generation. The mating pool is used as the basis for creating the next generation

Table 2.2: An Example Population

String	Fitness Value	Probability
110101	2	2/10 = 0.20
110111	5	5/10 = 0.50
011010	1	1/10 = 0.10
100010	2	2/10 = 0.20

Fittest = 110111 and should be selected for reproduction approximately 50% of the time.

Weakest = 011010 and should only be selected 10% of the time.

There are a large variety of reproduction operators in use. These include rank selection, roulette wheel selection, tournament selection, uniform stochastic sampling, and similarity-based selection. Most have in common the trait of selecting the fittest and discarding the worst, and statistically selecting from the remainder of the population.

The most commonly used reproduction method in GA's is the Roulette Wheel method (Figure 2.30). This method chooses strings purely on their relative (i.e. percentage) fitness values. Using the values from Table 2.2 we can construct a roulette wheel. To select the four strings to be placed in the mating pool, the wheel is spun four times. It is expected that the string 110111 be selected more often than the other weaker strings. Multiple copies of a string are allowed.

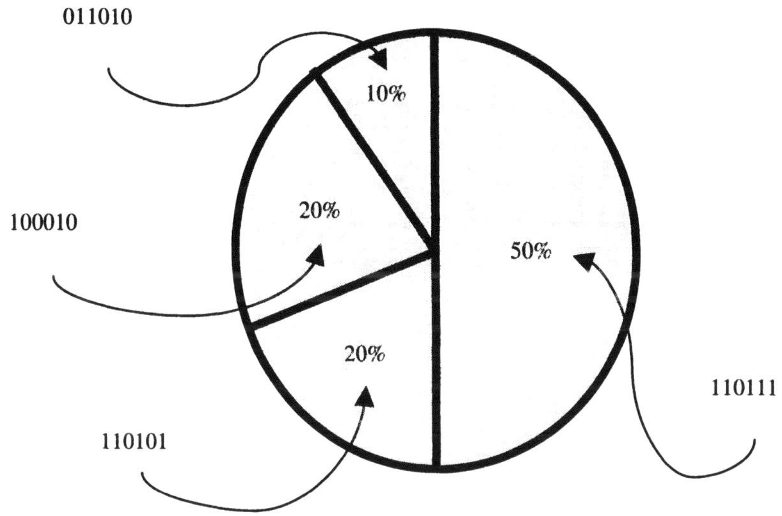

Figure 2 30: Roulette Wheel Representation of Table 2.2

2.6.5.3 Crossover

The values of the two strings are exchanged up to this point (see Figure 2.31). Crossover is analogous to the blending of chromosomes from the parents to produce new chromosomes for the offspring in biology. Two individuals (strings) are chosen from the mating pool. The strings may either be the same or may differ. A parameter called the crossover probability is used to decide if crossover should take place. The crossover probability, p, is set by the user. A typical value of p=0.6. If crossover is not performed the two selected strings are copied to the new population. When crossover takes place, a point along the bit strings is randomly chosen. The two strings are split at this point (crossover point) and the split regions are swapped to create two new strings that are composed entirely of genetic material from their two parents. These strings are then put into the new population. Crossover is continued until the new population is created.

2.6.5.4 Mutation

Identical copies of very fit individuals, that may not necessarily be the optimum solution, may come to dominate a population leading to premature convergence. This problem can be overcome by introducing a mutation operator into the GA. Mutation takes place when a gene in a genome is altered. The probability for this mutation is

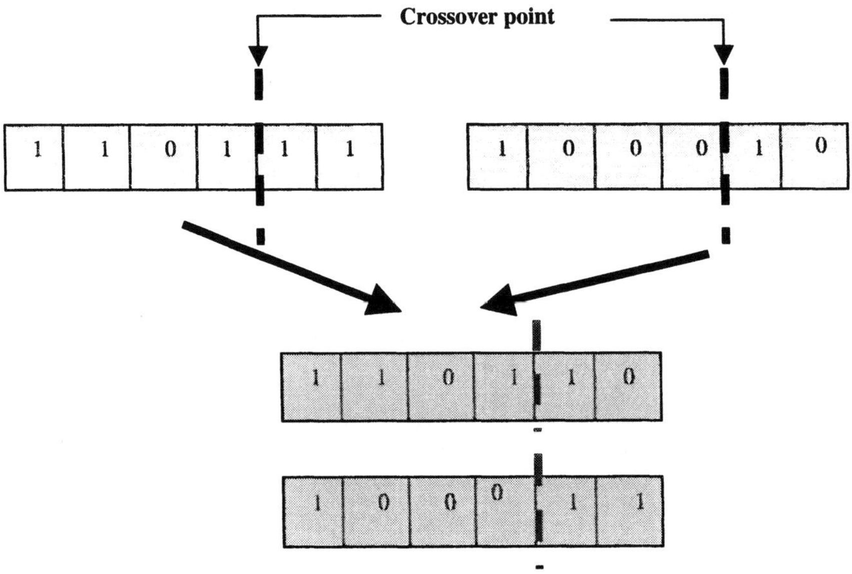

Figure 2.31: Crossover Operation

called mutation rate. It is performed during crossover, although it can be performed during selection instead of crossover. The GA checks each string in the mating pool to see if it should perform a mutation. If it is decided to mutate the string then a **mutation point** along the string is chosen at random, and the single character at that point is randomly changed. In binary strings the character is flipped. For example if we start with the string 10100 and mutate the third bit we get an altered string: 10000

The mutated individual is then copied into the next generation of the population. Mutation is very rarely used in most genetic algorithms and its probability should be kept very low (usually about 0.001%). A high mutation rate will degenerate the GA algorithm into a random walk, with all the associated problems. Then the cycle starts again with selection.

2.6.5.5 The Stopping Criterion

Determining when to stop the evolution process is extremely important. This iterative process continues until a user specified criteria are met. One common method is to stop when the population has converged. Since the offspring in such a situation are very similar to the parent's reproduction is pointless. Another approach is to stop when the fitness value has reached some predetermined value. This requires some knowledge of the theoretical limit of fitness for the problem domain.

2.6.5.6 Premature Convergence

A common problem with Genetic Algorithms is that the population can occasionally converge too rapidly. Rapid convergence is usually an indication that the GA is stuck in a suboptimal solution. The following features can be applied to reduce this problem:

Population

Several sub-populations can be created by dividing the original population. The GA treats each of these subpopulations exactly as it would treat the original population (i.e. reproduction, crossover and mutation are used). The only difference being that a small amount of crossbreeding between the subpopulations can exist. The crossbreeding ensures that there is enough varying genetic material being added to the subpopulations so that premature convergence is unlikely.

Size of Mating Pool

The reproduction process can be varied according to the specific problem being solved. One variation is in the size of the subset from which the parents are chosen (the mating pool). Some strings may not initially have high fitness values but may still have very good offspring. Choosing a subset that is too small can lead to such strings being lost to the ensuing generations. On the other hand, a subset that is too large can lead to slow convergence.

Selection of Parents

Parent strings may be selected in a variety of ways. The simplest form is by randomly selecting two parent strings from the population (sampling without replacement). As mentioned earlier, the Roulette Wheel method involves assigning probabilities to each string based on their respective fitness value. This method tends to lead to a higher convergence rate than the first.

Mutation Rate

Since mutation is the only way new genetic material is introduced into a population, it plays an important role in a genetic algorithm. If the initial population is relatively small compared with the search space, then it is highly possible that many genes are not represented from the start. Mutation can help overcome this but a very high rate can lead to extreme difficulties for the GA to converge due to the added randomness. A very low mutation rate can lead to suboptimal solutions.

2.6.6. Intelligent Fusion, Transformation and Combination

Intelligent technologies such as Expert Systems, Neural Networks and Generic Algorithms have also been used in various hybrid configurations. These hybrid configurations have been grouped into four classes, namely, fusion, transformation, combination and associative systems. The structure of these configurations is described in chapter 3. These classes of systems, and their knowledge and task modeling issue stages, have been described in Khosla and Dillon (1997).

2.7 Software Engineering Technologies

There are two software engineering technologies used in this book.

- Object-Oriented Technology
- Agents and Agent Architectures

2.7.1.Object-Oriented Software Engineering

The recent research in object-oriented software engineering and databases has shown objects provide a powerful and comprehensive mechanism for capturing the relationships between concepts not only in terms of their structure but also their behavior (Cox 1986; Booch 1986; Kim et al. 1988; Myer 1988; Unland et al. 1989; Coad et al. 1990, 92; Rumbaugh 1990; Dillon and Tan 1993, and others). Computationally, they offer more powerful encapsulation than other knowledge representation formalisms like frames (Dillon and Tan 1993). They also have special features like message passing and polymorphism which make them attractive computationally than other symbolic knowledge representation formalisms semantic networks and frames.

As a result of research in these two communities and in artificial intelligence, a common set of characteristics which define the general object-oriented model unique object identifier, data and behavior (i.e. operation/method/procedure) abstraction or encapsulation, inheritance, composition, message passing and polymorphism.

Object-oriented methodology has been used in this book in the context of its knowledge modeling features like inheritance and composability, and software implementation features like encapsulation, message passing and polymorphism. These features are now briefly described in the following subsections.

2.7.1.1. Inheritance and Composability

The structured representation of real world concepts includes various kinds of relationships. Inheritance and composition are two constructs which have given expressive power to knowledge representation formalisms for relating real world concepts in a meaningful fashion. These two relational constructs are also important features of the object-oriented methodology.

Inheritance allows real-world objects to be organized into classes so that objects of the same class can have similar properties, and more specific classes or subclasses may inherit properties of the more general classes. In fact inheritance is also used as a mechanism for default reasoning in computer applications where knowledge is organized hierarchically. Put another way inheritance makes extensive use of abstraction. The classes at the higher levels in the hierarchy are expressed as generalizations of the lower level classes (which are their specializations). The relationship is expressed through an *IS-A* link. The two basic modes in which inheritance can be realized are single and multiple inheritance. In single inheritance, there is a single *IS-A* or *INSTANCE-OF* link from a class or instance at a lower level to class at a higher level, whereas in multiple inheritance there can be multiple *IS-A* links from a class at a lower hierarchical level and classes at higher level/s. Aggregation or composition is another common form of relationship observed in hierarchical structures. It represents the whole-part concept used in our everyday life (Britannica 1986) and is incorporated in the object-oriented model. A composite object consists of a collection of two or more heterogeneous, related objects referred to as component objects. The component objects have a *PART-OF* relationship to the composite object. Each component object may, in turn, be a composite object, thus resulting in a 'component-of' hierarchy. There are other forms of non-hierarchical relationships like *ASSOCIATION* (Dillon and Tan 1993) and others obtained from entity-relationship models (Coad and Yourdon 1990; Hawryszkiewyz 1991) which are also modeled as extensions to the object-oriented methodology.

2.7.1.2. Encapsulation

Encapsulation is a property of object-oriented models by which all the information (i.e. data and behavior) of a object is captured under one name, that is the object name. For example a real world object like *Chair* encapsulates attribute values that define the *Chair*, methods that are applied to change the attributes of *Chair*, and other related information. This notion of encapsulating information related to a particular concept does not distinguish between the type of attributes or methods used to define that concept. In other words, it is a useful software implementation methodology for realizing heterogeneous architectures involving more than one intelligent methodology.

2.7.1.3. Message Passing

When integrating two fundamentally different paradigms it becomes important to ascertain the communication mechanism between the two from a computational point of view. The object-oriented model provides a uniform communication mechanism between objects. In order to communicate, objects pass messages. A message defines the interface between the object and its environment. Essentially, a message consists of the name of the receiving object, a message name or method selector and arguments of the selected method.

2.7.1.4. Polymorphism

In large-scale domains, genericity is an important element to promote comprehensibility and intelligibility of the domain. Polymorphism (Pressman 1992; Dillon and Tan 1993) is another feature of the object-oriented models that brings about the genericity in terms of the behavior of different objects or concepts in the domain. It is one of the key features of object-oriented programming (Blair et. al. 1989; Pressman 1992; Dillon and Tan 1993). It allows object-oriented systems to separate a generic function from its implementation. These generic functions or virtual functions (as they are called sometimes) provide the ability to carry out function overloading (Berry 1988; Dillon and Tan 1993).

2.7.2. Agents and Agent Architectures

Intelligent agents and multi-agent systems are one of the most important emerging technologies in computer science today. A dictionary definition of the term "agent" is: *An entity authorized to act on another's behalf.* The definitional term "another's behalf" in this book refers to a problem solver or a user. The definitional term "entity" refers to the agent which maps percepts (e.g. inputs) to actions for achieving a set of tasks or goals assigned to it in a largely nondeterministic environment. The four ingredients Percept, Action, Goal and Environment (PAGE) of an agent have been derived from Russell and Norvig (1995). Table 2.3 provides a PAGE description of systems modeled as agent types. In fact Russell and Norvig (1995) define an agent as consisting of an architecture and a program *(agent = architecture + program).* As a software program it maps percepts to actions and in the process exhibits the following characteristics:

- **Autonomy:** An agent should be able to exercise a degree of autonomy in its operations. It should be able to take initiative and exercise a non-trivial degree of control over its own actions.
- **Collaboration:** An agent should have the ability to collaborate and exchange information with other agents in the environment to assist other agents in improving their quality of decision making as well as its own.
- **Flexibility and Versatility:** An agent should be able to dynamically choose which actions to invoke, and in what sequence, in response to the state of its external environment. Besides, an agent should have a suite of problem solving methods from which it can formulate its actions and action sequences. This facility provides versatility as well as more flexibility to respond to new situations and new contexts.
- **Temporal History:** An agent should be able to keep a record of its beliefs and internal state and other information about the state of its continuously changing environment. The record of its internal state helps it to achieve its goals as well as revise its previous decisions in light of new data from the environment.
- **Adaptation and Learning:** An agent should have the capability to adapt to new situations in its environment. This includes the capability to learn from new situations and not repeat its mistakes.
- **Knowledge Representation:** In order to support its actions and goals with an agent should have the capabilities and constructs to properly model structural and relational of the problem domain and its environment.
- **Communication:** An agent should be able to engage in complex communication with other agents, including human agents, in order to obtain information or request for their help in accomplishing its goals.
- **Distributed and Continuous Operation:** An agent should be capable of distributed and continuous operation (even without human intervention) in one machine as well as across different machine for accomplishing its goals.

An agent program with above characteristics can be a single agent system or a multi-agent system. Multi-agent systems are concerned with coordinating problem solving behavior amongst a collection of agents. Each agent in a multi-agent system represents a specific set of problem solving skills and experience. The intention is to coordinate the skills, knowledge, plans and experience of different agents to pursue a common high-level system goal.

Table 2.3: PAGE Description of Agent Types

Agent Type	Percepts	Actions	Goals	Environment
Fruit Storage Control System	Temperature, Humidity Reading	Control Fruit Weight Loss	Retain Fruit Freshness	Controlled Storage
		Control Fruit Disease		
Oil Dewaxing System	Oil Type, Oil Inflow Rate, Tank Oil Level	Adjust Oil Inflow Rate Valve, Adjust Oil Outflow Rate Valve	High Quality Dewaxed Lubricant Oil	Petroleum Plant
Inventory control System	Sales Forecast Existing Stock	Stockpile, Liquidate, Replenish	Minimize Storage Cost	Inventory and Sales Databases, User

An agent program describes the behavior of an agent in the sense that for a given set of percepts or inputs a particular action is performed. A number of agent programs can be found to assist an user in e-mail filtering, on line news management, and in various other manufacturing and business areas (Maes et al. 1994; Dinh 1995; Lee 1996). Agent applications can also be found in the areas of air-traffic control, network resource allocation, and user-interface design. On the other hand, an agent architecture outlines how the job of generating actions from percepts to actions is organized (Russell and Norvig 1995). Maes (1994) has provided a more elaborate definition. Maes defines an agent architecture as a particular methodology for building agents. It specifies how the agent can be decomposed into the construction of a set of component modules and how these modules should be made to interact. The total set of modules and their interactions has to provide an answer to the question of how the sensor data and the current internal state of the agent determine its actions and future internal state of the agent. Architecture encompasses techniques and algorithms that support this methodology.

2.8 Multimedia

Media can exist in various forms, namely, text, video, sound and music. The term multimedia is typically applied to use of some sort of interaction across media (or carriers) and concerns are focussed on integrating carriers (image, text, video and audio). The media characteristics shown in Table 2.4 are used for mapping media to the data characteristics and information content to be communicated to the user. The temporal dimension defines the permanent (Perm in Table 2.4) or static and transient (Trans in Table 2.4) or dynamic nature of the media. The granularity is indicative of the continuous or discrete form of the media. On the other hand, baggage characteristics reflect the level or interpretation associated with the media. These and other characteristics are used for designing multimedia as a means for interpreting the computer-based artifact. We look at these aspects in more detail in chapter 5.

Table 2.4: Media Characteristics

Medium	Carrier Dimension	Temporal Dimension	Granularity	Medium Type	Default Delectability	Baggage
Map	2D	Perm	Continuous	Visual	Low	High
Picture	2D	Perm	Continuous	Visual	Low	High
Table	2D	Perm	Discrete	Visual	Low	High
Form	2D	Perm	Discrete	Visual	Low	High
Graph	2D	Perm	Continuous	Visual	Low	High
Ordered List	1D	Perm	Discrete	Visual	Low	Low
Sliding Scale	1D	Perm	Continuous	Visual	Low	Low
Written Sentence	1D	Perm	Continuous	Visual	Low	Low
Spoken Sentence	1D	Perm	Continuous	Aural	Mhigh	Low
Animation	2D	Trans	Continuous	Visual	High	High
Music	1D	Trans	Continuous	Aural	Mhigh	Low

Further, modeling data using media artifacts involves a number of terms. Some of the terms that are used in this book are outlined here:

Consumer: a person interpreting a communication.

Medium: a single mechanism by which to express information, e.g. spoken and written natural language, diagrams, sketches, graphs, tables, pictures.

Exhibit: a complex exhibit is a collection or composition of several simple exhibits. A simple exhibit is that which is produced by one invocation of one medium, e.g. a diagram, computer beep.

Substrate: is a background to a simple exhibit. It establishes to the consumer the physical or temporal relationship and the semantic context within which new information is presented to the information consumer. For example, a piece of paper or screen (on which information may be drawn or presented) or a grid (on which a marker might indicate the position of an entity).

Information Carrier: is that part of the simple exhibit which, to the consumer, communicates the principal piece of information requested or relevant in the current communicative context, e.g. a marker on a map substrate, prep phrase within sentence predicate substrate.

Channel: the total number of channels gives the total number of independent pieces (dimensions) of information the carrier can convey, e.g., a single mark or icon (say, ship icon) can convey information by its shape, color, position and orientation in relation to a background map.

2.9 Summary

E-business as a discipline represents a whole range of new and known concepts and technologies. The first half of this chapter introduces the reader to different types of e-business systems, e-business strategies and e-business models. E-business systems include enterprise communication and collaboration systems, e-commerce systems, decision support systems, knowledge management systems and multimedia/hypermedia information systems. E-Business strategies include channel enhancement, value-chain integration, industry transformation and industry convergence. These strategies are used by organizations to attain competitive advantage using the Internet. Indirectly these strategies also represent the level of sophistication of IT capabilities of an organization and their corresponding ability to be engaged in e-business. The second half of the chapter introduces the reader to a range of technologies including Internet and web technologies, intelligent technologies, software engineering technologies and multimedia. These technologies include XML, expert systems, artificial neural networks, fuzzy systems and genetic algorithms. Expert systems, artificial neural networks, fuzzy systems and genetic algorithms are the four most widely used intelligent technologies. Case based reasoning systems are also introduced. These are used in domains like law where it is not possible to represent the knowledge using rules or objects. Software engineering technologies which have used in the book include object-oriented and agents and agent architectures..

Object-oriented software engineering technology today is one of the premium technologies for building software systems. Besides its ability to structure data through inheritance and composability relationships and other non-hierarchical relationships, its encapsulation, and polymorphic properties make it attractive from a software implementation viewpoint. Agents and agent architectures are one of the most important emerging technologies in e-business today. They provide a means to function in dynamic environments by mapping percepts to actions and in the process incorporate very sophisticated characteristics in a software program, namely, autonomy, collaboration, flexibility and versatility, adaptation and learning, complex communication, and others. Finally, multimedia technologies are being used for developing perceptual representations of data and enhancing the effectiveness of use of computer-based artifacts

References

Adler S. (1998), "Initial Proposal for XSL", available from: http://www.w3.org/TR/NOTE-XSL.html

Aitkins, J. (1983), "Prototypical Knowledge for Expert Systems," *Artificial Intelligence*, vol. 20, pp. 163-210.

Balzer, R., Erman, L. D., London, P. E. and Williams, C. (1980), "Hearsay-III:A Domain-Independent Framework for Expert Systems," in *First National Conference on Artificial Intelligence* (AAAI), pp. 108-110

Berry, J. T. (1988), *C++ Programming, Howard W. Sams and company*, Indianapolis, Indiana, USA.

Blair B. and Boyer J. (1999), "XFDL: Creating Electronic Commerce Transaction Records Using XML", *Proceedings of the WWW8 Intl. Conference*, Toronto, Canada, pp. 533-544

Bray T. et al. (ed.) (1998), "Extensible Markup Language (XML) 1.0", available at http://www.w3.org/TR/1998/REC-xml-19980210

Encyclopedia Britanica, (1986), Articles on "Behaviour, Animal," "Classification Theory," and "Mood," Encyclopedia Britanica, Inc.

Chandrasekaran, B. (1990), *What Kind of Information Processing is Intelligence*, The Foundations of AI: A Sourcebook, Cambridge, UK: Cambridge University Press, pp. 14-46.

Coad, P. and Yourdon, E. (1990), *Object-Oriented Analysis*, Prentice Hall, Englewood Cliffs, NJ, USA.
Coad, P. and Yourdon, E. (1991), *Object-Oriented Analysis and Design*, Prentice Hall, Englewood Cliffs, NJ, USA.
Coad, P. and Yourdon, E. (1992), *Object-Oriented Design*, Prentice Hall, Englewood Cliffs, NJ, USA.
Cox, B. J. (1986), *Object-Oriented Programming*, Addison-Wesley.
Dillon, T. and Tan, P. L. (1993), *Object-Oriented Conceptual Modeling*, Prentice Hall, Sydney, Australia.
Erman, L. D., Hayes-Roth, F., Lesser, V. R. and Reddy, D. R. (1980), "The Hearsay-II Speech-Understanding System: Integrating Knowledge to Resolve Uncertainty," *ACM Computing Surveys*, vol. 12, no. 2, June, pp. 213-53.
Erman, L. D., London, P. E. and Fickas, S. F. (1981), "The Design and an Example Use of Hearsay-III," in *Seventh International Joint Conference on Artificial Intelligence*, pp. 409-15.
Finin T., Fritzson R., MacKay D. and MacEntire R. (1994), "KQML as an Agent Communication Language, *Proceedings of the Third International Conference on Information and Knowledge Management*, pp.112-124
Greffenstette, J.J. (1990) "Genetic Algorithms and their Applications" *Encyclopedia of Computer Science and Technology,* vol. 21, eds. A. Kent and J. G. William, AIC-90-006, Navla Research laboratory, Washington DC, pp. 139-52.
Goldberg, D.E. (1989), *Genetic Algorithms in Search, Optimization and Machine Learning*, Addison-Wesley, Reading, MA, pp. 217-307.
Hamilton S., "Electronic Commerce for the 21st Century", IEEE Computer, vol. 30, no. 5, pp.37-41
Hamscher, W. (1990), "XDE: Diagnosing Devices with Hierarchic Structure and Known Failure Modes," *Sixth Conference of Artificial Intelligence Applications,* California, pp. 48-54.
Hawryszkiewyz, I. T. (1991), *Introduction to System Analysis and Design*, Prentice Hall, Sydney, Australia.
Hayes-Roth, F., Waterman, D. A. and Lenat, D. B. (1983), *Building Expert Systems,* Addison-Wesley.
Haykin, 1994 *Neural Networks: A comprehensive foundation.* IEEE Press, New York.
Hebb, D. (1949), The Organization of Behavior, Wiley, New York.
Holland, J. (1975), *Adaptation in Neural and Artificial Systems*, University of Michigan Press, Ann Arbor, Michigan, USA.
Inmon, W.H., and Kelley, C., (1993), Rdb/VMS, *Developing the Data Warehouse,* QED, Publication Group, Boston, USA.
Jong, K.D. (1988) "Learning with Genetic Algorithms: An Overview," *Machine Learning*, vol. 3, pp. 121-38
Kim, Ballou, Chou, Garza and Woelk (1988), "Integrating an Object-Oriented Programming System with a Database System," *ACM OOPSLA Proceedings*, October.
Kohonen, T. (1990), *Self Organization and Associative Memory*, Springer-Verlag.
Kolodner, J. L. (1984), "Towards an Understanding of the Role of Experience in the Evolution from Novice to Expert," *Developments in Expert Systems,* London: Academic Press.
Kraft, A. (1984), "XCON: An Expert Configuration System at Digital Equipment Corporation," *The AI Business: Commercial Uses of Artificial Intelligence*, Cambridge, MA: MIT Press.
McClelland, J. L., Rumelhart, D. E. and Hinton, G.E. (1986), "The Appeal of Parallel Distributed Processing," *Parallel Distributed Processing,* vol. 1, Cambridge, MA: The MIT Press, pp. 3-40,
Michalewicz, Z. (1992) *Genetic Algorithms + Data Structures = Evolution Programs*, Springer-Verlag, Berlin.

Minsky, M. and Papert, S. (1969), *Perceptrons*, MIT press.
Minsky, M. (1981) "A Framework for representing Knowledge," *Mind Design*, Cambridge, MA: the MIT Press, pp. 95-128.
Myer, B. (1988), *Object-Oriented Software Construction,* Prentice Hall.
Neibur, D. and Germond, A. J. (1992) "Power System Static Security Assessment Using The Kohonen Neural Network Classifier," *IEEE Transactions on Power Systems*, May, vol. 7, no. 2, pp. 865-72.
Newell, A. (1977), "On Analysis of Human Problem solving," *Thinking: Readings in Cognitive Science,* Cambridge UK: Cambridge University Press.
Ng, H.T., 1991, "Model-Based, Multiple-Fault Diagnosis of Dynamic, Continuous Physical Devices," *IEEE Expert*, pp. 38-43.
Norris, G. et. al., (2000), *E-Business and ERP: transforming the enterprise*, New York Chichester: John Wiley
O'Brien, J., (2002), *An Internetworked e-Business Enterprise*, McGraw Hill Publishers, USA.
Pardi W. J. (1999), *XML In Action*, Microsoft Press
Pressman, R. S. (1992), *Software Engineering: A Practioner's Approach*, McGraw Hill International, Singapore.
Quillian, M. R. (1968), "Semantic Memory," *Semantic Information Processing*, Cambridge, MA: The MIT Press, pp. 227-270.
Rumbaugh, J. et al. (1990), *Object-Oriented Modeling and Design*, PrenticeHall, Englewood Cliffs, NJ, USA.
Rumelhart, D. E., Hinton, G. E. and Williams, R. J. (1986), "Learning Internal Representations by Error Propagation," *Parallel Distributed Processing,* vol. 1, Cambridge, MA:The MIT Press, pp. 318-362.
Russell, S., and Norvig, P. (1995), *Artificial Intelligence - A Modern Approach*, Prentice Hall, New Jersey, USA, pp. 788-790.
Schank, R. C. (1972), "Conceptual Dependency," *Cognitive Psychology,* vol. 3,pp. 552-631.
Schank, R. C. and Abelson, R. P. (1977), *Scripts, Plans, Goals and Understanding*, Hillsdale, NJ: Lawerence Erlbaum.42
Sejnowski, T.J., and Rosenberg, C.R. (1987), "Parallel Networks that Learn to Pronounce English Text," *Complex Systems*, pp, 145-168.
Shortliffe, E.H. (1976), *Computer-based Medical Consultation: MYCIN*, New York: American Elsevier.
Smolensky, P. (1990), "connectionism and Foundations of AI", *The Foundations of AI: A Sourcebook*, Cambridge, UK: Cambridge University.
Steels, L. (1989), "Artificial Intelligence and Complex Dynamics," *Concepts and Characteristics of Knowledge Based Systems*, Eds., M. Tokoro, et al., North Holland, pp. 369-404.
Unland, R, and Schlageter, G. (1989), "An Object-Oriented Programming Environment for Advanced Database Applications," *Journal of Object-Oriented Programming*, May/June.
Weill, P. Vitale, P., *Place to Space*, MIT Press, 2001.
Wang, X. and Dillon, T. S. (1992), "A Second Generation Expert System for Fault Diagnosis," in *Journal of Electrical Power and Energy Systems*, April/June, 14 (2/3), pp. 212-16.
Widrow, B., and Hoff, M.E. (1960), "Adaptive Switching Circuits," *IRE WESCON Convention Record*, Part 4, pp. 96-104.
World Wide Web Consortium (1998), "Extensible Markup Language (XML) 1.0" (W3C Recommendation) http://www.w3.org/TR/1998/REC-xml-19980210
World Wide Web Consortium (1999), "Namespaces in XML" (W3C Recommendation) http://www.w3.org/TR/1999/REC-xml-names-19990114/
Zadeh, L.A. (1965), "Fuzzy sets," *Information and Control*, vol. 8, pp. 338-353.

3 CONVERGING TRENDS TOWARDS HUMAN-CENTEREDNES AND ENABLING THEORIES

3.1. Introduction

In the past decade human-centeredness has become an important enabling concept in information system development. The fast growth of the Internet and WWW and partial failure of the dot coms has further accelerated development in this area. The need for human-centeredness has been felt in practically all areas of information systems and computer science. These include e-business, intelligent systems (traditional and web-based), software engineering, multimedia data modeling, data mining, enterprise modeling and human-computer interaction. In this chapter we discuss the pragmatic issues leading to human-centeredness in these areas and the enabling theories which are converging towards human-centered system development. These enabling theories include theories in philosophy, cognitive science, psychology and work-oriented design for human-centered e-business system development framework. We conclude the chapter with a discussion section that outlines the foundations of the human-centered system development framework described in the next chapter.

3.2. Pragmatic Considerations for Human-Centered System Development

In chapter 1 we quoted Norman (1997) as saying that the computer industry is still in its rebellious adolescent stage where technology provides all the excitement of youth as compared to the staid utility of maturity. Pragmatic considerations are about how various information technologies areas are evolving towards bridging this chasm between youth and maturity. The

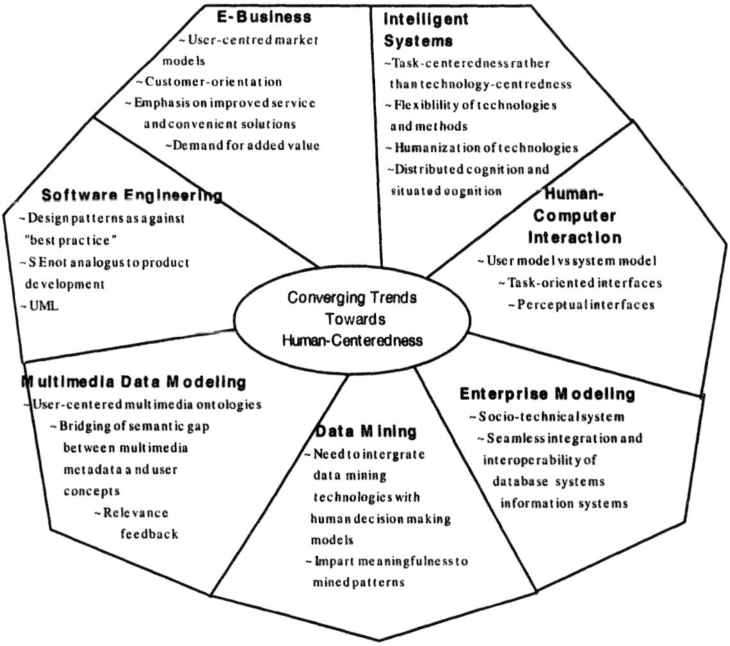

Figure 3.1: Converging Trends Towards Human-Centeredness

pragmatic considerations represent the practical problems associated with use of various technologies. These practical problems are underpinned in epistemological limitations (and strengths) which human and computers have, human vs. technology mismatch, relationship between technology and people and the impact of this relationship on the use of technology, social, organizational and task context in which technology is used, and some others.

The various areas looked into are:

- e-Business
- Intelligent Systems
- Software Engineering,
- Multimedia Data Modeling
- Data Mining
- Enterprise Modeling, and
- Human-Computer Interaction

3.2.1. e-Business and Human-Centeredness

E-business has revolutionized the way an organization functions today. From being just another channel a few years ago e-business has become a competitive necessity today. This revolution or change in thinking can be traced along four dimensions. These are the technology, competition, deregulation and customer expectations. The Internet technology has led to "death of distance", digitization of practically everything, improvement in the information content of product and services. Along the competition dimension, customer orientation and service and global reach have become competitive imperatives. Deregulation of telecommunication industry and other industries, single currency zones and ever changing business boundaries have further increased the potential for e-business. Finally, the changes along the first three dimensions have led to high customer sophistication and expectation. The demand for cost effective and convenient business solutions, high level of customization, and added customer value has led to change of focus from product-centric to customer-centric e-business designs. The customer-centric e-business designs are leading the development towards customer-centric market models (described in chapter 8) as against product-centric market models and human or consumer-centered brokerage architectures, online data mining of users behavior (described in chapter 7), and customization of web sites. At another level, development of knowledge management systems represents customization which is based on skill sets and tasks closely linked to the needs of the users or employees within an organization or wider communities (described in chapter 9).

The scenario in which vendors, brokers and buyers interact on private networks or, more frequently, on the global Net to execute commercial transactions has become increasingly familiar to the general public. Many software architectures have been proposed for supporting such networks in the past few years; in Hands, et. al., (1998) some of them are presented, addressing issues such as sales, ordering and delivery of products in the framework of the global Internet.

Indeed, Internet based electronic commerce is currently a driving force behind the evolution of many *Web-based technologies* such as HTTP, HTML, Java, CGI and others (Hamilton 1997), all of which were originally conceived for different applications. A further step toward open markets standardization has been envisioned in *eCo* (refer Figure 3.2), a reference architecture for electronic commerce proposed by the CommerceNet Consortium (including Actra, Bank of America, Visigenic, World Wide Web Consortium, Mitsubishi, NEC and Oki), which exploits Web-based technologies such as HTML, and Java/CORBA (Tenenbaum et. al. 1998).

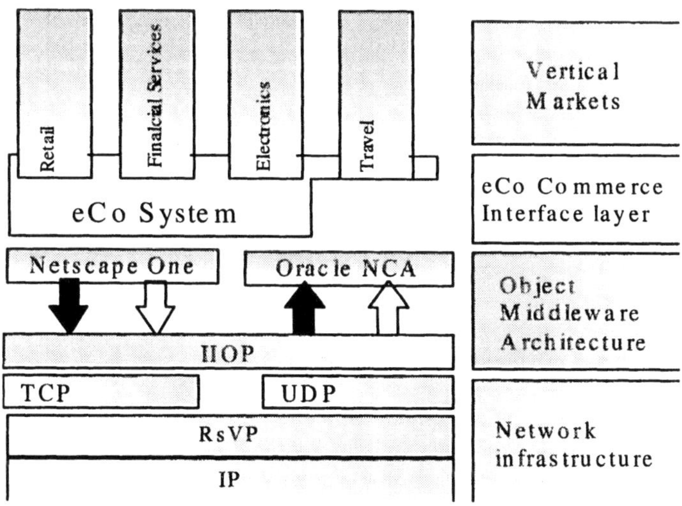

Figure 3.2: Electronic Commerce Framework

The eCo platform was originally a framework of reusable software components based on CORBA middleware standard, (Orfali, R. and Harkey, D. 1997) that can be used to build electronic commerce applications.

It includes a high-level domain specific language, *Common Business Language (CBL)* allowing software modules to communicate much like humans involved in commercial transactions, but exchanging *EDI-compliant object documents* instead of traditional paper documents.

Industry-wide standardization of eCo objects should allow companies to build *open markets* for business-to-business electronic commerce. Objects can be created in all the main proprietary environments, including IBM, Oracle, JavaSoft and Netscape.

In 1997, eCo-system was entirely recast on an XML foundation, due to XML adoption by all key vendors of the CommerceNet Consortium.

The eCo system framework overcomes a long-standing barrier to the development of electronic commerce, as XML documents provide, at least in principle, an incremental path to business automation, whereby browser-based tasks are gradually transferred to software agents. This development might allow traditional supply chains to evolve into open markets, while agents interact with business services through object documents.

However, traditional commerce, the existing electronic commerce architectures on the Internet are supplier-centered. XML's human readability, while an advantage over CORBA (Glushko 1999), does not eliminate the risk of a supply-side market model, where the structure and content of metadata are modeled w.r.t. the needs of vendors and distributors, leaving it to the brokers to transform them into a form more suitable for the buyers.

In this setting, nearly every electronic commerce purchase is preceded by a *network search* or *product brokering* phase (Tenenbaum et al. 1998). when the customer navigates the trading network looking for the needed products or services.

However, the avalanche of on-line suppliers and multimedia information about goods and services currently available, makes it difficult to locate, purchase and obtain the desired products at the best prices. General-purpose Internet search engines seem wholly unfit for this task.

A solution to this problem is the definition of a human or consumer-centered brokerage architecture which will locate all the vendors carrying a specific product or service, then query them in parallel to locate the best deals.

3.2.2 Intelligent Systems and Human-Centeredness

The four most commonly used intelligent methodologies in the 90's are symbolic knowledge based systems (e.g. expert systems), artificial neural networks, fuzzy systems and genetic algorithms.

Symbolic knowledge based systems have served varied purposes in industry and commerce during the last three decades. The most widely used versions being expert systems which have found their way into industry and commerce, including manufacturing, planning, scheduling, design, diagnosis, sales and finance. In these applications, the unitary architecture of production rules, normally enhanced by frames or objects, has been used to capture human expertise and to solve different problems. The different knowledge representation techniques like semantic networks, frames, scripts and objects have been able to capture some of the ways in which humans utilize knowledge. However, practitioners have also identified some of the limitations of symbolic knowledge based systems. These include among others, slow and constricted knowledge acquisition processes, inability to properly deal with imprecision in data, inability to process incomplete information, combinatorial explosion of rules, retrieval problems in recovering relevant past cases, and inability to reason under time constraints on occasions.

People deal every day with imprecision and fuzziness in data. This imprecision may be represented by linguistic statements. A number of fuzzy systems have been built based on fuzzy concepts and imprecise reasoning. Fuzzy systems have been used in a number of areas including control of trains in Japan, sales predictions, and stock market risk analysis. A major disadvantage of fuzzy systems and expert systems is their heavy reliance on human experts for knowledge acquisition. This knowledge may be in the form of rules used to solve a problem and/or the shape of the membership functions used for modeling a fuzzy concept. Besides the knowledge acquisition problem, these systems are restricted in terms of their adaptive and learning capabilities.

The limitations in knowledge based systems and fuzzy systems have been primarily responsible for the resurgence of artificial neural networks. In the financial sector, neural networks are used for prediction and modeling of markets, signature analysis, automatic reading of handwritten characters (checks), assessment of credit worthiness and selection of investments. In the telecommunication sector, applications can be found in signal analysis, noise elimination and data compression. Similarly, in the environment sector, neural networks have been used for risk evaluation, chemical analysis, weather forecasting and resource management. Other applications can be found in quality control, production planning and load forecasting in power systems. In these applications, the inherent parallelism in artificial neural networks and their capacity to learn, process incomplete information and generalize have been exploited. However, the stand-alone approaches of artificial neural networks have exposed some limitations such as the problems associated with lack of structured knowledge representation, inability to interact with conventional symbolic databases and inability to explain the reasons for conclusions reached. Their inability to explain their conclusions has limited their applicability to high-risk domains (e.g. real-time alarm processing). Another major limitation associated with neural networks is the problem of scalability. For large and complex problems, difficulties exist in training the networks and also in assessing their generalization capabilities.

Optimization of manufacturing processes is another area where intelligent methodologies like artificial neural networks and genetic algorithms have been used. Genetic algorithms are being used for solving scheduling and control problems in industry. They have also been successfully used for optimization of symbolic, fuzzy and neural network based intelligent systems because of their modeling convenience. One of the problems associated with genetic algorithms is that they are computationally expensive, which can restrict their on-line use in real-time systems where time and space are at a premium.

In fact, real-time systems add another dimension to the problems associated with the various intelligent methodologies. These problems are largely associated with the time and space constraints of real-time systems. Some examples of real-time systems are command and control systems, process control systems, flight control and alarm processing systems.

These computational and practical issues associated with the four hard and soft computing methodologies have made the practitioners and researchers look at ways of hybridizing the different intelligent methodologies from an applications viewpoint. However, the evolution of hybrid systems is not only an outcome of the practical problems encountered by these intelligent methodologies but is also an outcome of deliberative, fuzzy, reactive, self-organizing and evolutionary aspects of the human information processing system (Bezdek 1994).

Intelligent hybrid systems can be grouped into three classes, namely, fusion systems, transformation systems, combination systems (Khosla et al. 1997b). In fusion systems (Edelman 1992; Fu & Fu 1990; Hinton 1990; Sethi 1990; Sun 1994), the representation and/or information processing features of intelligent methodology A are fused into the representation structure of another intelligent methodology B. In this way, the intelligent methodology B augments its information processing in a manner which can cope with different levels of intelligence and information processing. From a practical viewpoint, this augmentation can be seen as a way by which an intelligent methodology addresses its weaknesses and exploits its existing strengths to solve a particular real-world problem. The hybrid systems based on the fusion approach revolve around artificial neural networks and genetic algorithms. In artificial neural network based fusion systems, representation and/or information processing features of other intelligent methodologies like symbolic knowledge based systems and fuzzy systems are fused into artificial neural networks. Genetic algorithm based fusion systems involve fusion of intelligent methodologies like knowledge based systems, fuzzy systems, and artificial neural networks.

Transformation systems (Gallant 1988; Ishibuchi et al. 1994) are used to transform one form of representation into another. They are used to alleviate the knowledge acquisition problem by transforming distributed or continuous representations into discrete representations. From a practical perspective, they are used in situations where knowledge required to accomplish the task is not available and one intelligent methodology depends upon another intelligent methodology for its reasoning or processing. For example, neural nets are used for transforming numerical/continuous data into symbolic rules which can then be used by a symbolic knowledge based system for further processing. Transformation systems have also been used for knowledge discovery and data mining (Khosla et al. 1997b).

Combination systems (Chiaberage et al. 1995; Fukuda et al. 1995; Hamada et al. 1995; Srinivasan et al. 1994) involve explicit hybridization. Instead of fusion, they model the different levels of information processing and intelligence by using intelligent methodologies that best model a particular level. Intelligent combination systems, unlike fusion systems, retain the separate identity of each intelligent methodology within a module. These systems involve a modular arrangement of two or more intelligent methodologies to solve real-world problems.

These three different classes of intelligent hybrid systems and their industrial applications have been researched and reported in Khosla et al. (1997b).

The concepts of fusion, transformation, and combination have been used in different situations or tasks, and by applying a top-down and/or bottom-up knowledge engineering strategy. All these hybrid architectures have a number of advantages in that the hybrid arrangement is able to successfully accomplish tasks in various situations. However, these hybrid architectures also suffer from some drawbacks. These drawbacks can be explained in terms of the quality of solution and range of tasks covered as shown in Figure 3.3. Fusion and transformation architectures on their own do not capture all aspects of human cognition related to problem solving. For example, fusion architectures result in conversion of explicit knowledge into implicit knowledge, and as a result lose on the declarative aspects of problem solving. Thus, they are restricted in terms of the range of tasks covered by them. The transformation architectures with bottom-up strategy get into problems with increasing task complexity. Therefore the quality of solution suffers when there is heavy overlap between variables, where the rules are very complicated, the quality of data is poor, or data is noisy. Also, because they lack explicit reasoning, the range of tasks covered by them becomes restricted. The combination architectures cover a range of tasks because of their inherent flexibility in terms of selection of two or more intelligent methodologies. However, because of lack of (or minimal) knowledge transfer among different modules the quality of solution suffers for the very reasons the fusion and transformation architectures are used.

As fusion, transformation, and combination architectures have been motivated by and developed for different problem solving tasks/situations, it is useful to associate these architectures in a manner so as to maximize the quality as well as range of tasks that can be covered. These class of systems are called associative systems (or associative hybrid systems) as shown in Figure 3.3.

The groundwork related to associative hybrid systems has been reported and explored in a book by Khosla et al. (1997b) and other publications (Khosla 1997c-f; Main et. al 1995; Tang et al. 1996 1995). As may be apparent from Figure 3.3, associative systems consider the four intelligent methodologies and their hybrid configurations, namely, fusion, transformation, and combination as technological primitives that are used to accomplish tasks. The selection of these technological primitives is contingent upon satisfaction of task constraints (e.g. presence/absence of domain knowledge, noisy incomplete data, learning, adaptation, etc.) which in Figure 3.3 have been grouped under the quality of solution dimension.

In summary, it can seen from the discussion in this section that intelligent associative systems have evolved from a technology-centered approach to intelligent systems where standalone intelligent technologies (e.g. neural networks, fuzzy logic, etc.) have been used for building intelligent systems to a task-centered approach where various intelligent technologies are used as primitives rather than prime drivers for building intelligent systems. The task-centered approach intends not only to model user/stakeholder tasks and capture deliberate, fuzzy, reactive, self-organizing and evolutionary aspects of human information processing through use of various technological primitives but also account for epistemological limitations which humans and computers have through satisfaction of various pragmatic task constraints.

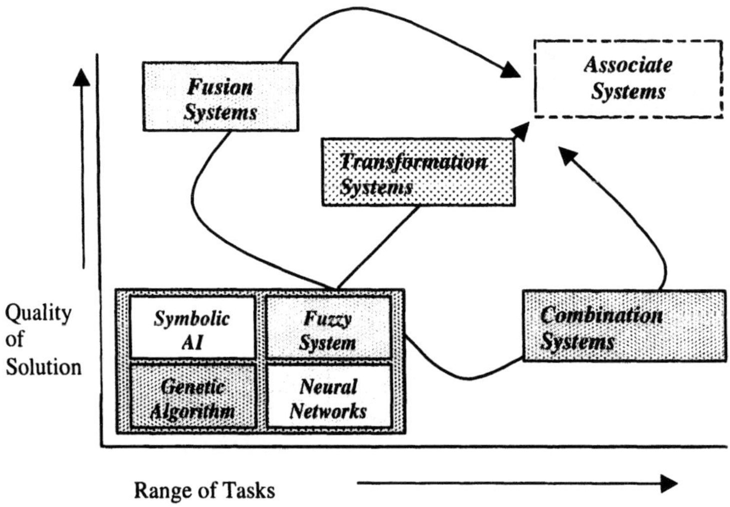

Figure 3.3: Intelligent Task-Centered Associative Systems

3.2.2. Software Engineering and Human-Centeredness

Software engineering can be defined as a layered technology that encompasses a definition phase, a development phase, and a maintenance phase. The development phase involves analysis, design, implementation and testing phases, respectively. In the past two decades it has evolved through three software engineering methodologies, namely, structured design or data flow methodology (Yourdon 1978), object-oriented methodology (Coad and Yourdon 1991; Jacobson 1995; Gamma et al. 1995; Pree 1995), and agent methodology (Wooldridge and Jennings 1994; Weilingaet.al. 1993).

Analysis and design phases are the main focus of the three software engineering methodologies. Analysis involves modeling of the information, functional, and behavioral aspects of a domain. On the other hand, software design is the technical kernel of software engineering. It is based on design characteristics like modularity, high cohesion, and low coupling. It is a multi-step process that involves data, architecture, procedure and interface design of a domain.

The traditional structured analysis and design methodology involves functional modeling using data flow methodology. Transformation and transaction flow methods are used to convert the data flow analysis into structured (architectural) design. One of the problems with the structured design methodology is the non-isomorphic transition between analysis and design phases. It can result in loss of information between analysis and design phases. The object-oriented methodology alleviates this problem by retaining the same vocabulary of objects and classes in the analysis and design phases respectively. Unlike the functional characteristics of the data flow methodology, object-oriented methodology intuitively captures the structural aspects of a domain. By definition, from a software design and programming perspective, the object-oriented methodology provides strong encapsulation and information hiding characteristics. In order to enrich the functional modeling aspects of the O-O methodology, some researchers (e.g. Rumbaugh 1991) have integrated the data flow methodology with the O-O methodology. More recently design patterns have been added to the armor of O-O methodology (Gamma et al. 1995; Pree 1995; and others).

A design pattern names, abstracts, and identifies the key aspects of a common design structure that makes it useful for creating a reusable object-oriented design (Gamma et. al. 1995). However these key aspects or abstractions are primitives, which are not expected to design an entire application or subsystem (Gamma et al. 1995). Further, the vocabulary of design patterns is primarily suited to meet the needs of software designers and not users. Many such additions to the O-O methodology in the last decade are much like "add more features" strategy of technology-centered products. As a result, today we have more than a dozen definitions of objects and classes, many of which (unlike the earlier stages of this paradigm) are not intuitive or user-centered for system modeling purposes. Moreover, from problem solving and human-centered perspectives, O-O paradigm does not provide an intuitive means of modeling goals and tasks.

Recently questions have been raised on the appropriateness of considering software analysis and design as two distinct processes. In fact the development of software design pattern construct is being seen as a means of alleviating this problem associated with software analysis and design process. The problem is primarily related to the fact that software engineering development process is not necessarily analogous to product development process in more mature traditional engineering disciplines. Thus, software design patterns which abstract software design structure from existing applications to be reused in a new one are being seen as means of ensuring software quality which is the main aim of the software engineering process. Although, the design patterns are a useful construct, their present state-of-the-art is still limited to the component level rather than an entire application. Further, their definition suggests a technology-based focus (i.e., they are likely to carry the limitations of the technology along with them) which makes them somewhat unsuitable for human-centered systems.

Unlike O-O methodology, agent methodology is primarily driven by problem solving, tasks and task-based behavior (Jennings et al. 1996; Khosla and Dillon 1997; and others). In fact, agents have transformed the Internet's character and mission. They are being used for searching and retrieving information for users from distributed sources on the Internet in a collaborative manner. However, besides their collaborative and task characteristics, they lack the structural characteristics of the O-O methodology. Traditionally, agent modeling is embedded in laws of thought, that is, classical AI logic. Most of the agent based systems on the Internet and in the field model tasks based on logic. This is at cross roads with the human-centered objectives, like activity-centeredness, focus on practitioner's goals and tasks, and the need to model tasks based on how users accomplish them rather than force fit a particular technology (like AI logic) on to the tasks.

Thus although, the three distinct approaches discussed in this section have made significant contributions towards achieving the primary goal of software engineering, namely, software quality, it is apparent they have not contributed in the same vein towards human-centeredness. The technology-centeredness of these approaches constrains them to model all aspects of a domain using a particular technology. This undermines to some extent the syntactic and semantic quality of a computer based artifact (software system) from a human-centered viewpoint. The syntactic quality determines the intuitiveness of the constructs used to model a domain. That is, how close arc the constructs used by a particular technology to those used by humans (i.e. users/stakeholders and not system designers). On the other hand, semantic quality determines how people use various artifacts to solve problems. That is, how close is the software design of a human problem to the human solution of that problem.

3.2.3. Multimedia Databases and Human-Centeredness

In recent years, large amounts of data in structured (e.g., relational/object-oriented), unstructured (e.g., image) and sequential (e.g., audio) formats has been collected and stored in thousands of repositories or multimedia databases. These repositories which exist in organizations as well on the Internet (e.g., World Wide Web) are used for locating and accessing multimedia data.

The progress made in locating and accessing data related to a single media type (e.g. image, audio, video or text) has been significant. Most of the recent techniques (Grosky 1994; Anderson et al. 1994; Chen et al. 1994; Glavitsch et al. 1994; Kashyap, Shah and Seth 1995; Jain 1996; Jain et al. 1994, and others) for searching and accessing digital data have employed the concept of metadata. Metadata represents implicit information about the data in individual databases and can be seen as an extension of the concept of schema in structured databases (Kashyap, Shah and Seth 1995). It can be classified as content-dependent metadata, content–descriptive metadata, and content-independent metadata (Kashyap Shah and Seth 1995). Content-dependent metadata depends only on the content of the original data. For example, in an image database color, texture, and shape are content-dependent metadata where information is determined by the content, e.g., hue and saturation values (for color). Content-dependent data can be automatically extracted from the contents. Content-descriptive metadata on the other hand, is determined exclusively by looking at the content, employs cognitive processes and can be domain-dependent or domain-independent. Domain-dependent metadata employs domain-specific concepts like retrieving all mammals or tigers from an animal kingdom multimedia database. Domain-independent metadata would be the one which captures the structure of a multimedia document (Bohm and Rakow 1994). However, as emphasized by Kashyap, Shah and Sheth (1995) and Sheth (1996) the above classifications are not sufficient to capture the semantic correlation[1] (as done by humans) for problems which involve more than one media (e.g., image, video and audio).. Even for a single media type like image, a number of models can be used for image indexing and retrieval. A user is constrained to use one model for querying, indexing and retrieval which may be entirely based on content-dependent and content-independent data. A user in actual practice may be employing more than one model for querying, indexing and retrieval and may actually be using a mixture of content-descriptive, content-

[1] Semantic correlation is defined as meaning and usage of data.

dependent and other metadata. Here again, from a human-centered perspective there is a scarcity of models or architectures that address this problem. Thus from a human-centered and semantic correlation perspectives there is a need for defining another level, namely, the ontological level above the metadata level as shown in Figure 3.4.

An ontology is a representation vocabulary, typically specialized to some technology, domain or subject matter. However, here we are dealing with upper ontology, i.e., ontology that describes generic knowledge that holds across many domains. Further, we are dealing with problem solving knowledge (e.g. tasks) about problem solving. As shown in Figure 3.4 the ontology can be domain independent and media independent or domain dependent and media independent. The domain independent and media independent ontology is based on generic tasks that are mapped on to the domain tasks and associated conceptual data structures (e.g., classes and objects). The domain dependent ontology on the other hand is based on specific domain tasks and associated conceptual data structures. Given the ontology level, one can adopt a top-down or bottom-up strategy for designing the metadata. The top-down strategy for designing metadata is also called ontology driven metadata design strategy because it will be influenced by the problem tasks in a domain understudy. However, the bottom-up strategy will be primarily media data driven rather than task driven.

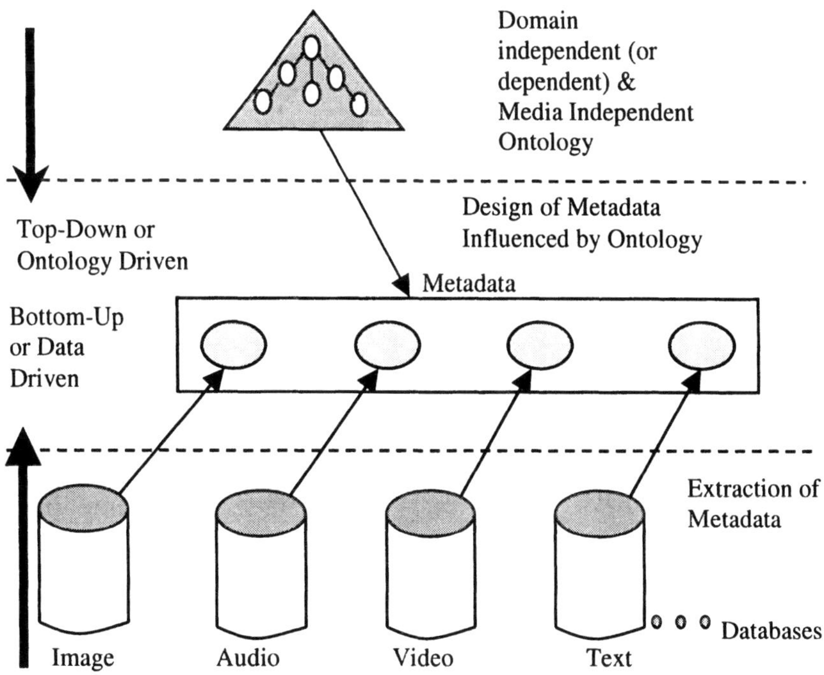

Figure 3.4: Multimedia Databases, Metadata and Ontology Levels:

3.2.5. Data Mining and Human-Centeredness

An important aspect of data mining is to impart meaningfulness (or meaningful knowledge) to the mined patterns from large databases (Khosla et al 1997b pp. 150-185).

One way of imparting meaningfulness is to integrate the task-based problem solving model of the user with the data mining process. That is, the problem solving model can be used to provide a priori knowledge to data mining techniques like summarization, clustering, association, prediction, and classification and enhance the quality and applicability of results of the computing mechanisms (e.g., data warehouse, object-oriented, neural networks, etc.) employed by these techniques. Further, this way data mining can become an integral part of the decision-making processes of stakeholders/user). The task based modeling process will also enable one to account for different user perspectives associated with data in the data mining process. For example, information related to a customer in an electric distribution utility is viewed by forecasting and pricing manager in terms of their energy consumption (for forecasting) and credit rating (for pricing) and other perspectives depending the task and the task model.

3.2.6. Enterprise Modeling and Human-Centeredness

The rapid growth in the use of computers in organizations in the past twenty years has reflected the important role played by information technology in a business enterprise. Most organizations, including businesses, government agencies, industrial firms, and hospitals, now depend on computers as an integral part of their operations.

Whatever form of information technology is utilized, the fact is that the management of business relies heavily on information throughout the business process where data, information, and knowledge are the three main resources to support that business process. In terms of organizational levels, the demand for data is very high at the operational level as shown in Figure 3.2. The demand for information and knowledge increases as we move up from operational level to the strategic level. This is because degree of unstructuredness of problems increases as we move up from operational level to the strategic level. Further, like information systems exist at all levels, there is also evidence that intelligent systems exist at all levels. The evidence can be seen in the development of intelligent systems such as intelligent airline reservation systems at the operational level (Nwana and Ndumu 1997), intelligent e-mail and news management systems at knowledge work level (Maes 1994), intelligent production scheduling systems at the management level (Hamada et al. 1995), and intelligent forecasting and prediction systems at the strategic level (Khosla and Dillon 1997b).

Figure 3.5: Applicability of Data, Information and Knowledge w.r.t. Organizational

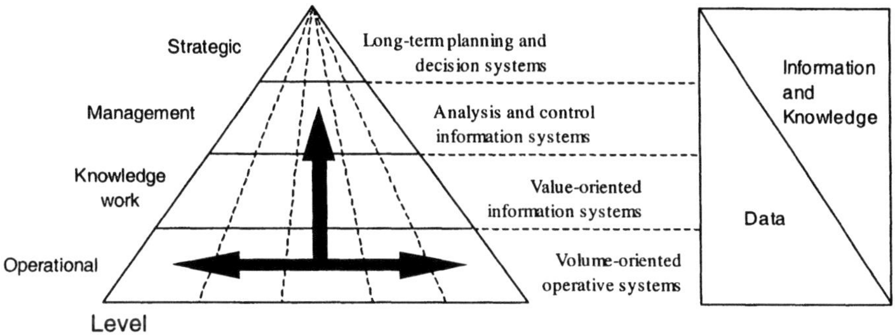

Like other areas covered in this chapter, technology-centered perspective has also dominated the development of enterprise systems at the operational, management and strategic levels in the last two decades. Although, database systems, information and intelligent systems represent different stages of evolution of enterprise systems, the distinctions between these systems to some extent today are technology-centered. Database systems are modeled using data abstraction technologies like entity – relationship diagrams, information systems rely on technologies based on functional abstraction like data flow diagrams, and intelligent systems rely on technologies like expert systems, fuzzy-logic, neural networks, and genetic algorithms which model different aspects of human-cognition, brain and evolution. As outlined in the previous paragraph, these three types of systems exist at all levels of an enterprise. This has created an obvious need for integration and interoperability of these systems. However, the technology mismatch is the one of the major obstacles today for their integration and interoperability. More so, fields like knowledge discovery and data mining have demonstrated that one type of system (i.e. a standard database system with DBMS capabilities) can evolve into another type of system (i.e. an intelligent system) to provide sophisticated intelligent decision support. Thus there is a need to build enterprise systems which are problem driven and which have capabilities to evolve with time. Such enterprise systems will need to have architectures which facilitate use of range of technologies for different tasks and needs which evolve with time. Thus in this scenario, technologies are more likely to be used based on their intuitive modeling strengths.

On the other hand, from a human-centered perspective (as outlined in chapter 1), in the past decade there has been an increasing emphasis on modeling of complex software systems which are based on synergy between human and the machine (Perrow 1984; Norman 1993). In the 70's and 80's information technology has been primarily used by organizations for automation (and enhancing the bottom line) without looking into its psychological and social side effects and the revolutionary impact it has had on the overall nature of workplace activity. In the 90's the disruptive effects of information technology had become all too visible and have forced the organizations to adopt a more balanced view where information technology and computers have to coexist (rather than necessarily replace) with people and their activities. In the 90's computers and information technology were being deployed based on the incentives they offer to workers in terms of their personal goals as well as the organizational goals. The computers and information technology in the 90's are seen as tools that assist people in their day-to-day activities and in breakdown situations rather than as prime drivers, which redefine workplace activities and tasks in an organization.

The development of knowledge management systems and enterprise portals in the last few years represent the latest stage in the seamless integration between database, systems, information systems and intelligent systems.

3.2.7. Human-Computer Interaction and Human-Centeredness

Human-Computer Interaction (HCI) is about designing computer systems that support people so that they can carry out their activities productively and safely (Preece, et al. 1997). Human factors engineering (which deals with factoring of human characteristics like limited attention span, faulty memory, etc. into the design of computer system) and usability engineering (which is concerned with making systems easy to learn and easy to use) are among a number of areas contributing to HCI. A lot has been said in the literature about making user interface human or user-centered. Most of the initial work done in the HCI has been based on interaction tasks. In this scenario, the user interface has been treated as a distinct entity detached from the underlying system design and/or model. As a result, the initial response of the software industry to the usability problems was to add more features to the user-interface and hope for the problems to go away. More recently, however, the HCI community has looked into areas like artificial intelligence, linguistics sociology, anthropology, sociology, design, engineering, social and organizational psychology and cognitive psychology to alleviate some of the problems associated with user-interface design. These areas have highlighted the need for considering user-interface design as being tightly integrated with overall system design. Thus today among other aspects, researchers are working on designing task-oriented interfaces, incorporating aspects related to industrial design in user-interface design, and integrating multimedia as means for reducing the cognitive load on users. The task-oriented interfaces specifically look into integration of the interaction tasks with the underlying problem domain tasks. However, complex software systems that clearly demonstrate such integration have still not emerged out of lab settings.

3.3. Enabling Theories for Human-Centered Systems

In the last section we have looked at how pragmatic considerations have resulted in the evolution towards human-centeredness of various areas of information technology. In this section, we discuss some theories from philosophy, cognitive science, psychology, and workplace that have influenced research and design of human-centered systems. These are:

- Semiotic Theory
- Cognitive Science Theories
- Activity Theory
- Work-oriented Design Theory

The rest of this section will describe these theories and their implications for design of human-centered systems.

3.3.1. Semiotic Theory – Language of Signs

The aim of this section is to establish the theoretical foundations for development of human-centered intelligent systems. For that matter, firstly theoretical aspects related to understanding of human intelligence from human science perspective (i.e. semiotic theory) and computer science perspective (artificial intelligence and computational intelligence) are outlined.

Human intelligence has always been of interest and curiosity in the scientific world. The understanding of human intelligence before the advent of computers was primarily rooted in human sciences and philosophy (Pierce 1960). After the advent of computers, the developments in this area have evolved under two fields, namely, artificial intelligence, and computational intelligence. The field of artificial intelligence is grounded mainly in symbolic logic and the physical symbol system (Newell 1980). The physical symbol hypothesis has led to development of class of intelligent agents embodied in symbols. The symbols represent knowledge at a higher level (also called the knowledge level) compared to ordinary computer programs. A number of knowledge level models of general intelligence were developed as a consequence including KL-ONE (Brachman et al. 1985), SOAR (Laird et al. 1987; Norman 1991) and ACT* and PUPS (Anderson 1989). An important aspect of these symbolic models has been the concept of inference and inference patterns.

While all computable problems can, in principle, be represented in symbolic terms as demonstrated by Turing's work on universal Turing machines, there is no reason to believe that aspects of the macrostructure of cognition (as opposed to the microstructure) are amenable to a purely symbolic treatment. This point is made clearly by McClelland, Rumelhart & Hinton (1986:12):

In general, from the PDP [parallel distributed processing] point of view, the objects referred to in macrostructural models of cognitive processing are seen as approximate descriptions of emergent properties of the microstructure. Sometimes these approximate descriptions may be sufficiently accurate to capture a process or mechanism well enough; but many times ... they fail to provide sufficiently elegant or tractable accounts that capture the very flexibility and open-endedness of cognition that their inventors had originally intended to capture.

Consequently, symbolic approaches at a macrostructural level tend to produce models that are brittle, all or nothing, solutions. Symbolic macrostructural approaches to problem solving (hereafter referred to simply as 'symbolic approaches') have a long history of success in the rigor of logic, mathematics and the physical sciences. Weizenbaum (1976) argues that this history has meant that many associate rigorous inquiry with symbolic formalisms to the effect that they are applied indiscriminately. Consequently, when the domain of a problem is inherently vague, either the vagueness is supplanted with concreteness or the problem is judged an inappropriate object of study.

Additionally, symbolic systems also suffer from what is known as the symbol grounding problem (i.e. the relationship between a word and the object it refers to is basically arbitrary). Modeling intelligence based on approximate descriptions and microstructure level of cognition has gained momentum to the emergence of computational intelligence (also known as soft computing). Additional aspects of intelligence, e.g. approximate or fuzzy reasoning, learning, prediction are being studied in this field (Khosla and Dillon 1997b; Zurada 1994). Unlike artificial intelligence, this field has largely grounded human intelligence in the human brain. A number of computational models have emerged including neural networks, genetic algorithms and fuzzy logic as outlined in the last chapter.

Although, the contributions made by artificial and computational intelligence fields have been significant, they still are fairly divergent contributions. These contributions have fallen short of providing a coherent view of human intelligence. Meanwhile, in the human sciences field there have also been significant efforts to model human intelligence. Well known contributions include the work of Boden (1983), and development of semiotics by Pierce and Morris (Pierce 1960; Morris 1971; Morris 1947).

Semiotics deals with basic ingredients of intelligence and their relationships. These ingredients are signs (representations), object (phenomenon), and interpretants (knowledge) as shown in Figure 3.6. The triple (sign, object, interpretation) represents a signic process, or semiosis (Morris 1971). Performing semiosis is to extract meaning of an object or phenomenon. In the process of extracting meaning it essentially studies the basic aspects of cognition and communication. Cognition means to deal with and to comprehend phenomena that occur in an environment. Communication means how a comprehended phenomenon can be transmitted between intelligent beings.

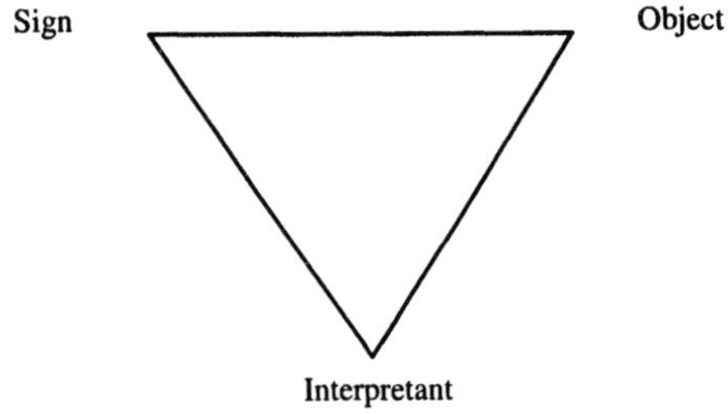

Figure 3.6: Triad of Signs

The basic unit of analysis in semiotics is a sign. Signs are representations, which are either internal or external to a cognitive system, which can evoke – in a cognitive system – internal representations called *interpretants* that represent presumable objects in the world. Interpretants too can act as signs evoking other interpretants. Interpretants only represent presumable objects because any cognitive system will not have absolute privileged access to knowledge about the world.

When we refer to 'dog' we are referring to a sign and not its referent, so 'dog' is a sign for dogs. Incidentally, this kind of sign is known as a *symbol* because it has a conventional and arbitrary relationship with its meaning.

While in some sense the meaning of something can be represented by a word, it is only through a process of decoding this representation that we understand it. To do this requires background knowledge about the meaning associated with it. Obviously, 'dog' does not mean anything unless one has had some kind of experience with dogs and is aware of the conventional relationship between the word and this experience.[2]

The experience of dogs is represented internally by a cognitive system and is distinct from a definition of 'dog' in terms of other high-level symbols. This is a point which seems to be only vaguely recognized by some, working on natural language or other symbolic systems who represent the decoded meaning (or interpretant) of a symbol exclusively in terms of other symbols (for example, a predicate calculus style representation). This practice only serves to specify the *relationships* between symbols in a symbol system without grounding their meaning in experience. One cannot recognize an object in the world without having some knowledge of what the sensory experience of that object (or the objects that comprise it) is like. This problem, called the 'symbol grounding problem' (Gudwin & Gomide 1997 a,b,c), is a recurrent problem in approaches to natural language and symbolic systems in general.

In his work Pierce (1960) developed three trichotomies of signs based on the original triad shown in Figure 3.6. In the first trichotomy a sign, according to Pierce (1960), is one of three kinds: Qualisign (a "mere quality or feeling"), Sinsign (an "actual existent or sensation") or Legisign (a "general law or rational thought"). The second trichotomy relates each sign to its object in one of three ways; as an Icon, Index or Symbol. Icon is "some character in itself", and can be classified as an image, diagram or metaphor. Index represents "some existential relation to an object," like a symptom is causally related to a disease. The symbol represents "some relation to the interpretant". Finally, in the third trichotomy each sign has an interpretant that represents the sign as a sign of possibility (Rheme), fact (Dicent) or reason (Argument). All the three trichotomies are shown in Table 3.1.

Pierce (1960) combined these three trichotomies to develop taxonomy of signs. A description of this taxonomy can be found in Sheriff (1989). Using the correspondence between signs and interpretants, Gudwin and Gomide (1997a) have adapted the taxonomy of signs drawn from semiotics to a taxonomy of associated knowledge types (see Figure 3.7. Figure 3.7 shows a modified version of the taxonomy as outlined by Gudwin and Gomicide (1997a). It includes the fusion, combination and transformation argumentative knowledge types described in section 3.2.2. We now provide a description of each of the knowledge types shown in Figure 3.7.

Table 3.1: Three Trichotomies of Signs (adopted from Sheriff (1989))

A sign is:	a "mere quality" QUALISIGN	an "actual existent" SINSIGN	a "general law" LEGISIGN
A sign relates to its object in having:	"some character in itself" (e.g. metaphor)	"some existential relation to that object" (e.g.	"some relation to the interpretant" SYMBOL

[2] Note that there are actually three distinct kinds of knowledge involved here. One relates to the experience of dogs, one to the experience of 'dogs' (the sign for dogs) and the other to the experience of the mapping between these two concepts.

	ICON	symptom to a disease) INDEX	
A sign's interpretant represents it (sign) as a sign of:	"possibility" RHEME	"fact" DICENT	"reason" ARGUMENT

3.3.1.1. Rhematic Knowledge

Rhematic knowledge as shown in Figure 3.7 has three types: symbolic, indexical and iconic. Symbolic rhematic knowledge is knowledge of arbitrary names like 'dog' or any symbol which has a conventional and arbitrary relationship to its referent. Indexical rhematic knowledge is knowledge of indices - signs that are not conventionalized in the way symbols are but are indicative of something in the way that smoke is indicative of fire. Indices as mentioned earlier are signs by virtue of their relationships with other phenomena. Such relationships can be causal, spatial, temporal or anything else that has the effect of associating a sign with a phenomenon.

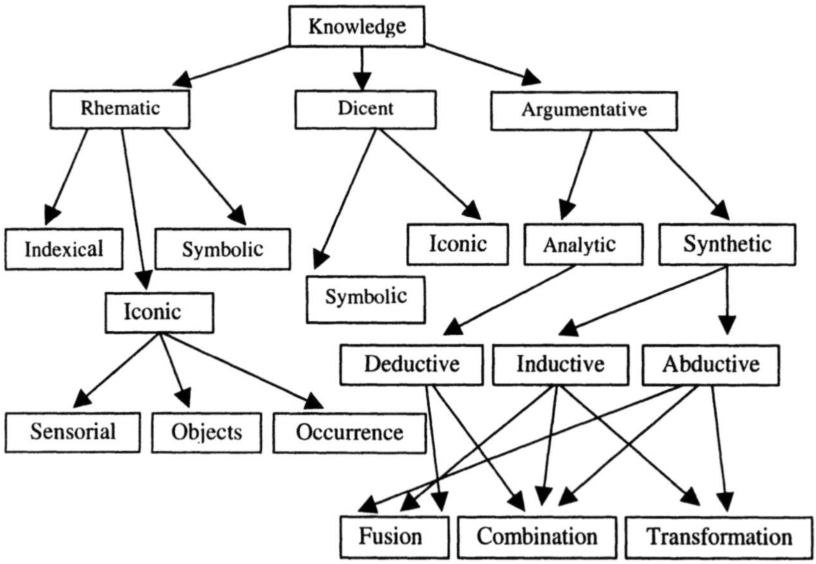

Figure 3.7: Knowledge Types (modified and adapted from Gudwin and Gomide 1997a)

Iconic rhematic knowledge is knowledge of signs that resemble their referents or provide direct models of phenomena. As such, icons unlike symbols are not arbitrarily related to their referents. There is a further subdivision of iconic rhematic knowledge into *sensorial*, *object* and *occurrence* knowledge types. Sensorial knowledge is knowledge from the senses or information to be sent to actuators. It involves interaction with the environment of the cognitive system. Object knowledge is an abstraction of sensory patterns representing an object in the world. Occurrence knowledge is knowledge of events, sequences of events, and involves actions.

3.3.1.2. Dicent Knowledge

Dicent knowledge employs truth-values (or degree of membership) to link sensorial, object or occurrence knowledge to world entities. It has two types: iconic and symbolic. Iconic propositions are propositions whose truth-values are derived directly from iconic rhematic knowledge (i.e., from experience). Symbolic propositions are names for other propositions, which may be either iconic or symbolic. Their truth-values match those of their associated propositions.

Symbolic propositions have been used in classical symbolic logic where we assume that the truth-value of the symbolic propositions are given. They have 0 or 1 truth-value, where truth-value of 1 means the proposition is a fact. They do not involve the semantic complexity (e.g. fuzzy membership) of iconic propositions where the truth-value lies in the interval 0 to 1.

3.3.1.3. Argumentative Knowledge

Finally, argumentative knowledge is knowledge used to generate new knowledge through inference or reasoning. There are three types: deductive, inductive and abductive. Deductive inference is categorized as analytic, meaning it does not require knowledge of the world. For example:

if *P* is equivalent to *Q*
and if *Q* implies *R*
then we can deduce that *P* also implies *R*.

This is true regardless of what *P*, *Q* and *R* actually represent.

Inductive and abductive knowledge are classed as synthetic because they do require verification in experience. Inductive inference involves inference from a large number of consistent examples and a lack of counter examples. For example, if all the crows that are observed are black and none are ever observed that are any other color, then by induction one can infer therefore that they are all black. Abduction is a method of inference that sees valid inferences as those that do not contradict previous facts. Knowledge based systems implicitly use deductive, inductive and abductive knowledge. Computational intelligence methods like neural networks are inductive in training/learning mode and deductive in trained mode. Genetic algorithms on the other hand use induction when performing crossover and mutation, and abduction when using selection. Figure 3.7 also shows the three hybrid configurations (fusion, combination, and transformation) of deductive, inductive and abductive knowledge types. These have been described in section 3.2.2.

Thus we can see from the above discussion that semiotics develops models which are deeper than those developed in artificial intelligence and computational intelligence. Unlike artificial and computational intelligence it considers multiple facets of intelligence through various knowledge types. It supports Weizenbaum's (1976) intuition that intelligent systems are better served by a variety of both symbolic and non-symbolic representational methodologies than by purely symbolic accounts of meaning. The suggestion is not that some aspects of cognition aren't best thought of as the manipulation of symbols, but rather that symbolic approaches cannot account for all aspects of human intelligence.

Gudwin and Gomide (1997a, b, c) have used the three knowledge types (rhematic, dicent and argumentative) in the interpretant space to develop a computational semiotics framework for building intelligent systems. They demonstrate the applicability of their semiotic framework through a control application. Although, the framework seems to be useful for small applications, for large-scale complex applications problems like combinatorial explosion, scalability and maintainability problems are likely to be encountered. Further, the use of primitive knowledge types does not throw any light on how to deal with complexity of large-scale problems. One can get lost in the details of interaction of various knowledge types.

3.3.2. Cognitive Science Theories

In the last section we have looked at human cognition based on semiotics which has its underpinnings in philosophy. In this section we discuss the developments in cognitive science and how they contribute to human-centeredness. We compare and contrast four approaches in cognitive science, namely, traditional approach, radical approach, situated cognition, and distributed cognition. The comparison primarily centers around factors related to human problem solving like external and internal representations, perceptual and cognitive processes, and task context (discussed in chapter 1). External representations are defined in terms of knowledge and structure of the external environment (Zhang and Norman 1994). They can be objects, physical symbols, or dimensions, and external rules, constraints or relations embedded in physical configurations (e.g., visual and spatial layouts of objects in an image, spatial relations between objects in an image). In comparison, internal representations are the knowledge and structure in memory (Zhang and Norman 1994). They can be propositions, productions/rules, schemas, neural networks, etc. Perceptual processes are used to analyze and process external representations, whereas cognitive processes are used to retrieve the information from the internal memory. The four approaches will now be discussed based on these factors.

3.3.2.1. Traditional Approach

The traditional approach (see Figure 3.8) developed by Newell (1990) primarily focuses on internal representations. According to the traditional view, external representations are merely inputs and stimuli to the internal mind. Thus when an intelligent agent has to accomplish a task which involves interaction with the environment, it creates an internal model of the environment through an encoding process, performs mental computations on the contents (symbolic or subsymbolic) in this internal model, and externalizes the output through a decoding process.

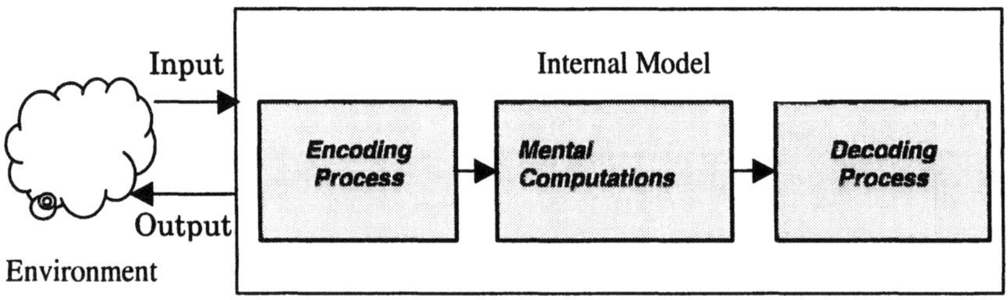

Figure 3.8: Traditional Approach to Cognitive Science

As noted by Zhang and Norman (1994), Kirlik et al. (1993) and Suchman (1987) most studies in traditional cognitive science do not separate external representations from internal representations or equate representations having both internal and external components to internal representations. This confusion often leads one to postulate unnecessary complex internal mechanisms to explain the complex structure of wrongly identified internal representation, much of which is merely a reflection of the structure of the external representation. More so, computer systems developed based on this traditional view often are cognitively rich and perceptually poor leading to a higher cognitive load on its users.

In general, traditional cognitive science based on the physical symbol hypothesis has other problems like the symbol grounding problem discussed in the previous section, frame problem, problem of 'situatedness' (idea that agent's actions are determined through the interaction of the agent with the current situation), lack of robustness (fault and noise tolerance, generalization capacity, adaptability to new situations), failure to perform in real time, and not sufficiently brain-like (Brooks 1991; Clancey 1989, 97 Dorffner 1996; Dreyfus 1992; McClelland and Rumelhart 1986; Harnad 1990; Suchman 1987).

3.3.2.2. Radical Approach

A radically different view (also known as the ecological view) proposed by Gibson (1966, 79) argues that perception is a direct process in which information is simply detected rather than constructed. It is based on the premise that brain is all there is and it is not a computer. According to Gibson, the environment is highly structured and full of invariant information. This invariant information in the environment is adequate to specify the objects and events in the environment, and thus it is sufficient for perception and action. Further, the invariant information can be directly perceived without the mediation of memory, inference, deliberation or other mental computations.

One of the central concepts of this approach is the notion of affordances. That is, what we see as the behavior of a system, object or event is that which is afforded or permitted by the system. For example, in Figure 3.9a the door handle affords grasping or pulling action whereas in the configuration shown in Figure 3.9b it affords a pushing action as against a grasping action. In other words, when the affordances are ambiguous, it is easy for us to make mistakes when trying to interact with an object.

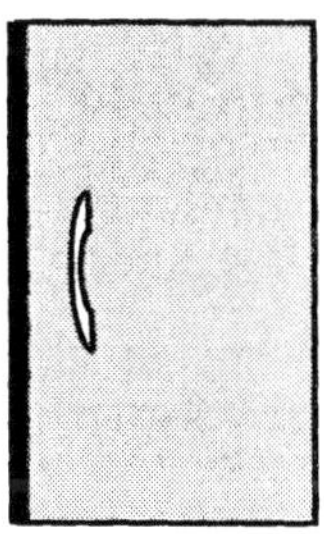

Figure 3.9a: Affordances of Door Handles – Grasping or Pulling Action

Figure 3.9b: Affordances of Door Handles – Pushing Action

The strength of the radical approach, from a human-centered perspective, is that it emphasizes the need to consider perceptual aspects of a domain which have been largely ignored by traditional cognitive science. The perceptual perspective can assist in developing systems that minimize cognitive load on its users through direct manipulation. Other strengths include their ability to address fundamental problems like symbol grounding and emergence, and performance problems like real time response and robustness.

The main weakness of this approach is its over emphasis on perceptual aspects of a domain. Systems built with perception and action approaches do not scale-up well to large and complex domains. In complex systems, in order to deal with complexity of the domain (e.g., through abstraction) and guide or prevent the perceptual processes from going astray, it becomes necessary to assist this approach with cognitive processes. The next section describes the situated cognition approach, an emerging field in cognitive science.

3.3.2.3. Situated Cognition

Situated cognition approach has been developed and advocated by a number of researchers (Clancey 1993 1997; Suchman 1987; Brooks 1990, 91; Nehmzow et al. 1989; Winograd and Flores 1986; Pfeifer and Redamakers 1991; Pfeifer and Verschure 1992a, 92b, 95). According to this approach, people directly access situational information and act upon it in an improvisatory, adaptive and emergent manner, rather than in a routine and predictable manner.

Situated action refers to the idea that an agent's actions are determined through the interaction of the agent with the current situation. Situated action directly grows out of the particularities of a situation. Thus the focus of study is the situated activity or practice rather than the formal or cognitive properties of artifacts (Nardi 1996). Situated action is not purely reactive as it depends on the agent's experience, which is not based on a prior knowledge but is acquired through interaction with a situation.

Situated agents, unlike traditional AI systems, are adaptive and can act in real time. Situated models or systems do not passively receive and process input but are inextricably embedded in their environment and in a constant sensori-motor loop with it via the system's own actions in the environment. Situated systems are developed at a very fine-grained level of minutely observed activities that are embedded in a particular situation. This is reflected in the work of Clancey (1997) and Suchman (1987). To quote from Suchman (1987):

> *The organization of situated action is an emergent property of moment-by-moment interactions between actors, and between actors and the environment of their action.*

The basic unit of analysis for situated action as identified by Lave (1988) is "the activity of persons-acting in setting." It is not the individual nor the environment, but the relation between the two. By paying attention to the flux of ongoing activity, situated action emphasizes improvizatory nature of human activity (Lave 1988). Lave (1988) illustrates such improvisation through the well known "cottage cheese" story.

A participant in a Weight Watchers program had the task of fixing a serving of cottage cheese that was to be three quarters of the two-thirds cup of cottage cheese.
The participant after puzzling over the problem a bit, filled a measuring cup two-thirds full of cheese dumped it out on a cutting board, patted it into a circle. Marked a cross on it, scooped away one quadrant, and served the rest of it.

Thus, by emphasizing particularities of a situation in minute detail, situated action de-emphasizes generalization and regularities which span across situations and are essential for dealing with large and complex systems.

Situated action analysis relies on recordable, observable behavior. In this analysis, since ongoing action directs the flow of human action, goals and plans are considered "verbal interpretations" (Lave 1988) and plans as "retrospective reconstructions" (Suchman 1987). As illustrated by Nardi (1996), a meteorologist and a bird watcher can both be looking at the sky with different goals in mind. A meteorologist may be looking skyward to determine the weather whereas, a bird watcher may be looking for birds. The situation is the same in both cases, however the goals are different. A video recording has no way of determining what is in the mind of two individuals.

The development of 'New AI' based on completely autonomous systems (Brooks 1990, 91a, 91b; Nehmzow et al. 1989; Pfeifer and Verschure 1992) and radical connectionism based on self-organization (automatic adaptation via feedback through the environment) subscribe to the purist view of ongoing interaction modeled by situated models. Radical connectionism and other bottom-up approaches (e.g., Edelman 1987; Reeke and Edelman 1988; Edelman 1989; Dorffner 1996) deny the need of internal models. The goal of these approaches is biased towards understanding the nature of natural behaving systems, like animals, than towards developing complex real world applications in design, diagnosis, scheduling, etc.

A more moderate or 'brain-like' version called connectionism has been advocated by Smolensky (1988). It advocates integration of the symbolic and subsymbolic (or microfeature) levels in a connectionist framework using artificial neural networks. The microfeatures, at the subsymbolic level, are distributed and do not have conceptual semantics individually. When considered together as patterns of activity, microfeatures are capable of producing emergent symbolic behavior. Using the massive parallelism and other properties of neural networks, connectionist models also help to alleviate performance-related problems of a traditional approach like real-time response, noise tolerance and generalization. A number of applications of the connectionist model can be found in natural language (Sejnowski and Rosenberg 1987) and other areas (Sun 1991,94). In general the connectionist approach helps to bridge the gap between existing computer models (based on traditional approach) and the brain. The moderate view however, is not without its criticisms. The encoded microfeatures, although subsymbolic, represent a thinner slice of the symbolic world and hence do not adequately address the symbol grounding problem. Further, connectionist models are seen to lack situatedness in the sense that ontology is given by the designer rather than developed independently by the network.

Overall, situated cognition theory has generated a lot of interest. However, it is still not fully developed and there is no set methodology for building real world applications. The research and application stances vary from a purist view of completely autonomous systems to recent attempts by situated cognition researchers to include "routine practices," "routine competencies," and abstraction theories (Sunchman and Trigg 1991; Suchman 1993; Clancey 1997) to account for the observed regularities in the work settings studied. Although, the purist view seems pretty much grounded in human-centeredness, focusing on moment-by-moment interaction, one can get involved into a myriad of details which can make building of large scale systems cumbersome.

Next, we look at another emerging field of cognitive science, namely, distributed cognition.

3.3.2.4. Distributed Cognition

Distributed cognition is an emerging framework which describes cognition as it is distributed across individuals and the setting in which it takes place (Hutchins and Norman 1988; Norman 1988, 91, 93; Zhang and Norman 1994). To quote from Flor and Hutchins (1991):

> *Distributed cognition is a branch of cognitive science devoted to the study of: the representation of knowledge both inside the heads of individuals and in the world ...; the propagation of knowledge between different individuals and artifacts....; and the transformations which external structures undergo when operated on by individuals and artifacts...; By studying cognitive phenomena in this fashion it is hoped that an understanding of how intelligence is manifested at the systems level, as opposed to the individual cognitive level, will be obtained.*

There are two parts in the above definition. The first part relates to the consideration of external (outside the head) and internal (inside the head) representations of artifacts. Problem solving then involves combination of perceptual and cognitive processes that involve external (perceptual) and internal (cognitive) representations (Hutchins 1991; Norman 1992; Zhang and Norman 1994) as shown in Figure 3.10. Zhang and Norman (1994) and Zhang (1997) have illustrated the effect of external and internal representations on problem solving and the cognitive work involved using the tic-tac-toe problem.

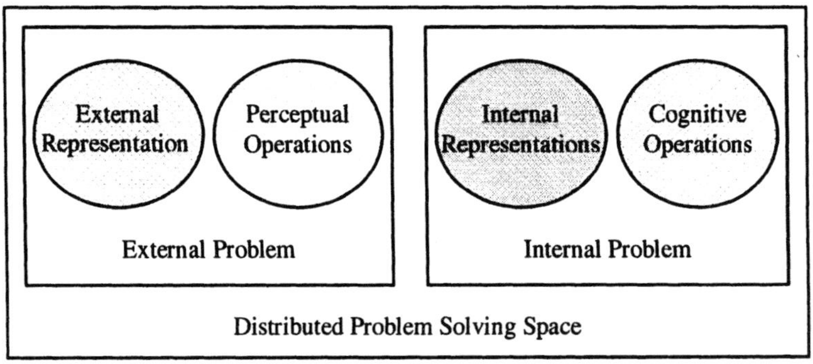

Figure 3.10: Distributed Representations and Problems Solving

Figure 3.11 shows two representations of the tic-tac-toe problem. In the first representation (on the right) a player has to color three squares in a straight line in order to win the game. In the second isomorphic representation (on the left) a player has to color three squares which add up to 15 in order to win the game. As also explained in chapter 1, problem solving in the first representation is accomplished using external representations or perceptual processes. The second isomorph involves cognitive operations (addition of three numbers). Thus depending on the representation chosen (also known as representational effect) the cognitive work involved will be different.

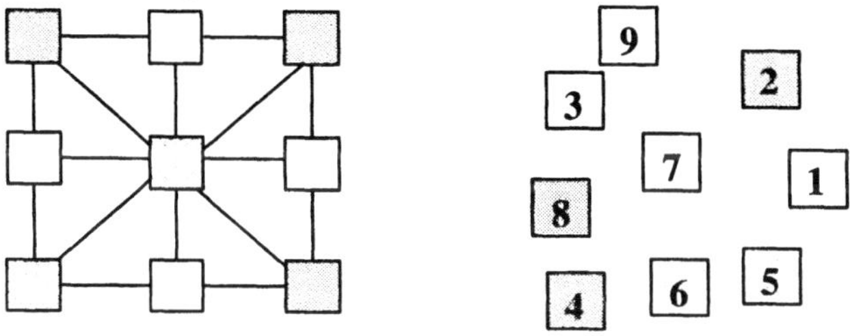

Figure 3.11: Tic-Tac-Toe

The second part of the distributed cognition definition relates to conceptualization of cognitive activities as embodied and situated within the work context in which they occur (Hutchins 1990; Hutchins and Klusen 1992). In other words, it involves describing cognition as it is distributed across individuals (as against its embodiment within an individual) and setting in which it takes place. It involves development of functional systems that determine the relations between a collection of actors or people, computer systems and other artifacts as situated in an environmental setting. Thus distributed cognition shifts the unit of analysis from an individual to the system and its components. At the systems level its primary goal is to analyze how different components of the functional system are coordinated. A number of functional systems like software programming teams (Flor and Hutchins 1991), ship navigation (Hutchins 1990), air-traffic control have been studied in this regard.

A common aspect of situated cognition and distributed cognition is the shift towards real activity in real situations. The difference is lack of goals in situated cognition as against system goals and motives. That is, in distributed cognition system goal or goals is/are the beginning point of analysis. In situated cognition the reference point in moving from one situation into another is not a goal or motive. In other words, condition for situated action does not have to be a goal but a response to dynamically changing conditions in the environment.

This completes the four main cognitive science theories. In the next section we delve into activity theory, an enabling theory from psychology.

3.3.3. Activity Theory

Activity theory has recently gained importance in human-computer interaction for analyzing user interfaces (Bodker 1991), Computer Supported Work Systems (Knutti 1991). Activity is generated by various needs for which people want to achieve a certain purpose or goal. The origins of activity theory can be found in the work done by psychologist Leont'ev (1974), Vygotsky (1978), and more recently by Nardi (1993, 96) and Kuutti (1996). The basic components of activity theory as outlined by Knutti (1996) are shown in Figure 3.12. Knutti (1996) defines an activity as a form of human doing whereby a subject works on an object (as in objective) in order to attain the desired outcome. An object can be a material thing (produce a new car), but it can also be less tangible (satisfying customer need). Activities are distinguished from each other according to their objects. Transforming the object into an outcome motivates the existence of an activity. The subject can be a person or a group of persons involved in an activity. An object (in the sense of objective) is held by the subject and motivates activity, giving it a specific direction (Leont'ev 1974). Behind the object there always stands a need or desire/motive, to which (the activity) always answers (Leont'ev *1974*). Tools or artifacts usually mediate activity. The tool in Figure 3.12 represents a transformation process employed by the subject (or subjects) to transform the object into a desired outcome. The tools can be material tools (e.g., axe, computer systems, procedures) and/or tools of thinking (e.g., plan). For example, in an automated supply system, the motive of a subject (e.g. database designer) may be, improved supply management, career advancement or gaining control over a vital organizational power source). In the supply system, a database designer who is modifying a database schema (object) so that all year columns are four digits (outcome) using a schema editor (tool).

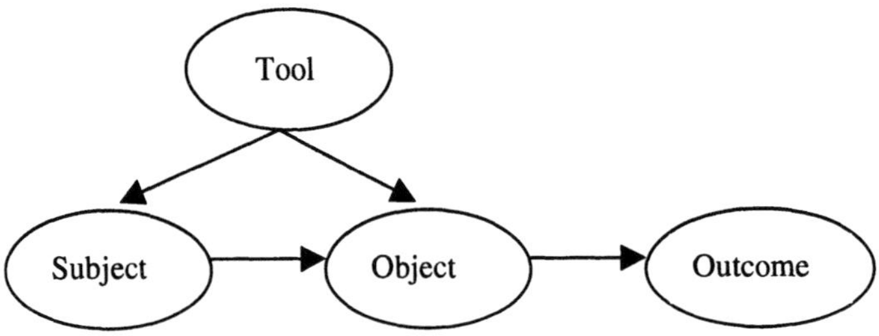

Figure 3.12: Components of Activity

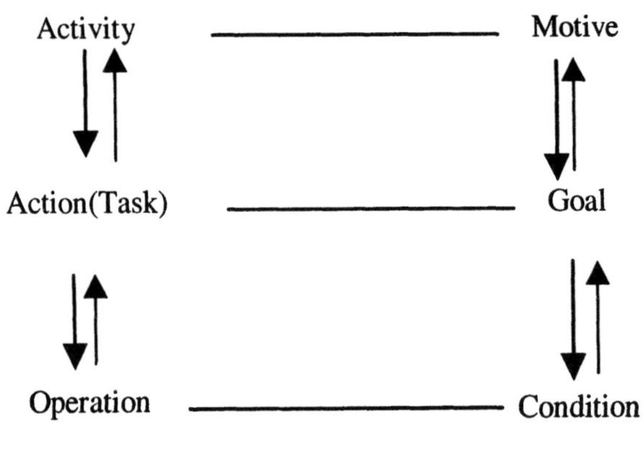

Figure 3.13: Levels of Activity

Activities as described by Leont'ev, (1974), Nardi (1993,96), Knutti (1996) and Kaptelinin (1996) are composed of actions and operations. The actions are goal-directed processes that are undertaken to fulfill an object. The actions are similar to tasks referred to in AI literature (Chandrasekaran et. al. 1992) and human-computer interaction literature (Norman 1991). Operations are low level refinements of actions. They can also be seen to represent unconscious, routinized or automated aspects of actions. For example, when learning to drive a car, changing the gears is a conscious action. However, with practice this conscious action becomes a routinized, unconscious operation.

The constituents of an activity can dynamically change as the conditions change. That is, all levels of activity can move up or down. For example, moving from a country with left-hand drive to a country with right hand drive can result in relearning certain operationalized aspects of driving (e.g. rules for turning left or right).

Like distributed cognition, the unit of analysis in activity theory is an activity or work system. However, unlike distributed cognition where the focus is on system goal or goals, the focus in activity theory is on individual goal or goals. One can say there is an overlap between individual goals and system goals (Nardi 1996), the focus in distributed cognition is to direct analysis at the systems level rather than the individual level.

One of the important contributions of activity theory is the tool mediation perspective. Besides activity theory, the cognitive approach has also introduced the mediation concept called "cognitive artifacts." Norman (1991) defines them as follows: "A cognitive artifact is an artifact designed to maintain, display, or operate upon information in order to serve representational function." Norman (1991) uses this definition to distinguish between the personal view and the system view to human-computer interaction. The personal view relates to the boundary between the user, and computer and the world. The system view encompasses all the components of a system including user, computer and other artifacts. According to Norman (1991), from a personal view, use of computers only changes the nature of the task (to the extent it can make a task easier for the user). It (i.e., use of computers) does not necessarily, empower a user (say, with a skill), from a personal view. The empowerment is true only from a systems view, where certain performance improvements can be realized through use of computers with people and other artifacts. On the other hand, activity theory subscribes to only one view and that is personal view. Further, it states that tools (like computers) not only change the nature of the task but also empower the user or individual even if the external tool is no longer used. Kaptelinin (1996) outlines three stages which lead to empowerment: a) the initial phase, when performance is the same, with or without the tool, because the tool is not mastered well enough to provide the benefits; b) the intermediate phase, when aided performance is superior to unaided performance, and c) the final phase, when performance is the same, with and without the tool, but now because the tool mediated activity is internalized and the external tool is no longer needed. For example, a fresh sales recruit may use a computer based training tool for enhancing their salesperson-customer interaction skills on a day-to-day basis. After a few years the salesperson may not need the training tool because of internalization of the training skills imparted by the tool.

The major limitation of activity theory is that it is not operationalized enough (Kaptelinin 1996). That is, methods and techniques are not rich enough to be directly utilized for developing workplace systems.

3.3.4. Workplace Theory

Till this point in the chapter we have looked at pragmatic considerations which establish a need for human-centered systems, and theories which can contribute towards development of human-centered systems. Another important aspect that has recently gained momentum is the need to situate computer system development in a work environment. That is, rather than engaging in an objective isolated rationalistic approach which may involve use of certain systems methodology (e.g. object-oriented, logic, etc.) there is a need to introduce certain subjectivity through a work-oriented design approach (Ehn et al 1989). This subjectivity entails involvement of stakeholders and end users in the system design process. This perspective has grown out of dissatisfaction experienced by practitioners and researchers (Ehn et al 1989; Greenbaum and Kyng 1991; and others) in workplace environments with traditional (formal) theories and methods of systems design. Workers or users see these approaches as politically motivated to deskill them. More so, human creativity and intelligence is restricted to the limited vocabulary of these methods.

Ehn et al (1989) has suggested a rethink in the existing design processes to include structures which ordinary people can use to incorporate their own interests and goals. Besides, descriptions in design should be flexible enough to enable users to express all their practical competence. Here again, two stances are emerging for developing such structures. One is largely based on ethnographic techniques and the other is based on Work-Centered Analysis (WCA) with emphasis on user and stakeholder expectations, and organizational culture. Both techniques have merit. The ethnographic techniques (which involve use of video and audio techniques for recording every minute aspect of work activity) seem to be grounded in human-centeredness, although the whole process can really become cumbersome for development of large and complex systems. The work-centered analysis and socio-technical framework developed in the information systems area by Alter (1996,99) and Laudon and Laudon (1995), respectively, have been derived from workplace settings and are based on a marriage between social and systemic aspects of computer system development. In this book, the latter approach has been adopted. These structures facilitate development of work-oriented systems by situating system development in organizational and stakeholder contexts.

The WCA framework defined by Alter (1996) is a comprehensive framework for analyzing a business process and use of information technology from a business as well as human perspective. However, for the purpose of building intelligent multimedia systems it does not provide an adequate framework for integrating the business and human perspective with the technical perspective of developing complex intelligent systems.

3.4. Discussion

In the preceding sections of this chapter, we have attempted to describe how pragmatic issues rather than purely technological innovation are driving the evolution of various areas in information systems and computer science. The enabling theories from philosophy, cognitive science, psychology, and workplace, which can help to address the human *vs.* technology mismatch and other pragmatic aspects, have been described. In this section, we think it is a good idea to recapitulate the pragmatic and theoretical aspects that will form part of the e-business human-centered framework developed in the next chapter.

In this book the fact that we want to develop e-business systems, the obvious starting point is e-business and human-centeredness. The discussion in section 3.2.1 highlights the fact that the business need for developing customer-centric e-business systems is going to elevate the need for user or human-centerdeness more than in traditional information systems. In the context of intelligent e-business systems, we show in section 3.2.2 that given the range of intelligent technologies, their strengths and weaknesses, their cognitive, neuronal and evolutionary underpinnings, task orientation can prove to be an important concept in harnessing the deliberative, fuzzy, reactive, self-organizing, parallel processing and optimizing properties of these intelligent technologies. Task orientation is also an essential component of human-centered software development. We intend to integrate this concept into the e-business human-centered framework

In a sense, like the intelligent technologies, various software engineering technologies have functional and structural underpinnings. The functional and structural underpinnings of these software engineering technologies impose restrictions on which aspects of a domain need to be captured, and how they are to be modeled. That is, as indicated in section 3.2.3 agents are intuitively suited for modeling of tasks and task based behavior and not for structural modeling, whereas, objects are intuitively suited for structural modeling of a domain. Thus, their inability to capture all aspects of a domain on their own impacts on the syntactic and semantic quality of a computer system from a human-centered standpoint. In our work, we intend to incorporate concepts from object-oriented and agent technologies in the human-centered framework to enhance the syntactic and semantic quality of the framework.

The development of multimedia databases has demonstrated that the conventional DBMS (DataBase Management Systems) are not adequate to handle queries associated with multimedia databases. This aspect is covered in more detail in chapter 10. These queries require semantic correlation between various media artifacts. This has resulted in a need for defining an ontological level above the metadata level associated with each media. This ontological level has more to do with the problem solving ontology of a domain rather the metadata aspects of the media or the media structure. Thus it is media independent and can be domain dependent or independent.

Data mining is an emerging field and is in high demand in the industry. However, the technology-centered methods used for data mining are beset with problems like meaningfulness and relevance of extracted rules. Here again, there is a need to integrate user-centered problem solving models with the data mining process in order to enhance the meaningfulness of its results.

The product vs customer-centric e-business systems, supplier *vs.* customer-centered models in electronic commerce systems, technology based vs. task based intelligent associative systems, human cognition based ontological level vs. metadata level in multimedia databases, meaningfulness problem associated with data mining, task and perception *vs.* feature oriented interfaces and underlying user tasks *vs.* underlying system tasks problem of existing user interfaces all suggest a need for task orientation and technology independent problem solving ontologies. Thus we intend to integrate concepts like task orientation, technology independent human-centered problem solving ontology and task based human-computer interaction as building blocks of the e-business human-centered framework. These concepts answer the question, "What needs to be done?" In order to answer the question "How can it be done," we have looked into enabling theories in philosophy, cognitive science, psychology and workplace.

The semiotic, cognitive science, activity and workplace system theories described in this chapter contribute significantly to the content of human-centered systems framework. These theories represent diverse aspects related to human-centeredness. The discussion and comparison of these theories leads us in the direction of amalgamation of concepts from these theories rather than committing ourselves to one particular theory. We feel amalgamation of concepts from various theories will help us to satisfy the pragmatic needs and develop a more comprehensive human-centered framework. In the rest of this section, we highlight various concepts developed by these theories which will form part of the human-centered systems framework.

Semiotic theory covered in this chapter describes a human cognitive system based on taxonomy of linguistic and non-linguistic signs. Any intelligent human-centered system should facilitate a symbiosis between the linguistic and non-linguistic nature of human communication and human-computer interaction. The four cognitive science theories discussed in this chapter model the linguistic and non-linguistic nature of human communication separately and collectively. The traditional approach is heavily biased towards the linguistic nature of human communication and relies on cognitive processes of humans. On the other hand, the radical and situated cognition approaches are more biased towards the dynamic and non-linguistic nature of human interaction. We subscribe to the dynamic aspects of situated cognition that involve, among other aspects, ability to adapt to novel situations and learn incrementally from them. The linguistic and non-linguistic nature of human communication is also linked to the cognitive and perceptual processes of humans. The distributed cognition approach models linguistic and non-linguistic aspects collectively through cognitive and perceptual models. Problem solving in distributed cognition takes place in a distributed problem space involving external and internal representations. Further, distributed cognition, like activity theory, is concerned with finding stable design principles across design problems (Norman 1988, 91; Nardi 1996; Nardi and Zarmer 1993). Like the workplace system theory, the unit of analysis in distribution cognition is a system. The system consists of people and artifacts working in a cooperative and coordinative manner to accomplish system goals. We also subscribe to these aspects of distributed cognition, activity theory and workplace, namely, system as the unit of analysis, system goals, distributed problem solving space, external and internal representations developing stable design principles across problems. However, unlike distributed cognition, we do not equate the human with the machine. We are more comfortable with the tool view as advocated by the activity theory. Computers are tools like other artifacts that enable people to accomplish their tasks. They can be programmed to exhibit certain intelligent properties like humans (and to that extent they can be considered as cognizing tools) but to a large extent are still not close to the range of intelligent behavior exhibited by humans, which includes emotions and other aspects.

Finally, the organizational and stakeholder context of workplace system theory described in section 3.3.4 provides us with a basis for putting people at the forefront of the system development process. These enabling theories however have to be contextualized in terms of e-business strategies and e-business models introduced in chapter 2. In the next two chapters we develop various components of the e-business human-centered framework based on the pragmatic and theoretical aspects described in this chapter and e-business strategies and models introduced in chapter 2.

3.5. Summary

This chapter looks into various pragmatic issues and the enabling theories for development of human-centered e-business systems in particular and human-centered systems in general. The pragmatic issues primarily center around the human *vs.* technology mismatch and the epistemological limitations (and strengths) which humans and computers have. It is shown how these pragmatic issues have become a pivotal point in the evolution in a number of areas including e-business, intelligent systems, software engineering, multimedia databases, enterprise modeling, data mining and human-computer interaction. The outcome of the discussion on pragmatic issues and their impact on various areas helps us to identify a set of critical properties that need to form a part of a human-centered system development framework. Whereas, the pragmatic issues help us identify some of the critical properties of a human-centered system development framework, they do not provide us with a theoretical basis for underpinning the framework. For that matter, the chapter then moves on to describe enabling theories in philosophy, cognitive science, psychology, and workplace for development of human-centered system development frameworks. The outcome of discussion on these theories is a set of theoretical concepts on which e-business human-centered system development framework is founded in the next chapter.

References

Albus, J.S. (1991). "Outline for a Theory of Intelligence," in *IEEE Transactions on Systems, Man and Cybernetics* 21(3), May/June.

Anderson, J. and Stonebraker, M. (1994), "Sequoia 2000 Metadata Schema for Satellite Images," in *SIGMOD Record, special issue on Metadata for Digital Media*, W. Klaus, A. Sheth, eds., 23 (4), December, http://www.cs.uga.edu/LSDIS/pub.html.

Aristotle. (1938). *De Interpretaione* (H. P. Cook, Trans.), London: Loeb Classical Library.
Bezdek, J.C. 1994, 'What is Computational Intelligence?' *Computational Intelligence: Imitating Life*, Eds. Robert Marks-II et al., IEEE Press, New York.
Boden, M.A. (1983). "As Ideias de Piaget," in Traducao de Alvaro Cabral – Editora Cultrix – Editora da Universidade de Sao Paulo.
Bodker, S. (1991). *Through the Interface: A Human Activity Approach to User Interface Design*, Hillsdale, NJ:Lawerence Erlbaum
Bohm, K., and Rakow, T. (1994). "Metadata for Multimedia Documents," in SIGMOD Record, special issue on Metadata for Digital Media, W. Klaus, A. Sheth, eds. 23 (4), December, http://www.cs.uga.edu/LSDIS/pub.html
Brooks, R.A. (1990). Elephants Don't Play Chess, in P. Maes, ed., *Designing Autonomous Agents*, Cambridge. MA: MIT Press, Bradford Books, pp. 3-16.
Brooks, R.A. (1991a). Intelligence Without Representation, *Artificial Intelligence* 47 (1-3), Special Volume: Foundations of Artificial Intelligence.
Brooks, R.A. (1991b). Comparitive Task Analysis: An Alternative Direction for Human-Computer Interaction Science. In J. Caroll, ed., *Designing Interaction: Psychology at the Human-Computer Interface*, J. Caroll, ed., Cambridge: Cambridge University Press.
Chandrasekaran, B., Johnson, T.R., and Smith, J.W. (1992), 'Task Structure Analysis for Knowledge Modeling,' *Communication of the ACM*, vol. 35, no. 9., pp. 124-137.
Chen, F., Hearst, M., Kupiec, J., Pederson, J., and Wilcox, L. (1994), "Metadata for Mixed-media Access," in SIGMOD Record, special issue on Metadata for Digital Media, W. Klaus, A. Sheth, eds., 23 (4), December, http://www.cs.uga.edu/LSDIS/pub.html.
Chiaberage, M., Bene. G.D., Pascoli, S.D., Lazzerini, B., and Maggiore, A. (1995), "Mixing fuzzy, neural & genetic algorithms in integrated design environment for intelligent controllers," *1995 IEEE Int Conf on SMC,*. Vol. 4, pp. 2988-93.
Clancey W.J. (1989). "The Knowledge Level Reconsidered: Modeling How Systems Interact," in Machine Learning 4, pp.285-92.
Clancey, W.J. (1993). "Situated Action: A Neuropsychological Interpretation (Response to Vera and Simon)," *Cognitive Science*, 17, 87-116.
Clancey, W.J. (1997). *Situated Cognition*, Cambridge, MA: MIT Press.
Clancey, W.J. (1999). "Human-Centered Computing – Implications for AI Research," http://ic.arc.nasa.gov/ic/HTMLfolder/sld001.htm.
Coad, P. and Yourdon, E. (1990) *Object-oriented Analysis,* Yourdon Press, Prentice-Hall, Englewood Cliffs, NJ.
Coad, P. and Yourdon, E. (1991) *Object-oriented Design,* Yourdon Press, Prentice-Hall, Englewood Cliffs, NJ.
Dorffner G. (1996). "Radical Connectionism - A Neural Bottom-Up Approach to AI," in *Neural Networks and New Artificial Intelligence*, G. Dorrfner ed., International Thomson Press.
Dreyfus H.L. (1992). *What Computers Still Can't Do*, Cambridge, MA: MIT Press.
Edelman, G. 1992, *Bright Air, Brilliant Fire: On the Matter of the Mind.* New York, USA, Raven Press.
Edelman, G.M. (1987). *Neural Darwinism: The Theory of Neuronal Group Selection*, New York: Basic Books.
Edelman, G.M. (1989). *The Remembered Present: A Biological Theory of Consciousness*, New York: Basic Books.
Ehn, P. & Kyng, M. (1989) *Computers and Democracy: a Scandinavian Challenge*, edited by Bjerknes, G., Ehn, P. and Kyng, M. Aldershot [Hanks, England]; Aveburg, pp 17-57.
Flor, N., and Hutchins, E. (1991). "Analyzing Distributed Cognition in Software Teams: A Case Study of Team Programming During Perfective Software Maintenance," in J. Koenemann-Belliveau et al., eds., *Proceedings of the Fourth Annual Workshop on Empirical Studies of Programmers*, Norwood, N.J.: Ablex Publishing.

Fu,L.M.& Fu,L.C. 1990, "Mapping Rule based Systems into Neural Architecture".*Knowledge-Based Systems*. 3(1): 48-56.

Fukuda, T., Hasegawa, Y. and Shimojima, K. 1995, 'Structure Organization of Hierarchical Fuzzy Model using Genetic Algorithm'. *1995 IEEE International Conference on Fuzzy Systems*. vol. 1, pp. 295-9.

Gallant, S. 1988, "Connectionist Expert Systems". *Communications of the ACM*. February 152-169.

Gamma, E et. al., (1995) "Design Elements of Object-oriented Software," Massachusetts: Adisson-Wesley.

Gibson, J.J. (1966). *The Senses Considered as Perceptual Systems*, New York: Houghton Mifflin Company.

Gibson, J.J. (1979). *The Ecological Approach to Visual Perception*, Boston: Houghton Mifflin.

Glavitsch, U., Schauble, P., and Wechsler, M., (1994) "Metadata for Integrating Speech Documents in a Text Retrieval System," in SIGMOD Record, special issue on Metadata for Digital Media, W. Klaus, A. Sheth, eds., 23 (4), December, http://www.cs.uga.edu/LSDIS/pub.html.

Glushko R., Tenenbaum J. and Meltzer B. (1999), "An XML-framework for Agent-Based E Commerce", Communications of the ACM, vol. 42 no. 3.

Goldberg, D.E. (1989), *Genetic Algorithms in Search, Optimization and Machine Learning*, Addison-Wesley, Reading, MA, pp. 217-307.

Greffenstette, J.J. (1990), "Genetic Algorithms and their Applications," *Encyclopedia of Computer Science and Technology*, vol. 2, eds. A. Kent and J. G. William, AIC-90-006, Naval Research Laboratory, Washington DC, pp. 139-52.

Grosky, B. (1994), "A Primer on Multimedia Systems, " IEEE Multimedia pp. 12-24.

Gudwin R. and Gomide, F. (1997a). "Computational Semiotics: An Approach for the Study of Intelligent Systems - Part I: Foundations," *Technical report RT-DCA 09 - DCA-FEEC-UNICAMP*.

Gudwin R. and Gomide, F. (1997c). "An Approach to Computational Semiotics," In *Proceedings of the ISA'97 - Intelligent Systems and Semiotics: A Learning Perspective, International Conference*, Goithersburg, MD, USA, 22-25, September, 1997.

Gudwin R.and Gomide, F. (1997b). "Computational Semiotics: An Approach for the Study of Intelligent Systems - Part II: Theory and Application," *Technical report RT-DCA 09 - DCA-FEEC-UNICAMP*.

Hamada, K., Baba, T., Sato, K. and Yufu, M. 1995, "Hybridizing a Genetic Algorithm with Rule based Reasoning for Production Planning,". *IEEE Expert*. 60-67.

Hamilton S., "Electronic Commerce for the 21st Century", IEEE Computer, vol. 30, no. 5, pp.37-41

Hands, J., Patel A., Bessonov M. and Smith R. (1998), "An Inclusive and Hands Extensible Architecture for Electronic Brokerage", Proc. of the Hawai Intl. Conf. on System Sciences, Minitrack on Electronic Commerce, pp.332-339.

Harnad, S. (1990). "The Symbol Grounding Problem," in *Physica D*, 42 (1-3), pp. 335-46.

Hinton, G.E. 1990, "Mapping Part-Whole Hierarchies into Connectionist Networks," *Artificial Intelligence*. 46(1-2): 47-76.

Hutchins, E. (1990). "The Technology of Team Navigation," in J. Galegher, ed., *Intellectual Teamwork*, Hillsdale, NJ: Lawerence Erlbaum..

Hutchins, E. (1991). *How a Cockpit Remembers its Speeds*. Ms La Jolla: University of California, Department of Cognitive Science.

Hutchins, E. (1995). *Cognition in the Wild*, Cambridge, MA: MIT Press.

Ishibuchi, H., Tanaka, H. and Okada, H. 1994, "Interpolation of Fuzzy If-Then Rules by Neural Networks,". *International Journal of Approximate Reasoning*. January, 10(1): 3-27.

Jacobson, I., (1995). *Object-oriented Software Engineering*, Addison-Wesley.

Jain, R. and Hampapuram, A. (1994). "Representations of Video Databases," in SIGMOD Record, special issue on Metadata for Digital Media, W. Klaus, A. Sheth, eds., 23 (4), December, http://www.cs.uga.edu/LSDIS/pub.html

Jennings, N. R. et al. (1996). "Using Archon to Develop Real-World DAI Applications, Part 1." *IEEE Expert* December, 64-70.

Kaptelinin, V. (1996). "Computer-Mediated Activity," in *Context and Consciousness*, B. Nardi, ed., MIT Press, pp. 17-44.

Kashyap, V., Shah, K., and Sheth, A. (1995). "Metadata for Building the Multimedia Patch Quilt," in *Multimedia Database Systems: Issues and Research Directions*, S. Jajodia and V. S. Subrahmanium, Eds., Springer-Verlag, p. 297-323

Kashyap, V., and Sheth, A.(1994) "Semantics-based Information Brokering," in Proceedings of the Third International Conference on Information and Knowledge Management (CIKM), November, http://www.cs.uga.edu/LSDIS/infoquilt

Kashyap, V., Shah, K., and Sheth, A. (1996). "Metadata for Building the Multimedia Patch Quilt," in SIGMOD

Khosla, R., 1997a, ***Tutorial Notes on Software Engineering methodology for Intelligent Hybrid Multi-Agent Systems,*** Int. Conf. on Connectionist Information Processing and Information Sys, Dunedin, New Zealand, November

Khosla, R. & Dillon, T.S. 1997b, ***Engineering Intelligent Hybrid Multi-Agent Systems.*** Boston, USA, Kluwer Academic Publishers.

Khosla, R. and Dillon, T.S. 1997c, "Neuro-Expert System Applications in Power Systems,". K. Warwick, A. Ekwue & R.K. Aggarwal, eds. ***Artificial Intelligent Techniques in Power Systems.*** UK, IEE press, pp. 238-58.

Khosla, R and Dillon, T., 1997d, "Task Structure Level Symbolic-Connectionist Architecture," chapter in ***Connectionist-Symbolic Integration: From Unified to Hybrid Approaches,*** edited by Ron Sun and Frederic Alexandre, Lawrence Erlbaum Associates in USA, pp. 37-56, November 1997.

Khosla, R. & Dillon, T. 1997e, "Fusion of Knowledge-Based Systems and Neural Networks and Applications,". Keynote paper. *1st Int. Conf. on Conventional and Knowledge-Based Intelligent Electronic Systems.* Adelaide, Australia, May 21-23, pp. 27-44.

Khosla, R and Dillon, T., 1997f, *"Learning Knowledge and Strategy of a Generic Neuro-Expert System Arch. in Alarm Processing,"* in IEEE Trans. on Power Systems, Vol. 12, No. 12, pp. 1610-18, November.

Khosla, R. and Dillon, T.S. 1995a, "GENUES Architecture and Application,". In J. Liebowitz, ed. ***Hybrid Intelligent System Applications.*** New York, Cognizant Communication Corporation, pp. 174-99.

Khosla, R. and Dillon, T.S. 1995b, "Symbolic-Subsymbolic Agent Architecture for Configuring Power Network Faults,". *International Conference on Multi Agent Systems.* San Francisco, USA, June., pp 451

Khosla, R. and Dillon, T.S. 1995c, "Integration of Task Structure Level Architecture with O-O Technology,". *Software Engineering and Knowledge Engineering.* Maryland, USA, June 22-24, pp. 95-7.

Kirlik et al. (1993). " tain Environment: Laboratory Task and Crew Performance," in IEEE Transactions on Systems, Man, and Cybernetics 11(4), pp.1130-38.

Knutti, K. (1991). "Activity Theory and its applications to Information systems research and Development," in H.-E. Nissen, ed., Information Systems Research, Amsterdam: Elsevier Science Publishers, pp. 529-549.

Knutti, K. (1996). "A Framework for HCI Research," in *Context and Consciousness*, B. Nardi, ed., Mit Press, pp. 45-68.

Koenemann-Belliveau et al., eds., *Proceedings of the Fourth Annual Workshop on Empirical Studies of Programmers*, Norwood, N.J.: Ablex Publishing.

Laird, J., Rosenbloom, P. and Newell, A. (1987), "SOAR: An Architecture for General Intelligence" *Artificial Intelligence*, vol. 33, pp 1-64.

Laudon, K.C. and Laudon, J.P., (1995) *Management Information Systems*, Prentice Hall.

Lave, J. (1988). *Cognition in Practice*, Cambridge: Cambridge University Press.

Leont'ev, A. (1974). "The Problem of Activity in Psychology," in *Soviet Psychology*, 13(2):4-33.

Maes, P. (1994) "Agent That Reduce Work and Information Overload," Communications of the ACM, July, pp. 31-40.

Main, J., Dillon, T.. and Khosla, R. (1995), "Use of Neural Networks for Case-retrieval in a System for Fashion Shoe Design,".*Eighth Int. Conf. on Industrial and Engg Apps of AI & Expert Systems*.Melbourne, June, pp. 151-8.

McClelland, J. L., Rumelhart, D. E. and Hinton, G.E. (1986), "The Appeal of Parallel Distributed Processing," Parallel Distributed Processing, vol. 1, Cambridge, MA: The MIT Press, pp. 3-40.

McClelland J., Rumelhart D., et al. (1986) *Parallel Distributed Processing: Explorations in the Microstructure of Cognition*, Cambridge, MA: MIT Press.

Morris, C.W. (1971). "Foundations for a Theory of Signs," *in Writings on the General Theory of Signs*, The Hague: Mouton.

Morris, C.W. (1947). *Signs, Language and Behavior*, New York: Prentice Hall.

Nardi, B. (1993). *A Small Matter of Programming: Perspectives on End User Computing*, Cambridge: MIT Press.

Nardi, B. and Zarmer, C. (1993). "Beyond models and metaphors: Visual formalisms in user interface design," *Journal of Visual Languages and Computing*, March.

Nardi, B. (1996). "Studying Context: A Comparison of Activity Theory. Situated Action Models, and Distributed Cognition," in *Context and Consciousness*, B. Nardi, ed., MIT Press, pp. 69-103.

Nehmzow, U., Hallam, J., Smithers, T. (1989) "Really Useful Robots," *Proceedings of Intelligent Autonomous Systems* 2, Amsterdam.

Newell, A., (1980), "Physical Symbol Systems" *Cognitive Science*, vol. 4, pp. 135-183.

Newell A. (1990). *Unified Theories of Cognition*, Cambridge, MA: Harvard University Press.

Norman, D. (1988). *The Psychology of Everyday Things*, New York: Basic Books.

Norman, D. (1991). "Cognitive Artifacts," in *Designing Interaction: Psychology at the Human-Computer Interface*, J. Caroll, ed., Cambridge: Cambridge University Press.

Norman, D. (1993). *Things That Make Us Smart*, Reading, MA: Addision-Wesley.

Norman, D. and Hutchins, E. (1988). "Computation via direct manipulation," Final Report to Office of Naval Research, Contract No. N00014-85-C-0133. La Jolla: University of California, San Diego.

Nwana, H. S. and Ndumu, D. T. (1997) "An Introduction to Agent Technology," In Nwana, H. S. and Azarmi, N. (eds) *Software Agents and Soft Computing: Towards enhancing machine intelligence; concepts and applications*, Spinger- Verlag, pp. 3-26

Orfali, R. and Harkey, D., *Client/Server Programming with Java and COBRA*, John Wiley Computer Publishing

Perrow, C.1984, *Normal Accidents: Living with High-Risk Technologies*, Basic Books, New York.

Pfeifer, R. and Rademakers, P. (1991). "Situated Adaptive Design," in W. Brauer and D. Hernandez eds., *Kunstliche Intelligence und Kooperatives Arbeitein. Proceedings of the International GI Conference*, Berlin: Springer, pp. 53-64.

Pfeifer, R. and Verschure, P.F.M.J. (1992a). "Distributed Adaptive Control: A Paradigm for Designing Autonomous Agents," in F.J. Varela, P. Bourgine eds.: *Toward a Practice of Autonomous Systems, Proceedings of First European Artificial Life Conference*, Cambridge, MA: MIT Press, Bradford Books, pp. 21-30.

Pfeifer, R. and Verschure, P.F.M.J. (1992b). "Beyond Rationalism: Symbols, Patterns, and Behavior," in *Connection Science* 4, pp. 313-25.
Pfeifer, R. and Verschure, P.F.M.J. (1995). "The Challenge of Autonomous Agents: Pitfalls and How to Avoid Them," in L. Steels., R. Brooks eds.: *The Artificial Life Route to Artificial Intelligence*, Hillsdale, N.J.: Erlbaum, pp. 237-63.
Pierce, C. (1960). "Collected Papers of Charles Sanders Peirce," – vol I – Principles of Philosophy; vol II – Elements of Logic; vol III – Exact Logic; vol IV - The Simplest Mathematics; vol V – Pragmatism and Pragmaticism; vol. VI – Scientific Metaphysics – C. Hartshorne and P. Weiss eds., Cambridge, MA: Belknap Press of Harvard University Press.
Pree, W. (1995), *Design Patterns for Object-oriented Software Development*, Massachusetts: Addison-Wesley.
Preece, J. et al. 1997, *Human-Computer Interaction*, Addison-Wesley.
Reeke, G.N., and Edelman, G.M. (1988). "Real Brains and Artificial Intelligence," in *Daedalus*, Winter, pp. 143-78.
Rumbaugh, J. (1991), *Object-oriented Modeling and Design*, New Jersey: Prentice Hall.
Sejnowski, T.J. and Rosenberg, C.R. (1987). "Parallel Networks that Learn to Pronounce English Text," *Complex Systems* 1, pp. 145-68.
Sethi, I.K. 1990, "Entropy Nets: from Decision Trees to Neural Networks,". Proc. of IEEE, vol. 78(10), pp.1605-13
Sheriff, J.K. (1989). *The Fate of Meaning*, Princeton, NJ: Princeton University Press.
Sheth, A. (1996) "Data Semantics: What, Where and How?," *in Proceedings of the 6th IFIP Working Conference on Data Semantics (DS-6)*, R. Meersman and L. Mark (Eds.), Chapman and Hall, London, UK
Smolensky, P. (1988). "On the Proper Treatment of Connectionism," *Behavioral and Brain Sciences* 11, pp. 1-73.
Srinivasan, D., Liew, A.C. and Chang, C.S. 1994, "Forecasting Daily Load Curves using a Hybrid Fuzzy-neural Approach,". IEE Proceedings on Generation, Transmission, and Distribution. 141(6): 561-567.
Suchman, L. (1987). *Plans and Situated Actions*, Cambridge: Cambridge University Press.
Suchman, L. (1993). "Response to Vera and Simon's Situated Action: A Symbolic Interpretation," in *Cognitive Science* 1:71-76.
Suchman, L., and Trigg. R. (1991). "Understanding Practice: Video as a Medium for Reflection and Design," in J. Greenbaum and M. Kyng, eds., *Design at Work: Cooperative Design of Computer Systems,* Hillsdale, NJ: Lawrence Erlbaum.
Sun, R. (1989), "Rules and Connectionism,", in *Technical Report No. CS-89-136*, Waltham, MA: Brandeis University, Dept. of Computer Science.
Sun, R. (1991), "Integrating Rules and Connectionism for Robust Reasoning," in *Technical Report No. CS-90-154*, Waltham, MA: Brandeis University, Dept. of Computer Science.
Sun, R. (1994), "CONSYDERR: A Two Level Hybrid Architecture for Structuring Knowledge for Commonsense Reasoning,". *Proc. of the1st Int. Symp. on Integrating Knowledge and Neural Heuristics*. Florida, USA, pp.32-9.
Tang, S.K., Dillon, T. and Khosla, R. 1995, "Fuzzy Logic and Knowledge Representation in a Symbolic-subsymbolic Architecture,". *IEEE International Conference on Neural Networks.* Perth,Australia, pp. 349-53.
Tang,S.K.,Dillon,T..and Khosla, R. 1996, "Application of an Integrated Fuzzy, Knowledge-based, Connectionistic Arch. for Fault Diagnosis in Power Systems,". *Int Conf on Intell. Sys App to Power Sys* Florida, Jan. pp. 188-93.
Tenenbaum J., Chowdhry T. and Hughes K. (1998), "eCo System: CommerceNet's Architectural Framework for Internet Commerce", *http://www.commercenet.org*
Vygotsky, L.S. (1978). *Mind in Society*, Cambridge, MA: Harvard University Press.

Weizenbaum, J. (1976) *Computer Power and Human Reason: From Judgment to Calculation.* W. H. Freeman, San Francisco.

Weilinga, J., Schreiber, and Breuker, J. A. (1993). "KADS: a Modeling Approach to Knowledge Engineering," in *Readings in Knowledge Engineering*, Academic Press, pp. 93-116.

Winograd, T., and Flores, F. (1986). *Understanding Computers and Cognition: a New foundation for Design*, Norwood, NJ: Ablex.

Wooldridge, M. and Jennings, N. R. (1994) "Agent Theories, Architectures, and Languages: A Survey," In *ECAI-94 Workshop on Agent Theories, Architectures, and* Languages, Amsterdam, Netherlands

Yourdon, E. Constantine, L.,(1978). *Structured Design: fundamentals of a discipline of computer program and Systems* Design, New York: Yourdon Press.

Zhang, J. (1997) "Nature of External Representations in Problem solving," in Cognitive Science, 21(2), pp. 179-217.

Zhang, J., and Norman, D. A. (1994). "Representations in Distributed Cognitive Tasks," in *Cognitive Science*, 18, pp.87-122.

4 HUMAN-CENTERED E-BUSINESS SYSTEM DEVELOPMENT FRAMEWORK

4.1 Introduction

This chapter builds on the foundations laid down in the previous chapter. It describes the human-centered e-business system development framework for multi-agent e-business systems based on human-centered criteria outlined in the first chapter and the pragmatic considerations and enabling theories discussed in chapter 3, which contribute towards realization of those criteria. The human-centered framework is described in terms of four components, namely, activity-centered e-business analysis, problem solving ontology, transformation agent, and multimedia interpretation, respectively. The three human-centered criteria are used as guidelines for development of the human-centered framework. The pragmatic considerations and contributing theories are used to develop the structure and content, or knowledge base, of the four components. The structure and content are described at the conceptual and computational (transformation agents) level. We start this chapter by describing the external and internal planes of human interaction which underpin the development of the human-centered framework. We follow it with the description of two components of the human-centered e-business system development framework, namely, activity-centered e-business analysis and problem solving ontology. In the next chapter we continue with the description of the problem solving ontology component and describe two other components, namely, the transformation agent and multimedia interpretation component. These four components have been used to define the external and internal planes of human interaction with the environment.

4.2 Overview

The human-centered framework developed and applied in this book involves a conceptual level and a computational level. The conceptual level determines how the three human-centered criteria discussed in the first chapter are going to be modeled, based on the enabling theories described in chapter 3. The computational level, on the other hand, looks at how the conceptual level can be realized using technology-based artifacts. The technology-based artifacts are chosen based on their semantic and syntactic quality, and the pragmatic considerations discussed in the previous chapter. In order to set the scenario, we firstly describe the external and internal planes of human interaction which among other aspects underpin the development of the framework. This is followed by description of various components of the framework.

4.3 External and Internal Planes of Human-Centered Framework

In this book we intend to design and develop computer-based artifacts or software systems based on a human-centered approach. In this section we wish to outline the philosophy behind this approach.

First and foremost, as indicated in chapter 3, we employ *system* as the unit of analysis in our human-centered e-business system development framework. Rather than looking at the system from a purely technical perspective, we look at a system as a unit of analysis from a social and stakeholder perspective. The social perspective, unlike the technical perspective (which is primarily based on principles of rationality and objectivity), emphasizes the role played by people and organizations (particularly organizational culture and policies) in a system and the impact of change (especially technology-based change) on people and incentives to people for accepting the change. In order to look at these aspects more closely, a system is seen as consisting of five components, namely, an activity (more specifically work activity), stakeholder, product, data and tool. An activity consists of goals, tasks and actions or operations. Stakeholders are people or groups who have a stake in the outcome of work activity. Stakeholders can be managers or regulatory bodies who sponsor a work activity (as shown in Figure 4.1). They can be the participants who enter, process and use information in a work activity, and they can be customers (internal or external to an organization) who use the product produced by the work activity. A product, as outlined by Alter (1996), represents an outcome of the activity and can be defined in terms of its physical content, information content and service content. Data used in a work activity can exist in various forms, namely, sensor readings (numerical), text, graphics, audio, video, etc.

Tool is an artifact, which is used to perform a task directly or is used to assist people in performing a task. A tool can be an external tool (e.g., hardware, software packages, etc.) or an internal tool (e.g., problem solving strategy or plan). A customer, as defined by Alter (1996), can be an internal customer or an external customer. An internal customer is within the same organization whereas an external customer is outside the organization.

From a social perspective, any changes in a system either through computerization or otherwise, are made as a result of optimization of all the five components rather than any one component (e.g., technology). In order to understand the meaning of this statement we need to look at the traditional system design approach. Traditionally, system design has been largely targeted towards meeting business goals. These product or business goals are management sponsored and are largely driven by quantitative improvements (e.g., reduced cost, reduced defect rate, reduced cycle time, increased efficiency, etc.). Technology is invariably used as a means for satisfying the business goals and a system's success is determined in a business context rather than a human context. Although technology today enables organizations to suitably respond to external (e.g., competition) and internal (e.g., efficiency) pressures, its underlying principles of rationality and objectivity are not adequate tools for dealing with social and organizational reality in which the technology & other system components operate. Further, it does not have adequate tools to deal with the subjective reality of the stakeholders. As a result, one is likely to end up with a successful technology rather than a successful system. A successful system, unlike a successful technology, not only considers management sponsored business goals but also attempts to marry these goals with the goals and incentives of its direct stakeholders and requirements based on organizational culture. The incentives can involve computer-modeled tasks, which would enhance direct stakeholder competence, increase the degree of involvement of the stakeholders in a work activity, or help them in breakdown situations in a work activity. Assisting the stakeholders in breakdown situations can provide the motivation to the stakeholders to engage with the computer-based artifact as an integral part of their work activity. As mentioned earlier, these breakdown situations relate to those tasks which stakeholders are unable to accomplish in a non-computerized work activity or find it difficult to accomplish. The direct stakeholder incentives and organization culture tend to emphasize important qualitative system improvements.

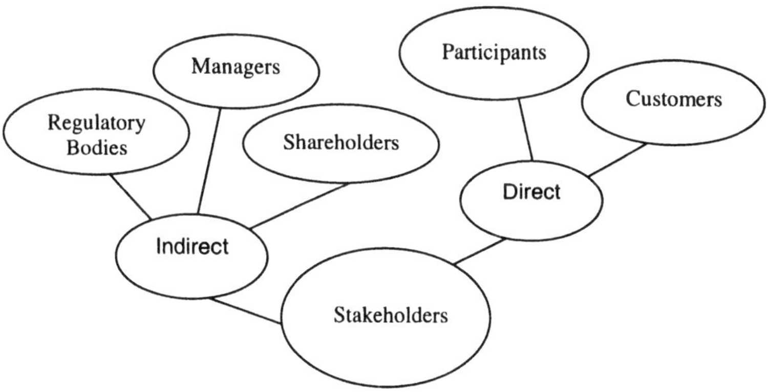

Figure 4.1. Direct and Indirect Stakeholders

In other words, business goals cannot be considered independently from direct stakeholder incentives and culture and vice versa[3]. That is, people cannot survive in organizations without satisfying business goals and organizations cannot survive for long without addressing stakeholder goals and incentives. Thus there is a need to

[3] For example a system goal might be reduce the cost of a particular work activity. However, a stakeholder may not participate in the work activity for realizing system goals unless some of their personal or professional goals are also satisfied.

integrate the two perspectives to realize successful systems (rather than just successful technologies).

In order to account for the business and social and stakeholder perspectives a system needs to be analyzed in an external context or plane of action and an internal context or plane of action. The external context defines the problem setting or context in which a system exists. The problem setting or the external environment can be defined in terms of objective aspects of the physical, social, and organizational reality in which a system exists. The physical reality primarily identifies various system components involved in the system. The social and organizational reality on the external plane involves the social, competitive, technical, and regulatory environment in which the system operates. It includes the division of labor between the stakeholders and tools (e.g., computers), overall business or product goals, competitive forces, and organizational policies. The workplace and, to an extent, situated cognition theories which emphasize the inclusion of physical, social and organizational realities, can be considered as enablers in modeling the external context or plane of action.

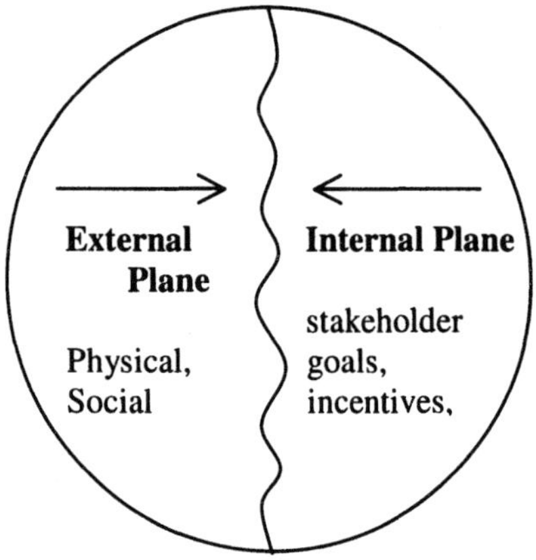

Figure 4.2. External and Internal Plane of Human-Centered Systems

The internal context, unlike the external context, involves subjective reality. This subjective reality can be studied at the individual or group level in terms of stakeholder goals, incentives, internal representations and external representations (as advocated by the distributed cognition theory) of system components (particularly the data component), and the problem solving strategy. Since we are dealing with systems that include computer-based artifacts in the external plane, the problem solving strategy can also be seen as a means of integrating and transforming the human solution or model to a software solution. The human solution can involve both perceptual tasks (based on external representations of data) and cognitive tasks (based on internal representations) involving deliberate structure and deliberate or automated reasoning. Thus, distributed aspects (representational and problem solving) of distributed cognition theory, stakeholder goal-oriented nature of the activity theory, task and problem driven ontology (discussed in section 4.5) can be considered as enablers for modeling the internal plane.

The use of computer-based artifact also brings into focus the problem of human-machine communication and interpretation of computer generated artifacts (e.g., software system results) by the stakeholders in the external plane. Multimedia artifacts like text, graphics, video and audio, and perceptual aspects of the distributed cognition theory can be considered as enablers for modeling the human-computer (and machine-machine) interface.

It may be noted that the external and internal planes represent two ends of the system development spectrum. These two planes also satisfy human-centered criteria for system development. Firstly, the external plane situates the use of computer-based artifacts among other system components in a work activity. This broadening of the scope of analysis of a human-centered system is more conducive to a problem or work driven design rather than a purely technology driven design. Secondly, the emphasis on stakeholder goals and incentives and problem solving strategy on the internal plane broadens the role of stakeholders from human factors to human actors. Thirdly, the consideration of internal (cognitive) and external (perceptive) representations and the role multimedia artifacts can play in modeling external representations assists in accounting for the representational context in which humans operate. From a human-centered system development perspective these two contexts or planes need to be bridged in a seamless manner for building successful systems.

4.4 Components of the Human-Centered e-Business System Development Framework

The discussion on the external and internal planes in the preceding section has set out the broad framework for development of human-centered systems as shown in Figure 4.3. In order to focus our attention on various aspects of this broad framework we have conceptualized it into four components. These are the activity-centered e-business analysis component, problem solving ontology component, transformation agents and the multimedia based interpretation component. The purpose of the activity-centered e-business analysis is to account for the physical, social and organizational reality on the external plane and the stakeholder goals, tasks, incentives and organizational culture on the internal plane. We have chosen to separately account for the problem solving strategy in terms of the problem solving ontology component for two reasons. Firstly, we think the role of problem solving generalizations and routines grounded in experience play an important role in systematizing and structuring complex computer-based systems. Thus by accounting for it separately, we can more effectively employ these generalizations on the outcomes of the activity-centered e-business analysis component that primarily focuses on the existing problem setting or situation. The problem solving generalizations employed by us are also used as a means for transforming a human or stakeholder solution to a software solution. This means that the problem solving ontology will interface with conceptual or task aspects of the activity-centered e-business analysis component as well as computational or transformation aspects of the computer-based artifacts. These transformational aspects are modeled by the third component transformation agents and involve use of various technology-based artifacts. Finally, the multimedia interaction component focuses on the human-computer interface in terms of how multimedia artifacts can be effectively used to model external representations, reduce the cognitive load of the computer-based artifacts on the stakeholder and enhance the perceptive aspects of problem solving. These four components are shown in Figure 4.3 as part of the human-centered e-business system development framework. The ontology of each of these components is described in this chapter and the next chapter.

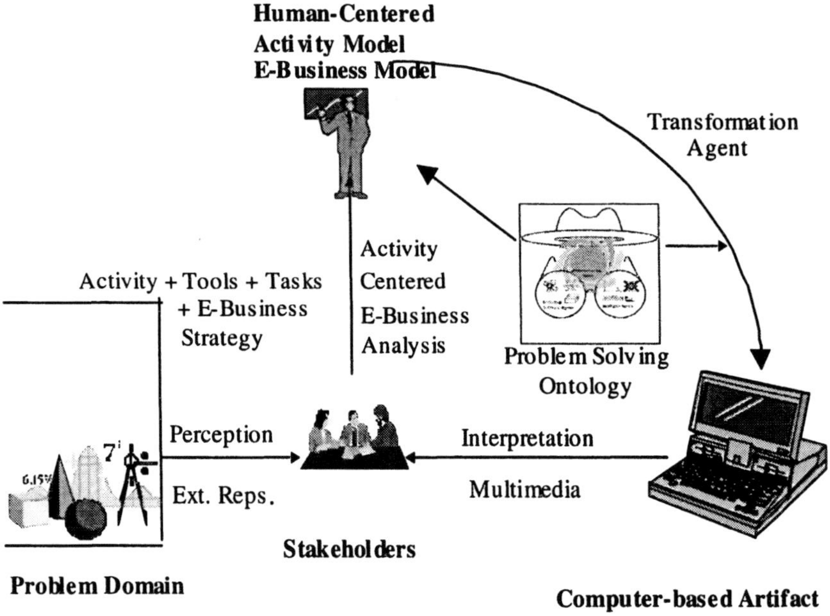

Figure 4.3. Components of Human-Centered e-Business System Development Framework

4.5. Activity-Centered e-Business Analysis Component

The purpose of the activity-centered e-business analysis is primarily to determine product and stakeholder goals and tasks, and tools and data required in accomplishing the tasks. There are six steps involved in the activity-centered e-business analysis component.

- Problem Definition and Scope.
- Performance Analysis of System Components
- Context Analysis of System Components
- Alternative System Goals and Tasks
- Human-Task-Tool Diagram
- Task-Product Transition Network.
- e-Business Strategy and Model
- e-Business Infrastructure Analysis

4.5.1. Problem Definition and Scope

This step primarily involves discussions with the sponsors (e.g., management, regulatory bodies, etc.) of the work activity in the context of e-business risks and opportunities. The discussions provide the background and motivation behind the need for reengineering an existing work activity.

In order to determine e-business risks and opportunities Weill and Vitale (2001) develop a macro level approach. In their macro level approach they firstly determine future strategic intent and core competencies of the organization. Secondly, they determine the e-business risks and opportunities by rating ten e-business related questions (shown in Table 4.1) on a scale of 1 to 5. In this book we have applied the questions to determine the e-business risks and opportunities at a micro or work activity level.

Table 4.1: e-Business Threats and Opportunities (adapted from Place to Space by Weill and Vitale, 2001, MIT Press)

Digitally Describe or Deliver – How large is the potential to digitally describe or deliver your products?	**Dynamic Pricing** - How large is your potential loss to the firm if its product is not sold by a certain time?
Price/Cost Structure – Relative to the current way of doing business, how important are Internet technologies for reducing costs in creating and delivering product to your customers?	**Knowledge Management** – How large is the potential for your firm to benefit from better knowledge management?
Customer Loyalty – How large is the potential for competitors to undermine the loyalty of your customers.	**Online Customer** – What percent of your current customers are already online at work, at home, or both?
Customer Self-Service Gap – How large is the gap between your current and potential customer self-service?	**Customisation** - How large is the opportunity for on-line customisation of your product?
Geographical Reach – What is the difference between your firm's current geographical reach and its potential reach via the Internet?	**Channel and Intermediary Power** – How large is the power or importance of channel intermediaries *in your traditional business?*

The e-business risks and opportunities are scoped in terms of system components like product, activity, and customer as shown in Figure 4.4. The system components are also used for defining the content and scope of the problem. That is, what steps/tasks are undertaken in the work activity at present to produce the product, what is the physical, information and service content of the product, who are the internal and external customers of the product, who are the direct stakeholders (i.e. day-to-day participants directly responsible for the outcomes/products of the activity) and indirect stakeholders (e.g., sponsors), what data and information are being used in the activity, and what tools are being employed to realize the outcomes.

It can be noticed from Figure 4.4 that the e-business risks and opportunities primarily relate to three system components, namely, product, customer and work activity. The product and customer components determine the effectiveness of an enterprise as perceived by the external business environment. The work activity component determines the internal efficiency of an enterprise and the three inputs, namely, participants (people), data and tool or technology play an important role in improving internal efficiency.

The bi-directional arrows in Figure 4.4 indicate that all system components influence the work activity and are influenced by it. Further, besides the work activity, the other system components can also be influenced by each another. For example, the outcomes of an activity and its tasks may be influenced by the stakeholder/participant component in terms of satisfaction/dissatisfaction of stakeholder goals. The type of data (e.g. multimedia, noisy and incomplete) may influence the tasks in the activity and type of technological tools used to process the data.

The type of tool (e.g., computers) may influence the participation of the stakeholders in the activity based on their perceptions and knowledge of the tool. The content of various system components provides the framework for their analysis. In the next step we do the analysis in terms of performance of various system components and the context (social, organizational, technical and competitive) in which these components operate.

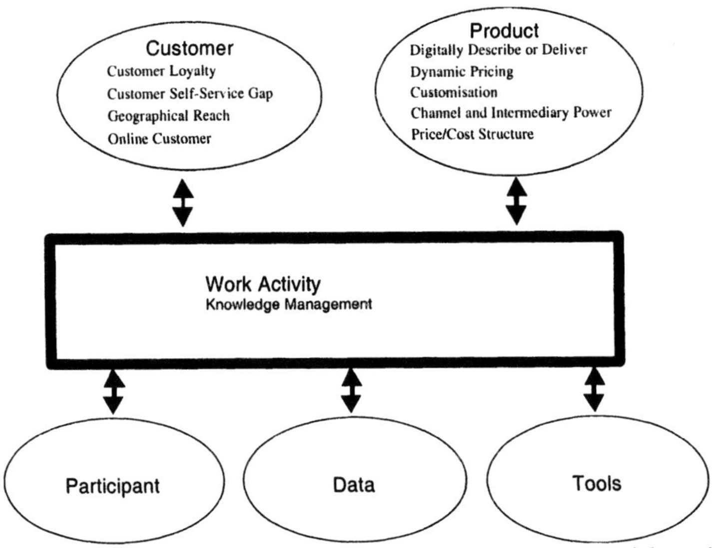

Figure 4.4: Activity-Centered System Components and e-business Risks and Opportunities

4.5.2. Performance Analysis of System Components

The performance of various system components is analyzed with a view to identify the role and the goals of the computer-based artifacts in an alternative system. The performance parameters of various system components provide an objective basis for determining a comprehensive set of goals, leading to improvement in not one or two but all system components.

The performance of a system can be analyzed in terms of its effectiveness and efficiency. Effectiveness is related to the product really being what the customer wants. In other words, is it the right product? It measures the performance of the product component in terms of cost, quality, responsiveness, reliability, and conformance to standards. Cost is measured in terms of money, time, and effort required using the product. Quality encompasses the customer's perception of a product's quality and measures such as defect rate. For, physical products, customer's perception of the quality relates to the function and aesthetics (e.g., climate control, and computerized directions through global positioning satellites in cars). For information based products, quality is perceived in terms of accessibility and presentation of data and information. The quality of service based products is perceived in terms of the level of customer satisfaction.

On the other hand, efficiency involves doing things the right way and is related to the optimal use of resources of the tool, data and participant components by the activity component for producing the product. The performance variables related to an activity are rate of output, productivity, cycle time, and flexibility. The rate of output involves an estimation of the number of units (e.g., cars) produced per hour or per week. Productivity is typically measured by evaluating output per labor hour, ratio of outputs to inputs, and cost of rework. Cycle time is measured in terms of the turnaround or start to finish time for producing the product. Flexibility, on other hand tests the rigidity of the work activity in terms of the number of product variations the work activity can handle. It determines the extent to which the product of a work activity can be customized to varying customer specifications. It may be noted that in different work activities one set of performance variables may be considered more relevant than others and hence different work activities may consider different performance variables.

Although the performance improvements in product and activity components are the most important, the performance of data, stakeholder and tool components also need to be analyzed for total system improvement.

The performance of data component is measured for its quality, accessibility, presentation and security. The quality is measured in terms of accuracy, precision and completeness of data. Accessibility is determined in terms of ease of data manipulation. Presentation is determined by how effectively various media is used to communicate data/information content. Finally, security involves the extent to which information is controlled and protected from inappropriate, unauthorized access and use.

The stakeholder component performance is determined in terms of the skills and involvement of the participants in the activity. Skills relate to the extent of experience of the participants in the activity.

The involvement relates to the extent to which participants have been involved in determining the tasks and tools to be used in activity. The involvement can range from no involvement to a very high involvement, where all the participants have been consulted in identifying tasks, tools, and data to be used in a work activity.

Finally, the performance of the tool component is determined in terms of its functional capabilities, and their use compatibility and ease of use, and maintainability.

4.5.3. Context Analysis of System Components

The performance analysis identifies the desired goals of the system. The context analysis determines the context in which these goals need to be realized. It determines the nature of tasks which need to be modeled in a computer-based artifact for realization of the goals and acceptance of the computer-based artifact, incentives and goals, technical, competitive and security realms in which these components exist. Unlike the performance analysis where quantitative measures are used, this analytical step involves largely those qualitative constraints that impact upon the successful operation and use of the system. It is important to consider these constraints as they can make a difference between a successful or unsuccessful system. They help to reengineer the tasks and tools in a work activity that lead to the development of a successful system. In the rest of this section the qualitative constraints are determined through analysis of each component.

4.5.3.1. Work Activity Context

The activity context is studied in terms of organizational culture and policies. Organizational culture represents the fundamental set of unwritten assumptions, values, and ways of doing things that have been accepted by most of its members (Laudon and Laudon 1998). For example, in universities it is assumed and accepted that teachers have more knowledge than the students, and that self-learning computer-based artifacts on the Internet are not easily accepted by the traditional academics. On the other hand, because of deregulation of many service based industries like electrical utilities and domestic and international couriers, putting service to the customer first is an aspect of organizational culture which can be found in many customer based computerized systems like paying your bills through phone and Internet and hour to hour details to customers about the progress of their documents from one destination to another. By studying organizational culture, one can determine not only what tasks can be computerized but also how task modeling needs to be sensitized to various assumptions, values and policies of the organization. These sensitivities may introduce additional tasks and constraints that need to be modeled in the computer-based artifact. The analysis is done in terms of their impact on the tasks being performed in the activity. The outcome of this analysis forms constraints on how various tasks are to be accomplished.

4.5.3.2. Direct Stakeholder Context (Participants and Customers)

The direct stakeholders are participants and customers who enter, process and use information in a work activity and are directly effected by its outcomes. Since our motivation for doing activity-centered analysis is to determine the applicability and use of computer-based artifact in a work activity, we analyze the stakeholder context in terms of the incentives the computer-based artifact has to offer the to participants and customers to facilitate its acceptance and use. In the e-business realm the customer incentives are analyzed in terms of customer loyalty, filling customer self-service gap, geographical reach of product and services, and on line product and services for on line customers. These incentives can result in additional goals and tasks for an alternative e-business system. The participant incentives are primarily determined in terms of job performance and job satisfaction. That is, to what extent the use of computer based artifact will result in improved job performance and satisfaction of participants. Unlike the business perspective where traditionally the primary motive for use of a computer-based artifact is reduced cost, automation, and efficiency the direct stakeholder incentives from a social perspective are analyzed among other aspects, in terms of the breakdowns encountered by the direct stakeholders in accomplishing their tasks in a work activity. These breakdowns can involve those decision-making points in a task where the work activity participants and customers need assistance, and computer-based artifact can be effectively used to model/complete that task. For example, in a salesperson recruitment activity, a sales manager or a recruitment consultant may find it difficult to distinguish between two equally good candidates or in fact determine their goodness w.r.t. the existing successful salespersons during an interview. A sales recruitment software can be used (as will be illustrated in chapter 6) to benchmark existing successful salespersons or compare the profiles of two equally good candidates. In this way computer-based artifacts are likely to be used as partners by the direct stakeholders rather than as technologies which are imposed on them through user manuals and principles of rationality. Further, the accomplishment of goals is analyzed in terms of the stakeholder's perspective. This may result in incorporating flexibility in the computer-based artifact to facilitate its acceptance and use. The outcome of context analysis is a set of direct stakeholder-centered tasks to realize the goals identified.

4.5.3.3. Product Context

The product context is studied in a e-business competitive realm. It is determined whether the product or products produced by the activity can be done away with altogether by the customers or substituted by other products produced outside the present activity. The product related e-business risks and opportunities like digitization, dynamic pricing, customization, channel and intermediary power and price/cost structure shown in Figure 4.1 are analyzed in terms of new goals and tasks. The outcome of this analysis is whether to go ahead with the activity and/or the tasks and constraints which need to be incorporated in the existing activity to make it worthwhile.

4.5.3.4. Data Context

The data is analyzed in terms of the structure of the data used, and policies and practices for information sharing and privacy in an organization. For example, in the Internet banking area the privacy constraints on customer's data are far more stringent than student's data in a university. These privacy and information sharing constraints need to be properly respected by a computer-based artifact for its acceptability and use. The outcome of this analysis also results in tasks and constraints on processing and use of data.

4.5.3.5. Tool Context

The tool context is studied in the technical realm. That is, whether the existing technology is good enough or new technological artifacts need to be considered for more intuitive modeling of tasks in a work activity. For example, multimedia artifacts are being used today to enhance the perceptual design of tasks accomplished by a computer-based artifact.

4.5.4. Alternative System Goals and Tasks

This step builds upon the outcomes of the performance and context analysis step in terms of the goals and corresponding tasks for an alternative computer-based system. These goals and tasks form the basis for developing a human-centered activity model shown in Figure 4.3.

In order to develop such a model we firstly need to determine the division of tasks between the participants/customers and the computer-based artifact. Further, we need to determine the underlying assumptions or preconditions for accomplishment of these human-centered tasks. This is done in the next two steps.

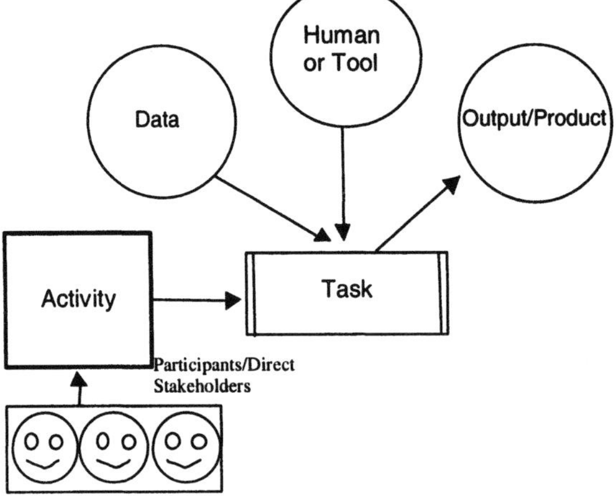

Figure 4.5: Human-Task-Tool Diagram

4.5.5. Human-Task-Tool Diagram

The purpose of the human-task-tool diagram is to determine the division of tasks between the participants/customers and the computer-based artifact. It assists in identifying the human interaction points with the computer-based artifact and data involved in the interaction. This data is later on used by the multimedia interpretation component for selecting suitable media artifacts. The notations used in the human-task-tool diagram are shown in Figure 4.5. It shows the data used by each task and the intermediate/final product produced after completion of the task. This information is useful for organizing the task-product transition network and in determining the correspondence between task and data to be used later on by the problem solving ontology component.

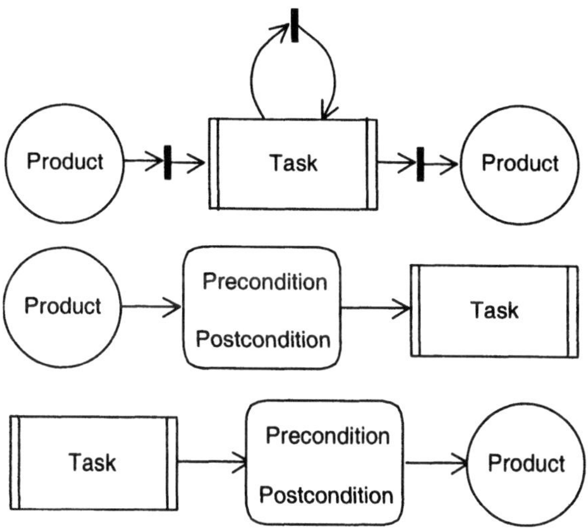

Figure 4.6: Task-Product Transition Network

4.5.6. Task Product Transition Network

The task-product transition network shown in Figure 4.6 defines the relationship between the tasks and elementary, intermediate and final products of a work activity. It can also help us in identifying parallelism, sequentiality between tasks and cyclic or repetitive tasks. Further, the precondition of the transition assists us in defining the assumptions under which the task will be accomplished. The postcondition reflects not only the new product state but also the level of competence required from the technological artifact or tool used for accomplishing the task.

4.5.6. e-Business Strategy and Model

The preceding steps have accomplished two important goals. Firstly, in the preceding steps we have carried out an e-business analysis based on identification of e-business risks and opportunities related to a work activity and associated system components, and performance and context analysis of the system components. Secondly, based on the e-business analysis we have identified the goals and tasks of an alternative e-business system. In order to realize the goals and tasks of the alternative e-business system we need to determine the e-business strategy and model compatible with the goals and tasks of the e-business system. The e-business strategy can be any one (or combination) of channel enhancement, value-chain integration, industry transformation and industry convergence as outlined in section 2.3 of chapter 2. Further, in order to realize e-business Information Technology (IT) based solution one has to decide on the e-business model (as outlined in section 2.4 of chapter 2) to be employed. The choice of e-business model will also influence the IT infrastructure analysis which is discussed next.

4.5.7. e-Business Infrastructure Analysis

The design of any new information system invariably imposes new infrastructure needs on various system components. This may include changes in the organization and training of participants, existing data models may need to supplemented with new data definitions, and information technology infrastructure may need to be enhanced so that it meets the requirements of the e-business model. The most critical of these infrastructure needs is that of the IT infrastructure. For example, a value-net integrator model may impose IT infrastructure requirements which connects an enterprise with its supplier databases, databases of its freight carrier company and their delivery centers, and databases of other business partners. E-Business infrastructure analysis looks into all these issues

This step completes the activity-centered e-business analysis of the human-centered e-business system development framework. The next describes the motivations behind the problem solving ontology components and its structure.

4.6. Problem Solving Ontology Component

The problem solving ontology component shown in Figure 4.3 is used to transform a human solution (obtained through activity-centered analysis) to a software solution (in form of a computer-based artifact). In this section, we firstly review some of the work done on problem solving ontologies in the literature. We follow it with the description of problem solving ontology employed in this book.

An ontology is a representation vocabulary, typically specialized to some technology, domain or subject matter. However, here we are dealing with upper ontology, i.e., ontology that describes generic knowledge that holds across many domains. Further, we are dealing with problem solving knowledge or generic (e.g., tasks) about problem solving. In this section we start by covering problem solving ontologies and determining their strengths and weaknesses. We then describe the problem solving ontology used in this book.

4.6.1. Strengths and Weaknesses of Existing Problem Solving Ontologies

The research on problem solving ontologies or knowledge-use level architectures has largely been done in artificial intelligence. The research at the other end of the spectrum (e.g., radical connectionism) is based more on understanding the nature of human or animal behavior rather than developing ontologies for dealing with complex real world problems in control, diagnosis, design, etc. It is well acknowledged that to deal with these complex problems one cannot completely rely on the particularities of a real world problem (as suggested by the situated cognition approach). One also has to be in a position to benefit from the generalizations or persistent problem solving structures that hold across domains. It is with this motivation we look into some of the work done in artificial intelligence on the knowledge-use level, as against application level.

The work on knowledge-use level in artificial intelligence can be traced back to the work done by Clancey (1985) on heuristic classification. Clancey analyzed the inference structure underlying a series of expert systems and cognitive models in general. He found that the reasoning pattern of these programs involved a) abstracting descriptions of situations in the world (also called data abstraction), b) heuristically (by cause, frequency, or preference) relating these abstractions to a second classification (also called solution abstraction), and then c) refining the second description to a level suggesting particular actions. He called this reasoning or inferencing pattern heuristic classification. Heuristic classification represents a significant empirical generalization of expert system development. These three stages (data abstraction, solution abstraction through heuristic match and refinement) of heuristic classification have been found useful in focussing expert system development at the knowledge-use level. However, the highly abstract generalizations do not provide enough application vocabulary for the problem solver.

Besides, there are certain omissions like lack of contextual validation of data (its absence can result in nonproductive abstractions) before abstracting it, and lack of consideration of epistemological limitations that humans and computers have and pragmatic constraints associated with complex real world problems. The epistemological limitations relate to the need for making decisions in finite time, finite memory and storage structure of computers, imprecision associated with human observations and the need for inductively derived models (to improve model accuracy and prediction) based on real world data and interactions with humans.

Around this time, another approach, namely, model based approach towards system modeling was being developed (Hart 1984, Steels 1985; Steels and Van de Velde 1985; Simmon 1988). The model based approach focussed on the domain models underlying expertise rather than the inferencing pattern used in heuristic classification. The model-based systems emphasized the need for deep or complete knowledge of the domain of study rather than surface or shallow knowledge that focussed only on portions of deep knowledge. Based on deep knowledge, part-whole, geometric and functional models of a domain were developed. Although, by definition the model-based approach sounds comprehensive, it suffers from certain weaknesses. First of all, it assumes that exact domain theory is known. This is not the case especially, in complex domains where it becomes difficult to develop complete domain models. Secondly, it relies on the correctness of observed data, whereas in complex real world problems, the data is often noisy and incomplete. Finally, the main strength of model based systems i.e., deep or complete knowledge, can work against itself especially in real time situations where exploration of large spaces or combinatorial explosion of rules can lead to unacceptable response times.

In 1988, McDermott developed the problem solving method approach which is somewhere in between model based approach and data base approach. A problem solving method is a knowledge-use-level characterization of how a problem might be solved. For example, a medical diagnostic problem can be solved using a cover-and-differentiate method in which, firstly, explanations covering the observed symptoms are determined, and then the cause is determined by differentiating among various explanations (Eshelman 1988).

A problem solving method specifies the domain knowledge required from the expert to solve a particular problem. For example, in a medical diagnostic system the domain knowledge is represented as a infection model that explicitly represents relations between symptoms (e.g., fever, cough) and infections (e.g., bronchitis). The specified domain knowledge may only form a small portion of the complete domain knowledge as defined in model based systems. Thus the problem solving method approach accounts for some of the problems (e.g., combinatorial explosion of search space) associated with model based systems. However, its strength can also become a drawback in establishing the completeness of the system. Further, problem solving methods also suffer from what Steels (1990) calls the grain size problem. In other words, because a problem solving method intends to solve the complete problem, it may use other problem solving methods for handling various subtasks in the problem domain that may be somewhat different in structure than itself. For example, propose-and-revise method (Chandrasekaran 1990) can involve use of a classification method for proposing different designs in the propose phase. This leads to a proliferation of problem solving methods for a solving a particular problem. More recently, Fensel and Groenboom (1996), Fensel (1997) and Chandrasekaran, Josephson and Benjamins (1998) have suggested use of adapters as a means of mapping a problem solving method on to a task domain ontology. These adapters are different than those used by the Gamma et al. (1995) in software engineering. In software engineering design patterns and adapters are defined as low level primitives that link two software design artifacts. On their own these adapters are not sufficient to solve the complete problem. Besides, they are designed from the perspective of software design rather than problem solving. The adapters defined by Fensel (1997), and Chandrasekaran, Josephson and Benjamins (1998) are used for modeling complete solutions for complex real world problems. These complex problems are solved using intelligent methods which (unlike adapters define by Gamma et. al. (1995)) require assumptions to be made in terms of type domain knowledge needed. However, the adapter based approach of Fensel, and Chandrasekaran, Josephson and Benjamins apparently presupposes use of one or the other problem solving method, domain ontology and domain model for solving a problem besides being only suited for knowledge based systems. In many complex problems more than one domain ontology and domain model may be used (Steels 1990). Thus the adapters should facilitate use of multiple domain-models and domain ontologies.

Another line of research, namely, task structure analysis developed by Chandrasekaran (1983), Chandrasekaran and Mittal (1983), Chandrasekaran, Johnson and Smith (1992) focuses on modeling domain knowledge using generic tasks and methods as mediating concepts. Typical generic tasks are classification, diagnosis, interpretation, and construction. For each generic task (say diagnosis) a task structure analysis is done. The task structure analysis represents the interplay between methods (e.g., abduction) and subtasks for a given generic task. The task structure analysis as outlined by Chandrasekaran, Johnson and Smith (1992) does alleviate, to some extent, problem solving method granularity problems with the problem solving method approach. However, it only employs methods as mediating concepts for task accomplishment and not representations. The distributed cognition approach described in the previous chapter clearly establishes the role of external and internal representations in problem solving. The task structure analysis approach implicitly assumes internal representations and does not take into account external representations.

Table 4.2 : Problem Solving Ontologies – Strengths and Weaknesses

Approach	***Strengths***	***Weaknesses***
Heuristic Classification (inference pattern) Clancey 1985	Good empirical generalization	No distinction between different classification methods. (e.g. weighted evidence combination). Not enough vocabulary. Pragmatic constraints not considered.
Model Based Systems (part-whole, causal, geometric, functional) Steels 1985; Simmons 1988	Principled domain models, complete knowledge	Combinatorial explosion, assumes all observations are correct & exact domain theory is known.
Problem Solving Ontologies (between model based and data based) based on Problem Solving Methods - (cover-and-differentiate, propose-test-refine, etc) McDermott 1988	Helps to determine type of domain knowledge required for problem solving, eases the knowledge acquisition bottleneck.	When to stop the knowledge acquisition, when is the system complete. Do not consider the role of representations or tasks Problem Solving Ontologies.
- Generic Task Based (classification, interpretation, diagnosis & construction/design) Chandrasekaran 1983, Chandrasekaran & Josephson 1997, Chandrasekaran & Johnson 1993, Steels 1990.	Reuse, basis for interpreting acquired data, can build generic software environments.	Generic task categorization is not generic enough because they (e.g. diagnosis) can be accomplished using many different domain models, and different methods (depending on problem granularity), pragmatic constraints not considered. Tasks only mediated by methods.
Generic Ontology – KADS methodology (domain layer, inference layer, task layer, strategy layer) Breuker and Weilinga 1989,91 Weilinga et al 1993.	Segregates knowledge modeling into four layers.	System modeling done with low level primitives. Suitable for knowledge based problems only. Does not consider pragmatic constraints.

In the preceding paragraphs we have outlined four distinct knowledge level approaches to problem solving. The first one developed by Clancey (1985) employs inference structure or pattern as an empirical approach to problem solving. Hart (1984), Steels and Van de Velde 1985 on the other hand use causal, structural and functional domain models to solve problems. McDermott (1988) and Simmon, (1988) adopt a problem solving method approach towards problem solving. Finally, Chandrasekaran, Johnson and Smith (1992). In Europe, Breuker and Weilinga (1989, 1991) have developed Knowledge Acquisition and Design System (KADS) methodology, which includes pertinent aspects of the four approaches. The expertise model of the KADS approach defines three layers, namely, domain layer, inference layer, and task layer to model knowledge based systems. It defines a set of primitives for each of these three layers and employs them in a bottom up fashion in a problem domain to develop higher level of analysis. It has been used successfully to develop a number of expert systems in the field. However, it is not clear as to how the KADS approach accounts for external representations in problem solving, epistemological limitations of humans and computers, and pragmatic constraints associated with real world problems. Further, none of the approaches provides insight into how to deal with the complexity of large-scale real world problems. That is, to what extent applications developed by using these problem solving methods or ontologies will be scalable, evolvable and maintainable. Table 4.2 shows a summary of various problem solving approaches discussed in this section, along with some of their weaknesses.

Besides the above limitations, the existing approaches do not lend themselves towards human-centered research and design and more specifically towards satisfying criteria 1, 2 and 3 of human-centeredness outlined in the first chapter. That is, most of these approaches facilitate an objective way to model solutions to real world problems. They are motivated by answering the following question: what is (or are) the most appropriate approach (s) for solving a particular problem or task? They do not necessarily answer the question: what are the underlying user's goals and tasks, or what problem solving strategy does the user. Further, because these ontologies are defined at a high level of abstraction, they do not provide adequate vocabulary (e.g. Activity Centered Analysis component in this book) or assistance for a non-specialist to solve a particular problem. Additionally, most of the above approaches in Table 4.2 are embedded in the knowledge based system technology. They (e.g., some Generic Task Based approaches), tend to subscribe to best practice approach, an approach which has been recently criticized in the software development community (emergence of patterns is a consequence of the best practice myth). Further, they do not adequately address the pragmatic task constraints modeled or satisfied by other technologies like neural networks, fuzzy logic, and genetic algorithms. A lack of this consideration has resulted in unsatisfactory results (in terms of satisfaction of constraints and quality of solution) from implementation of these problem solving methods in the field.

4.7. Summary

This chapter builds on the foundations laid down in the previous chapter. It describes a human-centered e-business system development framework for developing multi-agent e-business systems. The human-centered approach involves a seamless integration of external and internal planes or contexts of action.

The external context defines the problem setting or context in which a system exists. The problem setting or the external environment can be defined in terms of objective aspects of the physical, social and organizational reality in which a system exists. The internal context, unlike the external context, involves subjective reality. This subjective reality can be studied at the individual or group level in terms of stakeholder goals, incentives, organizational culture, internal representations and external representations of data in a work activity, and problem solving strategy that is adopted by stakeholders in individual or group work activity.

The external and internal planes represent two ends of the system development spectrum. These two planes are conceptually captured with the help of four system development components, namely, activity-centered e-business analysis component, problem solving ontology component, transformation agent component, and multimedia interpretation component. The activity-centered e-business analysis component is based on identification of e-business risks and opportunities in terms of system components like product, customer and work activity. It defines the scope of the problem by identifying the content of six system components, namely, product, data, customer, work activity and tool. It conducts a performance and context analysis of the existing situation as defined by the six components. The outcome of the performance and context analysis is a set of e-business goals and tasks for a computer-based artifact that forms a part of an alternative e-business system. These goals and tasks form the basis for a human-centered activity model. The terminology and notations for a human-task-tool diagram are outlined in order to determine among other aspects, the division of labor between the direct stakeholders and computer-based artifact. It also helps to define the human interaction points in a computer-based system which are used later on by the multimedia interpretation component. A task-product transition network is also drawn to define among other aspects, the preconditions and postconditions for each task.

The e-business goals and tasks are used to determine the e-business strategy and e-business model. The choice of the e-business model establishes the IT infrastructure needs for an e-business IT based solution.

The results of the activity-centered e-business analysis and the task-product transition network are used by the problem solving ontology component to develop a human-centered activity model. Another role of the problem solving ontology component is to systematize and structure the tasks outlined in the task-product transition network. This chapter covers some existing work done by researchers in the evolution and development of problem solving ontologies. It outlines the strengths and weaknesses of some of the problem solving ontologies. The next chapter describes the problem solving ontology used in this book and transformation agent and multimedia interpretation components.

References

Alter, S., (1996), Information systems – A Management Perspective, second edition, Benjamin/Cummings Publishing Company.

Breuker, J.A. and Weilinga, B.J., (1989) "Model Driven Knowledge Acquisition" in B. Guida & G. Tasso eds. *Topics in the Design of Expert Systems*, Springer-Verlag, pp 239 – 280.

Breuker, J.A. and Weilinga, B.J., (1991) *Intelligent Multimedia Interfaces*, Edited by Mark Maybury, AAAI Press, Menlo Park, CA.

Chandrasekaran B. and Josephson, J.R., (1997) "Ontology of Tasks and Methods", *AAAI 97 Spring Symposium on Ontological Engineering,* March 24-26, Stanford University, CA California, USA.

Chandrasekaran, B. (1983), "Towards Taxonomy of Problem Solving Types", *AI Magazine* Vol 4 No. 1, Winter/Spring pp 9-17.

Chandrasekaran, B., and Johnson, T.R. (1993), "Generic Tasks and ask Structues: History Critique and New Directions", *Second Generation Expert Systems*, G.M. Davies, J.P. Krivine and R. Simmons.

Clancey, W.J., (1985) "Heuristic classification", Artificial Intelligence, 27, 3 (1985), 289-350.

Eshelman, L. (1988). "Mole: A Knowledge Acquisition Tool for Cover-and-Differentiate systems" in *Automating Knowledge Acquisition for Expert Systems*, Ed. S. Marcus, 37-79. Boston: Kluwer

Fensel, D (1997), "The Tower-of-Adapter Method for Developing and Reusing Problem-Solving Methods," *EKAW*, pp. 97-112

Fensel, D. and Groenboom, R., (1996), "MLPM: Defining a Semantics and Axiomatization for Specifying the Reasoning Process of Knowledge-based Systems,".*ECAI*, pp 423-427

Gamma, E et. al., (1995) "Design Elements of Object-Oriented Software," Massachusetts: Adisson-Wesley.

Hart, P. (1984). "Artificial Intelligence in Transition" in *Knowledge-Based Problem Solving*, Ed. J. Kowalik, 296-311. Engelwood Cliffs, N.J. Prentice-Hall.

Laudon. K.C. and Laudon, J.P., (1998), Management Information Systems, Prentice Hall International.

McDermott, J., (1988) Preliminary steps toward a taxonomy of problem solving methods. In *Automated Knowledge Acquisition for Expert Systems,* S. Marcus, Ed., Kluwer Academic, pp. 225-256.

Simmons, R. 1988. "Generate, Test, and Debug: A Paradigm for Solving Interpretation and Planning Problems". Ph. D diss., AI Lab, Massachusetts Institute of Technology.

Steels, L. (1990) "Components of Expertise", AI Magazine, 11, 28-49., 11, 28-49

Steels, L. 1984. "Second-Generation Expert Systems" presented at the *Conference on Future Generation Computer Systems,* Rotterdam. Also in *Journal of Future Generation Computer Systems* (1)4: 213-237.

Steels, L., and Van de Velde, W. 1985. Earning in Second-Generation Expert Systems" in *Knowledge-Based Problem Solving*, Ed. J. Kowalik. Englewood Cliffs, N.J.: Prentice-Hall.

Steven, S.S. (1995). "On the Psychological Law", *Psychological Review*, 64(3), 153-181

Weilinga, B.J., Ath. Schreiber and J.A. Breuker, 1993 "KADS: A Modelling Approach to Knowledge Engineering", Readings in *Knowledge Acquisition and Learning*, eds. Buchanan, B.. & Wilkins, D., San Mates California, Morgan Kaufmann pp 92-116.

Weill, P., and Vitale, M., (2001), *Place to Space*, MIT Press, 2001.

5 HUMAN-CENTERED VIRTUAL MACHINE

5.1. Introduction

The objective of this chapter is to outline the computational framework of multi-agent e-business systems based on the human-centered approach. The title human-centered virtual machine encapsulates the integration of conceptual components of the human-centered e-business system development framework and the technology based artifacts used to realize the conceptual components at the computational level.

In chapter 4 we described some of the existing problem-solving ontologies, their strengths and weaknesses. In this chapter we start with the description of the problem-solving ontology component. We follow it with description of the transformation agent component and multimedia interpretation component. The transformation agent component is constructed through integration of the problem solving ontology with various technological artifacts like intelligent technologies, agent and object-oriented technologies, multimedia presentation, XML and distributed processing technologies. The multimedia interpretation component, on the other hand, deals with interpretation of data content by the direct stakeholders/users. It does that by mapping the data characteristics to media characteristics and media expressions of different media artifacts. An application of the multimedia interpretation component in an intranet based clinical diagnosis system is also described. The chapter concludes by outlining the emergent characteristics of the human-centered virtual machine.

5.2. Problem Solving Ontology Component

As mentioned in the previous chapter the main aim of the problem solving ontology component is to develop a human-centered activity model based on the stakeholder goals and tasks model (outcome of activity-centered e-business analysis), stakeholder representational model, and stakeholder domain model for various tasks. As shown in Figure 5.1, it does that by systematizing and structuring these aspects using five information processing phases, namely, preprocessing, decomposition, control, decision, and postprocessing.

The information processing phases and their generic tasks have been derived from actual experience of building complex systems in engineering, medicine, bioinformatics, management, Internet and e-commerce. Further, they have been based on number of perspectives including neurobiology, cognitive science, learning, forms of knowledge, user intelligibility, and others (Khosla et. al. 1997).

Each information processing phase in turn is defined in terms of generic goals, generic tasks, constructs for analyzing external representations and sensor data, underlying assumptions on the domain data, knowledge engineering strategy (top down or bottom up), soft (e.g., non-symbolic methods like neural networks and genetic algorithms) and/or hard (e.g., symbolic rule based systems) computing techniques used for accomplishing various tasks. Although, the five information processing phases represent domain independent tasks, domain dependent tasks can also be integrated into these phases.

Each phase is encapsulated using a problem solving adapter construct. A problem solving adapter construct besides distinguishing between different information processing phases is used to establish a signature mapping between user's or practitioner's goals and task (as determined in the by the activity-centered e-business analysis component), external (perceptual) and internal (interpreted/linguistic and non-linguistic) representation ontology and the domain model. The problem solving adapter definitions do not constrain the user or practitioner in terms of domain model or models employed, problem solving technique employed.

In the remainder of this section, we outline the problem solving vocabulary of the five problem solving adapters. Before we do that, it is useful to define the terms used in the vocabulary.

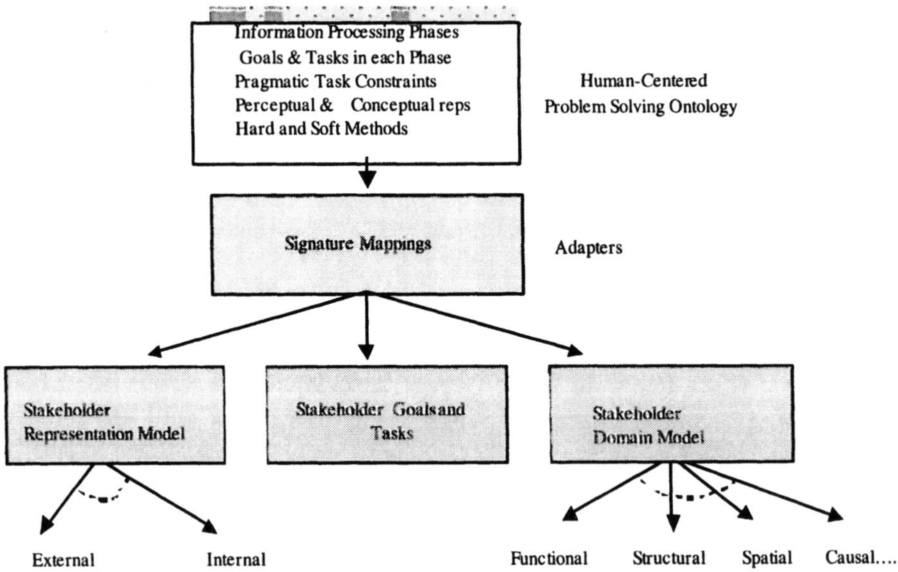

Figure 5.1. Human-Centered Problem Solving Ontology

5.2.1. Definition of Terms Used

Information Processing Phase:
- a distinct step or event in problem solving

Goal:
- a desire or desired outcome or state

Task:
- Tasks are goal directed processes in which people consciously or unconsciously engage.

Task Constraints:
- are pragmatic constraints imposed by the stakeholders and the environment for successful accomplishment of a task. The task constraints primarily determine the selection knowledge required for selecting a technological artifact (e.g., a computing technique) for accomplishing a task. The task constraints are a byproduct of epistemological limitations that humans and computers have and the environment in which a computer based software artifact will operate (Steels 1990). Human limitations relate to the need to make decisions in finite time. Thus those models or techniques which lead to deep solution hierarchies (e.g., symbolic rule based systems) and large response times cannot be used in software systems supporting humans in real world tasks requiring fast response times (especially internet based e-business applications). Similarly, computers have finite space and memory. Therefore, models and techniques (e.g., breadth first search) requiring large search spaces cannot be used. Other human limitations include lack of domain knowledge in certain tasks which means techniques like self-organizing neural networks need to be used to inductively learn the domain model and concepts used to accomplish such tasks. Finally, human or sensor observations may be imprecise. Therefore hard computing artifacts which rely on precision cannot be used. That is, the epistemological limitations lead to a number pragmatic considerations or constraints for selection of appropriate techniques. These include dealing with information or data explosion, noisy and incomplete data, need to avoid search or use search techniques which are not constrained by necessary and sufficient conditions. Besides the above constraints imposed by epistemological limitations, human ability to adapt also constrains use of those technological artifacts, which can adapt like humans do in new or similar situations. Therefore, techniques that do not have adaptive behavior cannot be used to model tasks that require adaptation. In summary human and computer related task constraints can be knowledge and data related (e.g., imprecise/incomplete data, learning), conceptual and software design related (e.g., scalability, maintainability), and domain performance related (e.g., response time and adaptation).

Precondition:
- helps us to define underlying assumptions for task accomplishment.

Postcondition:
- defines the level of competence required from the technique or algorithm used for accomplishing the task.

Represented Features:

- are linguistic (e.g., symbolic, fuzzy) and non-linguistic (e.g., numeric) features in a domain.

Representing Dimension:

- is the physical or abstract dimension used to represent a feature. It can be seen as capturing the perceptual representation or category of a feature. The perceptual representation is a stable signature (e.g. oval shape of a face or pattern in a raw sensory signal). These representing dimensions can be shape, color, distance, location, orientation, density, texture, etc

Psychological Scale:

- is the abstract measurement property of the physical or abstract dimension of a represented feature. There are four types of scales, namely, nominal, ordinal, interval and ratio. The four psychological scales devised by Steven (1957) are based on one or more properties, such as category, magnitude, equal interval and absolute zero. The category refers to the property by which the instances on a scale can be distinguished from one another. The magnitude denotes the property that one instance on a scale can be judged greater than, less than, or equal to another instance on the same scale. The equal interval refers to the property that the magnitude of an instance represented by a unit on the scale is the same, regardless of where on the scale the unit falls. Finally, absolute zero: is a value that indicates the nonexistence of the property being represented. The nominal scale is based on the category property only. The ordinal scale includes the category as well as magnitude properties. The interval scale includes category, magnitude and equal interval properties. Finally, the ratio scale includes all the four properties (i.e., category, magnitude, equal interval and absolute zero).The purpose of using the representing dimension and scale information is twofold. Firstly, from a human-centered perspective the representing dimension and scale information provide insight into distributed representations (external and internal) used in problem solving (Zhang & Norman 1994; Stevens 1957). The distributed representations account for the representational context of human-centered criteria no. 2. Through the representing dimension and scale information, we can determine what part or parts of a task can be accomplished perceptually. For example, in a energy forecasting domain, the represented features of a energy consumption profile are the hourly energy consumption data points. The representing dimension of the energy consumption profile is its shape (on the nominal scale). The shape can be seen to represent the external representation whereas numeric data values of the data points are internal representations of the profiles. Thus, certain tasks like eliminating noisy consumption profiles involving valley or straight line shapes can be done perceptually using the representing dimension of shape. Secondly, the representing dimension and scale information can assist in developing more efficient and effective means of communicating the data content perceptually to the user/direct stakeholders of a computer-based artifact. This will also help in reducing the cognitive load on the users

Technological Artifact:

- can be a software artifact like an agent, object and/or a hard or soft computing technique to accomplish a given task. Objects and classes can be used to structure the represented features/data and/or the devices/components/objects used by different problem solving adapters to accomplish various tasks. Thus the technological artifacts and relations are defined in the task context as outlined by users. Agents can be used to model various tasks associated with the adapter. Soft or hard computing techniques can be used for accomplishing various tasks. The selection of a soft or hard computing technique will depend upon the knowledge engineering strategy and the task constraints. For example, in case domain knowledge is not available then soft computing techniques have to be used. On the other hand, if domain knowledge is available (top-down knowledge engineering strategy) then hard computing techniques can suffice.

Knowledge Engineering Strategy:

- Top down or bottom up knowledge engineering strategy is simply indicative of the availability or non-availability of domain knowledge, respectively, for accomplishing a task. A bottom-up strategy is contingent upon use of soft computing techniques for accomplishing a given task, whereas a top-down strategy can use hard computing technique like a symbolic rule based system for accomplishing a task. Further, in a bottom-up strategy, learning and adaptation are a necessity, whereas, in a top-down strategy learning and adaptation may be used for enhancing performance of a task. A number of complex problems employ a mixture of top-down and bottom-up strategy for accomplishing different tasks.

5.2.2. Problem Solving Adapters

In the this section we define the problem solving adapters based on the terms defined in the preceding section. These are preprocessing, decomposition, control,, decision, and postprocessing adapters. These adapters are built on five information processing phases developed by Khosla et. al. (1997).

5.2.2.1. Preprocessing Phase Adapter:

- The preprocessing adapter shown in Figure 5.2 can be used by all the phase adapters except the postprocessing phase adapter.

Goal: As shown in Figure 5.2, the goal of the preprocessing adapter is to improve data quality.

Task: Noise Filtering

- employs heuristics or other algorithmic/non-algorithmic techniques for removing noise from a domain at a global or a local level of problem solving. The non-algorithmic techniques can involve perceptual or visual reasoning (e.g. distinguishing a irregular shape from a regular one). The noise represents peculiarities that are specific to a problem domain and need to be removed in order to improve the quality of data. It can involve removing irrelevant parts of a natural language query, eliminating irrelevant data in a web mining problem, eliminating skin look-alike regions from actual skin regions in a face recognition problem, eliminating highly irregular shaped energy consumption profiles from standard profiles in a energy prediction problem, eliminating nuisance alarms, faulty alarms in a alarm processing and diagnosis problem, etc.

Task: Input Conditioning

- this task may require simple formatting of the input data and/or transforming the data from one format to another (e.g., transforming different image formats, etc.), dimensionality reduction (e.g., combining and/or removing ineffective data points, using existing domain knowledge to aggregate/partition data, etc.).

Task: Problem Formulation

- involves sequencing of various actions required to accomplish the above tasks.

Tasks: Other Domain Dependent Tasks

- This includes those tasks which are peculiar to a domain

Task Constraints:

- Domain and application dependent

Represented Features:

- Since the task like noise filtering is heuristic in nature, the represented features in the domain can be qualitative/linguistic (binary, structured and fuzzy) or continuous in nature. For example, in a alarm processing problem, a alarm may be filtered based on its existence (binary), based on multiple occurrences of it or based on the topology of the network (structured). Further, fuzzy variables (e.g., adjectives in a natural language query) may be used to eliminate particular type of queries. In domains like signal processing fast forward transforms are applied on continuous numeric data.

Psychological scale:

- The represented features can be analyzed based on the nominal, ordinal, interval or ratio scales. These psychological scales which have been developed by Steven (1957) are used by humans to derive perceptual and conceptual semantics of real world objects.

Perceptual Representing Dimensions:

- The perceptual dimensions on which the psychological scales are applied could be shape (e.g., eliminating noisy energy consumption profiles based on shape), distance (e.g., suppressing sympathetic alarms emerging from parts of network beyond certain threshold distance from the faulty component), color, etc.

Knowledge Engineering Strategy

- Top-down or bottom-up.

Technological Artifacts: hard or soft computing techniques.

- In our problem solving ontology we consider computational or algorithmic techniques as well as perceptual or non-algorithmic techniques. Besides, we also consider software-engineering techniques like object-oriented methodology as a means of accomplishing a task. For example, a dimension reduction task can be accomplished using an object-oriented technique by aggregating or partitioning the data. The computational techniques can be hard or soft, depending upon the task constraints and the represented features. On the other hand, perceptual techniques exploit the perceptual representing dimensions of the represented features.

The preprocessing phase adapter definition based on the goal, task, precondition/postcondition and other definitions, as outlined in this section, is shown in Figure 5.2. Figure 5.3 shows the representation and task signature mapping for preprocessing adapter. The signature mappings represent those aspects (e.g., goals and tasks) of the preprocessing adapter definition in Figure 5.2, which are invariably used by computer-based applications. The tasks indicated as optional or not shown in Figure 5.3 and shown in Figure 5.2 are optional and may or may not be used in a particular application

Phase: Preprocessing
Goal: Improve data quality
Task: problem Solving Context – Global; Input Context – raw symbolic or continuous data`
Task: Noise filtering – form – time based noise filtering, content and task context based noise filtering
Task: Input conditioning – form – Dimensionality reduction, Data transformation (e.g. color transformation), input formatting
Task: Problem formulation – form – conceptual ordering of actions
Task Constraints: Domain/application dependent
Precondition: Raw or processed data
Postcondition: Conditioned data
Represented Features: *Qualitative/linguistic* – binary, structured
Non-Linguistic – continuous features
Psychological Scale: Nominal; Ordinal, Interval, Ratio
Representing Dimension (Perceptual): Shape, Location, Position, Color, etc.
Knowledge Engineering Strategy: Top-down or bottom up
Technological Artifacts: Hard (e.g. symbolic rule based), soft (e.g. neural networks), etc.

Figure 5.2: Preprocessing Phase Adapter Definition

Domain Representation Signature	Domain Task Signature
Phase: Preprocessing	**Phase**: Preprocessing
Goal: Improve data quality	**Goal:** Improve data quality
Represented Features:	**Precondition:** raw or processed data
Qualitative/linguistic- binary, structured,	**Task :** Noise filtering (optional)
Non-Linguistic- continuous features	**Task:** Data conditioning - form - Dimensionality reduction, Data transformation (e.g. color transformation), data formatting
Psychological Scale: Nominal; Ordinal, Interval, Ratio	**Task Constraints** domain/application dependent
Representing Dimension (Perceptual): Shape, Location, Position, Color, etc.	**Domain Model:** functional, structural, spatial, Causal, spatial, etc.
Knowledge Engineering Strategy top-down or bottom-up	**Postcondition** conditioned data
	Knowledge Engineering Strategy: top-down or bottom-up

Figure 5.3. Signature Mapping for Preprocessing Adapter

5.2.2.2. Decomposition Phase Adapter

Goal:

- The primary goal of the decomposition phase adapter is to restrict the context of the input from the environment at the global level. The secondary goals are to reduce the complexity and enhance overall reliability of the computer-based artifact.

Task: Restrict input context

- The input context at the global level is restricted in terms of user's or stakeholder's perception of the task context. The user's task context can be used to restrict the input in terms of different types of users (e.g., medical researcher, and evolutionary biologist in a human genome application), different perspectives employed by a business manager in customer relationship management application (e.g., product based data mining, customer based data mining), different player configurations in a Internet based computer game application, different control models in an optimum control system modeling application, different categories of alarms in a real-time alarm processing application or different subsystems in a sales management application. Thus user's task context is captured with the help of concepts that are generally orthogonal in nature. This also enables a reduction in the complexity of the problem as well as enhancement of the reliability of the computer-based artifact. Further, these concepts are abstract and do not provide a direct solution to the task in hand.

Task: Concept Validation

- In a number of multimedia applications (e.g., Internet based image retrieval applications involving relevance feedback) the search is guided by feedback from the user during run time. That is, the nature of the user query or input data in general may not be adequate and feedback from the user in terms of pursuing the search in one of many directions may help to reduce the search time as well as enhance the quality of the results. For example, in an electronic commerce application, an initial user query may only specify buying a shirt. It may not specify what type of shirt and/or collar. This information can be ascertained by prompting the user to select from a range of shirts with different types of collars.

Task Constraints: The generic task constraints associated with the decomposition phase adapter are scalability and reliability. The concepts used to restrict the input context in the decomposition phase should be scalable vertically as well as horizontally. One way of satisfying this task constraint is to ensure that the concepts defined in this phase are orthogonal or un-correlated. This will also enhance the reliability and quality of results produced by other phase adapters (e.g., control), which depend on the competency of the decomposition phase adapter. It may be noted that these task constraints also serve a useful purpose in terms of future evolution, maintenance and management of the computer based artifact.

Represented Features:

- The qualitative or linguistic features employed in this phase by the user are coarse-grain features. These coarse-grain features may have binary and/or structured values. For example, coarse-grain binary features to partition a global concept like an animal (into mammal, bird) in the animal kingdom domain, may be has_feathers, gives_milk, has_hair, etc. On the other hand, structured features like player_configuration (with values like 1, 2, 3,4) may be used in a computer game application.

- The features representing concepts in this phase can also be numeric or continuous in nature. For example in an e-business security based biometric application involving face recognition, orthogonal concepts, like skin regions and non-skin regions, can be distinguished based on the skin color pixel data.

Domain Models:

- As shown in Figure 5.4 the domain models used for restricting the context and identifying the represented features can be structural, functional, causal, geometric, heuristic, spatial, shape, color, etc.

Psychological Scale:

- The psychological scale used by the decomposition phase adapter is the nominal scale. The nominal scale is the lowest psychological scale with formal property category. It is suitable for determining orthogonal concepts represented by binary and structured qualitative features.

Representing Dimension:

- The representing dimension of the represented features can be shape, position, color etc. measured on the nominal scale. For example, in a face recognition application, the representing dimension for distinguishing between orthogonal concepts like skin-region and non-skin-region is the skin-tone color.

Name Decomposition

Goal: Restrict Data Context, Reduce complexity, enhance reliability

Precondition : Conditioned or transformed/ filtered data

Task : Determine abstract orthogonal concepts - form - subsystems, categories, regions, control models, game configurations, system user-based configurations, etc.

Task: concept validation (for relevance feedback systems, e.g. multimedia product search)

Domain Model structural, functional, causal, geometric, heuristic, spatial, shape, color, etc

Task: Problem formulation

Task Constraints orthogonality reliability, scalability,

Represented Features: *Qualitative/linguistic-* binary, structured
Non-Linguistic- continuous features

Psychological Scale: Nominal

Representing Dimension (Perceptual): Shape, Location, Position, etc. on the nominal scale

Knowledge Engineering Strategy top-down or bottom-up

Problem Solving Methods hard (e.g. symbolic rule based), soft (e.g. neural networks)

Postcondition Domain decomposed into orthogonal concepts.

Figure 5.4. Decomposition Phase Adapter Definition

Knowledge Engineering Strategy:

- Top-Down or Bottom-up

Technological Artifacts:

- Objects and classes can be used to structure the represented features/data and/or the devices/components/objects used by the decomposition problem solving adapter to accomplish a task. Agents can be used as software artifacts to model various tasks associated with the adapter. Soft or hard computing mechanisms can be used for accomplishing various tasks. As explained earlier, the selection of a soft or hard computing technique will depend upon the knowledge engineering strategy and the task constraints.

Precondition:

- Conditioned or transformed/noise filtered data

Postcondition:

- Domain decomposed into orthogonal concepts

Domain Representation Signature	Domain Task Signature
Name : Decomposition	**Goal:** Restrict Data Context, Reduce complexity, enhance reliability
Represented Features:	**Precondition:** Conditioned or transformed/ filtered data
Qualitative/linguistic - binary, structured	**Task :** Determine abstract orthogonal concepts - form - subsystems, categories, regions, control models, game configurations, system user-based configurations, etc..
Non-Linguistic - continuous	**Task:** concept validation (Optional - for relevance feedback systems, multimedia product search)
Psychological Scale: Nominal; *Formal Property*: category	**Domain Model**: structural, functional, causal, geometric, heuristic, spatial, shape, color, etc.
Representing Dimension (Perceptual): Shape, Location, Position, etc. on the nominal scale	**Task Constraints**: orthogonality, scalability, reliability
	Postcondition: Domain decomposed into orthogonal concepts
	Knowledge Engineering Strategy: top-down or bottom-up

Figure 5.5. Signature Mapping for Decomposition Adapter

5.2.2.3. Control Phase Adapter

The control phase adapter definition is shown in Figure 5.6.

Goal: Establish the decision control constructs for the domain based decision classes as identified by stakeholders/users.

As explained in the decomposition phase adapter definition, the goal of the decomposition phase adapter is to reduce the domain complexity by restricting the input context. However, the decomposition phase adapter does not account for the specific problem being solved in terms of decisions/outcomes required from the computer-based artifact. The primary goal of the control phase adapter is to establish the decision control constructs for the domain based decision classes as identified by stakeholders/users. The decision classes are defined for each abstract concept defined in the decomposition phase.

Task: Noise filtering and input conditioning

- The preprocessing phase adapter, as mentioned earlier, accomplishes these tasks. Whereas, the preprocessing phase adapter is used in the global context prior to the decomposition phase, in the control phase it is used in the local context to filter out noise and condition the data within each abstract concept defined in the decomposition phase.

Task: Determine decision level classes

- Decision level classes are those classes inference on which is of importance to a stakeholder/user. These classes or concepts represent the control structure of the problem. These decision-level classes generally exist explicitly in the problem being addressed. These decision level classes could represent behavioral categorization strategies in e-sales recruitment problem or group of network components in a telecommunication network, possible faulty section/s in a electric power network, possible face regions in a face recognition application, possible set of control actions in a control application, potential set of diagnosis in a medical diagnostic application, etc. These concepts can be determined using functional, structural, causal, or other domain model/s used by the stakeholder/user.
- The granularity of a decision level class can vary between coarse and fine. The coarseness and the fineness of a decision level class depend on the context in which the problem is being solved and the decision level class priority in a given context. In one context, a decision level class may be less important to a problem solver, and thus a coarse solution may be acceptable, whereas, in another context the same decision level class may assume higher importance and thus a finer solution may be required. That is, if the decision level class priority is low, then its granularity is coarse, and the problem solver is satisfied with a coarse decision on that class. Otherwise, if the decision level class priority is high then the decision-level class has fine granularity and the problem solver wants a fine set of decisions to be made on the decision-level class, which would involve a number of microfeatures in the domain space. In case of coarse granularity distinct control and decision phase adapters (described in the next section) may not be required and can be merged into one.

Task: Concept validation

- Like in the decomposition phase adapter, this task is required in applications where problem solving is largely guided by relevance feedback from the stakeholder/user. This is especially true in a number of image retrieval applications on the Internet.

Task: Conflict Resolution

- It is possible that the decisions made by a decision level class may conflict with the decisions by another decision level class. For example, an application like e-sales recruitment may involve two or more behavioral categorization strategies or models. In case of conflicting behavior categories from two or more models, conflict resolution rules need to de designed. Similarly in a telecommunication network diagnostic problem, two decision level classes may represent two sections of a telecommunication network. If these sections predict fault in two different network components (given that only one of them can be actually faulty), then there is a conflict.

  The conflicts can also occur with respect to previous knowledge or in situations involving temporal reasoning. In the case of temporal reasoning the previous result may become invalid or conflict with the result based on new data. The conflict may be resolved by looking at the structural, functional, spatial indisposition of the decision level classes or their components or even through concept/decision validation (which would involve validation/feedback from the stakeholder/user on the conflicting set decisions).

Task: Problem Formulation

- involves sequencing of various actions required to accomplish the above tasks.

Task Constraints:

- Learning and adaptability are the additional domain independent task constraints in this phase, besides scalability and reliability.

Represented Features:

- *Qualitative/linguistic* - binary, structured, fuzzy

The qualitative or linguistic features employed by the control phase adapter include semi-coarse grain binary, structured and fuzzy features. The granularity of the binary and structured features used by the control phase adapter is finer than those used in the decomposition phase. In the decomposition phase binary and structured features are used for determination of abstract independent orthogonal concepts at the global level. In the control phase adapter the binary and structured features are used at the local level within each abstract concept. More so, the binary and structured features are used many times with fuzzy features in order to identify the decision level concepts in a domain. The fuzzy features are used in the control phase instead of the decomposition because fuzzy features cannot be used to distinguish between abstract orthogonal concepts. For example, let us assume mammal and bird are two abstract concepts in an animal classification domain. Then the interpretation of a large mammal is not the same as a large bird. That is, the fuzzy variable *large* qualifying a mammal and bird carry different perceptual as well as conceptual meanings and thus cannot be used universally at the global level for discriminating between abstract concepts.

- *Non-Linguistic - continuous features*

Continuous valued features used by the control phase adapter are limited to a abstract concept determined in the decomposition phase. For example, in a face recognition application pixel data related to the skin region concept is analyzed.

Domain Models:

- The domain model used for accomplishing various tasks and identifying the represented features can be structural, functional, causal, geometric, heuristic, spatial, shape, color, etc. For example, a functional model may be used by a business manager in a customer relationship management application for defining data mining decision support concepts like customer association and product similalrity. Similalrly, in the face recognition application, shape and area models are used to determine the decision classes. On the other hand, in a genome classification application a functional model may be used to determine gene decision (classification) classes based on their functionality or in an alarm processing application, structural configuration of various components in the network may be used for determining the faulty sections.

Psychological Scale:

- Besides the nominal scale, ordinal, interval and ratio scales can used by the control phase adapter. The fuzzy features used by the control phase adapter can be seen to represent information on the ordinal, interval or ratio scales.

Representing Dimension:

- The representing dimension of the represented features can be shape, position, color etc. measured on the nominal and/or ordinal, interval and ratio scales. For example, in a face recognition application, area and shape of the skin-regions are the representing dimensions of the various face-recognition decision classes.

Name : Control

Precondition : orthogonal concept defined, concept data/expertise available

Goal: Establish domain decision control constructs for orthogonal concepts based on desired outcomes from the system

Task: Local noise filtering (done by Preprocessing Adapter) – form – time based noise filtering, content and context based noise filtering

Task: Determine decision level concepts – form - secondary codes, potential fault sections/regions, potential explanation sets/ cause sets/diagnosis sets, decision categories based on structural, functional shape, color, location, spatial and heuristic domain models

Task: Decision level concept validation (optional – for relevance feedback systems)

Task: Conflict resolution (optional) – form – decision conflicts between decision categories,

Task: Problem formulation

Task Constraints: scalability, reliability, maintainability, learning, adaptability,

Domain Models : structural, functional, causal, geometric, heuristic, spatial, shape, color, etc.

Represented Features: *Qualitative/Linguistic* - binary, structured, fuzzy data
Non-Linguistic - continuous data related to an orthogonal concept

Psychological Scales: Nominal, Ordinal, Interval, Ratio

Representing Dimensions (perceptual): shape, size, length, distance, density, location, position, orientation, color, texture

Knowledge Engineering Strategy : top-down or bottom-up

Technological Artifacts: hard (symbolic), soft (e.g. neural networks, fuzzy logic, genetic algorithms) or their hybrid configurations

Postcondition: decision level concepts defined, decision control constructs/actions defined.

Figure 5.6. Control Phase Adapter Definition

Knowledge Engineering Strategy:

- top-down or bottom-up knowledge engineering strategy can be used.

Technological Artifacts:

- The computing technique can be hard (e.g., symbolic) or soft (e.g. neural networks, fuzzy logic, genetic algorithms) or a hybrid configuration of hard and soft computing techniques (Khosla et. al. 1997) depending upon the task constraints and the knowledge engineering strategy. We have also shown structural relationships in Figure 5.7 which can be used for identifying the relationships between data entities. It can also be used in other problem solving adapters.

Precondition:

- The control phase adapter assumes that orthogonal concepts in the domain have been defined. Further, if top-down strategy is employed, it is assumed that qualitative data is available. However, if bottom-up strategy is used it is assumed raw case data is available. Based on the above description, the signature mappings of the control phase adapter are shown in Figure 5.7.

Postcondition:

- Defines the competence of the control adapter in terms of defining the decision control constructs for the decision level concepts.

Domain Representation Signature	Domain Task Signature
Name: Control **Represented Features:** *Qualitative/Linguistic*- binary, structured, fuzzy data *Non-Linguistic* -continuous data related to an orthogonal concept **Psychological Scales:**Nominal, Ordinal, Interval, Ratio **Representing Dimensions (perceptual):** shape, size, length, distance, density, location, position, orientation, color, texture **Knowledge Engineering Strategy:** top-down or bottom-up **Structural Relationships (optional):** Inheritance, composition, association	**Name:** Control **Goal:** Establish domain decision control constructs for orthogonal concepts based on desired outcomes from the system **Precondition:** orthogonal concept defined, concept/ case data **Task:** Determine decision level concepts – potential fault sections/regions, potential explanation sets/ cause sets/diagnosis sets, decision categories based on structural,functional shape, color, location, spatial and heuristic domain models **Task:** Decision level concept validation (optional – for relevance feedback systems) **Task:** Conflict resolution (optional)– decision conflicts between decision instances **Task Constraints:**scalability, reliability, maintainability, learning, adaptability, **Domain Models:** structural, functional, causal, geometric, heuristic, spatial, shape, color, etc. **Postcondition:** decision level concepts defined, decision control constructs/axioms defined

Figure 5.7. Signature Mapping for Control Phase Adapter

5.2.2.4. Decision Phase Adapter

Goal:

- Provide decision instance results in a user/stakeholder defined decision concept. Whereas, the control phase adapter primarily controls the invocation of various decision level classes and conflicts between them, the decision phase adapter is responsible for providing specific outcomes required by the user/s or stakeholder/s in each decision class. These outcomes can include transaction frequency patterns of e-banking customers in a customer relationship management application, specific faulty component/s in a telecommunication network, actual faces in a face recognition problem, legal move in a computer game, product with desired features in a electronic commerce application, and so on.

Task: noise filtering and input conditioning

- The preprocessing phase adapter, as mentioned earlier, accomplishes these tasks. In the decision phase adapter, the preprocessing phase adapter is used to filter out noise and condition data in a decision class.

Task: Determine decision instance

- This task entails determination of specific decisions or decision instances required by the user/stakeholder(s). Decision instance or instances represent partly or wholly user defined outcomes from a computer-based artifact. These outcomes are realized within each decision class invoked by the control phase adapter. For example, in a customer relationship management application this may involve determining the association between a customer's transaction behavior and demographics. In a face recognition problem, this task may involve identification of a face (or faces) among various face candidates (which represent the decision classes) or in telecommunication this may involve determination of a faulty component or components in the candidate section or sections (decision classes) of the telecommunication network. Similarly, in an alarm processing and fault diagnosis application in a power system control center, this task may involve determination of various fault instances like single line fault, multiple line fault, etc. in candidate sections (e.g., 220kv, 66kv, etc.) of the power network. On the other hand, in a control system application, this task may involve selecting a control action among various candidate control actions.

Task: Viability/Utility of Decision (optional)

- In some real time systems it may become necessary to compute the computational resources and the time required by different decision level classes to determine the solution. Thus, certain decision level classes may not be considered viable under these constraints and thus may not be activated.

Task Constraints:

- scalability, reliability, maintainability, learning, generalization, adaptability, domain dependent

Domain Model:

- Here again, one or more domain models like structural, functional, causal, geometric, heuristic, spatial or location, shape, color, etc. can be used for determining the decision instances. For example, in the face recognition problem, shape and location domain models of the face and facial features like eyes, nose and mouth are used. In the alarm processing and fault diagnosis problem structural and spatial models are used for determining the fault instances in different sections of the network. The structural domain model is used in terms of the connectivity of different components in a given section of the power network. The spatial model is used in terms of spatial proximity of the alarms emanating from different parts of a network from the faulty component. That is, the further away an alarm is from the location of the faulty section or component, the lesser is its importance.

Represented Features:

- *Qualitative/Linguistic*- binary, fine grain fuzzy data,

  The qualitative or linguistic features employed can be fine grain fuzzy or even binary. For example, in a e-sales recruitment problem after determining the behavior category of a sales candidate, the intensity of the behavior category is determined a high (or very high), medium (or medium-high) and low.

- *Non-Linguistic - continuous decision data*
  For example, in the face recognition problem, color pixel data related to a face candidate and spatial coordinates of facial features (like eyes, mouth and nose) are used to identify actual faces and track eye movements in the decision phase.

Psychological Scales: Nominal, Ordinal, Interval, Ratio or none

- The nominal scale can be used to measure binary features (like existence or non-existence of an alarm) whereas fine grain fuzzy features can be measured on the ordinal, interval or ratio scales, depending on the scale properties, by the fuzzy features. For example some of the scale properties of fuzzy feature heavy cheek hair are category (cheek hair), magnitude (heavy > light) and absolute zero (no cheek hair). These properties represent the ratio scale.
- Representing Dimensions (perceptual): shape, size, length, distance, density, location, position
- As mentioned earlier representing dimension is useful for determining the perceptual aspects of data and reasoning in a problem domain. For example, in the animal classification domain, the representing dimension of the fuzzy feature is density.

Knowledge Engineering Strategy:

- The decision to use top-down, bottom-up or a mix of both will depend upon availability/non-availability of domain knowledge for various tasks.

Technological Artifacts:

- hard (symbolic), soft (e.g. neural networks, fuzzy logic, genetic algorithms), hybrid configurations, or other statistical/mathematical algorithms.

  Broadly hard symbolic computing mechanisms (like rule based systems) can be used for high level tasks (like problem formulation) subject to availability of qualitative domain knowledge for the task. On the other hand soft computing mechanisms can be used for decision instance task which may involve pattern recognition, learning, generalization and adaptability. As a consequence of satisfying task constraints (like learning, generalization and adaptability) optimization may be another constraint that may need to be satisfied. Genetic algorithms are ideal for satisfying the optimizing learning and generalization characteristics of soft computing mechanisms (like neural networks). More details on use of various soft computing mechanisms in isolation and in hybrid configuration can be found in Khosla and Dillon (1997). Similarly, hard symbolic techniques can be used for accomplishing the task.

Precondition: raw and/or qualitative case data, user specified decision instances.

Postcondition: Unvalidated Decision instance results from the computer-based artifact based on user/stakeholder defined decision concepts/classes.

The adapter definition and signature mapping are shown in Figures 5.8 and 5.9, respectively.

Phase: Decision
Goal: Provide decision instance results based on user/stakeholder defined decision concepts/classes from the computer-based artifact
Precondition Decision concepts defined (for top-down KE strategy), decision control constructs defined (optional), decision concept data/expertise available
Task: Context validation – Problem Solving context – Decision level; Input context: Local decision concept data
Task: Decision concept noise filtering (done by preprocessing adapter)
Task: Define specific decision instances for each decision concept
Task: Validate/Utility of decision
Task: Other user/stakeholder defined decision instance related tasks
Task: Problem formulation
Task Constraints: Learning, generalization, adaptability, domain dependent
Precondition: Raw or processed data
Postcondition: Conditioned data
Represented Features: *Qualitative/linguistic* – binary, fine grain fuzzy decision concept data
Non-linguistic – continuous decision concept data
Psychological Scale: Nominal; Ordinal, Interval, Ratio or none
Representing Dimension (Perceptual): Shape, size, length, distance, density, location, position, orientation, color, texture
Knowledge Engineering Strategy: Top-down or bottom up
Technological Artifacts: Hard (symbolic), soft (e.g. neural networks, fuzzy logic, genetic algorithms), hybrid configuration or other statistical/mathematical techniques Structural relationships based on object-oriented technology can also be used.
Postcondition: Unvalidated decision instance results

Figure 5.8. Decision Phase Adapter Definition

Domain Representation Signature	Domain Task Signature
Name : Decision	**Name** : Decision
Represented Features: *Qualitative/Linguistic* - binary, fine grain fuzzy decision concept data, *Non-Linguistic* - continuous decision concept data	**Goal:** Decision instance results based on user/stakeholder defined decision concepts/classes **Task :** Determine decision instance
Psychological Scales: Nominal, Ordinal, Interval, Ratio or none	**Domain Model**: - functional, structural, causal, spatial, color, etc.
Representing Dimensions (perceptual): shape, size, length, distance, density, location, position, orientation, color, texture	**Task Constraints**: learning, generalization, adaptability
Structural Relationships (optional) Inheritance, composition, association	**Precondition:** Decision concepts defined (for top-down) decision control constructs defined (optional), decision data/expertise available
	Postcondition: Unvalidated decision Instance results
	Knowledge Engineering Strategy: top-down or bottom-up

Figure 5.9. Signature Mapping for Decision Phase Adapter

5.2.2.5. Postprocessing Phase Adapter

Goal: Establish outcomes as desired outcomes, Satisfy user/stakeholder. Logic and provability are the hallmarks of our conscious interactions with the external environment. Thus, the goal of the postprocessing phase adapter is to validate outcomes from the decision phase adapter as desired or acceptable outcomes. The postprocessing adapter like the preprocessing adapter can be used in decomposition (e.g., concept validation by the user), control and decision phases of the problem solving ontology component.

Task: Decision instance result validation – form – model based instance result validation.

- For example, in a face recognition application the actual faces and facial movements as determined by the decision phase adapter, need to be validated by the user. Similarly, in a web based multimedia application (chapter 11) relevance feedback from the user is employed to optimize the search process. In a e-sales recruitment application the recruitment manager may validate or invalidate candidate's behavior category predicted by the system based on their own evaluation of the candidate. In a control system application, feedback from the environment establishes whether the selected/executed control action has produced the desired results. For example, a control action taken by the inverted pendulum control system may result in the pole balancing or falling over. This result is the feedback from the environment validating or invalidating the control action by the inverted pendulum control system. In an alarm processing application, the operator may instruct the system or computer based artifact to explain how certain components in the network have been identified as faulty.
- The validation task can be accomplished by perceptual and/or hard/soft computing mechanisms. For example, in a real time alarm processing application a power system control center operator may validate a decision made in the decision phase by using graphic display of the power network and by querying the system on the fault model of the faulty component. On the other hand a control system application may validate a control by using perceptual mechanisms (e.g. the location/position of the inverted pendulum) task model base.

Name: Postprocessing
Precondition: specific unvalidated decision outcomes available, decision data available. (optional).
Goal: Validate decision outcomes as desired outcomes, Satisfy user/stakeholder
Task: Context validation - Problem solving context - Postprocessing ; Input context: decision instance result data and/or model
Task: Decision instance result validation through domain model, user/stakeholder or environment
Task: Decision instance result explanation
Task: Problem formulation
Task Constraints: provability, reliability
Represented Features *Qualitative/Linguistic* - binary, fine grain fuzzy,
: *Non-Linguistic* - continuous
Psychological Scales: Nominal, Ordinal, Interval, Ratio or none
Representing Dimensions (perceptual): shape, size, length, distance, density, location, position, orientation, color, texture
Knowledge Engineering Strategy: top-down or bottom-up
Technological Artifacts : hard (symbolic), soft (e.g. neural networks, fuzzy logic, genetic algorithms)
Postcondition: Decision results validated and explained to the user

Figure 5.10. Postprocessing Phase Adapter

In control systems and multimedia based relevance feedback problems the postprocessing phase adapter can be seen as part of the feedback loop where validation on the outcomes of the decision phase is provided by the environment or the human user. In other domains if validation models are not available, they can be developed for each decision concept or class (defined by the control phase adapter.) by employing learning artifacts like neural networks.

The validation and explanation tasks in the postprocessing phase (shown in Figure 5.10) can also be seen to represent logic and provability which are the hallmarks of our conscious interactions with the external environment.

5.3. Human-Centered Criteria and Problem Solving Ontology

The problem solving ontology component developed by us has been designed to satisfy criteria 1and 3 of human-centeredness outlined in the first chapter. That is, it is derived from the problem solving pattern or consistent problem solving structures/strategies employed by practitioners while designing solutions to complex problems or situations (criteria 1: Human-centered research and design is problem/need driven as against abstraction driven (although there is an overlap)). It facilitates use of perceptual (external) as well as conceptual (internal) representations for problem solving (as also advocated by the distributed cognition approach and criteria 3: Human-centered research and design is context bound). Further, it constrains the perceptual and conceptual representations of the environment in the context of the activity being studied with the help of five information processing phases. From a situated cognition viewpoint, the five information processing phases represent the routines or problem solving structures people employ when solving complex problems. These phases are situated in the context of the work activity being studied and the technological artifacts employed to accomplish various tasks can be adaptive and evolutionary in nature. In other words, the ontology facilitates use of a range of intelligent technologies for satisfying different pragmatic task constraints and thereby minimizing task generation. Finally, the problem solving structures of the problem solving ontology component have been derived from studying complex problems both inside and outside knowledge based systems area and include problems in image processing, data mining, process control, electronic commerce, diagnosis, forecasting, and sales recruitment.

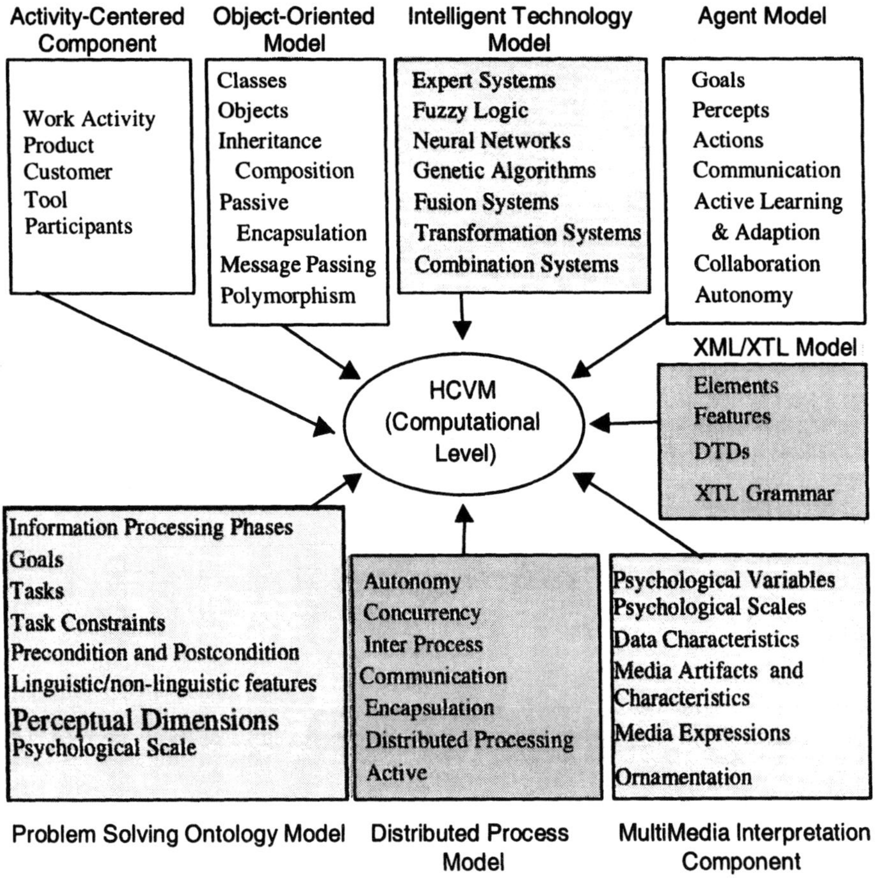

Figure 5.11. Human-Centered Virtual Machine (HCVM)

5.4. Transformation Agent Component

This component's purpose is to transform the systematized human-centered activity model developed through application of the problem solving ontology component into a computer-based software artifact. It does that through integration of the activity-centered e-business analysis and problem solving ontology components of the human-centered framework with technological artifacts related to the intelligent technology model, agent model, object-oriented model, multimedia (described in the next section) and distributed process model as shown in Figure 5.11. The outcome of this integration is a Human-Centered Virtual Machine (HCVM) shown in Figure 5.12. It consists of five layers, namely, the object layer, which defines the data architecture or structural content in the context of the work activity, the software agent layer, which helps to define the distributed processing constructs, the multimedia design and generation constructs and the XML/XTL based constructs used for transforming task and representation constructs of the problem solving adapters into an XML representation for e-business transaction based (e-commerce) applications (chapter 8). The intelligent agent layer defines the constructs for intelligent technologies (Khosla and Dillon 1997). The hybrid or optimization layer defines constructs for intelligent fusion, combination and transformation technologies. Finally, the problem solving agent layer defines the constructs related to the problem solving adapters described in section 5.2. The five layers facilitate a component based approach for agent based software design. The generic agent definition used for defining the transformation agents in the problem solving agent layer, intelligent hybrid agent layer, intelligent agent layer and software agent layer is shown in Figure 5.13. Based on the generic agent definition, a neural network agent is shown in Figure 5.14.

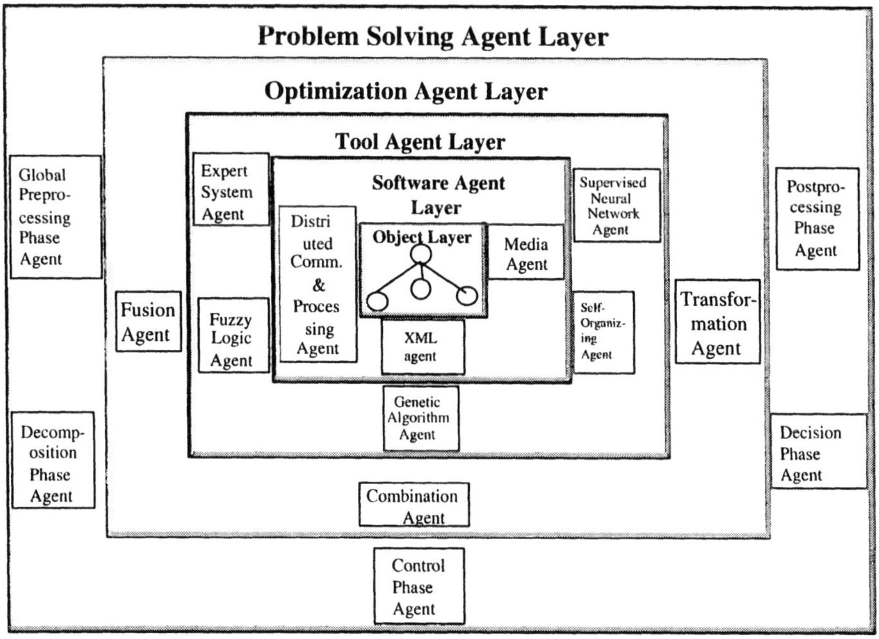

Figure 5.12: Five Layers of HCVM

The generic definition of the transformation agent includes communication constructs employed by the transformation agent. These communication constructs are based on human communicative acts like request, command, inform, broadcast, explain, warn and others (Maybury 1995). The linguistic and non-linguistic features represent the sensed data from the external environment as well as computed data by the agent. The sensed and computed data are used by the multimedia interpretation component (described in the next section) to gather data from the environment (in this case human is the data source) and also assist the direct stakeholders in interpreting the computing data.

The *parent agent* construct identifies the generic agents in the four agent layers, whose constructs and services have been inherited by a particular application or domain based transformation agent. The *communication with* construct in Figure 5.13 identifies all the agents and objects that a transformation agent communicates with in the five layers. The *external tools* construct in Figure 5.13 refers to those computer-based or other tools that are external to the definition of an agent. On the other hand, *internal tools* are those tools that are defined internally by a transformation agent. For example, Figures 5.14 and 5.15 shows the agent definition of a neural network agent and fuzzy-neuraln network agent respectively. The *external tools* include simulated training data files used by the agent. On the other hand, the sensitivity algorithms and the back propagation rule are *internal tools* defined and used by the neural network agent. Since the neural network agent is a generic agent it does not have any parent agent or communication constructs.

The *internal state* construct refers to the beliefs of a transformation agent at a particular instant in time. Finally, the actions construct is used to define the sequence of actions for accomplishing various tasks.

Name:
Parent Agent:
Goals:
Tasks:
Task Constraints:
Precondition:
Postcondition:
Communicates With:
Communication Constructs:
Linguistic/non-linguistic Features:
Psychological Scale:
Representing Dimensions:
External Tools:
Internal Tools
Internal State:
Actions:

Figure 5.13: Generic Agent Definition

•**Name:**
- •Neural Network

•**Goals:**
- •create NN model of the domain

•**Tasks:**
- •perform backpropagation to learn weights
- •test convergence with test data

•**Tasks Constraints**
- •computing resources

•**Precondition:**
- •Training data available (continuous/discrete)
- •Initial network structure available
- •Training data normalized
- •convergence criteria

•**Post Condition:**
- •Converges on global minimum

•**Represented features:**
- •Training data
- •Training/ Test set error
- •convergence criteria

•**Psychological Scale:** Ratio
•**Representing Dimension (Perceptual):**
Shape (graph, plot)

•**External tools**
- •simulated data files

•**Internal tools**
- •Sensitivity algorithms
- •Backpropagation
- •Parallel distributed learning

•**Actions**
- •Feed weights parameters to network
- •return model parameters
- •return training set error

Figure 5.14. Neural Network Agent

Name: Fuzzy Neural Network Agent
Parent Agent: Fuzzy, neural network
Goals: Optimization, adaptation

Tasks (some): Create Fuzzified neural-network model , Perform backpropagation
Test convergence with test data
Tasks Constraints: Normalized Training data available, Fuzzified inputs available,
optimized Fuzzy-neural model not known
Precondition: Training data normalized, Convergence criteria is known
Post Condition: Converges on global minimum, Optimized fuzzy-neural model
Communicates with: Decision Agent, Distributed process agent
Communication constructs: Receive data from decision agent, Inform model parameters
to user, Receive feedback data from environment
Represented Features: Fuzzified data, training/test set error, convergence criteria
Representing Dimensions (Perceptual features): Training / test set error shapes,
Convergence graphs
Linguistic/nonlinguistic percepts: Fuzzified input, Fuzzy-neural model output
External tools: Simulated data files, Intelligent NN Agent
Internal tools: Sensitivity algorithms
Actions: Feed fuzzified input to network, return training set error, return optimized results
(e.g., fuzzy rules)

Figure 5.15: Fuzzy-neural Network Agent

5.5. Multimedia Interpretation Component

From a social perspective, the role that computer-based artifacts play in mediating work activity is the result of social interaction between users and their environment and between the users and the artifact. The social interaction determines the way the users perceive, use and learn the artifact. This social interaction is determined by the psychological apparatuses or structures employed by the users and computer-based artifacts can be seen as extensions of the psychological apparatuses of their users (However, this is not intended to mean that humans and computer-based artifacts are necessarily cognitively equal). In this chapter and the last one we have studied these psychological apparatuses through the problem solving ontology component and the activity-centered e-business analysis component. The role of the multimedia interpretation component is to make the psychological apparatuses mapped in the computer-based artifact transparent to its users. This transparency will provide an immersive environment for the users and enable uninhibited interaction between the users and the artifact.

Keeping in view that computer-based artifacts are extensions of the psychological apparatuses of their users, their interpretation should be based on among other aspects, the psychological scales and representing dimensions employed by the users on the psychological variables of interest rather than physical variables used and computed by the computer-based artifacts to do the computations (Norman 1988). For example, in a sales recruitment system (used for determining the selling behavior profile of a salesperson and described in chapter 6) the computer-based artifact computes a behavioral category score (a physical variable) based on a number of physical variables (like numerical values of answers to various questions, weights of various questions, etc). However, the psychological variable of interest to a sales manager (a user) is the degree of fit of the salesperson's behavioral profile into a frontline sales job or a customer service role or, for that matter, the training needs of the salesperson for different roles, similarity/dissimilarity with benchmark profiles, etc. This is an example where psychological variables determine the information content of the physical variables, to be presented to the user for interpreting the outcomes or results of a computer-based artifact. Additionally, the physical variables used for computing the results (e.g., questions, answers in the sales recruitment example) also need to be modeled based on the psychological scales and representing dimensions employed by the users/direct stakeholders in the work activity. That is, for effective data gathering, appropriate psychological scales and representing dimensions have to be used. Given this background, the main focus of the multimedia interpretation component is to identify and analyze the psychological scales and representing dimensions employed by direct stakeholders for gathering and providing information (e.g. to a computer-based artifact) as well as psychological variables of interest used for interpretation of results. Based on the analysis, media artifacts like graphics, text video and audio are then used to model the data perceptually in order to reduce the cognitive load on the users. This process is encapsulated in the following three steps. They are also shown in Figure 5.16.

1. Data Content Analysis
2. Media, Media Expression and Ornamentation Selection, and
3. Media Presentation Design and Coordination

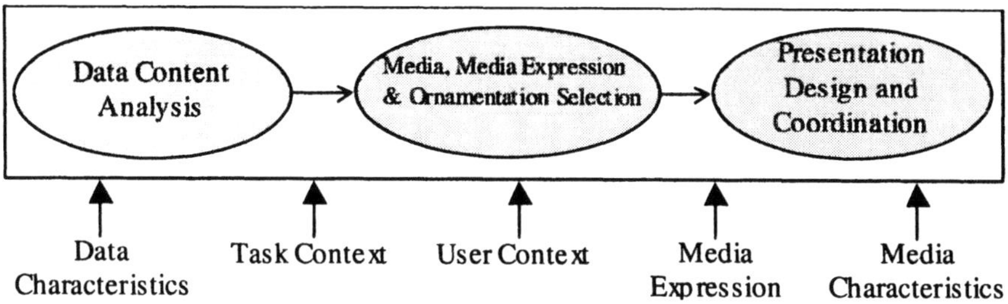

Figure 5.16: Media Analysis, Selection and Design Steps

5.5.1. Data Content Analysis

Data content analysis involves firstly, the identification of data for various tasks in a work activity context. Secondly, it involves determination of content of data to be communicated to the stakeholders based on its dimensionality, psychological scales, and representing dimensions as perceived by its users in the work activity and task context. Finally, it involves analysis of other data characteristics like granularity, transience, urgency and volume as defined by Arens et. al (1994). Figure 5.16 shows the influence of the task context, user context and data characteristics on the data content analysis stage.

The tasks in a work activity establish the context in which data is to be interpreted and used. The human-task-tool diagram and the task product transition network assist in identifying the human-computer interaction tasks and other computational tasks. The primary aim of the multimedia interpretation component is to model the data content linked to human-computer interaction tasks. These tasks define the human-computer interaction points for data gathering as well as interpretation of computed results.

The five phases of the problem solving ontology systematize the tasks and assist in identifying data at different levels of abstraction. These different levels of abstraction in problem solving can also be mapped to different levels of media expression in order to situate the users or direct stakeholders in the computerized system and make information processing in these transparent to them. This aspect of media representation will be explained in the next section.

The psychological scales and representing dimensions have been defined by the problem solving adapters of the problem solving ontology component. These psychological scales and representing dimensions are associated with data used for different tasks. The primary purpose of using the psychological scales and representing dimensions in the problem solving component was to determine whether perceptual reasoning techniques could be used for accomplishing the tasks. However, these psychological scales and representing dimensions of data that have been identified in the user and task context can also be used for data content analysis by the multimedia interpretation component. An application of the scale information and representing dimensions for data content analysis will be shown later in the this chapter.

The other data characteristics used for data content analysis include dimensionality, granularity, transience, urgency, and volume. These are described in the rest of this section.

Dimensionality: of a data item refers to the number of degrees of freedom on which a data item is perceived by the user in a particular task context. For example, a medical symptom like *ear drum red or yellow and bulging* is perceived by the user on **two** dimensions namely, color and shape.

Granularity: determines the granularity of variation in data value that carries meaning for the user. Granularity can be continuous or discrete. Continuous is a class in which small variations along a dimension of interest carry meaning. Information in such a class is best supported by a medium that supports continuous change. Discrete is a class in which there exists a lower limit to variations on the dimension of interest (e.g. types of cars made in Australia).

Transience: refers to whether the information to be presented expresses some current/changing state or not. The changing state can be *live* or *dead*. Live information consists of a single conceptual item of information that varies with time along some linear ordered dimension. On the other hand, dead information does not reflect current state but rather past state.

Urgency: Urgent information requires presentation in such a way that it draws the user's attention. The characteristic takes the values *urgent* or *routine*. For example, in a medical symptom like high blood pressure, patient's blood pressure reading of 210/130 may be represented by a media with high or medium to high default detectability to draw doctors' attention.

Volume: A batch of information may contain various amounts of information to be presented. If it is single fact (e.g., name), it is called *singular*; If more than one fact (e.g., a database record) but still little relative to some task and user-specific threshold - it is called *little*; otherwise (e.g. on-line help) it is called *much.* A batch of information with volume *much* (like on-line help) will require use of medium like written text with a transient property *dead.* Whereas, a single fact can be represented by a medium with transient property *live.*

5.5.2. Media, Media Expression and Ornamentation Selection

The main aim of this step is to map the data to the appropriate media, media substrate and media expression. The data characteristics described in the preceding section primarily influence the media, media substrate and media expression selection. Media, as is obvious, specifies the type of medium used (e.g., text, graphics/image, video, audio, etc.). Media substrate is a background to a simple exhibit. It establishes to the consumer, physical or temporal relation and the semantic context, within which new information is presented to the information consumer or user, e.g., piece of paper or screen (on which information may be drawn or presented); a grid (on which a marker might indicate the position of an entity).

Media expression on the other hand, determines the abstraction level of media. The three abstraction levels, elaborate, representative and abstract for text, graphics/image, sound, and motion are shown in Table 5.2 (Heller and Martin 1995). For example, in order to display a particular medical symptom, elaborate or representative image and text may be used as the media or medium, a sliding scale may be used as a substrate with continuous granularity for indicating the severity of the symptom.

The three levels of media expression shown in Table 5.2 also influence the media characteristics shown in Table 5.1. That is, the abstract level of media expression has discrete granularity and high baggage, whereas, the elaborate level of media expression has continuous granularity and low baggage.

The medium and substrate are then selected based on the correspondence between data characteristics and media characteristics (shown in Table 5.1). In order to do the mapping firstly, the psychological scale information and representing dimension characteristic of the data is matched with the internal semantics of the media artifacts. For example, a representing dimension like location can be represented by a picture or map which has internal semantics of spatial location or animated picture with internal semantics of spatial location and motion. Secondly, we look at other characteristics of data like transience and urgency to enhance or upgrade the existing selected medium. For example, if a location has a transient property live then an animated picture rather than a simple picture would be used. Further, if the object or information carrier in the animated picture has an urgency property as urgent then besides animation (which has high detectability) it may have to be further enhanced with flashing bright color. Arens et al (1994) defines a set of transformation rules for selecting the medium and substrate. Some of these rules are defined below.

Transience: If the transience property is live, as a carrier, use a medium with the temporal endurance characteristic transient if the update rate is comparable to the lifetime of the carrier signal. If the data update rate is much longer, as a carrier, use a medium with the temporal endurance characteristic permanent. As substrate, unless the information is already part of an existing exhibit, use neutral substrate.
If the transient property is dead use a carrier/media with permanent temporal endurance.

Urgency: If the urgency property is urgent then if the information is not yet part of a presentation instance, use a medium whose detectability has the value high either for substrate or carrier. If the information is already displayed as part of a presentation instance, use the present medium but switch one or more of its channels from fixed to the corresponding temporally varying state, e.g. flashing. On the other hand, if the property is routine, choose a medium with low default detectability and a channel with no temporal variance.

Thirdly, we look at how we can complement selected media with one or more media by integrating the selected media with other media at different levels of media expression or abstraction. That is, an elaborate selected media can be integrated with abstract or representative forms of other media to enhance understanding and develop a more immersive environment for the users.

The level of media expression also facilitates mapping the media to different levels of problem solving. At higher levels of problem solving it is likely that abstract or representative levels of media expression will be mapped to data. whereas, at lower levels of abstraction elaborate levels of media expression are likely to be used. Further, as mentioned in the last section, the three levels of media expression can be effectively used to situate the user appropriately among the information processing phases of the computer-based artifact.Finally, we also look into the ornamental aspects of the overall presentation from an industrial design perspective. For example, laptops and pagers have traditionally come in black or grey colors. These colors have been associated with top level corporate executives and professionals. Similarly the color background of a computer-based presentation should reflect the social characteristics of the direct stakeholders and the environment in which they work. A medical diagnostic system presentation, for example, should use serene colors instead of bright colors (e.g. yellow) to reflect the social characteristics of the medical practitioners and clinical environment they work in.

Thus conceptually, the various aspects of data content analysis, media and media expression selection discussed in this section and the preceding section are meant to reduce cognitive load on the users through perceptual presentations. They are meant to facilitate direct manipulation of data through multimedia artifacts, and situate users in the information processing phases of the computer-based artifact through use of multiple levels of media expression.

Table 5.1: Media Characteristics

Medium	Carrier Dimension	Temporal Dimension	Granularity	Medium Type	Default Detectability	Baggage
Map	2D	Perm	Continuous	Visual	Low	High
Picture	2D	Perm	Continuous	Visual	Low	High
Table	2D	Perm	Discrete	Visual	Low	High
Form	2D	Perm	Discrete	Visual	Low	High
Graph	2D	Perm	Continuous	Visual	Low	High
Ordered List	1D	Perm	Discrete	Visual	Low	Low
Sliding Scale	1D	Perm	Continuous	Visual	Low	Low
Written Sentence	1D	Perm	Continuous	Visual	Low	Low
Spoken Sentence	1D	Perm	Continuous	Aural	Mhigh	Low
Animation	2D	Trans	Continuous	Visual	High	High
Music	1D	Trans	Continuous	Aural	Mhigh	Low

Table 5.2: Levels of Media Expression © IEEE

MEDIA TYPE	ELABORATE MEDIA EXPRESSION	REPRESENTATIVE MEDIA EXPRESSION	ABSTRACT MEDIA EXPRESSION
Text	Fully expressed written text	Abbreviated text, titles, bulleted items	Shapes, Icons
Graphics	Fully expressed photograph	Abbreviated blueprint, layout	Graphic icon
Sound	Fully expressed speech	Abbreviated tones	Sound effects
Motion	Fully expressed film footage	Abbreviated animation, news clips, film preview	Animated model/icon

5.5.3. Media Presentation Design and Coordination

Once the various media artifacts have been selected for various data items, their generation, display and coordination at the computational level is modeled by media agents. These media agents are defined using the generic agent definition shown in Figure 5.13. The media agents coordinate their action with the problem solving agents of the problem solving agent layer.

5.6. Application of Multimedia Interpretation Component in Medical Diagnosis

In this section we describe the application of three stages of the HCVM multimedia interpretation component in a intranet based clinical diagnosis support system for medical practitioners. The application is in the area of infectious diseases (Gorbach et al. 1998; Barrows et al. 1991) and addresses problems related to the gathering of patient symptomatic data, providing diagnostic assistance, and finding inconsistencies in practitioner prescribed treatments compared to those recommended by therapeutic guidelines (TG 1998).

A Patient Diagnosis and Treatment Data (PDTD) form used by medical practitioners in the "Inner South Eastern Division of General Practice," of Alfred Hospital, Melbourne, Victoria is shown in Figure 5.17. The patient symptom data (e.g., toxic looking, acute sore throat) shown in Figure 5.17, by definition, is fuzzy and imprecise. However, the symptoms are shown in Figure 5.17 in discrete form using check boxes. The ticks or crosses entered in the check boxes are an inaccurate representation of a medical practitioner's feedback on a patient's symptom. This inaccuracy in the symptomatic data can lead to inaccurate treatments.

Inner South East Melbourne Division of General Practice

Patient ID	Patient Sex	Patient Age ....
Date of Visit	GP Initials	Office Use Only ....

Diagnosis, symptoms & signs

A ☐ **Undifferentiated upper respiratory tract infection**
1 ☐ Fever
2 ☐ Cough
3 ☐ Runny nose
4 ☐ Mild sore throat

B ☐ **Acute sore throat**
5 ☐ Hard to swallow
6 ☐ Toxic looking
7 ☐ Follicular or exudative tonsillitis
1 ☐ Fever
8 ☐ Tender lymph nodes
9 ☐ Age over 4
10 ☐ Existing rheumatic heart disease
11 ☐ Absence of cough
12 ☐ Aboriginality
13 ☐ Scarlet fever

C ☐ **Acute otitis media**
14 ☐ High fever
15 ☐ Sore ear
16 ☐ Child screaming
17 ☐ Child tugging ears
18 ☐ Eardrum mild reddening or dullness
19 ☐ Eardrum red or yellow and bulging
20 ☐ Discharging ear
21 ☐ Past history of perforation
22 ☐ Has grommets

D ☐ **Otitis media with effusion**
23 ☐ Glue ear < 3 months duration
24 ☐ Glue ear > 3 months duration
25 ☐ Poorly moving drum

E ☐ **Acute sinusitis**
26 ☐ Nasal discharge clear
27 ☐ Nasal discharge purulent
28 ☐ Prolonged fever
29 ☐ Facial pain
30 ☐ Tenderness over the sinuses
31 ☐ Headache

Treatment

1 ☐ **None**

2 ☐ **Paracetamol and rest**

3 ☐ **Antitussives or decongestants**

4 ☐ **Bronchodilators**

Antibiotic
5 ☐ Amoxycillin/ampicillin
6 ☐ Amoxycillin and clavulanate
7 ☐ Cephalexin/cephradine/cefaclor
8 ☐ Dicloxacillin/flucloxacillin
9 ☐ Erythromycin/roxithromycin
10 ☐ Phenoxymethyl penicillin/phenethicillin/procaine penicillin
11 ☐ Sulphamethoxazole and trimethoprim
12 ☐ Tetracyclines/doxcycline
13 ☐ Other

14 ☐ **Antibiotic script if symptoms worsen**

15 ☐ **Antibiotic samples if symptoms worsen**

16 ☐ **Other (specify)**
....
....
....

Reasons for choice

1 ☐ **Symptoms and signs**

2 ☐ **Intuitive feeling**

3 ☐ **Coexisting illness/smoker**

4 ☐ **Age risk**

5 ☐ **Prolonged illness**

6 ☐ **Past history of recurrent infections**

7 ☐ **Patient expectation**

8 ☐ **Lack of time to explain**

9 ☐ **Child unexaminable**

10 ☐ **Just in case / diagnosis unsure**

11 ☐ **Other cases in community/family**

12 ☐ **Microbiology**

13 ☐ **Recent hospitalisation**

14 ☐ **Not responding to the antibiotic prescribed**

15 ☐ **Other (specify)**
....
....
....

P.t.o.

Figure 5.17: A Sample PDTD Form

5.6.1. Patient Symptom Content Analysis

The psychological variables employed by humans are invariably distinct from the physical variables used for computations by a computer-based artifact. For effective patient symptomatic data gathering in the drug prescription monitoring activity, it is useful to look at symptoms as psychological variables from a medical practitioner's perspective (the person interpreting and entering the information) rather than as physical variables used for computation. In this section, we analyze the data characteristics of symptoms for Acute Otitis Media infection. We use the analysis to map the symptoms to various media artifacts.

The symptoms related to acute Otitis Media are *fever, sore ear, ear drum mild reddening or dullness, child screaming, child tugging ears, ear drum red or yellow and bulging, discharging ear, history of perforation*, and *has grommets*.

Data characteristics, like dimensionality, psychological scale, representing dimension, granularity, transience and urgency have been used for the analysis. The data characteristics of symptoms like *fever, sore ear, ear drum red or yellow and bulging, discharging ear,* and *has grommets* is shown in Table 5.3. The psychological scale used is based on perceptive and cognitive or interpreted representation of the symptoms by the medical practitioners in the context of the drug prescription monitoring activity. The analysis of the symptoms has been done in the context of the drug prescription monitoring activity. It is briefly discussed now.

Fever: is measured or determined on a single dimension of temperature. Medical practitioners measure the temperature in the range of 37 degrees centigrade to 40 degrees centigrade. Thus, the psychological scale information is on the interval scale, and the representing dimension is the position of mercury on this scale. The granularity of the fever symptom is considered as continuous (ranging from 37 degrees centigrade to 40 degree centigrade). There is no urgency in terms of communicating the above information in the context of the drug prescription monitoring activity and thus is classified as routine.

Sore Ear: is measured on two dimensions, namely, location (i.e. ear) and color of the ear. The representing dimension of color is density which represents different color shades like skin (normal ear) color, pink (mild sore ear) color and red (sore ear) color in a continuous range. Here the red color represents higher severity than pink or skin color in terms of magnitude. Although, perceptually the soreness is indicated by the red color (or shades of red color) of the ear, which is indicative of the ordinal scale, the psychological scale used is ratio. This is because medical practitioners interpret the degree of soreness on a continuous scale, ranging from no soreness (zero) to yes (1 - indicated by the red color of the ear), to determine the strength of the treatment. The granularity is continuous and urgency is routine.

Child Screaming: Consists of two dimensions, namely, location and density. These two dimensions are measured on the nominal and ratio scales, respectively. The location dimension relates to location of the screaming sound. The density dimension represents the screaming intensity, which is measured on a continuous scale of zero (no) to one (yes). The transient property of a scream is transient.

Ear Drum Red or Yellow and Bulging: consists of three dimensions, namely, location, color and shape. These three representing dimensions are perceived and interpreted on nominal, nominal and ratio scales, respectively. The location dimension relates to the ear drum location. The color of the eardrum (i.e. red or yellow) is perceived and interpreted on the nominal scale based on the category property. However, the bulging shape or degree of bulge of the eardrum is perceived and interpreted on ratio scale ranging from zero (flat) to 1 (bulging) with a continuous granularity.

Discharging Ear: is measured on three dimensions, namely, location (i.e. ear), color of the discharge and texture (purulent or clear discharge). These are also the representing dimensions of the symptom. The location dimension is based on the nominal scale, which includes the category property. The color dimension is based on the nominal scale and includes clear/transparent color discharge, yellow or green discharge. Finally, the texture dimension is based on the ordinal scale where the purulence of the discharge and the extent (magnitude) of discharge is determined. The granularity of this symptom is continuous and urgency is routine.

Has Grommets: represents two dimensions, namely, location and shape. These two dimensions are based on the nominal scale. The medical practitioner is looking for absence or presence of grommets only. Given the nominal scale on both the dimensions, the granularity is discrete.

In this section we have described the characteristics of a subset of symptoms used for diagnosing acute Otitis Media. The characteristics of these symptoms have been analyzed based on characteristics like dimension, psychological scale, representing dimension, granularity, and transience. These characteristics are most relevant to the Acute Otitis Media symptoms. A similar analysis has been done for treatment data and other data used by decomposition, control, decision and postprocessing agents. Additional data characteristics like volume, and urgency have also been used in the analysis of treatment and other data. For example, the volume of symptoms is mostly represented by single facts (e.g. *sore ear*) and thus is *singular*, whereas, volume of treatment text based on therapeutic guidelines is *much* and requires elaborate text description.

Table 5.3 : Data Characteristics of Acute Otitis Media Symptoms

Data Characteristics	Fever	Sore Ear	Child Screaming	Ear Drum Red or Yellow and Bulging	Discharging Ear	Has Grommets
Dimension	1D	2D	2D	3D	3D	2D
Psychological Scale	Interval	Nominal,	Nominal and Ratio	Nominal, Nominal and Ratio	Nominal, Ordinal and Ordinal	Nominal and Nominal
Representing dimension	Position	Location and Color	Location and Density	Location, Color and Shape	Location Color and Texture	Location and Shape
Granularity	Continuous	Continuous	Continuous	Continuous	Continuous	Discrete
Transience	Dead	Dead	Transient	Dead	Dead	Dead
Urgency	Routine	Routine	Routine	Routine	Routine	Routine

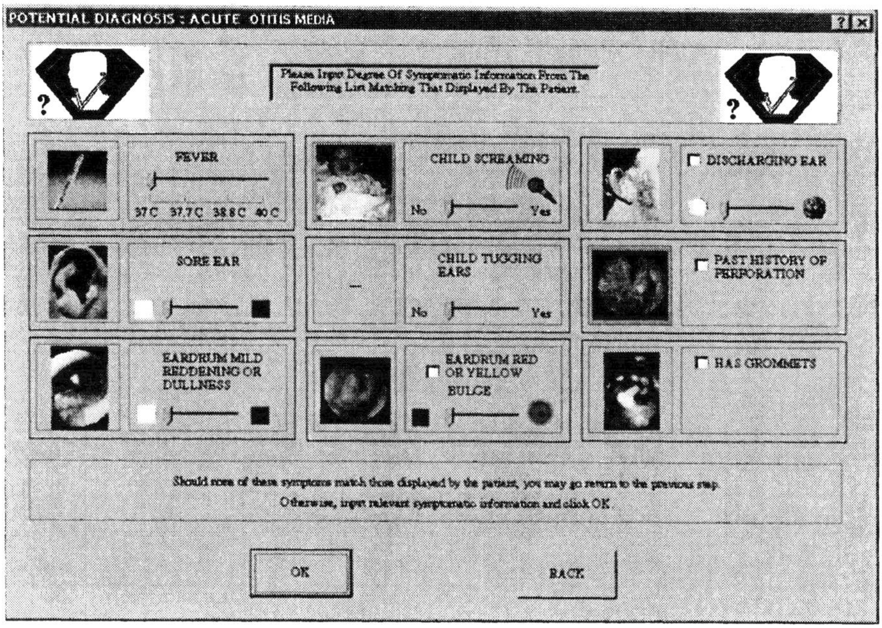

Figure 5.18: Multimedia Based Symptomatic Data and Gathering for Acute Otitis Media

5.6.2. Media, Media Expression and Ornamentation Selection

The characteristics of the symptoms outlined in the last section are used to select various media artifacts. Further, the modality or level of abstraction of various media is selected to facilitate complementation rather than duplication of media. In this section, we outline mapping of symptom characteristics to media types and the use of different levels of media expression.

Fever: A combination of text, image icon and a temperature sliding scale has been used to represent fever. A sliding temperature scale with an interval range of 37degrees to 40 degrees represents the single dimensionality and interval scale. The sliding scale in Figure 5.18 is used as a media substrate for determining patient's temperature. The scale pointer is the information carrier through which the actual physical value is recorded internally. The temperature sliding scale also represents continuous granularity of temperature.

As shown in Table 5.4 the text, thermometer icon and temperature scale represent different levels of media expression, which complement each other. The thermometer icon is an abstract image icon of temperature and complements the temperature scale.

The temperature sliding scale represents an elaborate level media expression of temperature and the word "fever" is a representative textual concept for temperature.

Sore Ear: Text, image and a sliding color scale are three media types employed to represent the two dimensions of the *sore ear* symptom as shown in Table 5.4. The degree of soreness or density is represented using a sliding color scale. It is used as the media substrate for measuring the degree of soreness. The color interval ranges from normal ear to a red sore ear. The image of the red sore ear represents the location dimension as well as an elaborate level of media expression. The sliding color scale also represents a representative level of media expression for the degree of soreness. The red sore image also complements the sliding color scale representation.

Table 5.4: Media Type and Media Expressions in Clinical Diagnosis Support

Media/Data Characteristics	Fever	Sore Ear	Child Screaming	Discharging Ear	Has Grommets
Media Type	Text, image, sliding scale	Text, image, sliding scale	Text, image and audio	Text image, sliding scale	Text image Check box
Media Expression	Text - representative Image - abstract Sliding temperature scale - elaborate	Text - representative Image - representative Sliding color scale - representative	Text - representative Image - elaborate Audio - elaborate Sliding scale - representative	Text – representative Image - elaborate Sliding texture scale - representative	Text - representative Image - elaborate Check box - representative

Ear Drum Red or Yellow and Bulging: is represented on three dimensions, namely, location, color and shape. The location dimension on a nominal scale is represented by the bulging eardrum image. The color dimension on the nominal scale is represented by the check box as well as the bulging ear drum image. The shape dimension on the ratio scale is represented using the bulge sliding scale ranging from a flat ear drum (indicating a physical value of 0) to bulging oval shaped ear drum (indicating a physical value of 1).

Child Screaming: has been shown in Table 5.4 for its variation in terms of use of text image and audio media artifacts. The image and audio artifacts shown in Figure 5.18 are an elaborate expression of a child's scream in the two media types. Although, they are at the same level they tend to complement rather than duplicate each other. Further, unlike perceptually oriented sliding scales used for other symptoms, a no/yes sliding scale has been used for this symptom. The aural nature of this symptom restricted us somewhat in providing a more perceptually meaningful sliding scale.

Discharging Ear: is represented using text, image, a texture based color sliding scale and a check box. The nominal scale of location dimension is represented using an elaborate level of the image artifact. The check box is used to confirm or negate presence or absence of the discharge. If the discharge is present the texture and color of the discharge is determined on a texture based color sliding scale. It may be noted that the sliding scale does not start with zero (0). The transparent or clear discharge on the left end of the sliding scale in Figure 5.18 represents a physical value of 1 whereas, the thick greenish discharge on the right end of the sliding scale represents a physical value of 5. Further, combining color and texture dimensions into one representation in Figure 5.18 is based on the assumption that color and texture vary concurrently and are interpreted together (rather than in isolation) for the purpose of determining severity of symptom and strength of the treatment.

Has Grommets: is represented using the image shown in Figure 5.18. The image is employed to represent the location and shape dimensions on the nominal scale. The check box is used to confirm or negate presence or absence of grommets.

The main purpose of this section has been to enhance the precision or quality of symptom data gathering. In this light, the multimedia representations shown in Figure 5.18 provide a richer medium for effective symptom data gathering than the PDTD forms shown in Figure 5.17. These representations, among others aspects, have been based on the psychological scales and representing dimensions employed by medical practitioners for determining the diagnosis and treatment of upper respiratory infections. The multimedia representations are expected to assist in a more clear explanation and detection of the differences and inconsistencies in the treatments prescribed by different medical practitioners.

In Figure 5.18 one can also notice two human faces with a question mark in the upper right and upper left-hand corners, respectively. These graphic objects have been for the purpose of situating the medical practitioners in terms of information processing and patient diagnosis and treatment in the system. The screen in Figure 5.18 shows that the computerized system is trying to ascertain symptoms related to a potential diagnosis of Acute Otitis Media. Finally, for ornamentation, cyan color has been used as a back ground color of the screen in Figure 5.18.

5.6.3. Multimedia Agents

In the last section we analyzed the data characteristics and selected the media artifacts for representing the data. At the computational level, multimedia agents are associated with each problem solving agent (e.g., decomposition, control and decision) for generation, display, layout and coordination of various media artifacts at problem solving, information processing and task level. These multimedia agents are also used for recording practitioner's feedback and feeding it to the corresponding problem solving agent. The definition of these multimedia agents, like the problem solving agents, facilitates learning, reasoning with respect to generation, display, layout and coordination of various media artifacts. A sample definition of a multimedia agent is shown in Table 5.5.

Table 5.5: Definition of upper respiratory decision media agent

Name :	Upper Respiratory Diagnosis Decision Media Agent C
Parent Agent:	HCVM media agent
Goals:	Effective/accurate symptomology gathering Establish practitioner's location in the system Correlate symptomatic data to argumentative diagnosis knowledge
Tasks:	Determine symptoms Map symptom characteristics to media artifacts Determine media layout Map symptomatic data to antecedents of rules and input vector of supervised neural networks
Task Constraints:	Medical practitioner's context, symptom data characteristics, media characteristics information processing /task context, media layout (e.g. visual, text)
Invoking Condition:	Request from upper respiratory diagnosis decision agent C
Precondition:	Trained Medical practitioner, Problem solving phase: decision diagnosis , availability of image/graphic, audio and text objects
Postcondition:	Multimedia upper respiratory diagnosis symptom display
Communicates with:	Upper respiratory diagnosis decision agent, graphic and audio objects
Communication Constructs:	Inform: upper respiratory symptomology to decision agent
Linguistic/non-linguistic features:	Psychological scale and representing dimensions of symptoms, symptom for upper respiratory infection cluster .
External and Tools:	**Software:** Graphic object, audio objects, text object **Domain:** Symptomology images, sound effects **Design:** Multimedia symptom analysis and design techniques
Internal Tools	Planning and sequencing media generation, display and coordination actions
Actions:	Generate and display upper respiratory symptomatic elaborate images, abstract sound effects and representative text, Generate & Display logarithmic sliding temperature scale and other perception based sliding scales for acute Otitis Media symptoms. Generate & Display abstract image icon to establish practitioner's location in the system (e.g., potential diagnosis state) Display feedforward neural network graphics for reasoning (not implemented)

5.7 Emergent Characteristics of HCVM

In order to get an overall picture of the HCVM, it is useful to look at its emergent behavior. We define the emergent behavior of HCVM by outlining its architectural, management and domain application characteristics.

5.7.1. Architectural Characteristics

The architectural characteristics define the significance of HCVM in terms of its emergent design characteristics. Some of the emergent design characteristics are outlined in this section.

5.7.1.1 Human-Centeredness

HCVM has been grounded in the three human-centered criteria outlined in the first chapter. These criteria have been built into the four components, namely, activity-centered e-business analysis, problem solving ontology, transformation agent and multimedia interpretation component. These four components have been used to define the internal and external plane of a system, respectively. The external plane captures the physical, social and organizational reality, whereas the internal plane captures the subjective reality related to stakeholder incentives, organizational culture and other aspects.

5.7.1.2 Task Orientation vs Technology Orientation:

The solutions to real world problems are determined by engineers, designers, accountants, sales managers, etc. in a task context (Chandrasekaran 1992; Peerce et al 1997) rather than a technological context. Various intelligent technologies, like knowledge based systems, fuzzy logic, neural networks and their hybrid configurations (fusion, transformation and combination), propose a technology-based solution to real world problems. The problem solving ontology component of HCVM is a task oriented system in which technological artifacts are considered as primitives for accomplishing various tasks. The use of one or more technological primitives is contingent upon satisfaction of task constraints. The task orientation enables HCVM to match a given task to one or more technologies among a suite of technologies rather than match a given technology to tasks in a work activity.

5.7.1.3 Flexibility:

Most complex real world problems require satisfaction of a number of task constraints ranging from incomplete and noisy information, learning, fast response time to explanation and validation and one technology is not enough to provide a satisfactory solution. A technology-based solution constrains a problem solver to force-fit particular software design onto a task or problem. The five problem solving adapters of the HCVM allow the problem solver to use multiple domain models. The optimization agent layer and the intelligent agent layer of the HCVM provide flexibility in terms of multiplicity of intelligent techniques and their hybrid configurations to develop optimum models that can be employed to satisfy various task constraints. Further, HCVM also provides flexibility in terms of pursuing different decision paths based on user competence and experience. That is, the user can use the five phases in different sequences for different situations. A decision making sequence can include five or less phases.

5.7.1.4 Versatility:

Technologies like expert systems and fuzzy logic rely heavily on availability of domain knowledge. In a number of real world problems (e.g.` data mining) explicit domain knowledge is not available or may involve a long and cumbersome knowledge acquisition process. HCVM is versatile in that they can model solutions in the presence or absence of domain knowledge.

5.7.1.5 Forms of Knowledge:
Real world problems involve use of multiple forms of knowledge (e.g. continuous, discrete symbolic and fuzzy). Unlike a number of intelligent technologies, associative systems are not limited to one or two forms of knowledge but can model any real world problem with continuous, discrete, fuzzy knowledge because of the multiplicity of techniques used by it.

5.7.1.6 Learning and Adaptation:
The ability to learn new tasks and adapt to novel situations are essential properties of HCVM. HCVM involve task based learning in which a problem solver employs multiplicity of learning techniques (e.g. supervised, self-organized, evolutionary, their variations and hybrid configurations) to match the needs of various learning tasks.

5.7.1.7 Distributed Problem Solving and Communication - Collaboration and Competition:
In order to deal with the complexity of real world problems (e.g. real-time alarm processing in a power system control center, building design) in general and World Wide Web (WWW) based problems (e.g. Web searching, Web mining, Internet games) in particular, distributed problem solving has become a necessity. The task oriented approach of HCVM not only enables distribution of tasks among different system components (which may be executed on remote machines) but also facilitates collaborative and competitive problem solving. That is, agents can collaborate with each other by performing different tasks. They can be mobile and perform computations on remote machines. On the other hand, because of availability of multiple techniques, agents can compete with each other on the same task (by performing it using different techniques like neural networks, knowledge-based systems, etc.) thus enhancing overall system reliability.

5.7.1.8 Component Based Software Design:
The five layers of the HCVM lead to a component based software design. The generic agents of the problem solving agent layer, intelligent hybrid agent layer, intelligent agent layer and software agent layer facilitate corresponding component definitions in the domain of study.

5.7.2. Management Characteristics

The management characteristics define the significance of HCVM in terms of management considerations that determine the use and maintenance of computer-based artifacts. Some of these characteristics are outlined next.

5.7.2.1. Cost, Development Time and Reuse:
The optimization of human and computing resources is an important management consideration for using information technology today. It has become an essential consideration in the deregulated industrial climate of the late 90's. In associative

systems the tasks can be distributed and implemented over various machines to enable optimization of computing resources as well as save valuable human time. The multiplicity of intelligent techniques employed by HCVM enables users (i.e., designers, engineers, etc.) to reduce the system development time. It also helps them to create an optimum system model (i.e., various intelligent techniques and their hybrid configurations can be employed simultaneously to save development time as well as assist in determining optimal system design). The component-based approach of HCVM facilitates reuse in terms of application-related objects (object layer), software agents, intelligent agents and problem solving agents. It reduces the need for building new applications from scratch.

5.7.2.2. Scalability and Maintainability:
The multilevel and component-based properties of HCVM enable the scalability (horizontal and vertical) and maintainability of the agents. The five problem solving adapters of the HCVM assists in systemizing and structuring software artifacts. This results in easier maintainability as well as scalability of the artifacts.

5.7.2.3. Intelligibility:
Humans form an important part of solutions to most real world problems. Thus it is imperative that any software system architecture should enable reduction of cognitive barriers between the user and the computer. This is vital for two reasons, namely, acceptability and effectiveness. That is, systems with low cognitive compatibility lead to low acceptability because the system's behavior may appear surprising and unnatural to the user. Further, systems with low cognitive compatibility will lead to low effectiveness because of lack of user involvement (resulting in unsatisfactory performance and major accidents (Perrow 1984)).

5.7.3. Domain Characteristics

The significance of an HCVM can also be seen in terms of the problems, which can be modeled with it. The architectural and management characteristics of HCVM and outlined in this section establish that HCVM can be used for a wide range of complex, data /knowledge intensive, distributed and time critical problems.

5.8. Summary

The objective of this chapter is to define the computational level of the human-centered e-business system development framework outlined in the chapter 4. It does that by developing the Human-Centered Virtual Machine (HCVM) through integration of activity-centered e-business analysis component, problem solving ontology component and multimedia interpretation component with various technological artifacts. These technological artifacts include intelligent technologies, agent and object-oriented technologies, distributed processing and communication technology and XML technology.

The problem solving ontology component is described with the help of five problem solving adapters, namely, preprocessing, decomposition, control, decision and postprocesssing. These adapters are grounded in the experience derived from developing various complex systems. They capture human generalizations and persistent structures used for modeling complex systems. They help in systematizing and structuring the human-centered tasks and representations in a form suitable for transforming a human solution into a scalable, evolvable and maintainable software solution. The transformation is realized by defining a set of transformation agents. These transformation agents are derived through integration of activity-centered e-business analysis component, problem solving ontology component and multimedia interpretation component with various technological artifacts. The outcome of the integration process is HCVM with a problem solving agent layer, intelligent hybrid agent layer, intelligent agent later, software agent layer and an object layer. The transformation agents in the four agent layers are modeled with the help of a transformation agent definition. The agent definition encapsulates characteristics of these transformation agents like goals, tasks and actions, representation, communication, external and internal tools used, and others.

The primary aim of the multimedia interpretation component is to model the data content of the human-computer interaction tasks using various media artifacts. It does that in three stages or steps. These are data content analysis, media, media expression and ornamentation selection, and presentation design and coordination. An application of the multimedia interpretation component in an Intranet based clinical diagnosis support is also described. Finally, in order to get an overall emerging picture of the HCVM, we outline its emergent behavior. We outline the emergent behavior in terms of its architectural characteristics, management characteristics and domain characteristics.

References

Arens, Y., Hovy, E.H., and Vosser, M. (1994) "On Knowledge Underlying Multimedia Presentations", *Intelligent Multimedia Interfaces*, Mark T. Maybury, Eds: AAAI Press, pp. 280-306.

Barrows, H.S and Pickell, G.C. (1991). *Developing Clinical Problem Solving Skills : A Guide To More Effective Diagnosis And Treatment.* W.W Norton, New York.

Chandrasekaran, B., Johnson, T.R., and Smith, J.W. (1992), 'Task Structure Analysis for Knowledge Modeling,' *Communication of the ACM*, vol. 35, no. 9., pp. 124-137.

Gorbach, S, Bartlett, J and Blacklowe, N. (1998). *Infectious Diseases.* Saunders, Philadelphia.

Heller , R. & Martin, B., (1995), "A Media Taxonomy, " *IEEE Multimedia*, pp. 36-45.

Khosla, R. & Dillon, T.S. 1997, ***Engineering Intelligent Hybrid Multi-Agent Systems***. Boston, USA, Kluwer Academic Publishers.

Maybury, M. T. (1994) "Planning Multimedia Explanation Using Communicative Acts", *Intelligent Multimedia Interfaces*, Mark T. Maybury, Eds: AAAI Press, pp. 60-74

Norman, D. A. (1988). The Psychology of Everyday Things. Basic Books: New York

Perrow, C.1984, *Normal Accidents: Living with High-Risk Technologies*, Basic Books, New York.

Preece, J., et al (1997), *Human-Computer Interaction*, Massachusetts: Addison-Wesley Pub.

Steven, S.S. (1995). "On the Psychological Law", *Psychological Review*, 64(3), 153-181

TG (Therapeutic Guidelines), (1998), Therapeutic Guidelines for Respiratory Infections, Victorian Medical Postgraduate Foundation Inc and Therapeutics Committee.

Zhang, J., and Norman, D. A. (1994). "Representations in Distributed Cognitive Tasks," in *Cognitive Science*, 18, 87-122

6 E- SALES RECRUITMENT

6.1. Introduction

The Internet has become a major driving force behind the development of computer based human resource management systems. This chapter describes e-business analysis, design and implementation of e-Sales Recruitment System (e-SRS) for a recruitment company. It illustrates the application of activity-centered e-business analysis component, problem solving ontology component and transformation agent component of the human-centered e-business system development framework. We begin this chapter with a brief description of human resource management e-business systems. It is followed by a brief discussion of motivation for using information technology in the area of sales recruitment, then followed by a detailed e-business analysis of the sales recruitment activity using the activity-centered e-business analysis component of the human-centered e-business system development framework. Finally, the e-business design of the e-SRS is described based on two alternative approaches. The first approach involves integration of a psychology based selling behavior model of artificial intelligence techniques like rule based expert systems. The selling behavior profiling and benchmarking results are outlined based on the artificial intelligence approach. The alternative approach is an adaptive approach, which involves integration of the selling behavior model with soft computing methods like fuzzy k-means clustering. In this incremental learning approach, the behavioral patterns are mined into meaningful selling behavior category clusters. This adaptive approach also allows a recruitment consultant or manager to change the behavior category of a candidate if it is strongly believed (based on their interaction with the candidate) that e-SRS has misclassified the candidate's behavior category.

6.2 Human Resource Management e-Business Systems

Human resource management involves the co-ordination of human resources through planning development, recruitment and training, evaluation, compensation and performance assessment (O'Brien 2002).

There are numerous human resource information systems designed to support the functions of the human resource department. Systems such as human resource planning to meet the needs of the business, personnel needs, development of employees, control of personnel and, policies and programs. Payroll and personnel systems help in the production of pay checks and payroll reports, maintaining personnel records and analyzing the use of personnel in the business. Recruitment and selection systems assist in recruitment, selection, hiring and job placement. More recently performance appraisals systems, employee benefits analysis systems, training and development systems, health safety and security systems have also been introduced (O'Brien, 2002).

The Internet has had a huge impact on the processes of recruitment and selection. Organizations use web sites such as my career, Seek and Monster to post vacant positions. Organizations' web sites are also used for recruitment purposes. This is a revolutionary process not only for the job hunters but also for the organizations themselves. Web sites can contain information such as reports, updates, interview tips and more. The types of systems that will be discussed in section two are online behavioral profiling and decision support systems that support the recruitment process of the organization.

The Intranet can support human resource activities by allowing employees to download training videos, providing educational information, allowing employees to enter and access personal details for human resource management files and supporting timesheet data.

Other systems, for example, CORE, which is an integrated performance management system, allows the human resource department to effectively monitor employee performance and training as well as keep track of job assignment compensation, holiday leave and also training needs.

6.3. Information Technology and Recruitment

Until recently, conventional and traditional methods and techniques were still preferred to automated or computerized techniques in a number of work activities (e.g. recruitment, etc.) in this important organizational function. One of reasons for the resistance to computerized techniques is the fact that work activities such as recruitment involve analysis of human behavior, which is considered too complex for any computerized system to model. This resistance also highlights a fact that if computer-based artifacts are to find a place in an area like human resource management they must provide enough motivation to the stakeholders in a human resource work activity for their use. We look at human breakdowns in work activities like recruitment as a means of motivating the stakeholders to use computer-based artifacts. These breakdowns represent those work situations where people are unable make a clear decision (e.g., selecting among two equally good sales candidates) either due to lack of sufficient information or expertise. That is, we use computer-based artifacts for modeling the human breakdowns in these work activities.

In the next section, we carry out an e-business analysis of the sales recruitment activity that, among other aspects, outlines the problems with the existing recruitment procedures, performance and context analysis of the recruitment activity, and goals for an alternative e-business system.

We also show in subsequent sections how the human breakdowns have been modeled and implemented in SRS. SRS has been used commercially for the last 5 years, primarily because of its ability to model these breakdowns.

6.4 Activity Centered e-Business Analysis of Sales Recruitment Activity

This section involves a detailed analysis based on the seven steps of activity centered analysis identified section of chapter 4.

6.4.1. Problem Definition and Scope of Sales Recruitment Activity

Sales management among other responsibilities includes forecasting demand (sales), managing salespersons, and establishing sales quotas. Managing salespersons involves such activities as recruiting of salespersons, supporting the salespersons in their work, meeting with customers, establishing territories and evaluating performance. Recruiting the right type of salesperson to match the organizational needs and ingraining them with proper selling attitudes has a critical impact on the performance of the sales force, sales manager, and the organization as a whole. Figure 6.1 identifies six components associated with the recruitment activity.

Most organizations (including recruitment organizations) rely on interviews as the main strategy for recruiting salespersons. Product knowledge, verbal skills, hard work, self-discipline, and personality are generally assumed to be well taken care of in the interview process. However, it is difficult to objectively determine a candidate's selling behavior during an interview.

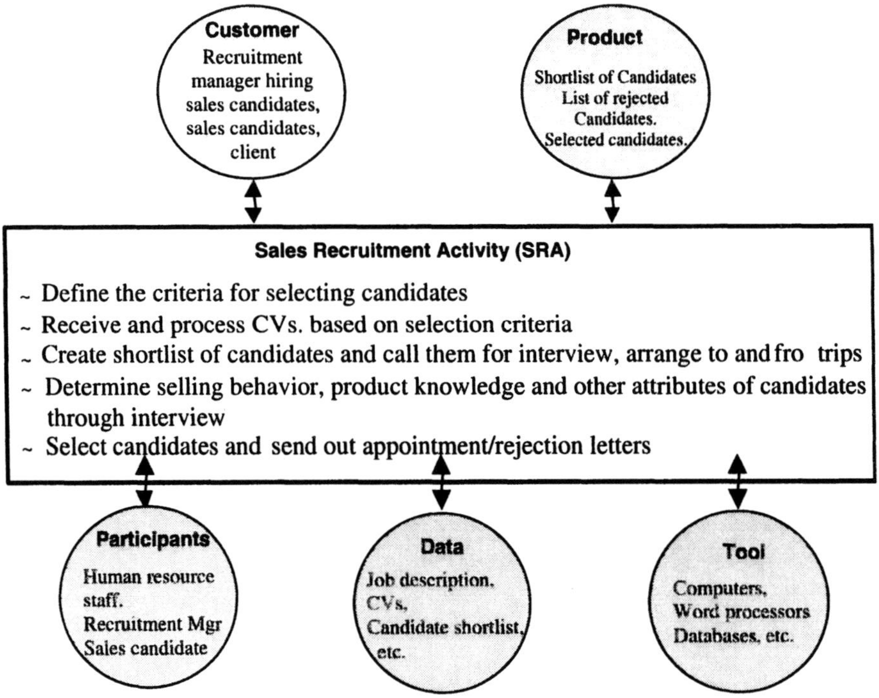

Figure 6.1: Scope of the Six Components of the Existing Sales Recruitment Activity

As a result, the existing recruiting procedures, though useful, have met with limited success. The high salesperson turnover and stress levels on sales managers while on the job are good indicators of the limited success of these procedures.

The fast growth of the Internet has added another dimension to the recruitment function. Table 6.1 identifies the e-business risks and opportunities for a recruitment company evaluating Internet technologies for making improvements in their recruitment function. In Table 6.1 a weight or score is indicated within brackets against each question. The score in brackets is on a scale of 1 (very small) to 5 (very large) against each e-business question.

In terms of the sales recruitment function the ability to digitally describe recruitment related product is considered as important. It is possible to conduct the interview over the Internet through video conferencing and also conduct a behavior profile test on the Internet. Further the initial correspondence (e.g., receiving candidate's CV, etc.) between the recruitment company and the candidate can also be done through the Internet. The cost savings in conducting the interview and other recruitment activities on the Internet are also great. A web site can assist the candidates to access information about their employers, their job requirements and also submit their CV's on line. These facilities can help to narrow the customer self-service gap.

Most people and organizations today have access to the Internet. Most recruitment companies have their own web sites to increase their geographical reach and revenue base. Thus clients and job seekers can be easily switch from one recruitment company to another through a click of a button. By the same token, the possibilities for on-line customization to satisfy client and candidate needs are also numerous. Finally, by using the Internet and intranet the recruitment company can maintain a database of clients, candidates, decisions made in matching client's needs with candidates and changing nature of clients and candidates over a period of time. This can assist the recruiter in the development of knowledge management systems and know how which can be shared with new employees for training and for retention of important clients.

The total score of 32.5 out 50 indicates substantial e-business opportunities (or risks) for the recruitment company available to add business and customer value. A score closer to 50 will indicate that a company must adopt the e-business route if it intends to stay in business. A score less than 20 indicates that the Internet does not play an important role in a company's business activities.

Thus an alternative system is sought to enhance the interview process as well avail a company of e-business opportunities for improving the overall effectiveness of the recruitment activity. In order to determine the role, goals and tasks of the alternative computer-based system, performance and context analysis of the existing sales recruitment activity is undertaken.

Table 6.1: e-Business Risks and Opportunities - E-Sales Recruitment

Digitally Describe or Deliver – How large is the potential to digitally describe or deliver your products? (4)	**Dynamic Pricing** - How large is your potential loss to the firm if its product is not sold by a certain time? (2)
Price/Cost Structure – Relative to the current way of doing business, how important are Internet technologies for reducing costs in creating and delivering product to your customers? (4)	**Knowledge Management** – How large is the potential for your firm to benefit from better knowledge management? (2.5)
Customer Loyalty – How large is the potential for competitors to undermine the loyalty of your customers? (4)	**Online Customer** – What percent of your current customers are already online at work, at home, or both? (3)
Customer Self-Service Gap – How large is the gap between your current and potential customer self-service? (3)	**Customization** - How large is the opportunity for on-line customization of your product? (4)
Geographical Reach – What is the difference between your firm's current geographical reach and its potential reach via the Internet? (5)	**Channel and Intermediary Power** – How large is the power or importance of channel intermediaries in your traditional business? (1)

6.4.2. Performance Analysis of Sales Recruitment Activity

The purpose of the performance analysis is to identify the role and goals of the computer-based artifact in the sales recruitment activity. In this section, we briefly outline the performance analysis of the relevant parameters related to the six components of the existing sales recruitment activity shown in Figure 6.1.

Product and Customer

The product performance variables are cost, quality, responsiveness, reliability and conformance to standards. The customer related performance variable is customer satisfaction. However customer satisfaction is measured in terms of the product performance variables.

Cost: At present the recruitment activity is largely non-Internet driven. That is, except for receiving CV's online, inviting and informing candidates over the phone, all other recruitment activities (including conducting tests and interviewing) are conducted face-to-face in a bricks and mortar environment. Direct and indirect costs in terms of senior management time, CV processing and short listing, traveling expenses of candidates, etc. run into hundred of thousands of dollars. In order to reduce traveling expenses 25% of inter-state candidates are not short-listed for interview.

The recruitment manager, client and the sales candidate are the three customer categories. In terms of customer satisfaction the Total Cost of Ownership (TCO) is considered. This includes money, time, effort and attention that could be used for other purposes by the customer. As far as the client is concerned the cost of acquiring the product (i.e. most suitable sales candidate) can be reduced by reducing the cost of producing the product (i.e., cost of selecting the most suitable sales candidate), and minimizing the cycle time from advertising to hiring. The recruitment manager is more concerned about optimizing their quality time spent on hiring the most suitable candidate. Finally, the sales candidate is concerned about optimizing the time and effort spent in going through the selection process.

Quality: approximately 35% of salespersons selected through a recruitment company leave the client organization within 2 years of employment. Further, there are no objective benchmarks for selecting the best candidate for a particular client.

Reliability: Decision to shortlist candidates for interview is entirely based on information provided in their CVs, which can be unreliable.

Conformance to Standards: The recruitment company employs a consistent set of interview questions while interviewing candidates for a particular job. The interview questions are selected from a question database based on needs of the client. The candidates, however, do not believe that the selection process is objective and that they are given adequate opportunity to provide all relevant information about themselves.

The performance analysis of the product component in this section identifies a need for a computer-based artifact with an aim to reduce direct and indirect costs of the sales recruitment activity through use of the Internet (Goal 1, G1),

- improve recruitment decision quality (G2),
- improve reliability of information related to sales candidates (G3), and
- provide uniformity and objectivity in the selection process (G4).

Work Activity

Cycle time: It takes approximately 10 to 15 person hours per candidate to complete the sales hiring activity. Given the heavy reliance on the CV's and unreliable nature of information in the CVs generally ten to twenty percent more candidates are short-listed. This also increases the total cycle for all the candidates.

Participants

Skills: Most recruitment managers have 10 to 15 years of experience in the profession, which is considered to be satisfactory.

Data

Quality: The methods used to determine the accuracy of the candidate data based on their CV are inadequate. The hiring decision in the sales activity involves, among other aspects, data related to the selling behavior of a candidate. This data is not readily available in the existing sales recruitment activity.

Accessibility & Presentation: The only accessible data is the job criteria and appropriateness of a candidate to suit those criteria. Other important data is not accessible in the exiting system, such as selling behavior data.

Tool

Functional Capabilities: The Internet technologies available to the company are only being used for receiving CVs, writing selection and rejection letters, and storing candidate information in a database. The Internet technologies are not being used for customization of the selection process (e.g., benchmarking of client's definition of a good candidate, on line testing/behavior profiling), and exploiting geographical reach of the Internet.

Some of the additional goals for the computer-based artifact based on the performance analysis of the work activity, participant, data and the tool are:

- reduce cycle time (G5),
- use Internet technologies to reduce costs, improve product and data quality and accessibility, and increase geographical reach. This will also assist in reducing the customer self-service gap for sales candidates and provide on-line customization of client's needs through benchmarking. (G6)

6.4.3. Context Analysis of the Sales Recruitment Activity

In order to understand the context in which the goals can be effectively realized, a context analysis of the six components of the sales recruitment activity is undertaken. This context is analyzed in terms of social (participants and tools) organizational (culture), data structure and security context, product substitution, and new emerging tools context. The outcome of the context analysis is a set of context-based tasks for an alternate computerized system.

Participant Goals and Incentives:

Recruitment Manager: The recruitment manager at present does not have an objective means of benchmarking the sales, customer service and telesales candidate's suitability against the organization's existing successful salespersons, customer service, sales support and telesales personnel. This is a human breakdown situation in the decision making process for sales recruitment. The recruitment managers are prepared to support the use of a computer-based artifact for improving recruitment decision-making if it could support benchmarking. The computer-based system should provide a means for benchmarking candidate behavior profiles with existing profiles of successful salespersons, customer service, sales support and telesales personnel. Further, for optimizing their time and making smarter hiring decisions they need high quality information pertaining to a candidate's behavior in selling situation.

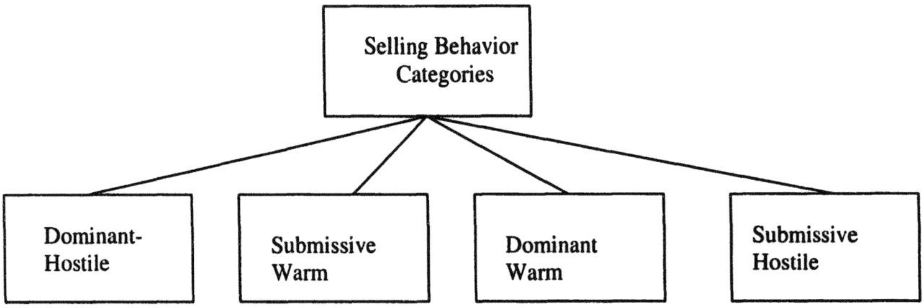

Figure 6.2: Selling Behavior Categories

Sales Candidate: The sales candidates are ready to support development of a computer-based recruitment decision support system if it asks them direct sales or customer service related information rather than indirect psychological questions (e.g., Myer's Briggs behavior profiling systems) which they do not understand.

Further, for improving data quality and accessibility, reducing cycle time, and providing incentives to recruitment managers and sales candidate, computer-based artifact should:

- relate behavioral category of sales candidates on areas directly related to the selling profession rather than use indirect methods of behavioral analysis. The behavioral analysis is based on four behavioral categories; dominant hostile, submissive warm, dominant warm, and submissive hostile as shown in Figure 6.2. These four categories are based on two dimensions, namely, "Submissive------Dominant, and Warm-----Hostile" as shown in Figure 6.3. These two dimensions are the two most significant dimensions in which selling behavior is expressed. More details on the behavioral dimensions and some earlier work done in the development of SRS are reported in (Khosla and Dillon 1992; Khosla and Dillon 1993; Khosla).
- to support ease of use and understanding, the language used for evaluating a sales candidate on various areas should reflect the language used by them in their day-to-day activities
- be able to identify their suitability to other sales related jobs such as customer service, and sales support. At present this information has to be evaluated by the hiring managers during the interview process.
- be able to provide not only the behavioral category but also the breakup of the behavioral profile based on various areas related to the profession, such as competition, customer, product, decisiveness, success and failure, rules and

regulations, job satisfaction. Overall, seventeen areas have been identified as shown in Figure 6.4.

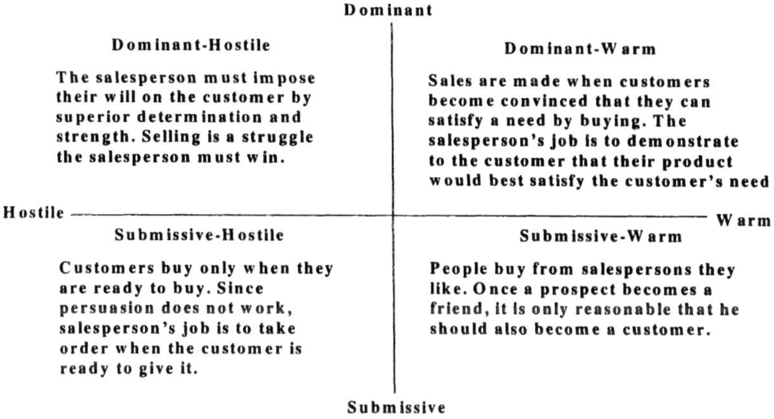

Figure 6.3: Selling Behaviour Category Dimensions

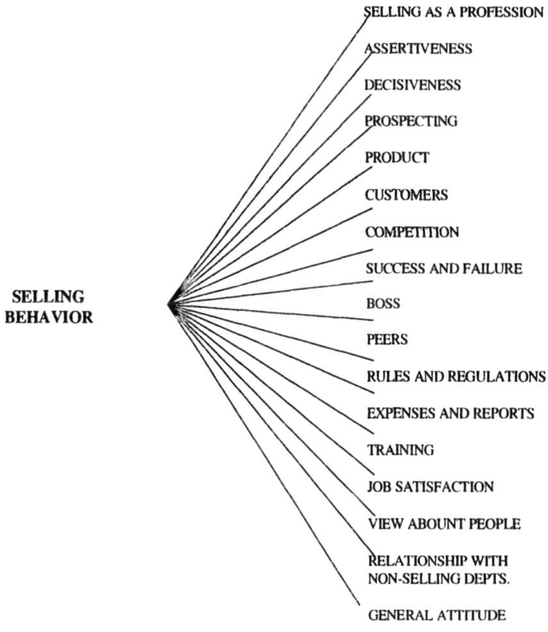

Figure 6.4: Evaluation Areas for Selling Behavior Categorization

- be able to benchmark candidate's selling behavior profile (including area wise breakup) with those of successful salespersons in client organizations.

Work Activity

Practitioner Cultural issue: Traditionally, recruitment managers have employed behavior profiling systems based on indirect methods like e.g., Myer's Briggs behavior profiling system. Besides their indirectness these systems require lot of analytical processing to be done by the recruitment manager or consultant can effectively use the results provided by the system. From a client's perspective, the sales managers do not have confidence with using computerized sales recruitment systems, especially those based on indirect methods.

Further, although sales managers do class salespersons in different behavioral categories, the selection of a sales candidate is a function of the behavioral category, culture of the organization and organizational policies for sales and marketing (e.g., high promotion aggressive strategy or sit back strategy). The culture of the organization can be interpreted in terms of what type of sales and customer service personnel are currently successful in that organization. Thus, here again the capability of an alternative system to benchmark a sales candidate against the existing successful salespersons is a motivating factor for using a computerized sales recruitment system.

Practitioner Concerns: The recruitment manager wants a facility of incorporating their own experience and gut feel in the e-business SRS. That is, the system needs to have an incremental learning strategy in which any misclassified candidate behavior category can be changed by the recruitment manager so that SRS does not make the same mistake again. Sales managers, from a client's perspective, are concerned about how a computerized system processes a candidate's information for determining the selling behavioral category of a sales candidate. In other words, the selling behavior model should correspond to the one used by them in their training programs.

Data

The data structure of various areas that relate to the selling profession is shown in Figure 8.19. The data security issues involve access of the behavioral profiles of the candidates. The access has to be restricted to the recruitment managers and senior management.

Tool

The new emerging tools are Internet technologies and e-commerce. The Internet can be used to provide access to a computer-based sales recruitment system for use by recruitment managers and sales candidates at different geographic locations. It will create uniformity and consistency in the recruitment activity. It will also help to reduce costs by allowing the behavior profiling of candidates from remote locations

6.4.4. Alternative e-Business System - Goals and Tasks

In this step, we consolidate the outcomes of the performance and context analysis in terms of the goals and corresponding tasks for an alternative e-business system.

The goals and corresponding tasks listed in this section form the basis for developing a human-centered activity model. The correspondence between some of the tasks and goal set is shown in Table 6.2. In order to facilitate formulation of a human-centered activity model, we need to firstly determine the underlying assumptions or preconditions for accomplishment of the human-centered tasks. Further, we also need to determine the division of labor (tasks) between the participants and computer-based artifact. These two issues are addressed through a human-task-tool diagram and the task-product network in the next two sections.

In this section, we list some of those tasks and cross-refer them with the goals identified in the performance analysis of the sales recruitment activity.

In order to improve the decision quality (G2), the following tasks need to be modeled:

- **T1**-The selling behavior profile of a sales candidate has to benchmarked against the behavior profiles of existing successful salespersons in the organization
- **T2**-The degree of fit of a candidate's profile to a frontline sales, customer service and sales support position has to determined
- **T3**- The training needs for frontline sales, customer service and sales support have to be determined

In order to improve the reliability of the information (G3) about sales candidates, data quality and accessibility, the following tasks need to be modeled:

- **T4**-The behavior categorization has to be based on selling related areas, as shown in Figure 6.4. The language used for evaluating the areas shown in Figure 6.4 has to reflect the language used by salespersons and managers in the profession.
- **T5**- Flexibility to change a candidate's behavioral category (as determined by SRS) based on recruitment manager experience

In order to reduce costs (G1 and G6), cycle time (G5) and improve conformance to standards (G4) the following task needs to be modeled:

- **T6**- Internet technologies should be used to facilitate behavior profiling of candidates from remote locations. Through consistent use of the computerized sales recruitment system, it will also assist recruitment managers in different geographical locations to conform to recruitment standards laid down by the organization.

Table 6.2: Grouping Goals and Tasks for an Alternative e-Business System

Goals	Corresponding Tasks
G1, G4, G5, G6	• **T6**-Behavior profiling of candidates from remote locations based on Internet technologies
G2	• **T1**-The selling behavior profile of a sales candidate has to benchmark against the behavior profiles of existing successful salespersons in client organization. • **T2**-The degree of fit of a candidate's profile to a frontline sales, customer service and sales support position has to be determined. • **T3**-The training needs for frontline sales, customer service and sales support have to be determined

G3	• **T5**-Flexibility to change a candidate's behavioral category (as determined by SRS) based on recruitment manager experience. In other words, provide incremental learning option in SRS. • **T4**-The behavior categorization has to be based on selling related areas and selling behavior model used in training programs

6.4.5. Human-Task-Tool Diagram

The human-task-tool diagrams in Figures 6.5, 6.6 and 6.7, respectively, show the division of labor between the computer-based e-SRS, recruitment manager, and the sales candidate. Figures 6.6 and 6.7 also show the human interaction points with e-SRS.

In the next section we show the implementation results of some of the tasks outlined in the last section.

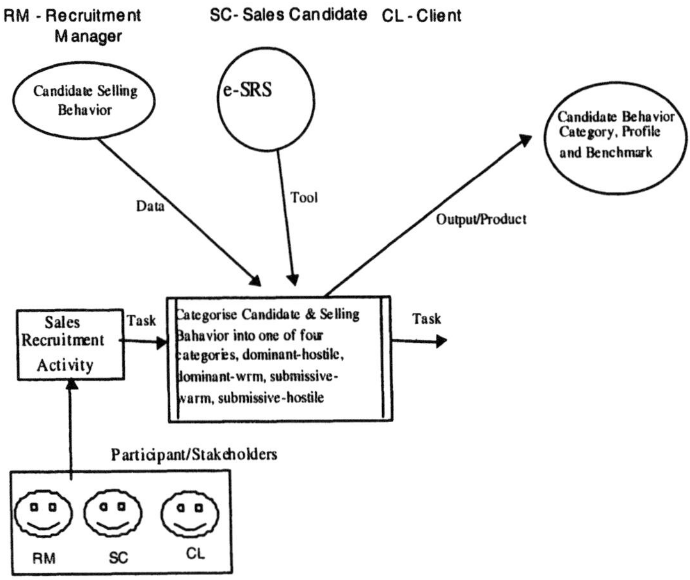

Figure 6.5: SRS Task

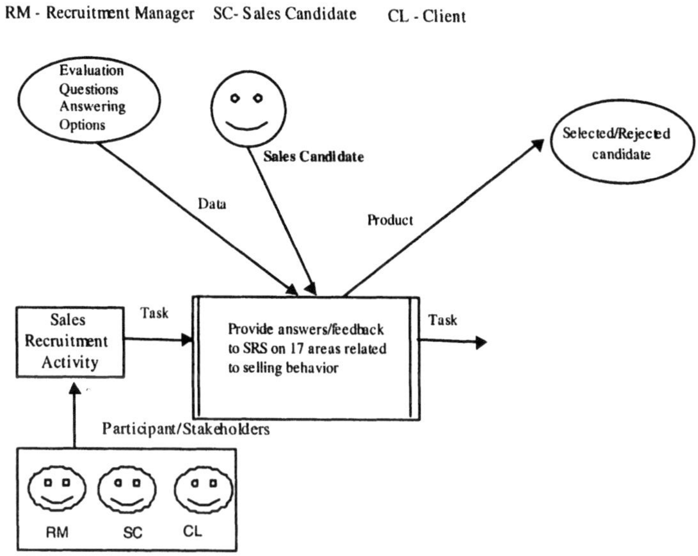

Figure 6.6: Sales Candidate Task

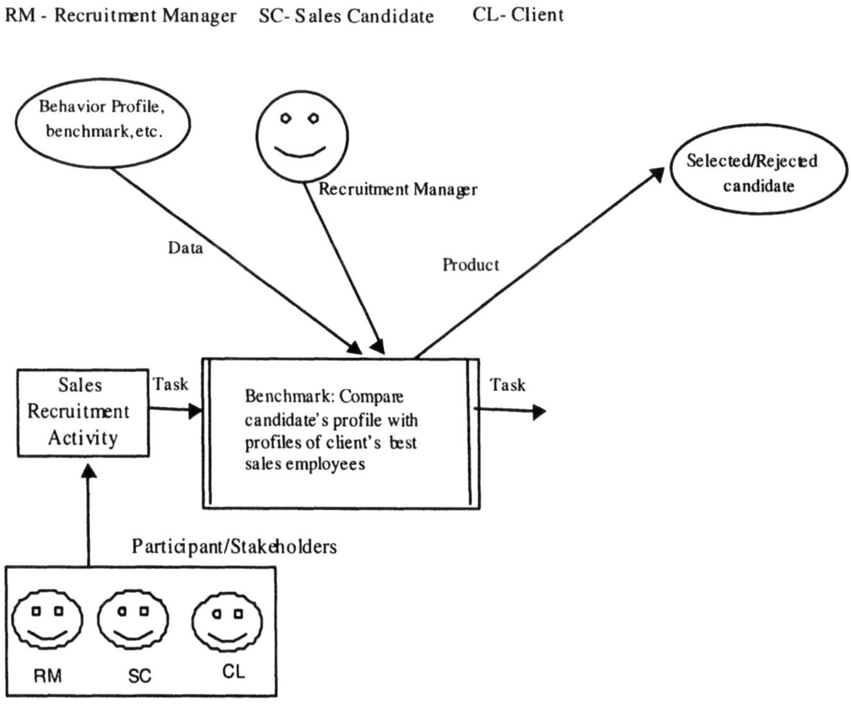

Figure 6.7: Recruitment Manager Task

6.4.6. Task Product Transition Network

A sample task-product transition network of the sales recruitment activity is shown in Figure 6.8. The product-task transition preconditions shown in Figure 6.8 assist us in defining the assumptions under which the task will be accomplished. For example, the preconditions shown in Figure 6.8 for the task " Compare candidate profiles with client's best sales employees (or benchmark profiles)" imply that candidate profile and benchmark profile data should be available for doing the comparison. The postcondition reflects not only the new product state but also the level of competence required from the method or algorithm used for accomplishing the task after the precondition has been satisfied. For example, the rules employed by an expert system or selling behavior clusters learnt by a clustering model should be cross-validated by relevant test data and also validated by the recruitment manager's own opinion about the candidate.

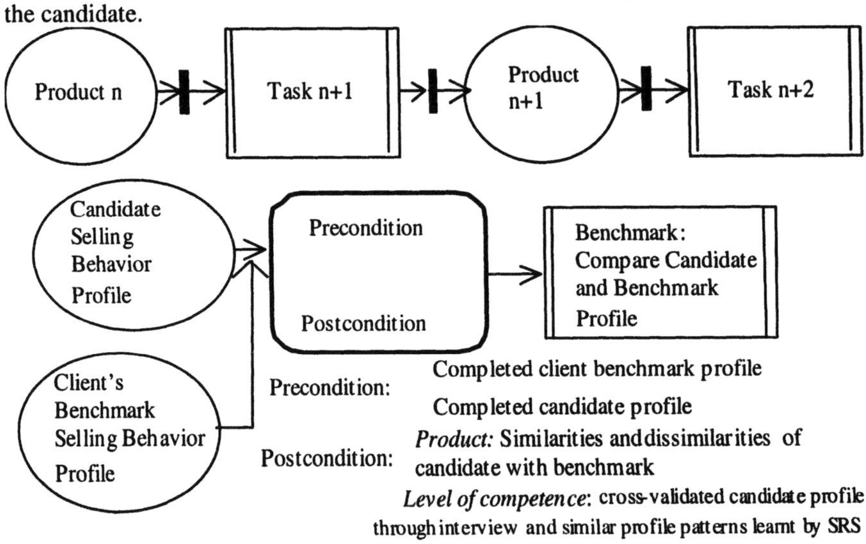

Figure 6.8: Sample Task-Product Transition Network of Sales Recruitment Activity

6.4.7. e-Business Strategy, e-Business Model and IT Infrastructure

Given the recent partial failure of the "dotcom" only companies the recruitment company have a preference for a hybrid clicks and bricks strategy (also known as "dotcorp" strategy). In other words, the company is adopting a channel enhancement e-business strategy. The channel enhancement e-business strategy will enable them to use their existing traditional channel for recruitment as well provide added customer value to their customers and clients through the web. Another reason for adopting this strategy is that their existing IT infrastructure will have to undergo a major overhaul if the company for instance, adopts a value chain integration strategy (which will require seamless integration of their databases). It is envisaged that the channel enhancement strategy will enable fill the customer self-service gap, reduce costs, increase geographical reach and facilitate on-line customization.

The e-business model employed is shown in Figure 6.9. The direct-to-customer model does not conflict with their existing e-business models (which in fact are also direct-to-customer models. In this model, the clients and sales candidates can pay for recruitment, behavior profiling, and reporting services on line.

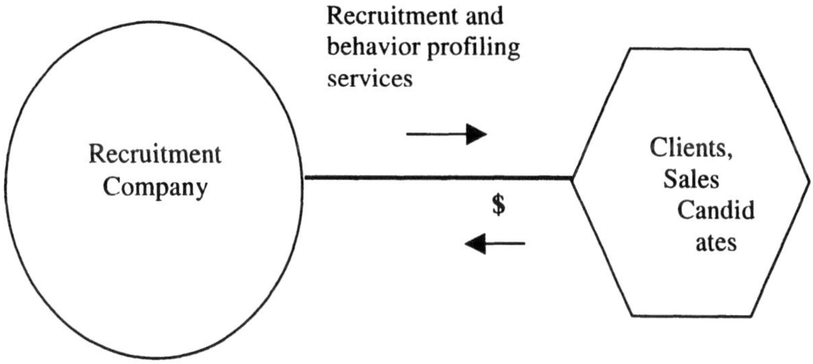

Figure 6.9: Direct to customer e-Business Model

6.5. Human-Centered Activity Model

The human-task-tool diagram and task-product transition network form the basis of the human-centered activity model. The computer-based tasks are systematized and structured using the five problem solving adapters of the problem solving ontology component. Human-centered activity model represents an integration of the activity-centered e-business analysis component with the problem solving ontology component. The five problem solving adapters represent generalized problem solving structures used to model the particularities of the sales recruitment activity within a computer-based environment. The computer-based tasks and data derived from the activity-centered e-business analysis are mapped on to the task and representation signatures of the five problem solving adapters. The rest of this section shows the mapping of the preprocessing adapter, decomposition and control adapters of the HCVM to the computer-based tasks in the sales recruitment activity.

6.5.1. Mapping Decomposition Adapter to SRA Tasks

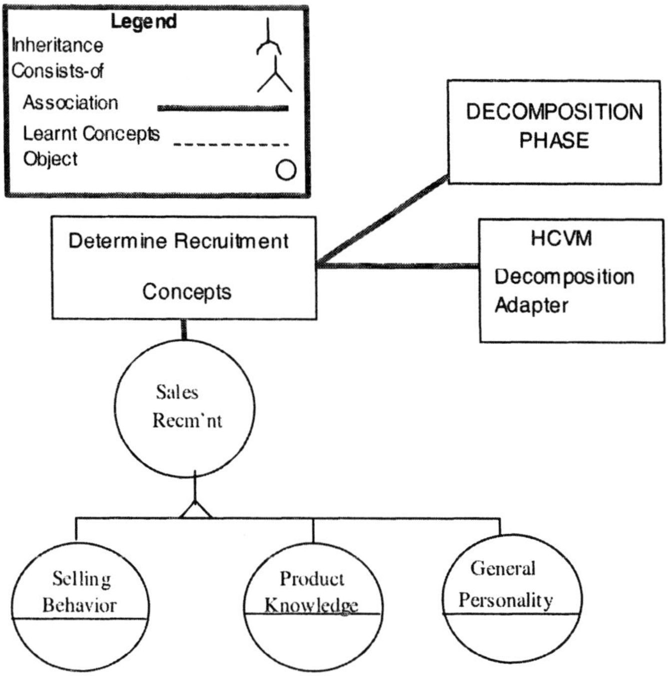

Figure 6.10:Mapping SRA Tasks and Objects to HCVM Decomposition Adapter

Figure 6.10 shows an association of the decomposition phase and decomposition adapter of the HCVM with the relevant tasks (refer work activity component in Figure 6.1) and objects of the sales recruitment activity. The objects in Figure 6.10 are representative of the object layer of the HCVM. The association between decomposition adapter and the sales recruitment activity is established based on the generic goals and tasks of the decomposition adapter and the corresponding task/s in the sales recruitment activity as shown in Table 6.3. There may exist one-to-one or one-to-many task mapping between the generic task of an adapter and the tasks of the sales recruitment activity. The one-to-many mapping reflects multiple levels of problem solving in the phase (e.g., decomposition phase). On the other hand, one-to-one mapping reflects single level of problem solving in a phase (e.g., in this case there is a single level). The task constraints shown in Table 6.3 are high level human related conceptual constraints of reducing problem complexity and computer related constraints of scalable software design.

The orthogonal concepts as shown in Table 6.3 are orthogonal in the sense that they represent independent aspects of the same problem. However, they are correlated in the sense that the recruitment manager takes into account candidate's attributes in all three areas before making an informed decision.

The domain model used for determining the orthogonal concepts like selling behavior, product knowledge and general personality is based on the functional model of a recruitment manager. Given that the task constraints are non-computational we can use perceptual artifacts, based on the representing dimensions, for representing the orthogonal concepts.

Table 6.3: Mapping Decomposition Adapter Signatures to SRA Goals, Tasks & Reps

HCVM and Representation Goal, Tasks, Signatures	Corresponding Goals, Tasks, etc. in Sales Recruitment Activity
Phase: Decomposition.	Decomposition
Goal: Restrict input context Reduce complexity.	Restrict Recruitment manager's hiring context Reduce salesperson recruitment domain space
Task: Determine abstract orthogonal concepts.	Determine sales recruitment concepts: • Selling Behavior • Product Knowledge • General Personality
Task Constraints: Orthogonality, reliability, scalability, domain dependent	Orthogonal sales recruitment concepts, scalable selling behavior categories
Precondition	Short listed candidates
Postcondition	Sales recruitment domain decomposed into orthogonal concepts --> Selling behavior, Product knowledge, General personality
Represented Features: Qualitative (linguistic)	Sales recruitment domain concept labels
Represented Features: Non-linguistic	Icons for Selling behavior, product knowledge and general personality concepts.
Domain Model: Structural, functional, casual, geometric, heuristic, spatial, shape, color, etc.	Functional (recruitment managers functional model)

6.5.2. Mapping Control Phase and Decision Phase Adapter to SRA Tasks

Figure 6.11 shows the mapping of the control phase adapter of the HCVM with the relevant tasks of e-SRS. The task "Determine Behavior Categorization Decision Strategy" defines the selection knowledge for pursuing one of the two analytical models (one based on Expert System (ES) model and the other based on behavioral pattern clustering model with incremental learning strategy). The conflict resolution rules task in Figure 6.11 models two scenarios. The first scenario relates to a situation when the two models do not infer or predict the same selling behavioral category. The second scenario relates to the situation when there is a conflict between the recruitment manager and (one or both) behavior categorization models. Although, not shown in Figure 6.11 the control adapter also identifies the decision level concepts based on the functional model of the recruitment manager. These are *selling behavior evaluation* and selling *behavior profiling and categorization* within each strategy. The *selling behavior evaluation* is functionally related to taking feedback (through questions and answers) from the candidate on seventeen areas

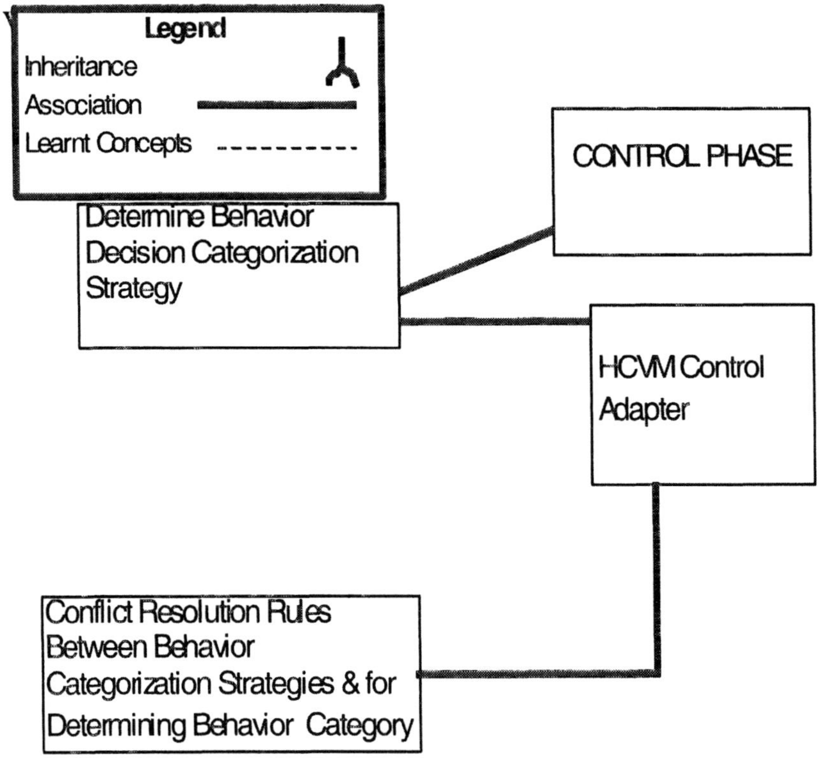

Figure 6.11: Mapping of Some SRS Tasks to HCVM Control Adapter

related to selling (and customer service) and calculating raw scores in behavioral categories like DHost (or DH), SHost (or SH), SW and DW. The e-SRS tasks in the control phase suggest a one-to-many mapping between control adapter task of determining decision level concepts and the corresponding e-SRS tasks.

The decision phase adapter task "Learn & Predict candidate behavior category," as shown in Figure 6.12 is based on the behavioral pattern clustering model. It is a task in the functional decision concept *selling behavior profiling and categorization* based on the clustering strategy. It learns and predicts one of six categories, namely, DH,

DW, SH, SW, SH-SW and Non-Determinant (ND) category. The SH-SW is a transitional category (indicating high scores in two categories). ND category indicates the SRS cannot infer or predict any category. Figure 6.13 shows the mapping of the decision phase adapter and tasks based on the ES model.

The HCVM post-processing adapter in the decision phase is used for comparing candidate's behavior profile with benchmark profile, producing detailed candidate evaluation reports (including area wise breakup of candidate's selling behavior profile, degree of fit, etc.)

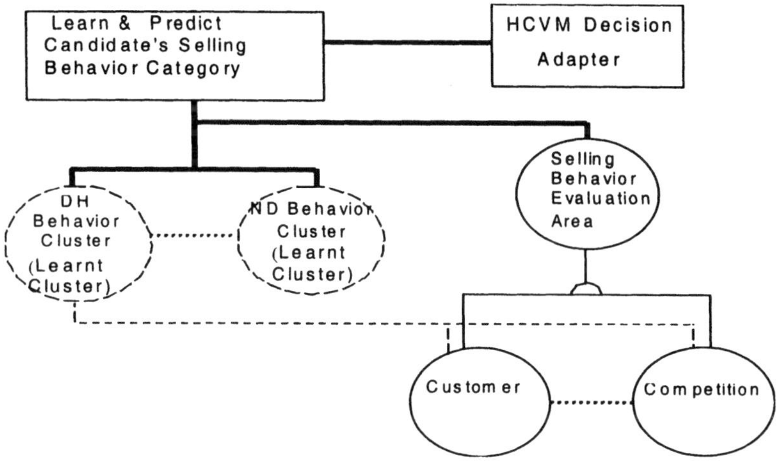

Figure 6.12: Overview of e-SRS and Some Tasks Associated with HCVM Decision Adapter Based on Clustering Model

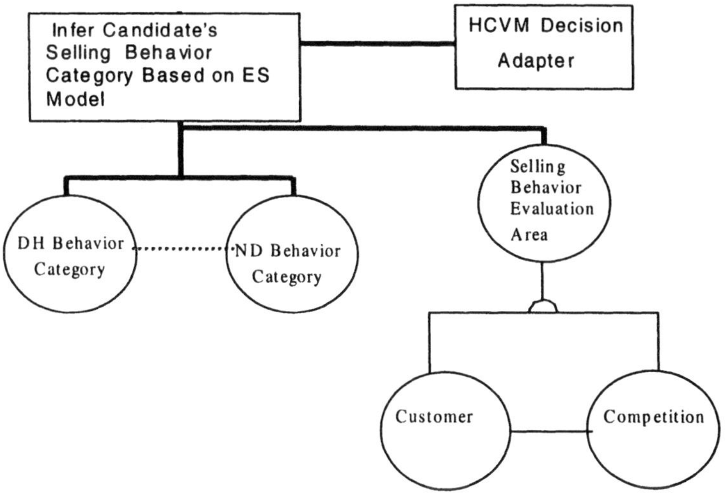

Figure 6.13: Overview of SRA and Some Tasks Associated with HCVM Decision Adapter Based on ES Model

6.6 Implementation and Results

The multi-agent design outline of some agents of the e-SRS is shown in Figure 6.14 and 6.15 respectively. The agent definition of the Selling Behavior Evaluation and Profiling Control Agent is shown in Figure 6.16. The two distinct approaches (i.e., ES and Clustering) to modeling of the candidate's selling behavior category are now described in this section. It is followed by description of the behavior profiling and benchmarking results of e-SRS.

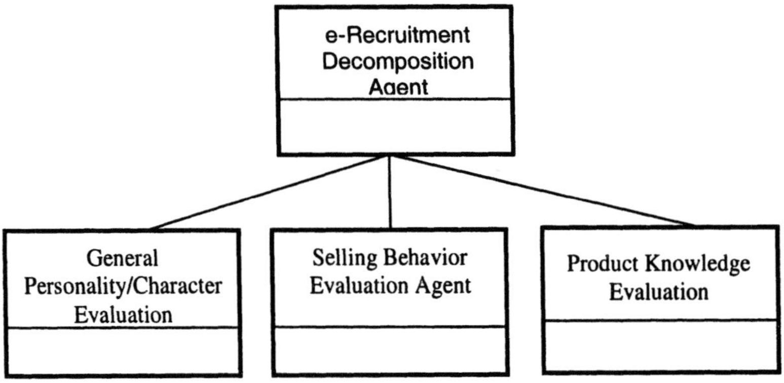

Figure 6.14: Agents related to Decomposition Phase of HCVM

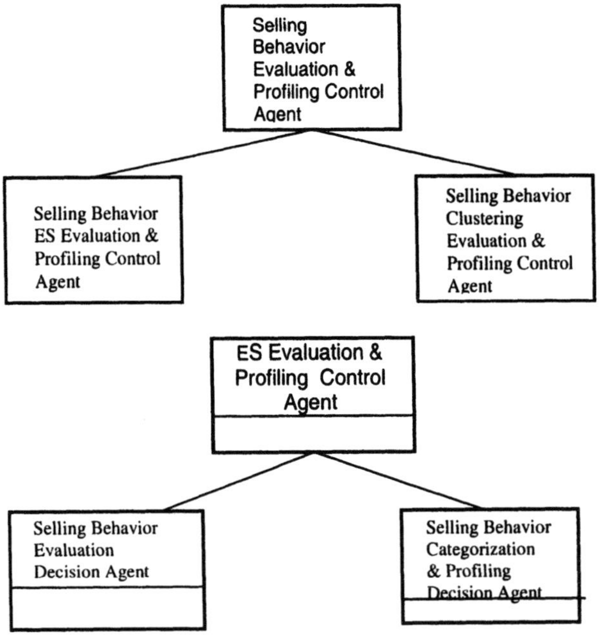

Figure 6.15: Agents related to Control and Decision Phases of HCVM

6.6.1. ES Model of Behavior Categorization

The various stages involved in the development of the ES model are shown in Figure 6.16.

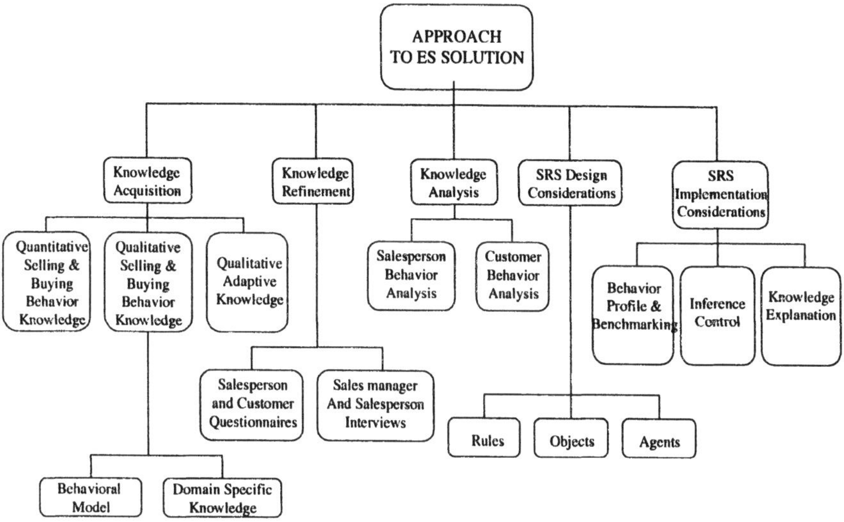

Figure 6.16: Five Stages of Development of ES Model of SRS

The knowledge acquisition stage involves qualitative and quantitative knowledge analysis of selling and buying behavior knowledge. As shown in Figure 6.16 the selling behavior knowledge involves integration of a selling behavior model with domain specific knowledge based on the experience of recruitment managers and sales managers in several industry sectors in Australia.

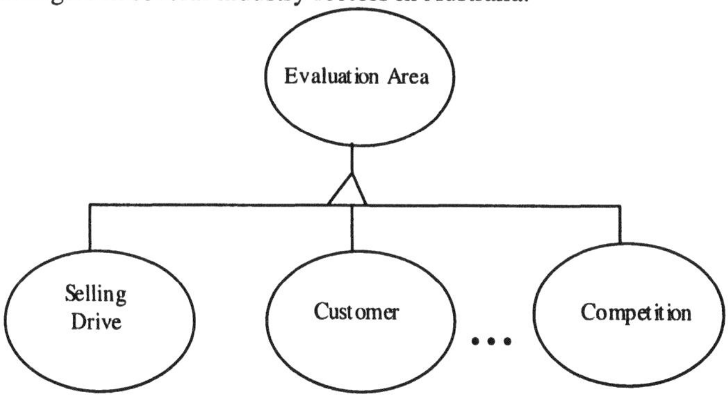

Figure 6.17: Areas for Evaluating Selling Behavior

The quantitative knowledge involves assigning weights to various areas for evaluation of selling behavior (as shown in Figure 6.17) based on Analytical Hierarchical Processing (AHP) technique. These areas are also shown in Figure 6.18 –

an e-commerce web site of a recruitment company. A sample set of questions related to the competition area are shown in Figure 6.19. The qualitative and quantitative knowledge has been iteratively refined through salesperson questionnaire surveys over period of 5 years.

The qualitative and quantitative analysis of customer behavior knowledge was also undertaken in the development of the initial ES prototype. The purpose of modeling the customer buying knowledge is to training new sales recruits in successfully closing deals with different types of customers.

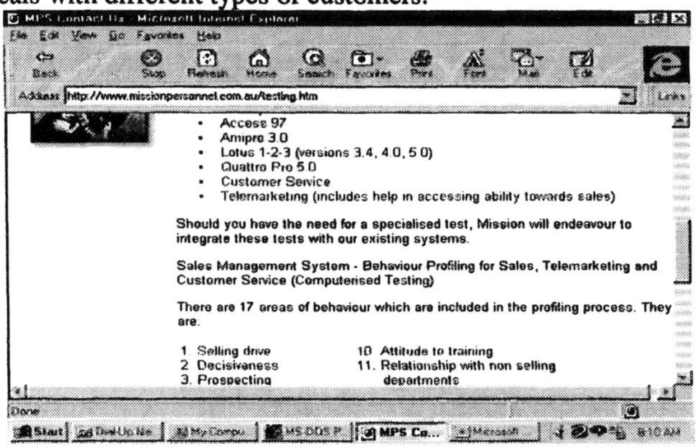

Figure 6.18: e-Business Web site of a Recruitment Company

1. In sales, the law of the jungle prevails. It's either you or the competitor. You relish defeating your competitors, and fight them hard, using every available weapon.	Behavioral Category:	DH
2. The best hope to outwork and outsell competitors is by keeping abreast of competitive activity and having sound product knowledge of your product.	Behavioral Category:	DW
3. You may not be aggressive otherwise, but when it comes to competition you are just the opposite. You spend good deal of your time to explain to the customer why he should not buy from the competitor.	Behavioral Category:	SH
4. You do not believe in being aggressive towards your competitors. Competitors are people like you and there is room for everybody.	Behavioral Category:	SW

Figure 6.19: Questions Related to the Competition Area

```
IF
    max (score DH, score SH, score SW, score DW) = score DW
  AND
    score DW / Total score < 0.65
THEN
    Pursue max (score DH, score SH, score SW)

IF
    Pursued category = DH
  AND
    score SH / score DH > 0.6
    score (SW + DW) / score (DH + DW) <= 0.9
    score (SH + SW) / score (DH + DW) >= 0.7
THEN
    Pursue max (score SH, score SW)
```

Figure 6.20: A Sample Selling Behavior Categorization Rule

The ES Behavior Categorization and Profiling Decision agent consists of 450 rules. The rules include behavior categorization rules for each category, meta-control rules and behavior pruning rules (which prune out contradictions in candidate's answers). One of the rules used for determining the predominant category in a candidate's selling behavior profile is shown in Figure 6.20.

Table 6.4 : Training Data Set of Behavioral Patterns Based on Pruned Scores

Sn	D-Host	S-Host	S-Warm	D-Warm
1	0.01	0.42	0.83	0.11
2	0.03	0.6	0.83	0.01
3	0.47	0.66	0.25	0.1
4	0.12	0.98	0.12	0.1
5	0.38	0.59	0.42	0.14
6	0.05	0.82	0.83	0.04
7	0.25	0.61	0.33	0.11
8	0.11	0.94	0.13	0.09
9	0	0.85	0.24	0.16
10	0.22	0.62	0.7	0.1
11	0.22	0.74	0.34	0.01
12	0.26	0.61	0.35	0.22
13	0.22	0.44	0.79	0.16
14	0.12	0.66	0.21	0.11
15	0.12	0.71	0.77	0.01
16	0.18	0.83	0.3	0.12
17	0.24	0.24	0.78	0.16
18	0.69	0.26	0.1	0.12
19	0.26	0.36	0.59	0.15
20	0.03	0.46	0.86	0.03

6.6.2 Predictive Model of Behavior Categorization

The predictive model is based on the need to develop an incremental learning model of selling behavior categorization (Task T5 in Table 6.2) and as an alternative to the ES model. Table 6.4 shows some of the selling behavior patterns used as training data set for developing two predictive models.

The first predictive model employs the K-NN (K-Nearest Neighbor) technique. The six selling behavior categorization clusters are shown in Figure 6.21.

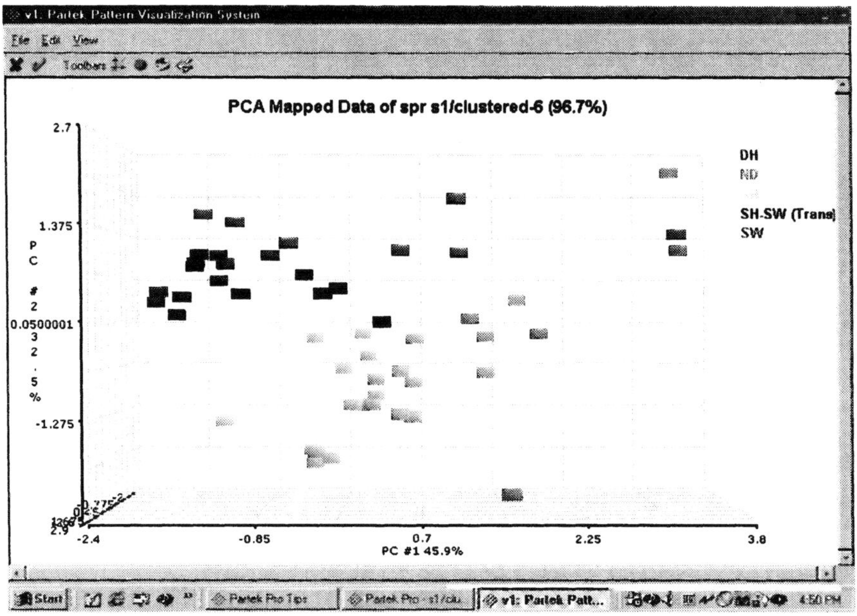

Figure 6.21: Six Selling Behavior Clusters

The second predictive model is based on the fuzzy k-means technique developed by Bezdek (1981). We use the fuzzy k-means technique to introduce further granularity in the behavior categories. That is, the four categories SH, SW, DH, and DW are refined using linguistic variable like high, medium and low. So, we have twelve clusters (SH (high, medium and low), SW (high, medium and low, and three each for the other two categories) instead of the original four. Qualitatively, the linguistic variables provide information on the intensity (or extent to which a candidate's behavior belongs to a category) of each category.

Fuzzy k-means is an iterative and non-hierarchical algorithm that aims to separate N objects into K clusters i.e., minimizing the intra-group dispersion of points. The fuzzy k-means algorithm is outlined in http://www.usyd.edu.au/su/agric/acpa and is as follows:

Table 6.5:Predicted Selling Behavior Categroies for candidates 35 to 50 Using Fuzzy-k-Means Clustering

PN	CAT	SH(High)	SW (High)	SH (Med)	SH(Low)	DH(High)	SW(Low)	DH (Med)	SW (Med)	DH(Low)
35	SH(Med)	0.00233	0.00003	0.57807	0.00008	0.00002	0.00005	0.39250	0.00029	0.02663
36	SH(Med)	0.00022	0.00000	0.98138	0.00000	0.00000	0.00000	0.01772	0.00001	0.00067
37	DH (Low)	0.00046	0.00005	0.00940	0.00006	0.0054	0.00039	0.23939	0.00029	0.74450
38	SW (Low)	0.00001	0.02870	0.00005	0.02692	0.0000	0.00212	0.0002	0.94189	0.00003
39	DH (Low)	0.00007	0.00001	0.00056	0.00001	0.0024	0.00005	0.00403	0.00006	0.99278
40	SH(Low)	0.00000	0.01246	0.00000	0.98366	0.00000	0.00003	0.00001	0.00384	0.00000
41	DH(High)	0.00002	0.00003	0.00009	0.00002	0.9980	0.00026	0.00041	0.00008	0.00104
42	SH(Med)	0.00033	0.00000	0.99874	0.00000	0.0000	0.00000	0.00087	0.00000	0.00005
43	SH (Med)	0.00352	0.00000	0.99435	0.00001	0.0000	0.00001	0.00192	0.00002	0.00017
44	SH(Low)	0.00000	0.00049	0.00001	0.99870	0.0000	0.00001	0.00001	0.00078	0.00000
45	DH(Med)	0.00301	0.00010	0.17098	0.00030	0.0000	0.00020	0.71591	0.00105	0.10838
46	SH(High)	0.99753	0.00000	0.00241	0.00000	0.0000	0.00000	0.00003	0.00000	0.00003
47	SH(Med)	0.00145	0.00001	0.94115	0.00002	0.0000	0.00002	0.05418	0.00006	0.00311
48	SH(Low)	0.00000	0.01621	0.00001	0.90083	0.0000	0.00017	0.00004	0.08272	0.00001
49	SH (Low)	0.00000	0.02146	0.00001	0.97030	0.0000	0.00010	0.00002	0.00811	0.00000
50	SH(Med)	0.04955	0.00002	0.92734	0.00006	0.0000	0.00004	0.01210	0.00010	0.01074

Table 6.5 shows the categories predicted by the fuzzy k-means model on unseen selling behavioral patterns. The prediction in Table 6.5 is based on fuzzy categories related to SH, SW and DH categories only.

6.6.3. Behavior Profiling and Benchmarking

The *ES Selling Behavior Categorization and Profiling Decision* agent shown in Table 6.6 models behavior categorization and benchmarking tasks of e-SRS. Figures 6.22 and 6.23 show the results of implementation of the sales candidate behavior profiling and benchmarking tasks of the e-SRS respectively. The screen shot in Figure 6.22 shows the implementation of tasks T2 and T3 shown in Table 6.2.

These two tasks involve several psychological variables of interest to the recruitment manager, namely, degree of fit, training needs, benchmarking, etc. Further, the selling behavior profile is shown at two levels of abstraction. The pie chart represents the overall distribution of four category scores, whereas, area wise behavior profile shown in the upper right hand corner of Figure 6.22 represents areawise breakup of the selling behavior profile.

Table 6.6: ES Behavior Categorization and Profiling Decision Agent

Name:	ES Behavior Categorization and Profiling Decision Agent
Parent Agent	HCVM Decision Agent, Expert System Agent
Goals:	Determine recruitment manager's defined decision outcomes (e.g., candidate behavioral category in terms of DH, SH, SW, DW, benchmarking, identifying degree of fit and training needs)
Some Tasks:	Infer candidate's selling behavior category Infer candidate's degree of fit for frontline, customer service and sales support jobs Infer candidate's training needs for frontline, customer service and sales support jobs Comparison of benchmark and candidate's profile Infer candidate's training needs based on benchmark profile
Task Constraints:	Unpruned and contradictory raw answers from candidate's on evaluation areas like competition, product, etc.
Precondition:	Candidate's raw scores from Selling Behavior Evaluation Decision Agent
Postcondition:	Candidate Selling behavior category and profile, training needs, degree of fit
Communicates with:	ES Evaluation and Profiling Control Agent, Behavior Profiling media agent
Communication Constructs:	Request: Raw Scores from Behavior Evaluation and Profiling Decision agents Tell: Pruned Scores to Behavior Profiling Media Agent
Linguistic/non-linguistic features:	Raw and pruned scores
External Tools:	Software: Graphic Pie Chart object, Button Object Domain: Competition, customer, product objects
Internal Tools:	Expert System
Actions:	Define rules for pruning candidate's behavior evaluation score Define rules for selling behavior categorization based on recruitment manager's experience and selling behavior model Define rules for determining degree of fit to other jobs corresponding training needs

That is, the upper right hand corner of Figure 6.22 shows the area wise breakup of a candidate's selling behavior as related to the Dominant Hostile (DH) category.

In Figure 6.23 we show a comparison of the candidate's profile (one with low dominant hostile score) with the benchmark profile (one with high dominant hostile score) of a particular organization. The hiring manager is particularly interested in the orientation of the two profiles. That is, are the two profiles parallel or do they cross each other (as in Figure 6.23)? They are less interested in the magnitude of difference between the two profiles (which if required can be deciphered from the Y coordinate dimension of the comparison of profile graph).

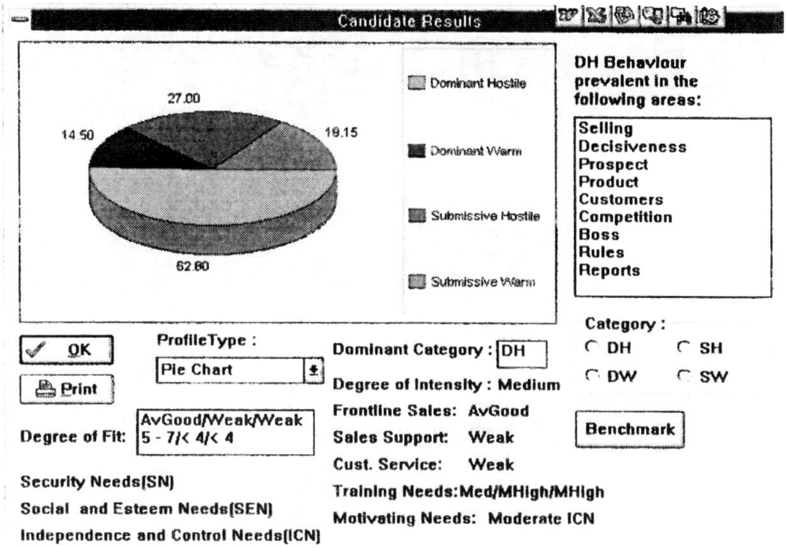

Figure 6.22 Candidate Result Screen (courtesy of Intelligent Software Systems,

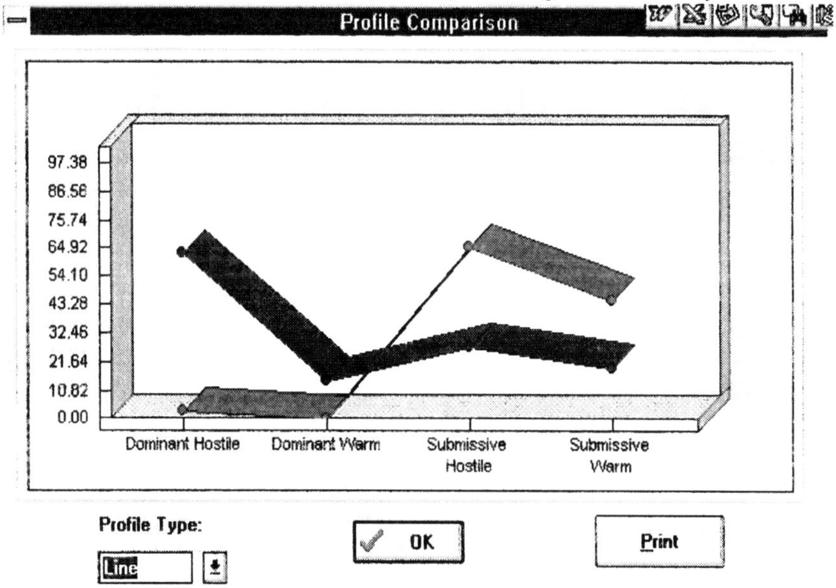

Melbourne Australia

Figure 6.23: Benchmarking of a Candidate's Behavior Profile (courtesy of Intelligent Software Systems, Melbourne, Australia)

5. In sales, the law of the jungle prevails. It's either you or the competitor. You relish defeating your competitors, and fight them hard, using every available weapon.	Behavioral Category:	DH
6. The best hope to outwork and outsell competitors is by keeping abreast of competitive activity and having sound product knowledge of your product.	Behavioral Category:	DW
7. You may not be aggressive otherwise, but when it comes to competition you are just the opposite. You spend good deal of your time to explain to the customer why he should not buy from the competitor.	Behavioral Category:	SH
8. You do not believe in being aggressive towards your competitors. Competitors are people like you and there is room for everybody.	Behavioral Category:	SW

Figure 6.24: Questions Related to the Competition Area

Figure 6.24 shows as an example of the language used for designing the four questions related to the *competition* area. It can be seen that the tone and words used mirror the language used in the selling profession. These questions form part of the *Selling Behavior Evaluation Decision* agent. This agent produces a candidate's selling behavior profile based on raw scores in different categories.

E-SRS is being present used in the industry for recruitment of salesperson, telesales personnel, customer service personnel and sales support personnel.

6.5. Summary

Traditionally, computer-based artifacts have not been a popular choice in human resource management function of an organization. The Internet is seen as a catalyst in development of computer based human resource management systems.

In this chapter we show how Internet can be used as medium for enhancing the geographical reach, reducing costs and improving efficiency and effectiveness of the sales recruitment activity. We describe how an e-business system can be used as an effective recruitment tool for hiring sales persons and overcoming breakdowns in human decision making situation in a sales recruitment activity. The breakdown modeled by e-Sales Recruitment System (SRS) relates to benchmarking the incoming sales candidates with the existing successful salespersons in an organization. Benchmarking has provided the motivation to the hiring/recruitment managers/consultants in the industry to make SRS an integral part of their sales recruitment activity.

References

Bezdek, J.C. 'Pattern Recognition with Fuzzy Objective Function Algorithms,' Advanced Applications in Pattern Recognition, Plenum Press 1981, USA

O'Brien, J., *An Internetworked e-Business Enterprise,* McGraw Hill Publishers, 11th Edition, USA, 2002.

Khosla, R., and Dillon, T., *'An Intelligent Assistant for Improving Sales/Customer Service Performance'* - in IEEE Workshop on Customer Service and Support, San Jose, California, U.S.A, July 1992

Khosla, R. and Dillon, T., *'A Knowledge Based Approach for Recruiting Salespersons',* Sixth Artificial Intelligence Technology Transfer Conference in Industry and Business}, Monterrey, Mexico, Sept. 1993, pp.83-9

Khosla, R., Dillon, T., and Parhar, A., *'Synthesis of Knowledge Based Methodology and Psychology for Recruitment and Training of Salespersons'*, in Lecture Notes in Computer Science (LNCS), Springer-Verlag, 18th German Annual Conference on Artificial Intelligence, Saarbr"ucken, Germany, September 1994

7 CUSTOMER RELATIONSHIP MANAGEMENT AND E-BANKING

7.1. Introduction

Businesses today are using the Internet as a genuine resource for gaining competitive advantage. On-line customization is one useful customer relationship management strategy adopted by e-businesses to add customer value and improve sales of their product and services using the Internet. People are inclined to believe those who have similar interests and living habits. In other words, determining the buying habit of customers on the Internet can benefit both customers and the e-business. From a customer's point of view, identifying customers with similar e-banking product buying habits may help that customer make their decision about a new product. On the other hand, knowing the buying habit of customers can help e-business practitioners to better package their products in an e-banking (or Internet banking) environment and design personalized services oriented towards each individual customer.

In recent years the customer relationship management area has usefully employed the data mining technology for developing customer-centric strategies. The purpose of this chapter is to outline a component based multi-layered multi-agent data mining architecture based on HCVM and describe its application in the area of Internet or e-banking.

The chapter is organized as follows. We firstly provide a brief background to the reader on data mining process and data mining algorithms. We then introduce the data mining strategies as applied on the Internet. We follow that with an outline of a component based multi-agent approach to data mining based on HCVM. We then describe an application of the component-based approach for profiling customer transaction behavior in the Internet or E-banking domain.

7.2. Traditional Data Mining and Knowledge Discovery Process

In the last two decades the digital revolution has invaded business enterprises. Computers have enabled organizations to store gigabytes of data related to stock markets, electricity consumption profiles (Khosla et. al. 2000), troubleshooting and diagnostic data, etc. As outlined by Fayyad and Uthuruswamy (1996a), in scientific endeavors, data represents observations carefully collected about some phenomenon under study. In business, data captures information about critical markets, competitors, and customers. On the other hand, in manufacturing, data captures performance and optimization opportunities, as well as the keys to improving process and troubleshooting problems. The reason organizations store or collect all this data is to enable them to extract some useful knowledge (at a later date!) which can make them more productive, efficient, and competitive. The terms, Knowledge Discovery in Databases (KDD), and Data Mining have emerged in the last five years from this need of extracting useful knowledge. KDD is a nontrivial process of identifying valid, novel, potentially useful, and ultimately understandable knowledge from data (Fayyad et al. 1996b).

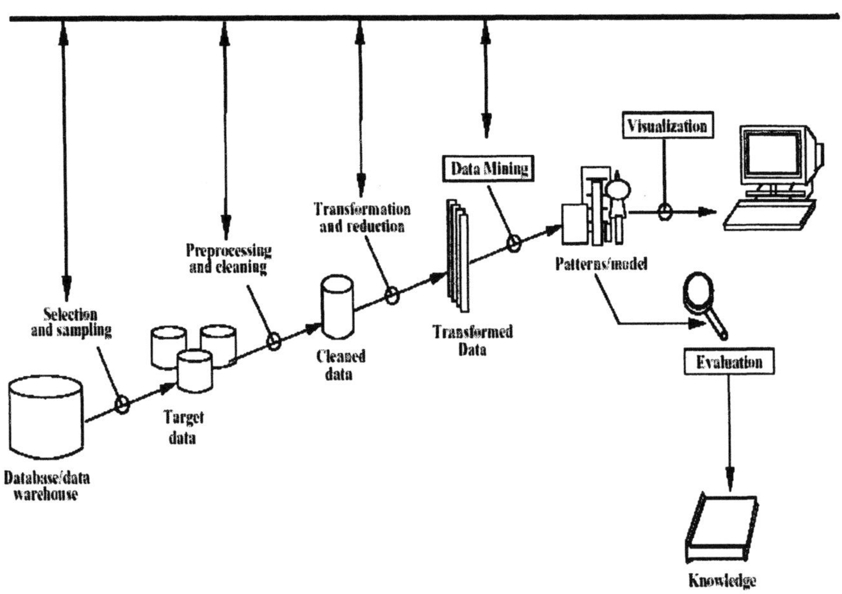

Figure 7.1. The KDD Process © 1996 IEEE

Data mining is a step in the KDD process that consists of applying data analysis process from the customer's viewpoint. The goals of the KDD process can be simply summarization of data or prediction, classification or clustering. That is, the goal of data mining is to obtain useful knowledge collections of data. Such a task is inherently interactive and iterative: one cannot expect to obtain useful knowledge by simply pushing a large amount of data sets into a black box. As a result, a typical data mining system will go through several phases. The phases shown in Figure 7.1 below start with the raw data and finish with the extracted knowledge, and include the following stages:

- *Selection* - selecting or segmenting the data according to some criteria e.g., all those people who own a car. In this way subsets of the data can be determined.
- *Preprocessing* - this is the data cleansing stage where certain information is removed, which is deemed unnecessary or noisy and may unfavorably affect the mined results or may slow down queries. For example, in a time-series prediction domain, the domain expert may consider profiles with abnormal patterns as noisy for the target data set. In other words, if the profile with abnormal pattern is included in the target data set it may unfavorably affect the mined results. In a medical domain, it may be unnecessary to note the sex of a patient when studying pregnancy. Also the data is reconfigured to ensure a consistent format as there is a possibility of inconsistent formats because the data is drawn from several sources e.g. sex may recorded as f or m and also as 1 or 0. Further, strategies for dealing with missing data are also configured at this stage.
- *Transformation* - the data is not merely transferred across but transformed in that overlays may add such as the demographic overlays commonly used in market research. The data is made useable and navigable.
- *Data mining* - this stage is concerned with the extraction of patterns from the data. A pattern can be defined as given a set of facts (data) F, a language L, and some measure of certainty C a pattern is a statement S in L that describes relationships among a subset Fs of F with a certainty c such that S is simpler in some sense than the enumeration of all the facts in Fs.
- *Interpretation and evaluation* - the patterns identified by the system are interpreted into knowledge which can then be used to support human decision-making e.g. prediction and classification tasks, summarizing the contents of a database or explaining observed phenomena.

7.3. Data Mining Algorithms

In this section we briefly outline the statistical, machine learning and soft computing techniques employed for data mining. The reader can find more detailed description of these techniques in Collier et al. al. (1998).

Association Rule Algorithms: An association rule identifies a combination of attribute values or items that occur together with greater frequency than might be expected if the values or items were independent of one-another. The rule association algorithms are grouped under the category of rule association such as Apriori and affinity grouping techniques.

Memory-based Reasoning (MBR) or Case-based Reasoning (CBR): In MBR/CBR systems expertise is embodied in a database of past cases, rather than being encoded in classical rules. Each case typically contains a description of the problem, plus a solution and/or the outcome. The knowledge and reasoning process used by an expert to solve the problem is not recorded, but is implicit in the solution.

Cluster Analysis: Clustering is the task of structuring segmenting a heterogeneous population into a number of more homogenous subgroups or clusters (collier et. al. 1998). Two types of clustering techniques are most commonly used, namely, K-Means and Nearest-Neighbor.

K-means clustering divides data into groups based on their expression patterns. The goal is to produce groups of data with a high degree of similarity within each group and a low degree of similarity between groups.

Nearest Neighbor (more precisely k-nearest neighbor, also k-NN) is a predictive technique suitable for classification models. As the term nearest implies, k-NN is based on a concept of distance, and this requires a metric to determine distances. All metrics must result in a specific number for comparison purposes. Whatever metric is used is both arbitrary and extremely important. It is arbitrary because there is no preset definition of what constitutes a "good" metric. It is important because the choice of a metric greatly affects the predictions. Different metrics, used on the same training data, can result in completely different predictions. This means that a business expert is needed to help determine a good metric.

Decision Trees and Rule Induction Algorithms: A decision tree is generated by dividing records in a data set into disjointed subsets. A number of decision algorithms are used in practice. These include ID3, CART, C4.5, and Chi-squared Automatic Interaction Detection (CHAID) developed by Hartigan (1975). Supervised Learning In Quest (SLIQ) developed by IBM's Quest project team, are some of the commonly used decision tree algorithms.

The Iterative Dichotomiser (ID3) algorithm (Quinlan 1986) is a decision tree building algorithm, which determines the classification of objects by testing the values of their properties. It builds the tree in a top down fashion, starting from a set of objects and a specification of properties. At each node of the tree, a property is tested and the results used to partition the object set. This process is recursively done until the set in a given subtree is homogeneous with respect to the classification criteria - in other words it contains objects belonging to the same category. This then becomes a leaf node. At each node, the property to test is chosen based on theoretic criteria that seek to maximize information gain and minimize entropy. In simpler terms, that property is tested which divides the candidate set into the most homogeneous subsets.

Classification and Regression Trees (CART) basically extends decision tree learning to incorporate numerical values and is able to induce regression trees.

The C4.5 Algorithm is an extension of the basic ID3 algorithm designed by Quinlan to address the following issues not dealt with by ID3:

- avoiding overfitting the data
- determining how deeply to grow a decision tree,
- reduced error pruning,
- rule post-pruning,
- handling continuous attributes (e.g., temperature),
- choosing an appropriate attribute selection measure,
- handling training data with missing attribute values,
- handling attributes with differing costs, and
- improving computational efficiency.

Chi-squared Automatic Interaction Detection (CHAID) is a multivariate segmentation technique which splits up respondents into groups. Supervised Learning In Quest (SLIQ) is a decision tree classifier that can handle both numeric and categorical attributes. SLIQ uses a pre-sorting technique in the tree-growth phase to reduce the cost of evaluating numeric attributes. This sorting procedure is integrated with a breadth-first tree growing strategy to enable SLIQ to classify disk-resident data sets. In addition, SLIQ uses a fast subsetting algorithm for determining splits for categorical attributes. SLIQ also uses a new tree-pruning algorithm based on the Minimum Description Length principle (Baxter et. al, 1994). This algorithm is inexpensive, and results in compact and accurate trees. The combination of these techniques enables SLIQ to scale for large data sets and classify data sets with a large number of classes, attributes, and examples. A further improvement on SLIQ is SPRINT (Scalable PaRallelizable Induction of Decision Trees) which removes all memory restrictions.

Soft Computing Techniques: Artificial neural networks and genetic algorithms are fast becoming popular soft computing techniques for data mining. Their inductive and abductive properties have especially been found useful in time series based energy consumption profiling (Khosla et al. 1997), bioinformatics and numerous other areas.

7.4. Data Mining and the Internet

The Internet consists of both structured data like databases of various formats and unstructured data or semi-structured data like web pages, server logs, etc. The users see the Internet as a way of minimizing their product acquisition cost. Thus they are interested in sourcing the right product and information from the Internet in the minimum possible time. Data mining from the viewpoint of helping Internet users is called Internet content mining. On the other hand, from the perspective of web sponsors, they are more interested in the user access pattern so as to better package and customize their product and services on the Internet. Data mining from this viewpoint is called Internet usage mining.

7.4.1. Internet Content Mining

With the popularity of Internet networking, the search engine has become an indispensable tool for people to get information from the Internet. However, the explosive expansion of the Internet in recent years gives rise to another contrary, serious problem—too much information. Filtering or cutting out unnecessary information from thousands of research results is a new challenge faced by researchers. The difficulty in Internet content mining is the lack of structure and quality control and the heterogeneity permeating the information source on the Internet (Liao1999, Cooley et.al. 1997).

There are two basic approaches for Internet content mining. The first one can be categorized as the database-based approach, which attempts to extend traditional data mining techniques to organize the semi-structured data available on the Internet. The second one is to develop more intelligent tools for information retrieval, such as intelligent agents. These two approaches are described next.

7.4.1.1 Database-Based Approach

Database approaches usually organize or integrate semi-structured or heterogeneous Internet data to structured collections of resources, which then can be processed or analyzed by traditional database querying mechanisms and data mining techniques.

Web-oriented Query Language

Many Web-oriented query languages have been developed. All of them try to extend standard database query languages such as SQL and even semi-natural language to collect data from the Web. Some examples are listed here. W3QL (D. Konopnicki and O. Shmueli 1998) combines structured queries, based on the organization of hypertext documents, and content queries, based on information retrieval techniques. SQUEAL (Ellen Spertus and Lynn Andrea Stein 2000) build a system on top of the most popular structured query language, to make powerful queries on the Web. WebOQL: provides a framework that supports a large class of data restructuring operations. WebLog (L. Lakshmanan, F. Sadri, and I. N. Subramanian 1996): Logic-based query language for restructuring extracted information from Web information sources.

Multilevel Databases

The main idea behind multi-level database approach proposed by several researchers is that the lowest level of the database contains primitive semi-structured information stored in various Web repositories, such as hypertext documents. At the higher level(s), meta data or generalizations are extracted from lower levels and organized in structured collections such as relational or object-oriented databases.

Some examples of this approach are: ARANEUS system (Merialdo et. al 1997) extracts relevant information from hypertext documents and integrates these into higher-level derived Web Hypertexts which are generalizations of the notion of database views; Khosla, et. al. (1996) propose the creation and maintenance of meta-databases at each information providing domain and the use of a global schema for the meta-database; King & Novak (1996) propose the incremental integration of a portion of the schema from each information source, rather than relying on a global heterogeneous database schema; Han, et. al. (1995) use a multi-layered database where each layer is obtained via generalization and transformation operations performed on the lower layers.

In addition to above approaches, researchers already developed some powerful query systems for Extensible Markup Language (XML) such as Ozone (Lahiri et al 1998) and XML-QL (Deutsch et al 1999). Because XML tags are customized and pages more structured than in SQL, these systems are able to support queries that focus more on semantics than syntax.

7.4.1.2 Agent-Based Approach

The agent-based approach is about the development of a system that can autonomously or semi-autonomously discover or collect useful information on behalf of a particular user. Liao (1999) has placed the agent-based Web mining systems into three categories, namely, intelligent search agent, Information Filtering/Categorization and Personalized Web Agents. A brief survey of applications under these three categories has been adapted from Liao (1999) and is described next.

Intelligent Search Agent

Many intelligent Web agents, which are able to search for relevant information using characteristics of a particular domain (and possibly a user profile) to organize and interpret the discovered information, have been developed and made available to the Internet users. Several agent examples such as, Harvest (Brown et. al. 1994), FAQ-Finder (Hammond et. al. 1995), Information Manifold (Kirk et. al. 1995), OCCAM (Kwok et. al. 1996), and ParaSite (Spertus et. al. 1997), are listed here. These all rely either on pre-specified and domain specific information about particular types of documents or on hard coded models of the information sources to retrieve and interpret documents. Other agents, such as ShopBot (Doorenbos et. al. 1996) and ILA (Internet Learning Agent) (Perkowitz et. al. 1995) attempt to interact with and learn the structure of unfamiliar information sources. ShopBot retrieves product information from a variety of vendor sites using only general information about the product domain. ILA, on the other hand, learns models of various information sources and translates these into its own internal concept hierarchy.

Information Filtering/Categorization

A number of agents try to automatically retrieve, filter, and categorize the discovered information by using various information retrieval techniques and characteristics of open hypertext Web documents. Such examples include HyPursuit (Weiss et. al. 1996) and BO (Bookmark Organizer) (Maarek et. al. 1996). HyPursuit creates cluster hierarchies of hypertext documents, and structure an information space by using semantic information embedded in link structures as well as document content to. BO (Bookmark Organizer) combines hierarchical clustering techniques and user interaction to organize a collection of Web documents based on conceptual information.

Personalized Web Agents

Personalized web agents have recently become very popular on the web. Amazon.com are using software from NetPerceptions to personalize the pages it presents to book buyers (Schafer et al. 1999). NetPerceptions try to obtain or learn user preferences and discover Web information sources that correspond to these preferences, and possibly those of other individuals with similar interests using collaborative filtering (Sarwar et al.2001). The information inferences are mainly based on previous personal history and data accumulated from customers with similar attributes. Some other examples of personalized web agents are the WebWatcher (Armstrong et al. 1995), and Syskill & Webert (Pazzani et al. 1996). Syskill & Webert is a system that utilizes user profile and learns to rate Web pages of interest using Bayesian classifier.

The up-to-date example is CMF web agent. The CMF Web Agent (Hellmann 2002) is an application that allows you to monitor the entire web (or as much as is indexed by several popular search engines, anyway) for new pages related to topics of interest. For example, monitor the web for any mention of your new startup company, and display the results as a news list on your company intranet. Alternatively, monitor the net for your own name or email address and keep the results in your private content management portal. This application makes use of the public web search engines (currently Google, http://www.google.com, and AllTheWeb, http://www.alltheweb.com) to detect new content.

7.4.2 Internet Usage Mining

In order to understand and better serve the needs of Web-based applications, Internet usage mining approach tries to get user's Internet access patterns. The key of Internet usage mining is the Internet server log data. By analyzing the log data using data mining techniques, it will be not very difficult to get usage patterns of Internet users. There are two kinds of tools available for Internet usage mining as outlined by Liao (1999). One is user pattern discovery; another is user pattern analysis.

7.4.2.1 User Pattern Discovery

The development of user pattern discovery tools to mine for knowledge from collected data is a sophisticated technique combination from AI, data mining, psychology, and information theory. In Chen et. al. (1996), algorithms are introduced for finding maximal forward references and large reference sequences. These can, in turn, be used to perform various types of user traversal path analysis such as identifying the most traversed paths thorough a Web locality. On the other hand, another team of researchers (Pirolli et. al.1996) use information foraging theory to combine path traversal patterns, Web page typing, and site topology information to categorize pages for easier access by users.

7.4.2.2 User Pattern Analysis

The user pattern analysis involves determination of tools and techniques to understand, visualize, and interpret discovered user access patterns. Examples of such tools include the WebViz system (Pitkow et. al. 1994) for visualizing path traversal patterns and the WEBMINER system (www.webminer.com) which proposes an SQL-like query mechanism for querying the discovered knowledge (in the form of association rules and sequential patterns).

The problem with the data mining techniques described in this section is that they are specific to a domain or specific to a certain data mining problem on the Internet and lack a problem solving approach. In this chapter we adopt a component based multi-layered approach to Internet mining. This approach is motivated by the human-centered approach and consistent problem solving structures/strategies employed by practitioners while designing solutions to complex problems or situations

In this approach we apply the problem solving component of the HCVM, for example, to systematize and structure the Internet mining in terms of information processing and decision making model of web sponsor or e-business manager. As outlined in the earlier chapters the problem solving component forms one of the five layers of a component-based data mining architecture is outlined in the next section. We illustrate the application of the component-based data mining architecture by profiling transaction behavior of Internet users in the Internet banking domain. In the next section we outline a multi-layered component based multi-agent architecture for data mining.

7.5. Multi-layered . Component-based Multi-Agent Distributed Data Mining Architecture

The component-based distributed architecture for data mining is shown in Figure 7.2. As can be seen in Figure 7.2, the distributed data mining architecture is an adaptation of the HCVM developed in chapter 5 The object or data layer of the HCVM is defined as a large database of records. The database could be relational or an object-oriented database. The clerical agent layer of the HCVM has been adapted to a parallel and distributed processing agent layer. The data mining applications in general and real time Internet mining applications in particular invariably require parallel and

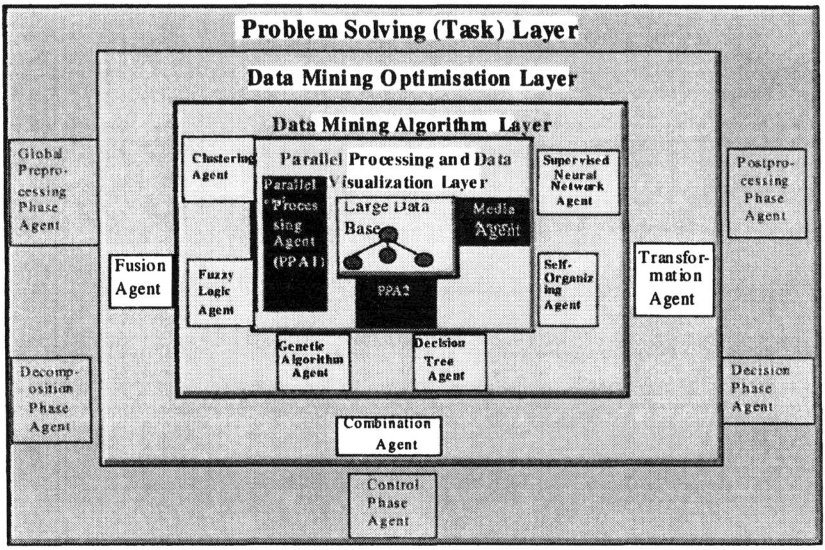

Figure 7.2: Component Based Distributed Multi-Agent Data Mining Architecture

and distributed processing facilities. The data mining algorithm layer in Figure 7.2 consists of intelligent as well as statistical data mining agents used for extracting meaningful patterns, finding associations and similarities in data. The data miming optimization layer shown in Figure 7.2 has its underpinnings in Figure 7.3. It is used for optimizing the performance of the data mining agents both in terms of the quality of their solution (e.g., accuracy) as well as the data mining tasks, which may be optimally handled by more than one data mining agent. The performance and task optimization can occur through fusion, transformation, combination or association (combination of fusion, transformation and combination). For example, GA agent can be used for optimizing the input data used by an artificial neural network agent for prediction.

The final layer, that is, the problem solving layer of Figure 7. 2 can be seen as the humanization layer of a data mining application. Humanization occurs in terms of modeling the tasks of the user (e.g., web sponsor/e-business manager or an Internet customer or user) at a technology independent level. The users tasks are modeled using the problem solving adapters namely, preprocessing, decomposition, control, decision and postprocessing of the HCVM The five problem solving adapters will facilitate structuring of user information as well as facilitate data mining at different levels of abstraction. The five layers thus facilitate a component-based and layered approach for developing Internet based data mining applications

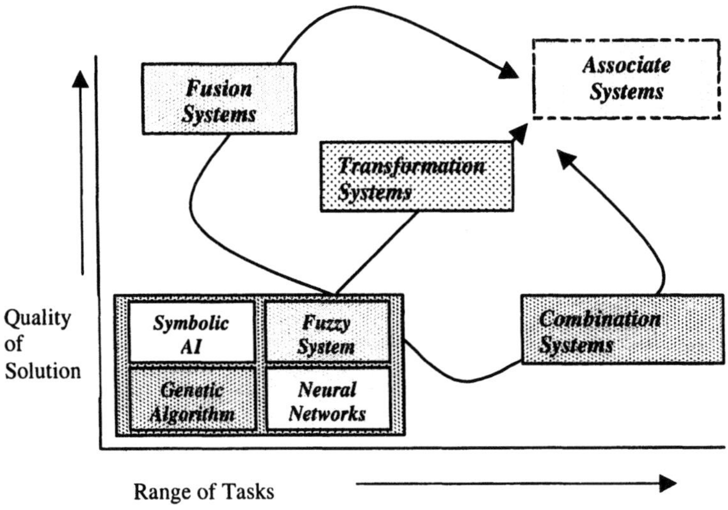

Figure 7.3: Optimization of Performance and Tasks in Data Mining

7.6. Application in e-Banking

The ability of the financial institutions like banks to collect data far outstrips their ability to explore, analyze and understand it. For that reason, in the past five years banks have moved aggressively towards applying data mining techniques especially in the Customer Relationship Management (CRM) area. Given the cost savings with Internet banking, the banks seem now keen to apply data mining techniques to study online transaction behavior of their clients and improve their on line product offerings. Figure 7.4 shows a highly simplified data model of a bank with both Internet and branch (face-to-face) banking facilities.

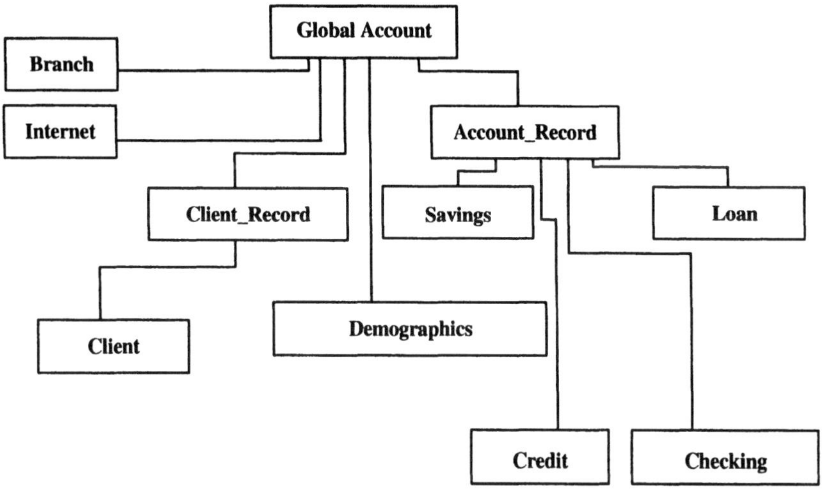

Figure 7.4 : Simplified CRM Model of Banking Domain

In this application we model the CRM aspects of the e-banking domain from a Web sponsor's or an e-business manager's viewpoint using the problem solving agent layer of the data mining architecture in Figure 7.2. We then show the application of the data mining agent and the parallel processing agent layers of the data mining architecture for profiling the on line transaction behavior of e-banking customers.

7.6.1. CRM Model of e-Banking Manager

The decision support model of an e-banking manager in CRM is constructed using the five problem solving adapters of the HCVM. A brief description of these adapters as applied to CRM in an e-banking domain is provided next.

7.6.1.1 Decomposition Phase

The goal of the decomposition phase is to restrict input context and reduce domain complexity. In the e-banking domain it is done by mapping the orthogonal concepts employed by the e-banking manager in CRM area to the decomposition adapter as shown in Figure 7.5.

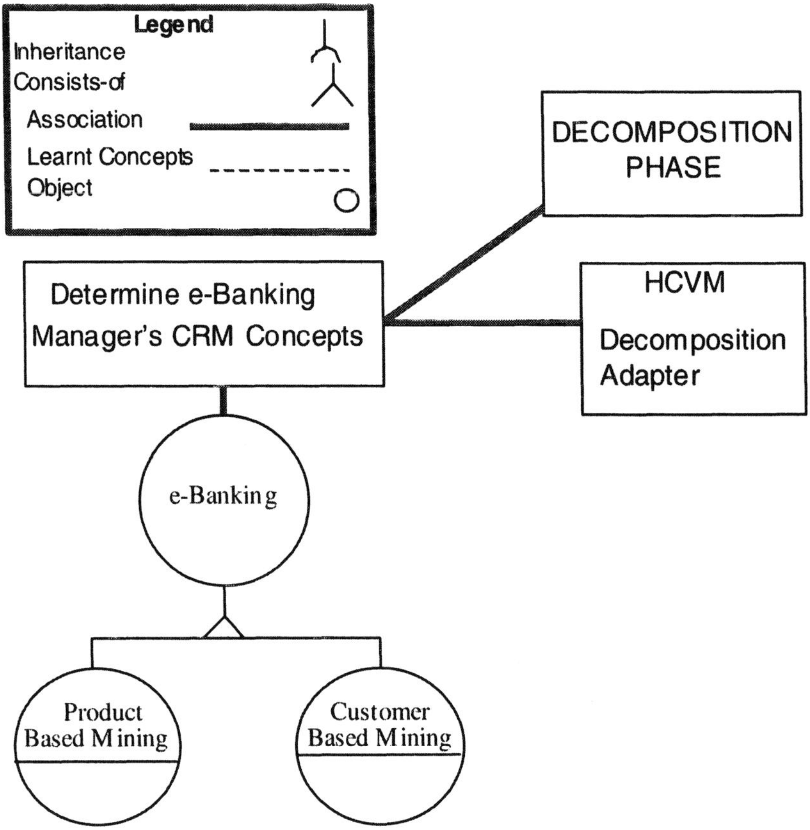

Figure 7.5: Mapping CRM Concepts to HCVM Decomposition Adapter

7.6.1.2 Control Phase

The role of the control phase is to determine decision level concepts of interest to the user. In the e-banking application the role of the control phase adapter is to determine decision level concepts related to product and customer based data mining in the context of CRM. The decision level concepts in the context of CRM are shown in Figure 7.6. The decision level concepts range from customer association, loan similarity and credit card similarity in product based mining, and account transfer pattern to demographic similarity in customer based mining. It may be noted these concepts are functional concepts based on the functional decision support model of the e-banking manager.

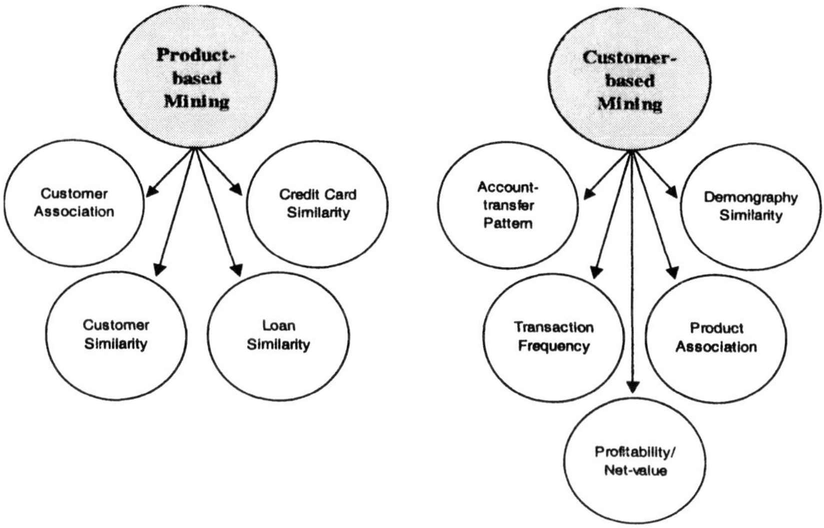

Figure 7.6 : Decision Level CRM Concepts in e-Banking

Preprocessing can occur in any of the three phases (i.e., decomposition, control and decision). In this application the preprocessing adapter is used to filter out the noisy or irrelevant data. For example, web-log data of e-commerce server, unrelated to transaction data is removed at the preprocessing stage.

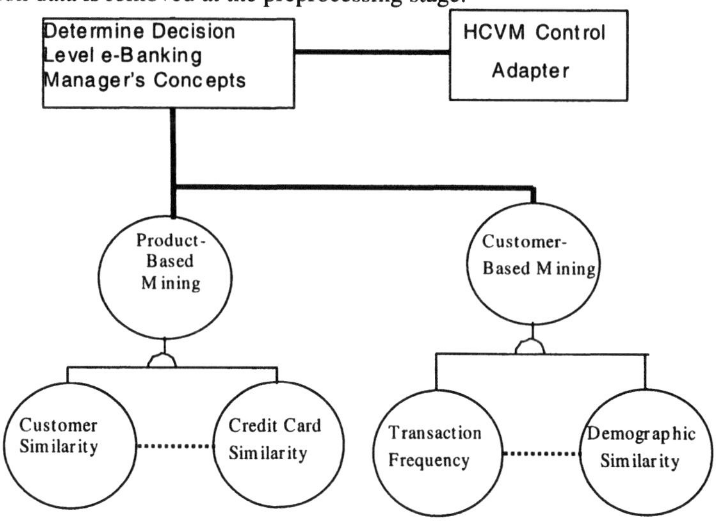

Figure 7.7: Mapping HCVM Control Adapter to e-Banking Application

A sample mapping of the HCVM control adapter with the e-banking task and concepts is shown in Figure 7.7.

7.6.1.3 Decision Phase

In the decision phase, we must identify the desired outcomes for the e-banking manager. That is, we must determine the decision instances or events of specific interest to the user. For example, an e-banking manager is interested to find out similarity among customers in terms of combination of bank products they purchase from the bank. This will facilitate on-line customization of bank products and higher profitability. On the other hand, by determining the transaction frequency of their customers, the bank can determine transaction costs to different type of customers as well as determine whether existing transaction costs need to be increased or decreased. Figure 7.8 shows a sample mapping of these concepts with the HCVM decision adapter.

The postprocessing adapter like the preprocessing adapter can be used in any of three phases (i.e., decomposition, control and decision). In the decision phase the postprocessing adapter is used to integrate and summarize the product combination and transaction frequency results for the e-banking manager.

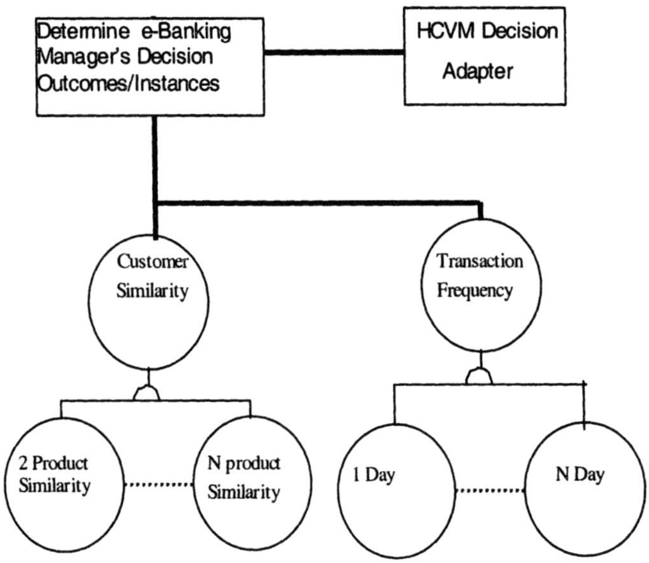

Figure 7.8: Mapping HCVM Decision Adapter to e-Banking Application

7.6.2 Agent Design and Implementation

In this section we outline the agent design of the data mining and parallel processing. An overview of the agent based design architecture is shown

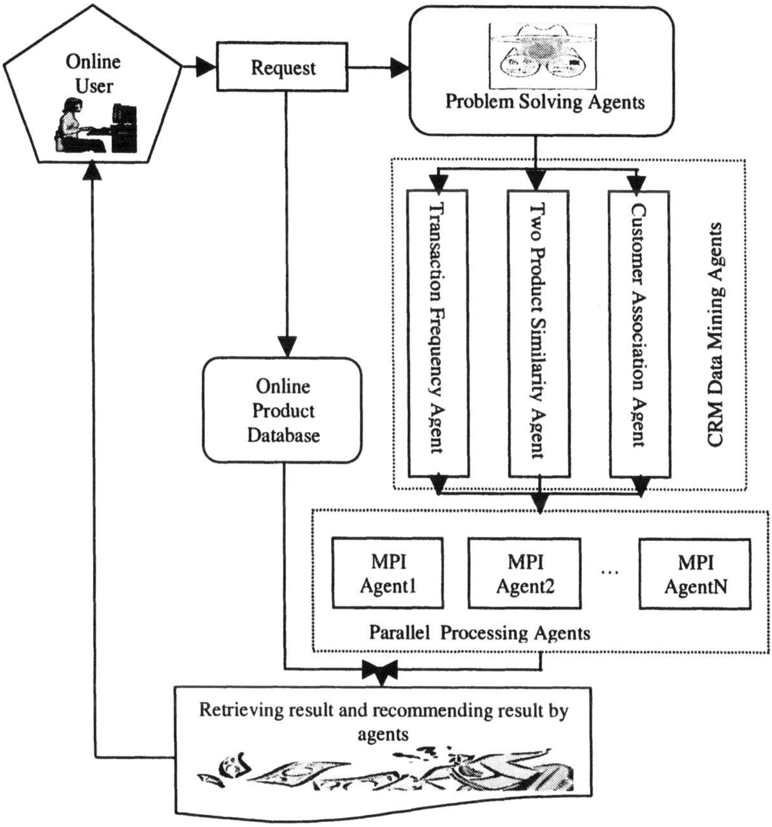

Figure 7.9: e-Banking Application Architecture

in Figure 7.9.

The agent definitions of agents in the problem solving agent layer, data mining agent layer and parallel processing layer are shown in Tables 7.1, 7.2 and 7.3 respectively. The *Two Product Similarity* agent is a decision phase problem solving agent. The *Nearest Neighbor* agent is a clustering agent of the data mining agent layer.

On-line applications must respond to their users in a very short time—usually less than 30 seconds. In addition, currently available data on e-commerce websites increase in the order of a Gigabyte on a weekly or monthly basis. Some have reached Terabyte and even Petabyte (Düllmann 1999). High Performance Computing (HPC) becomes a necessity in these situations because of their super computing ability in terms of memory, multiprocessors, and secondary storage. For these reasons, we have implemented the e-banking application using 128 processor Compaq Alpha Server (Alpha) SC, with 64 Gbyte of memory and 1.4 Terabyte of disk space on a Tru64 UNIX 5.1 Operating System .

Table 7.1: Agent Definition of Two Product Similarity Decision Agent

Name :	Two Product Similarity Agent
Parent Agent	HCVM Decision Agent ,
Goals:	Develop optimal cluster model based on customers with two product similarity
Some Tasks:	Select data mining agent to learn product clusters Select data visualization tool Present product clusters to e-banking manager
Task Constraints:	Optimal similarity model, 2 million data records
Precondition:	Preprocessed financial data
Postcondition:	Identification of 2 product clusters.
Communicates with:	Nearest Neighbor Clustering agent, Fusion Agent, Product Similarity Control Agent, e-Banking Multimedia Visualization Agent
Communication Constructs:	Command: Nearest Neighbor Agent Tell: e-Banking media agent
Linguistic/non-linguistic features:	Saving, credit and loan data
External Tools:	Software: Histogram Graphic object, Button Object Domain: Bank data Model and database
Actions:	Invoke nearest neighbor clustering agent Collect results from nearest neighbor clustering agent

Table 7.2: Agent Definition of Nearest Neighbor Clustering Agent

Name :	Nearest Neighbor Clustering Agent
Parent Agent	Clustering Agent,
Goals:	Learn two product clusters
Some Tasks:	Perform nearest neighbor to learn 2 product cluster Determine similarity coefficients
Task Constraints:	Homogeneous clusters
Precondition:	Preprocessed financial data for saving, loan and credit product data
Postcondition:	Cross-validated 2 product cluster model.
Communicates with:	Nearest Neighbor Clustering agent, MPI parallel Processing Agent, Two Product Similarity Decision Agent, e-Banking Multimedia Agent
Communication Constructs:	Command: MPI Parallel Processing Agent Tell: e-Banking media agent
Linguistic/non-linguistic features:	Saving, credit, and loan data, cluster data
Internal Tools	Nearest neighbor algorithm
External Tools:	Domain: Bank data model and database
Actions:	Change learning parameters Invoke MPI parallel process agent Collect results from MPI parallel process

Table 7.3: Agent Definition of Nearest Neighbor Clustering Agent

Name :	MPI Parallel Processing Agent
Parent Agent	Parallel Processing Agent
Goals:	Process financial data in minimum time
Some Tasks:	Determine optimum number of parallel processes Collate results from N-1 Processes
Task Constraints:	Minimal processing, uniform load distribution among processes
Precondition:	Dedicated N-1 processes available. Readable preprocessed product transaction data
Postcondition:	Collated processed results from N-1 processes in optimum time.
Communicates with:	Nearest Neighbor Clustering agent, N-1 MPI Parallel Processing Agents,
Communication Constructs:	Command: N- 1 MPI Parallel Processing Agents
Linguistic/non-linguistic features:	Saving, credit, and loan data
Internal Tools	MPI algorithm
External Tools:	Domain: Bank data model and database
Actions:	Invoke N - 1MPI parallel process agents Assign financial data to different processes

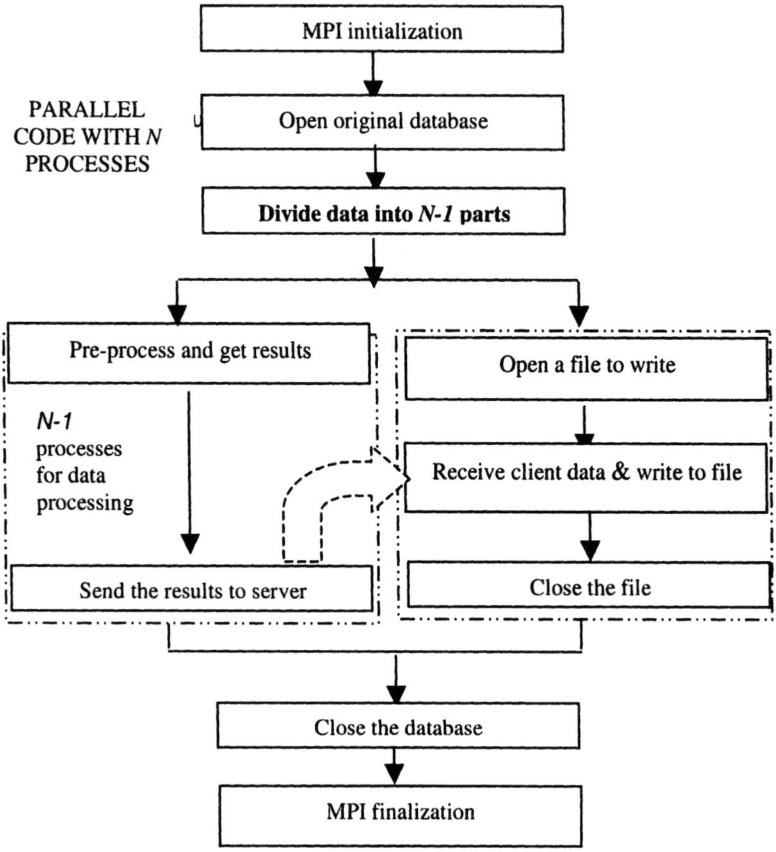

Figure 7.10: MPI Implementation Agent

We have used MPI (Gropp et al. 1999) command to divide the available data and feed to different processes in a multi-processor environment. The MPI Parallel Processing agent shown in Table 7.3 is used to collate data mining results from N-1 processes. The MPI implementation architecture used by the *MPI Parallel Processing* agent is shown in Figure 7.10.

7.7. Data Mining Implementation Results

The transaction frequency, customer association and product similarity agents in Figure 7.9 are decision phase agents of the HCVM problem solving agent layer and employ the services of data mining agents like clustering agent shown in Figure 7.2.

7.7.1. Transaction Frequency

Frequency of transaction occurrence for customer can be interpreted in different ways such as frequent repetition or regularity of customer or buying patterns of customer. Table 7.4 shows sample results calculated from 1056320 database transactions. The "av_trsf_in" and av_trsf_out" fields stand for average transactions involving transfer of money into all the accounts and average transactions involving transfer of money out of all accounts.

Table 7.4: Sample Results of Transaction Frequency of Customers

Client_id	account_id	district_id	frequency	av_trsf_in	av_trsf_out	tot_trans	last_bal
31	25	68	3.991	18224	7491	274	30199
458	378	68	3.845	19252	7866	344	38965
2141	1766	28	3.901	10458	2855	483	45731
2809	2322	33	3.799	13577	4383	460	16988
3984	3293	1	3.984	23878	5768	155	65249
4620	3834	54	3.971	7112	2156	665	30658
4621	3834	54	3.971	7112	2156	665	30658
7195	5952	50	3.806	18509	4430	628	72327
8667	7181	77	3.881	12375	4157	296	83607
9721	7861	34	3.899	9673	2559	414	90366

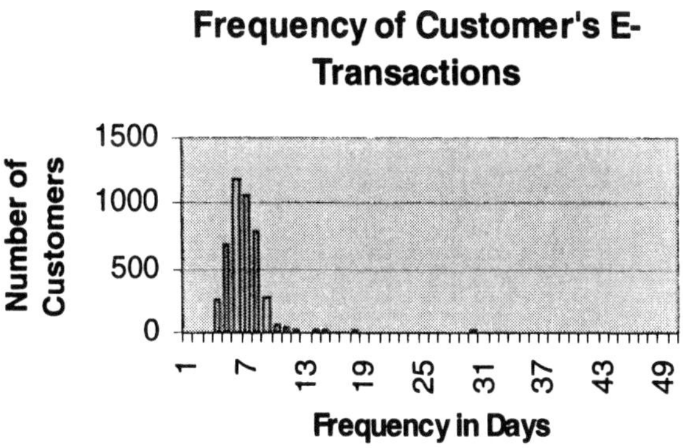

Figure 7.11: Visualization of Buying Frequency of Customers

It can be seen from Figure 7.11 that:

- there are 9 transactions, which occur frequently between 3-4 days. Now we can determine which clients are frequent. There are the ten clients who repeat transaction after 3-4 days. There are ten clients instead of 9 because there is one account id 3834 that has two users.

- the average transaction frequency for most customers is 6-7 days (Figure 7.11).
- calculations show that the percentage of people whose transaction are between four to nine days accounts for more than 80% of all customers in the site.

7.7.2. Product Similarity

The clustering agent is used to determine clusters of customers with similar transactional behavior. The loan account and credit account transaction records shown in Table 7.5 have been used to cluster similarities in two product transaction behavior. The fields "Loan_Dur" and "Loan-Stat"`stand for Loan duration and Loan status repsectively.

Table 7.5: Loan Account and Credit Card Transactions

Account_id	Card_Type	Av_Trans	Balance	Loan_Amt	Loan_Dur	Loan_Stat
790	1	7559	28826	208128	48	2
1843	1	4922	31652	105804	36	1
2167	1	8557	34109	170256	24	1
2824	2	5213	38281	50460	60	3
3050	1	7280	51572	82896	12	1
3166	1	5657	23730	177744	48	4
4337	1	11133	46132	51408	24	1
4448	1	6946	36681	192744	36	1
4894	1	9070	43671	117024	24	1

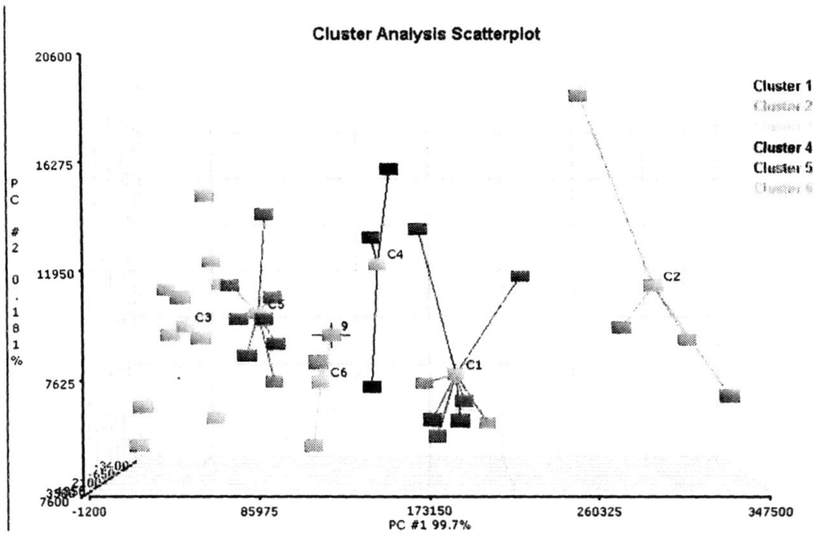

Figure 7.12: Visualization of Two Product Similarity Clusters

The cluster visualization is shown in Figure 7.12. Figure 7.13 shows visualization of similar transaction behavior across all transactions as summarized in Table 7.6.

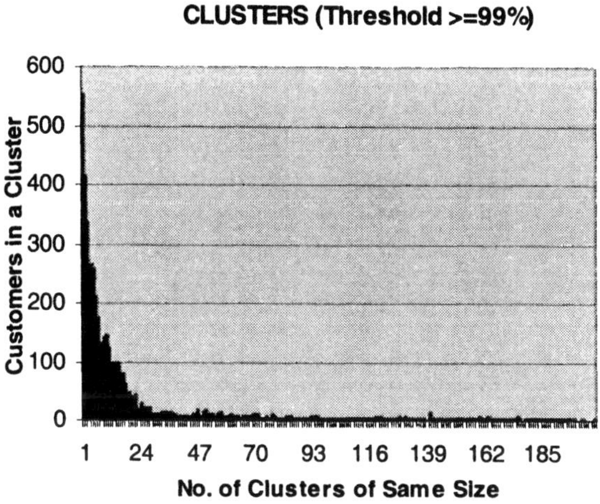

7.13: Number of Customers in a Cluster *vs* Cluster Size

Table 7.6: Summarized Customer Transactions

acc_id	frequency	av_trsf_in	av_trsf_out	Tot_tran	last_bal	Tot_trsf in&out	tot_trs in	Tot_trsf out
2322	3.799479	13576.57	4528.82	460	16988	62	116	344
5952	3.805882	18509.46	4874.40	628	72327	65	134	494
378	3.844828	19251.74	8066.29	344	38965	50	103	241
7181	3.880851	12375.49	4429.83	296	83607	37	83	213
7861	3.898844	9672.64	2559	414	90366	44	94	320

In conf	Out conf	mse
0.53	0.18	13.20
0.49	0.13	16.51
0.49	0.21	10.93
0.45	0.17	10.78
0.47	0.14	18.89

We can observe from Figure 7.13 that the largest cluster consists of about 550 customers and the cluster size is less than two (i.e., these clusters have customers with no similar interests). Further, the term "Threshold >= 99%" in Figure 7.13 means that the similarity coefficient of customers within a cluster is greater than or equal to 99 percent. In Table 7.6 , the fields "acc-id," av_trsf_in," av_trsf_out," "Tot_trsf," "In_conf," Out_conf," and "mse" stand for account_id, average money transferred into accounts, average money transferred out of accounts, total number of transfers, transfer in confidence, transfer out confidence and mean standard deviation of average frequency (frequency field) of internet banking transaction.

7.7.3. Customer Association

Customer Association agent determines the likelihood of association between two attributes, products or events. We list below some of the associations between customer transactions and customer demographics, customer account balance, loan transactions and credit card transactions.

- More transactions are done from the district where there are more inhabitants.
- More transactions are did by those clients whose average salary is also high.
- There are 10 clients who have both minus a/c balance and bad loans.
- We have 39 customers who have minus a/c balance. Out of them above 11 customers either have bad loans or credit card.
- Most of the customers used credit card for household payments.

7.7.4. Parallel Computing Performance

MPI Parallel Processing agents have been used to execute the decision agents. The transaction records in the various product and customer demographic databases are distributed among various processes and results are collated by the server process as shown in Figure 7.10. Figure 7.14 shows the speedup of parallel computing performance. It can be seen from Figure 7.14 that the execution speed of the e-banking application is less than 3 seconds if more than 12 processes are used. Therefore, parallel computing is suitable to the real-time requirement of online banking. There is no reduction in execution time after the 16th process. Process number 1 has not been plotted, as it is the server process.

7.8. Summary

This chapter models data mining as a part of a multi-layered multi-agent intelligent decision support architecture rather than as a stand alone technology. The multi layered multi-agent intelligent decision support architecture is applied in the CRM area of e-banking. The architecture humanizes the data mining process by adopting a multi-layered component-based approach. In this approach the problem solving or task layer of the HCVM is used to model the tasks and decision outcomes from an e-banking manager's perspective. This layer is technology independent. The lower level agent layers like distributed processing and visualization agent layer, data mining agent layer and optimization agent layer are used for parallel processing of 2 million customer transaction records, visualization of results, selection and modeling of data mining agents, and optimization of performance of the data mining agents. The agent modeling, design and implementation of the five layers of the data mining architecture are illustrated with the help of an e-banking application in terms of identifying on-line customer transaction frequency, similar product and transaction behavior, association rules between customer demographics and customer transactions. Parallel computing results on a 128 processor Compaq Alpha Server (Alpha) SC are also reported.

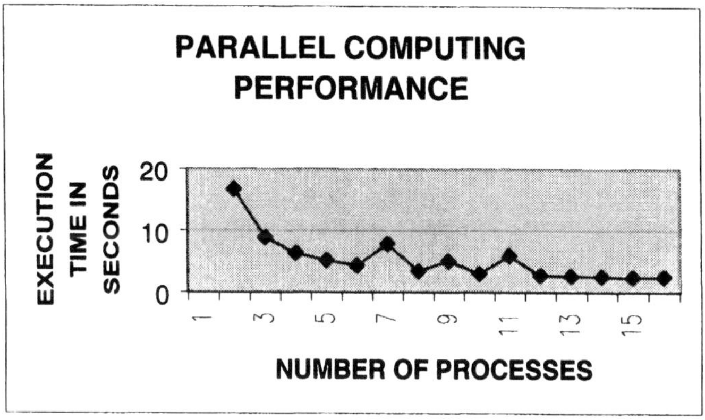

Figure 7.14: Speedup of Parallel Computing Performance

References

Armstrong R., Freitag D., Joachims T. & Mitchell T., (1995) "Webwatcher: A learning apprentice for the world wide web,". *in Proc. AAAI Spring Symposium on Information Gathering from Heterogeneous, Distributed Environments.*

Baxter, R.A., and Oliver, J.J. (2002), "MDL and MML: Similarities and Differences," Technical Report – TR 94/207, Dept. of Computer Science, Monash University, Aiustralia

Brown C. M., Danzig B. B., Hardy D., Manber, U. and Schwartz, M. F., (1994), "The harvest information discovery and access system," in *Proc. 2nd International World Wide Web Conference.*

Chen M.S., Park, J.S. and Yu P.S. (1996). "Data mining for path traversal patterns in a web environment," in *Proceedings of the 16th International Conference on Distributed Computing Systems*, pages 385—392.

Cooley, R., Srivastava, J., Mobasher, B., (1997),"Web Mining: Information and Pattern Discovery on the World Wide Web," *Proceedings of the 9th IEEE International Conference on Tools with Artificial Intelligence (ICTAI'97)*, November 1997. http://citeseer.nj.nec.com/cooley97web.html

December, John (1995) *Challenges for Web Information Providers in The World Wide Web*, Unleashed, Sams Publishing

Deutsch Alin, Fernandez Mary, Florescu Daniela, Levy Alon, and Suciu Dan, (1999), "A Query Language for XML,". *Eighth International Conference on the World-Wide Web.* Elsevier Science B.V., May..

Doorenbos R. B., Etzioni, O. and Weld D. S. (1996) "A scalable comparison shopping agent for the world wide web," *Technical Report 96-01-03*, University of Washington, Dept. of Computer Science and Engineering.

Düllmann D., "Petabyte databases," SIGMOD'99, ACM, 1999

Gropp William, Lusk Ewing, and Skjellum Anthony., (2000)., *Using MPI Portable Parallel Programming with Message-Passing Interface* second edition,The MIT press Cambridge, Massachusetts London England,

Hammer J., GarciaMolina H., Cho J., Aranha R., and Crespo A.. (1997), "Extracting semi-structured information from the Web,". In *Proceedings of the Workshop on Management of Semistructured Data,* Tucson, Arizona, May .

Hammond, K. Burke R., Martin, C. and Lytinen S., (1995), " Faq-finder: A case-based approach to knowledge navigation," In *Working Notes of the AAAI Spring Symposium: Information Gathering from Heterogeneous, Distributed Environments.* AAAI Press, 1995.

Hellmann Doug (2002). CMF Web Agent. Retrieved from *http://www.zope.org/Members/hellmann/CMFWebAgent* on 26 September 2002

Khosla I., Kuhn B., and Soparkar N.(1996), "Database search using informatiuon mining," In *Proc. of 1996 ACM-SIGMOD Int. Conf. on Management of Data.*

Khosla R. and Dillon T., Engineering Intelligent Hybrid Multi-Agent Systems, Kluwer Academic Publishers, MA, USA, 2000, 425 pages.

Khosla R., Sethi I. and Damiani E., Intelligent Multimedia Multi-Agent Systems: A Human-Centerd Approach, Kluwer Academic Publishers, MA, USA, 2000, 333 pages

Khosla Rajiv and Li Qiubang (2002), Component-based distributedarchitecture with Fuzzy Application in Electrical Power.

King R. and. Novak M. Supporting information infrastructure for distributed, heterogeneous knowledge discovery. In Proc. SIGMOD 96 Workshop on Research Issues on Data Mining and Knowledge Discovery, Montreal, Canada,1996.

Kirk, T. Levy A. Y., Sagiv Y., and Srivastava D. The information manifold. In *Working Notes of the AAAI Spring Symposium: Information Gathering from Heterogeneous, Distributed Environments.* AAAI Press, 1995.

Konopnicki David and Shmueli Oded (1998). "WWW Information Gathering: The W3QL Query Language and the W3QS System.," *ACM Transactions on Database Systems,* September 1998.

Kwok C. and Weld D. (1996) "Planning to gather information". In *Proc. 14th National Conference on AI.*

Lakshmanan L., Sadri F., and. Subramanian I. N., (1996) "A declarative language for querying and restructuring the web," In *Proc. 6th International Workshop on Research Issues in Data Engineering: Interoperability of Nontraditional Database Systems (RIDE-NDS'96),* 1996.

Li Qiubang and Khosla Rajiv, (2002) "Intelligent Agent-Based Framework for Mining Customer Buying Habit in E-Commerce," In *Proceeding of Fourth International Conference on Enterprise Information Systems.* Page 1016-1022, April 2002.

Liao Weidong.(1999) "Data Mining on the Internet," retrieved from *http://trident.mcs.kent.edu/~javed/DL/surveys/IAD99s-datamining/* on September 20, 2002

Maarek Y. S. and Ben Shaul. I.Z. (1996) "Automatically organizing bookmarks per content," In *Proc. of 5th International World Wide Web Conference.*

Merialdo P. Atzeni P., Mecca G., (1997), "Semistructured and structured data in the web: Going back and forth," *In Proceedings of the Workshop on the Management of Semistructured Data (in conjunction with ACM SIGMOD).*

Pazzani M., Muramatsu J. & Billsus D., Syskill & Webert: (1996), "Identifying interesting web sites," *In Proc. AAAI Spring Symposium on Machine Learning in Information Access.* Portland, Oregon.

Pazzani, M., Muramatsu, J. & Billsus, D., (1996). Syskill & ebert:" Identifying interesting web sites," *In Proc. AAAI Spring Symposium on Machine Learning in Information Access.* Portland, Oregon.

Perkowitz M. and Etzioni O.(1995) "Category translation: learning to understand information on the Internet," In *Proc. 15th International Joint Conference on AI*, pages 930--936, Montral, Canada.

Pirolli P., Pitkow J., and Rao R. (1996) "Silk from a sow's ear: Extracting usable structures from the web," In *Proc. of 1996 Conference on Human Factors in Computing Systems (CHI-96)*, Vancouver, British Columbia, Canada.

Pitkow J. and. Bharat Krishna K. (1994) "Webviz: A tool for world-wide web access log analysis," In *First International WWW Conference*.

Sarwar Badrul, Karypis, George Konstan Joseph, & Reidl John (2001), "Item-based collaborative filtering recommendation algorithms," *The tenth international World Wide Web conference on World Wide Web*. pp. 285 – 295.

Sarwar, Badrul, Karypis, George, Konstan, Joseph & Reidl, John, (2001). "Item-based collaborative filtering recommendation algorithms,". *The tenth international World Wide Web conference on World Wide Web*. pp. 285 – 295

Schafer J. Ben., Konstan Joseph & Riedl John, (1999) "Recommender Systems in E-Commerce," *In Proceedings of the ACM E-Commerce 1999 conference.*

Spertus E. (1997). "Parasite: mining structural information on the web," In *Proc. of 6th International World Wide Web Conference.*

Spertus Ellen and Stein Lynn Andrea (2000). "Squeal: A structured query language for the Web," In *Proceedings of the 9 th International World Wide Web Conference*, Amsterdam, Netherlands, May 2000.

Weiss R., Velez B., Sheldon, M. A. Namprempre C., Szilagyi P,. Duda A., and Gifford D. K..(1996) "Hypursuit: a hierarchical network search engine that exploits content-link hpertexxt clustering," In *Hypertext'96: The Seventh ACM Conference on Hypertext*, 1996

Zaiane O. R. and Han J.. (1995) "Resource and knowledge discovery in global information systems: A preliminary design and experiment,". In *Proc. of the First Int'l Conference on Knowledge Discovery and Data Mining*, pages 331--336, Montreal, Quebec, 1995

8 HCVM BASED CONTEXT-DEPENDENT DATA ORGANIZATION FOR E-COMMERCE

8.1 Introduction

Electronic Commerce (EC) can be broadly seen as the application of information technology and telecommunications to create virtual *trading networks* where goods and services are sold and purchased.

A number of software architectures have been proposed for supporting such trading networks in the past few years; in Hands et al. (1998) some of them are presented, addressing issues such as sales, ordering and delivery of products in the framework of the global Internet.

Besides greatly increasing the efficiency and the effectiveness of traditional commerce, EC techniques stimulated interest in new distribution techniques for multimedia digital *content*.

Interestingly, experience has shown that transition between physical products and digital ones is usually gradual rather than abrupt. E-commerce transactions involving so-called *smart products* (Figure 8.1) often require transfer or presentation of some sort of digital content to the customer in addition to the delivery of a conventional product or service.

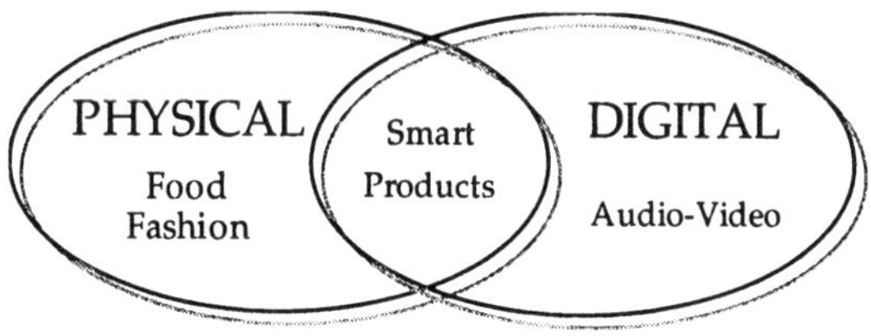

Figure 8.1. From physical to digital products

Digital content is conceptually very different from traditional physical products, being characterized by an increased interactivity and the possibility of multiple uses.

Also, digital content is seldom autonomous; rather, it needs to be executed (or displayed) using suitable devices. Figure 8.2 shows the main features of digital content fruition when compared to the consumption of traditional products.

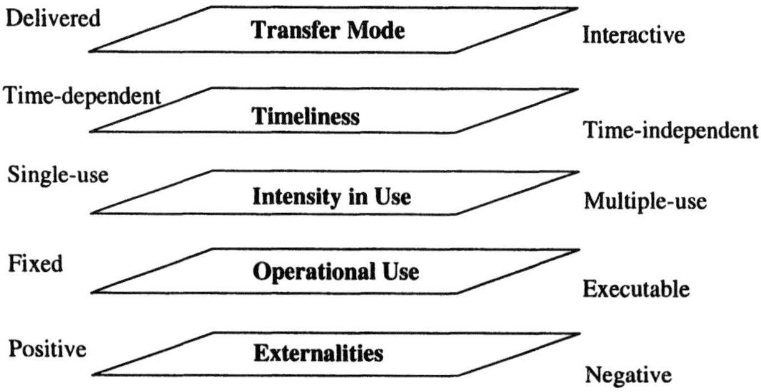

Figure 8.2 Features of the fruition of digital products

It is now widely acknowledged that Internet-based trading networks present a number of differences with respect to the linear *supply chains* of traditional commerce. First of all, the nature of interaction is different: Traditional supply chains were based on stable, long-lasting business relationships, while EC trading networks allow and indeed encourage a higher rate of change in commerce relations, causing customers to frequently change suppliers on the basis of short-term business opportunities.

It is widely acknowledged that this ever-changing business environment requires that content offered on the Internet be highly adaptive, even more so in comparison with other communication channels such as cable television. New user interfaces and devices keep emerging, the diversity of users is increasing, machines are acting more and more on behalf of humans, and Internet activities are becoming possible for a wider range of business, leisure, education, and research activities.

To achieve the high flexibility that this scenario requires, management of Internet content must be done at a much finer detail of granularity than traditional Web-based systems can provide. For example, content needs to be broken down into *tagged information items,* equipped with *metadata* providing enough contextual information.

Such semi-structured representation of context makes it possible to effectively combine and render data in the most appropriate way for the specific partners and tasks. Throughout the chapter, we shall refer to this technique as *context-dependent* content processing. The flexibility features of context-dependent content management are essential for an efficient e-business environment.

In this chapter we will discuss how semi-structured, XML-based data model can be exploited to create a *context-dependent* management of information. As we will see, XML-based metadata may enhance e-business systems flexibility, and new standards are emerging, such as the Semantic Web approach advocated by the World Wide Web Council (Berners-Lee, Hendler, and Lassila, 2001). However, we shall not commit to the Semantic Web approach nor to a specific metadata format; rather we shall discuss in some detail how XML metadata should be used to ensure e-commerce systems are human-centered. We outline a human-centered (as against *technology-centered*) approach to e-business, exploiting the *Human-Centered Virtual Machine* (HCVM) layered architecture.

The chapter is structured as follows: after this Introduction, the next section introduces the concept of context-dependent data management in human-centered e-commerce systems. It is followed by description of XML based context modeling and XML schema, and their integration with the client side context model based on HCVM. It includes a fuzzy agent based computation for flexible access to context information. Finally, a sample interaction with our context-aware e-business environment is outlined.

8.2 Context-dependent Data Management

In the past few years, several research groups have investigated information for electronic commerce brokering and some preliminary evaluation of agent-based technology was attempted with respect to that information (Connolly 1995; Maes et al. 1999). Recent developments, however, suggest a new assessment of the area's perspective.

The basic assumption we will rely on throughout the chapter is that each agent involved in e-commerce transactions operates in some sort of *context* (Almeida, Ribeiro and Ziviani 1999). Such context may consist in a complete *model of the market* expressed in a suitable formal language or just in some useful metadata about the environment the agent is operating in.

Generally speaking, context metadata is only loosely related to usual supply-side product classification; rather, it may be built cooperatively by the supplier, the customer agent itself or by suitable brokers as shown in Figure 8.3. Agent-based technologies help buyers to reduce search costs, find better matching products and gain efficiencies over physical market searches.

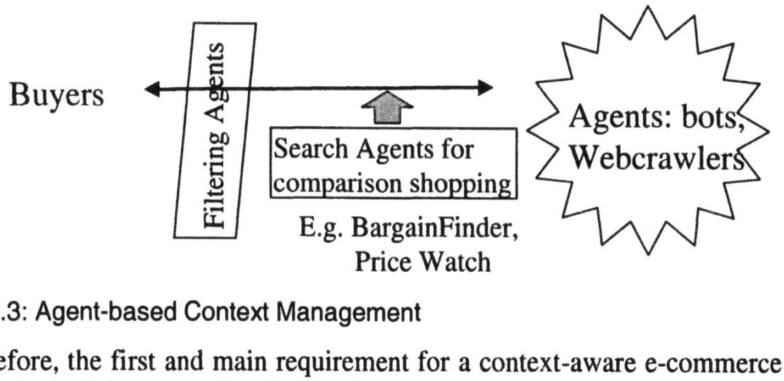

Figure 8.3: Agent-based Context Management

Therefore, the first and main requirement for a context-aware e-commerce system is to be able to fully comprehend available metadata and utilize them to shape content. The recently proposed notion of a *Semantic Web* relies on standard formats and common ontologies for metadata representation and sharing. Here, we use the HCVM approach to discuss simple, human-centered techniques aimed at extracting and organizing context information available in the form of heterogeneous XML documents coming from different sites, dealing flexibly with differences in structure and tag vocabulary.

8.2.1. Context Representation in E-Commerce Transactions

The purpose of context-aware data organization and management techniques is twofold. First of all, context-aware techniques are aimed at producing and maintaining accurate descriptions of customers' needs and of the context in which each transaction takes place, fostering the overall readability and effectiveness of e-business transactions. Secondly, context-aware data management should ensure the correct organization and presentation of the transaction's content.

Data models currently used for information' representation range from completely unstructured to fully structured models, such as the object oriented models (Bailin, 1989). Basically, context information can be represented in three ways:

- *Formal specifications* that define context by means of formal languages, e.g., description logic-based ones;
- *Structured data items* that illustrate context via object-oriented class hierarchies and their relationships. Semantic Web *ontology based* approach is considered by some as an evolution of the structured one (Fernandez, Gomez-Perez, and Juristo, 1997);
- *Textual documents* that use natural language.

While formal specifications of context are conceptually very important, few e-business or e-commerce developers, and virtually no users are familiar with formal notations. Surveys indicate that even the adoption of a structured data model for e-business metadata is still the exception rather than the rule. Unfortunately, lack of a simple and well-documented methodology has historically prevented many companies from adopting any kind of context representation and management policy when designing and implementing their information systems.

However, in recent times the ability of managing fast changes in context information turned out to be essential for small companies' survival and success, especially in Customer Relations Management (CRM) applications. Even for extremely well focused companies, volunteer efforts at knowledge sharing are often not enough, due to high personnel turnover. Our goal in this chapter is to define a technique able to support different notions of context according to changing application needs.

Namely, we shall describe a flexible context representation and management technique based on the eXtensible Markup Language (XML) semi-structured data model.

8.2.2 Human-Centered Context Modeling

Figure 8.4 shows how the HCVM framework can be straightforwardly instantiated in the case of XML-based context modeling. The information of the *object or data layer* on which HCVM distributed processing layer's agents operate is now encoded as semi-structured XML data, whose data types are defined via a suitable XML Schema (outlined in section 8.3).

In principle, nothing prevents using XML also as a data encoding format (i.e., in order to serialize the digital content); indeed, as we shall see, using XML Schema for context representation even encourages XML-based encoding of data. In this chapter, however, we focus on metadata rather than on content, as we are particularly interested in XML-based context representation in the context of HCVM.

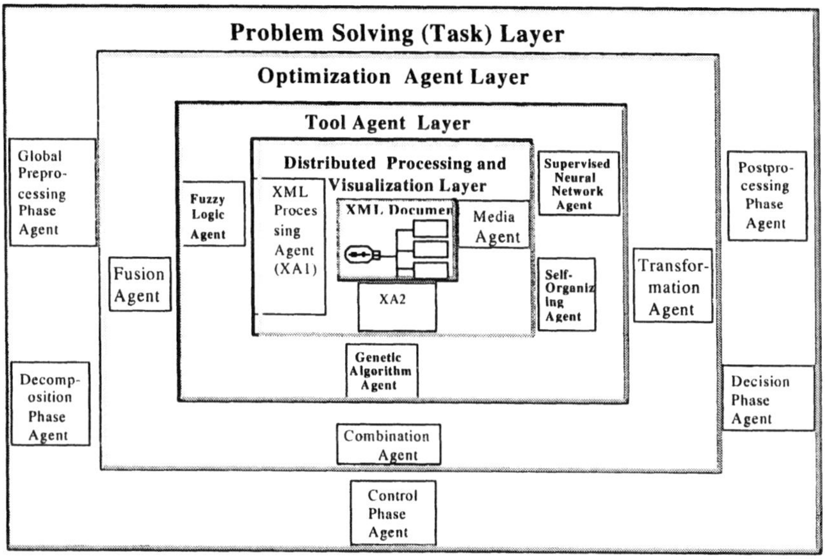

Figure 8.4: Multi-Layered Agent-Based Context Management

The XML *Processing* agent in the distributed processing and visualization agent layer of Figure 8.4 is used to transform contents based on context information about the user and the execution environment.

The output of joint processing of context and content on the part of the *XML Processing* agent is then made available to the Tool Agent Layer, where symbolic and sub-symbolic techniques (neural networks, fuzzy systems and the like) are used, for instance, for decision support based on input data.

As outlined in the introduction, companies' "naive" view of content management often involves lack of any flexibility in the presentation of multimedia content. Often, e-business and e-commerce transactions involve HTML files that hold flat multimedia commercial formats, like Flash Macromedia and others. The first Web documents contained only text, but support for multimedia data types was gradually added from 1993 onwards, especially through the use of a structuring and labeling mechanism called *Multipurpose Internet Mail Extension* (MIME). We call this approach *file-centered, as* it involves little more that using ordinary file system or database facilities for data storage and retrieval, while not providing any context-dependent searching and transformation functionality. On the other hand, a *human-centered* approach based on HCVM is the first step toward full support of a suitable life cycle for context information, which is hard to collect and may be expensive to maintain.

In human-centered E-business systems, contents are still logically seen as documents, pictures, or any other unstructured representation. However, human-centered systems provide more advanced content retrieval facilities inasmuch they explicitly support the notion of *context-based content organization* via the HCVM distributed and processing layer, including XML *Processing* agent. Figure 8.5 shows the architecture resulting in the application of the HCVM framework.

For the sake of conciseness, we shall not describe Figure 8.5 in detail; rather, we shall recapitulate the main steps that are relevant to our discussion. The first step in human-centered information management is *context initialization*, i.e. the process of obtaining information on or from the user.

Then, one or more *context elicitation* phases follow; techniques for eliciting context include interaction, questionnaires, and behavior analysis. The result of elicitation is the final context model. At this point, the context model is used by the E-business system as a basis for content organization and presentation. A *revision control* phase may also ensure that user feedback and reactions to context model are evaluated and taken into account for context refinement.

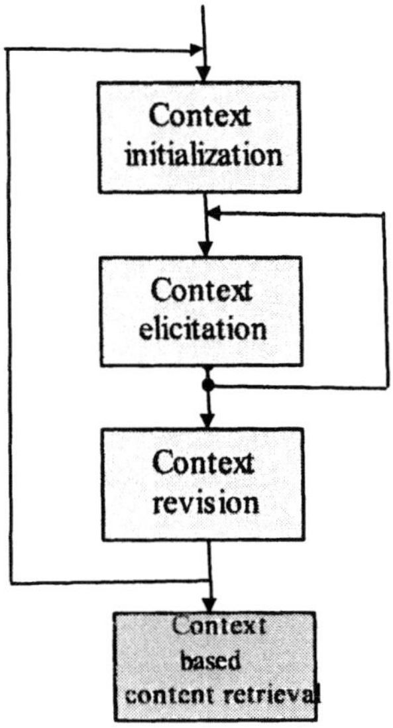

Figure 8.5 Context Exploitation in Digital Content Retrieval

As object-oriented techniques for software design became widespread, some researchers advocated using object-oriented techniques to become more human-centered, exploiting object-oriented technology for context definition. This approach met a certain degree of success at the design level, and many object-oriented tools for domain modeling are currently available, supporting methodologies for describing and managing context-information in an object-oriented fashion.

While it is very tempting to introduce object-oriented techniques commonly adopted for domain modeling to describe the context of a e-business transaction, e.g. to define who are the actors involved, either human users or software agents acting on behalf of organizations. However, this may prove very difficult in a business environment, when modelers are neither software designers nor programmers aware of O-O design methodologies.

8.3 Context Modeling in XML

Type support and commercial policies' enforcement can be made much easier by passing from a naive approach to content management to a document-centered, context-aware life-cycle; but this transition must be flexible and should not require learning new tools. Also, it is important to be able to support incomplete information in a declarative and reusable form.

Semi-structured data models like the *eXtensible Markup Language* (XML) allow for tackling this issue, supporting gradual enrichment of the context information's internal structure while preserving uniform navigation and query interfaces.

XML was originally designed to enable the use of SGML on the World Wide Web and standardized by World Wide Web Consortium (W3C) (Bray et al., 1998). A detailed, though preliminary, introduction to XML has been given in previous chapters.

As we have seen there, a XML document is composed of a sequence of nested elements, each delimited by a pair of start and end tags (e.g., <tag> and </tag>). XML documents can be broadly classified into two categories: well formed and valid. An XML document is said to be well formed if it obeys the basic syntax of XML (e.g., non-empty tags must be properly nested, each non-empty start tag must have the corresponding end tag). A sample well-formed XML document is presented in Figure 8.6. The structure of a *well formed* XML document can be represented as *a multi-sorted tree*[4], i.e. a tree whose nodes belong to different types (such as elements, attributes and content).

```
<?xml version="1.0" encoding="UTF-8" ?>
- <component>
    <maker>Componentwise Software</maker>
  - <version serialcode="12303B">
      <title>Satellite Parser 4200</title>
      <year>2002</year>
      <text>A new multi-platform parser
        component</text>
    </version>
  </component>
```

Figure 8.6 A Well-formed XML Document

[4] The XML structure tree becomes a *graph* when links are taken into account; we shall not deal with XML hypertext links in this chapter.

Well-formed documents are also *valid* if they conform to a proper *Document Type Definition* (DTD). A DTD is a file (external, included directly in the XML document or both) which contains a formal definition of a particular type of XML documents. Indeed, DTDs include declarations for elements (i.e. tags), attributes, entities, and notations that will appear in XML documents. Document type definitions clearly state what names can be used for element types, where they may occur, how each element relates to the others, and what attributes and sub-elements each element may have. Figure 8.7 shows the DTD associated with the XML document in Figure 8.6.

```
<!ELEMENT component (maker, version)>
<!ELEMENT maker (#PCDATA)>
<!ELEMENT text (#PCDATA)>
<!ELEMENT title (#PCDATA)>
<!ELEMENT version (title, year, text)>
<!ATTLIST version
  serialcode CDATA #REQUIRED
>
<!ELEMENT year (#PCDATA)>
```

Figure 8.7: DTD Associated with the Document in Figure 8.6.

While substantially longer than a DTD, an XML Schema definition carries much more information, inasmuch it allows the document designer to adopt a design style based on named types. This technique consists in defining XML data structures as reusable *simple* and *complex types* and then declaring XML elements as variables (called, as usual, *elements*) belonging to those types (Figure 8.8).

```
<xsd:schema xmlns:xsd="http://www.w3.org/2000/10/XMLSchema"
elementFormDefault="qualified">
  <xsd:element name="component">
    <xsd:complexType>
      <xsd:sequence>
        <xsd:element ref="maker"/>
        <xsd:element name="version" type="versionType"/>
      </xsd:sequence>
    </xsd:complexType>
  </xsd:element>
  <xsd:element name="maker" type="xsd:string"/>
  <xsd:element name="text" type="xsd:string"/>
  <xsd:element name="title" type="xsd:string"/>
  <xsd:complexType name="versionType">
    <xsd:sequence>
      <xsd:element ref="title"/>
      <xsd:element ref="year"/>
      <xsd:element ref="text"/>
    </xsd:sequence>
    <xsd:attribute name="serialcode" type= "xsd:string" use="required"/>
      </xsd:complexType>
  <xsd:element name="year" type="xsd:string"/>
</xsd:schema>
```

Figure 8.8 Use of Named Types in XML Schema

This capability, reminiscent of object oriented modeling techniques, makes the XML Schema language a very powerful tool for context representation. For this reason, XML Schema language is currently a solution of choice for defining XML-based formats for information interchange on the Internet, while DTDs are still widely used by the document management community.

XML schemata, unlike DTDs, are themselves XML documents. Besides the text syntax of Figure 8.8, they can be graphically represented as trees as shown in Figure 8.9. We shall use this style of representation throughout rest of the chapter.

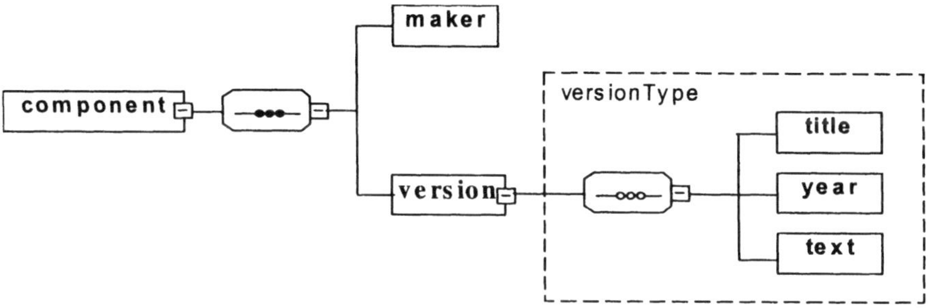

Figure 8.9 Tree-like Representation of XML Schema

A program called *XML validating parser* (Figure 8.10) performs the validation or syntax-checking procedure. Validation involves a well-formed XML document and a XML Schema: if the XML document is valid with respect to its schema, the validating parser usually produces a memory representation of the document according to a lower-detail data model, such as the tree-shaped Document Object Model (DOM) standard.

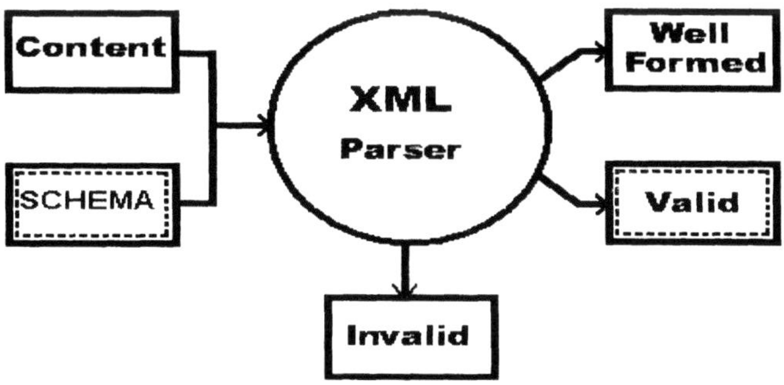

Figure 8.10: Schema Based Validation of Content

XML-based languages such as the Object Management Group's *XML-based Model Interchange* (XMI) have been proposed since long for representing and interchanging domain models between tools repositories and generators. On the other hand, domain information turned out to be too industry, company- and even product-specific for a standard to emerge. For this reason our proposal does not try to provide a general-purpose context Schema; rather, we shall rely on a multi-detail technique of schema definition.

Figure 8.11 graphically depicts our level-of-detail 1 XML Schema, according to which our business *context* is simply a sequence of generic pairs, each composed of an attribute name and the corresponding value. Such notion is perfectly consistent with the purely syntactical notion of context usually employed at operating system platform and programming language levels.

In our approach, the content of the value attribute is used to support *detail transition*, progressively adding semantics and structure to the context. When working at the initial level of detail (i.e., when the system parameter `detail` is set to 1), attribute value's content is managed as an opaque *text blob*, containing the context descriptor's text and any auxiliary information. When a context description document is validated against the Detail 1 Schema, its XML mark-up does not carry any information; all the semantics is expressed by the natural language terms, exactly like in human-centered environments.

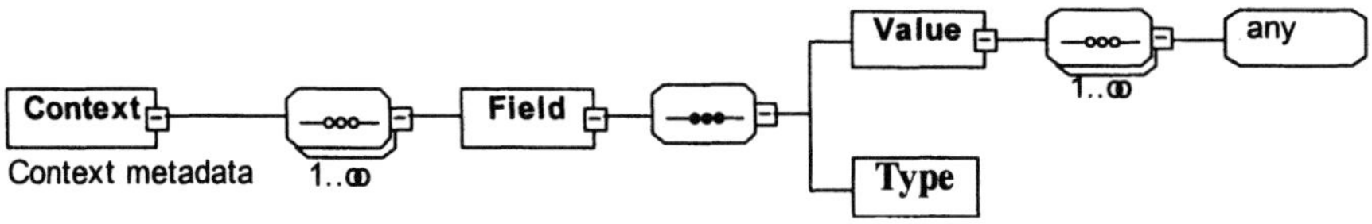

Figure 8.11 Context Representation via XML Schema, at Level Of Detail 1

The basic information' structure at level-of-detail 1 can be progressively enriched by using the <field> element value to store a whole XML document, that will be checked against a level of detail 2 schema only when the corresponding system parameter called detail is set at 2.

Note that this hidden second level document is considered simply a string when validating our level-of-detail 1 Schema, as the XML Schema specification does not allow an attribute to have Complex Content (Box, Skonnard and Lam, 2001)

Figure 8.12 shows a level-of-detail 2 Schema, designed to reproduce a company-specific context structure. This Schema specifies a more structured representation of context that is made available to the *XML Processing* agent of Figure 8.4.

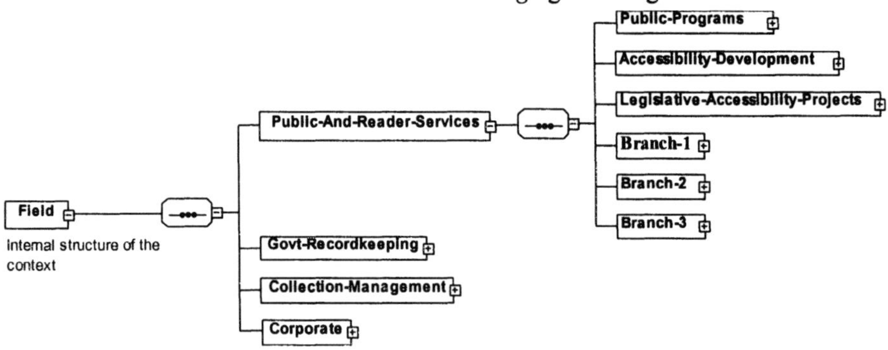

Figure 8.12: Level-of-Detail 2 XML Schema

The approach to XML representation of context shown in Figure 8.12 is aimed at defining the organizational coordinates of the source of the digital content being brokered or supplied in an E-business transaction. Taking into account the physical location of the requestor together with this context allows for fine-tuning content to the specific needs (or the regulations) of the customer requesting the data.

8.3.1 Using the Simple Object Access Protocol (SOAP) for Context Initialization

After having established that we shall represent the server-side context of an e-business transaction via XML documents containing instances of XML Schema data types (Figure 8.12), we are now concerned with client-side portion of the context itself. Both parts of the context are essential input to the HCVM *XML processing* agent (Figure 8.4). Conceptually there is nothing to prevent client-side context to be permanently stored at the server and retrieved each time a specific client (be it a human customer or a software agent acting on behalf of a partner organization) initiates a transaction. However, such an approach would be unrealistic on today's Internet.

Indeed, in the distributed scenario a XML Web service is a Web-based application that accepts requests from different systems across the Internet (or an Intranet) through the application of Web technology standards. Such contacts are occasional in nature and in many situations no assumption can be made on the client-side context of a transaction to be known to the server. Often, even the client identity is previously unknown. This situation is usually dealt with by encoding client-side context (seen, once again, as a set of instances of XML Schema data types) inside the request and providing enough authentication and security mechanisms to secure such context.

Besides XML, such standards include the *Simple Object Access Protocol* (SOAP), the *Windows Standard Description Language* (WSDL), and the usual protocol HTTP normally used for accessing Web sites. XML Web services are an increasingly successful paradigm for the development of complex Web-based applications; as we shall see SOAP carried over HTTP can be used for context initialization, providing the client-side part of a transaction's context.

The overall structure of a SOAP invocation is depicted in Figure 8.13: the outside *Multimedia Internet Mail Extension* (MIME) layer refers to the type of the message as reported in the HTTP header, namely text/XML.

The SOAP XML payload contains an encoded method invocation, i.e. a remote service request; its lexicon is defined by a standard XML namespace SOAP-ENV. In SOAP, the XML payload is used mainly to encode parameters' data types in a platform independent way.

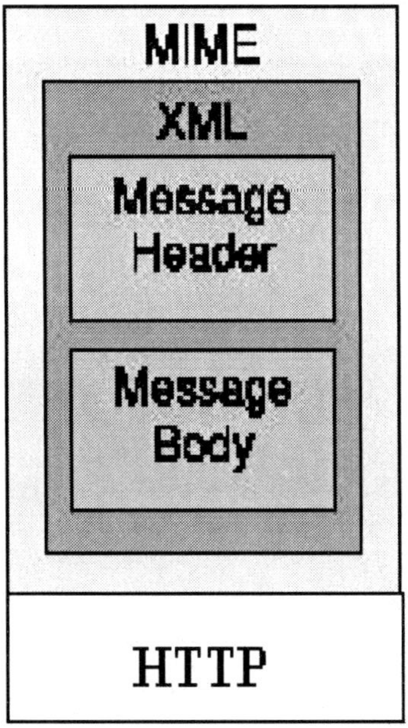

Figure 8.13: Overall Structure of a SOAP Invocation

The XML payload includes a root Envelope element and a child Body element, the latter having an optional sibling called Header. The SOAP payload's root element Envelope provides the serialization context for the method calls that follow. The Envelope element can contain additional attributes (qualified by a suitable XML namespace).

The SOAP Header element contains auxiliary information (called *header entries*) not functionally related to the method invocation, such as transaction management and payment. SOAP headers may contain the standard Actor and MustUnderstand attributes (as well as other optional, namespace-qualified ones), respectively stating the URI of the final destination of the message and whether header processing capability on the part of the recipient is mandatory (1) or not (0).

A SOAP response is much similar to a request, apart from the fact that it adds a Response suffix to the element name used for the request.

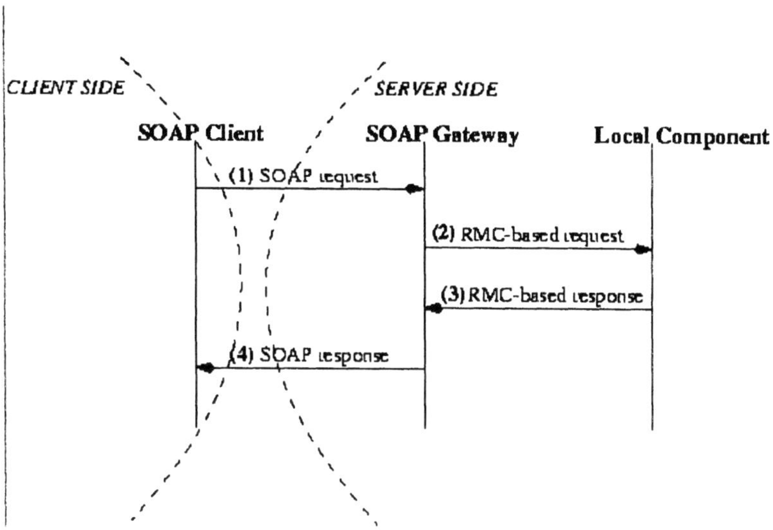

Figure 8.14: Execution Sequence of a SOAP Call

Figure 8.14 shows the execution sequence of a SOAP call. The SOAP header is used to hold generic meta information associated with the request, while the body is used to hold the service invocation and its parameters. In our HCVM-based approach to e-business communication, context initialization information (to be processed by HCVM XML agent, see Figure 8.4) is sent as XML-encoded data, which can be easily sent together with a SOAP message. [5] Such data contains instances of a XML Schema shared between the partners involved in the transaction.

8.3.2 Context-aware User Interface Based on HCVM

While SOAP-based communication is particularly suitable for business-to-business communication, in business-to-consumer interaction context must be initialized communicating with the user.

In our current implementation, a system parameter called detail is used to ensure adaptive context *initialization* and *elicitation* (Figure 8.5) via a flexible user interface. When communicating to humans, the HCVM *XML Processing* agent can achieve this goal by taking into account the context representation in order to shape the user interface itself.

The procedure goes as follows:

- At level of detail 1, a text-editor window with a single input field is used to type in each context facet. Before the context is stored, it is validated against the level-of-detail 1 XML Schema in order to ensure correct whitespace processing and canonicalization.

[5] Digital signatures can also be hosted in this field, making SOAP headers play an important role in SOAP authentication and security.

- At level of detail 2, an input/edit form is shown for each context facet. The form is generated on-the-fly according to the current Detail 2 Schema, i.e. the number and size of our input forms' fields are computed on the basis of the level of detail 2 schema.

Figure 8.15 shows the version of our user interface exploiting the XForm XML-based standard for declarative user interface definition. Our context-sensitive E-business environment computes the XForm definition of the user interface simply by visiting the DOM tree of the level-of-detail 2 XML schema. This approach requires a fully XML-compliant browser such as XSmiles (Vuorimaa, Rupponen, von Knorring and Honkala, 2002)

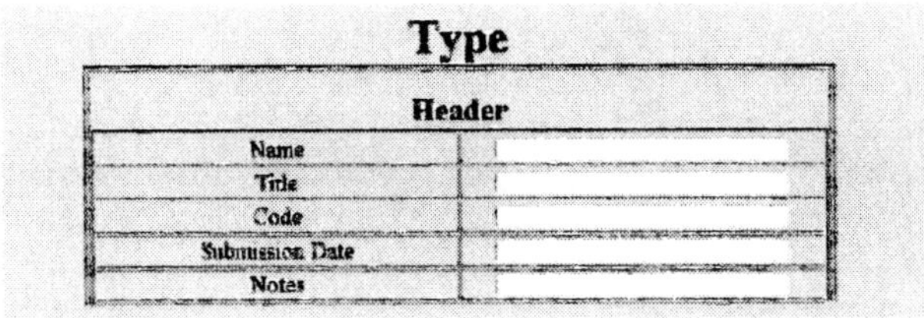

Figure 8.15: Context-dependent User Interface Generation Using XForm

An alternative and much more portable interface generation technique is shown in Figure 8.16. The context XML Schema at level of detail 2, being itself an XML document, is turned into a standard HTML form by applying a suitable XSLT transformation style sheet. Our current implementation of a HCVM-based e-business platform adopts this technique when dealing with browsers that cannot yet understand XForm definitions.

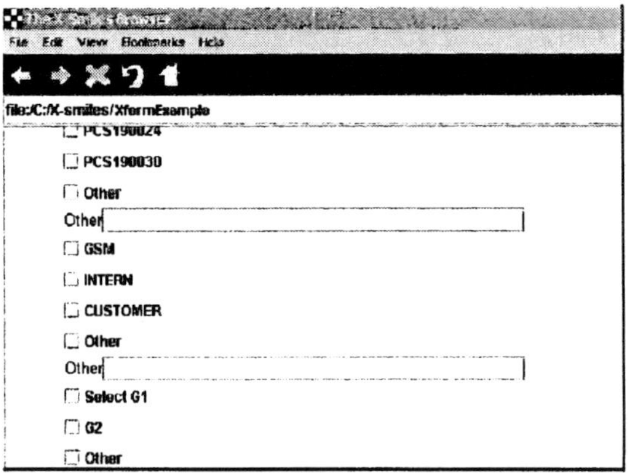

Figure 8.16: Context-aware User Interface Generation Using XSLT

8.4 Flexible Access to Context Information

Table 8.1 outlines the decomposition, control and decision phase content definitions of our context-aware, human centered e-business platform, taking into account both business-to-business and business-to-people styles of interaction. The shaded rows in

Table 8.1 show the mapping of HCVM content terms and attributes with those of the context-aware e-business application platform.
In the rest of the section we describe the fuzzy computations used by the HCVM *decision* agent (Figure 8.4) for choice and decision support. Our discussion will show how fuzzy matching of XML sub-trees can be used to this purpose.

Table 8.1: HCVM Phase Content Definitions of the E-BusinessPlatform

Content / Attribute	Decomposition	Control	Decision
Goal (Generic)	Restrict input context, reduce complexity, enhance reliability	Establish domain decision control constructs for context concepts	Provide user/stakeholder defined outcomes from the system
Goal (Application-specific)	*Restrict input to specific digital content*	*Define control knowledge for price-based decision classes.*	*Provide a list of digital content to satisfy the requested properties*
Task (Generic)	Determine orthogonal concepts	Determine decision level concepts	Determine decision instance
Task (Specific)	*Partition a global context of into orthogonal classes*	*Determine price based decision classes that can be used with required digital content*	*Retrieve digital content for the selected price*
Task Constraint (Generic)	Orthogonality, reliability, scalability	Imprecise and incomplete data, scalability, reliability, and other domain dependent	Imprecise, noisy data, generalization, adaptability, and other domain dependent
Task Constraint (Specific)	*Orthogonal types of context representation classes*	Imprecise, fuzzy features	Imprecise, fuzzy features
Precondition (Generic)	Filtered/conditioned domain data	Orthogonal concept defined, concept related data available	Decision class case data, decision detail concepts defined (optional)
Precondition (Specific)	*Domain-dependent filtered user query content data*	*Domain-dependent features, fuzzy membership functions for various features*	*Defined by user*
Postcondition (Generic)	Orthogonal abstract classes	Decision concepts/classes defined, control knowledge defined	Specific decision instance computed
Postcondition (SPECIFIC)	*Different types of contents to select from*	*Decision control knowledge for decision classes defined*	*Retrieved contents based on user specifications*
Technology Artifacts (Generic)	Symbolic rule based, neural networks, agent, multimedia	Agent, neural networks, fuzzy logic,	Agent, fuzzy logic
Technology Artifacts (SPECIFIC)	*Perceptual (multimedia)*	*Fuzzy logic*	*Fuzzy logic/*

Table 8.1 **(cont'd)**: HCVM Phase Content Definitions of the e-Business Platform

Content / Attribute	Decomposition	Control	Decision
Domain Model (Generic)	Structural, functional, causal, geometric, heuristic, spatial, color, shape, etc.	Structural, functional, casual, geometric, heuristic, spatial, shape, color, etc.	Structural, functional, causal, geometric, heuristic, spatial, shape, color, etc.
Domain Model (SPECIFIC)	*Content Structure model.*	*Fuzzy price model*	*Functional specification model*
Represented Features (Generic)	Qualitative/linguistic – binary, structured Non-linguistic – continuous features	Qualitative/linguistic – binary, structured, fuzzy data Non-linguistic – continuous data related to an orthogonal concept	Qualitative/linguistic – binary, fine grain fuzzy decision concept data Non-linguistic – continuous decision concept data
Represented Features (SPECIFIC)	*Structure (e.g. content type .gif,.jpeg,.png)*	*Fuzzy weight*	*Fuzzy (user selected characteristics)*
Psychological Scales (Generic)	Nominal; Formal property; category	Nominal, ordinal, interval, ratio	Nominal, ordinal, interval, ratio, or none
Psychological Scales (SPECIFIC)	*Nominal (e.g. different supplier)*	*Interval (e.g. price)*	*Interval (user selected characteristics)*
Representing Dimensions (Generic)	Shape, location, size, position, etc. on the nominal scale	Shape, size, length, distance, density, location, position, orientation, color, texture	Shape, size, length, distance, density, location, position, orientation, color, texture
Representing Dimensions (SPECIFIC)	*Shape, color* 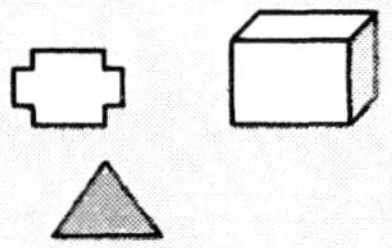	*Orientation* *Price band* 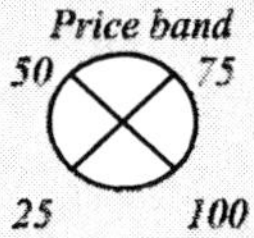 	*Shape, length, color of retrieved content.* *Functional specification sheets* 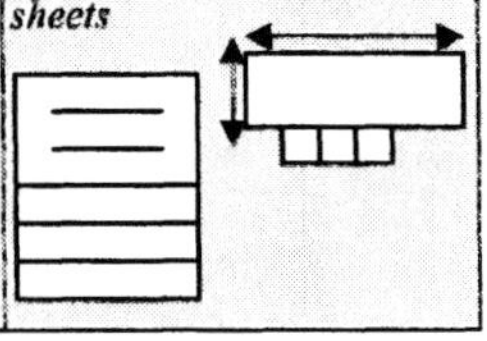

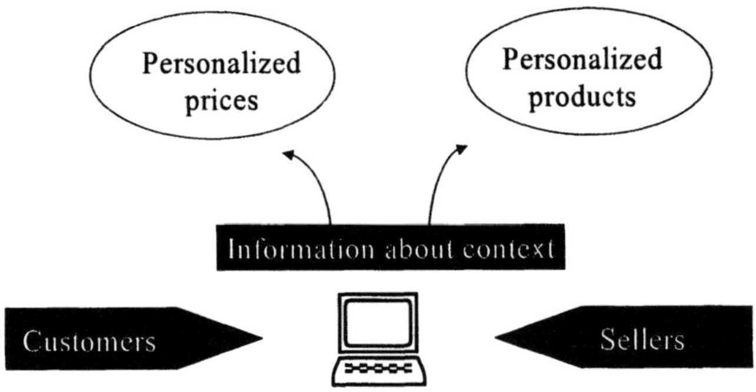

Figure 8.17: Accessing Context Representation

The decision computation carried out in our environment is aimed at flexibly computing the digital content to be presented to users (Figure 8.17) by taking into account both client and server portions of the context.

Once flexible context information has been stored in our system, flexible-searching facilities must be provided able to tolerate inherent variability in their structure. For this reason, our approach to querying information represented in XML is based on a flexible extraction and processing technique, capable of extracting relevant information from a (possibly huge) set of heterogeneous XML documents.

The relevant information is selected as follows:

- First, the user provides a XML pattern, i.e. a partially specified context sub-tree.
- Then, the arcs of the XML documents representing information are weighted and their structure is extended in order to increase pattern recall.
- Finally, information documents are scanned and XML fragments matching the search pattern are located and sorted according to their similarity to the pattern.

The problem of matching search patterns to the extended XML tree structure can be described as a fuzzy sub-graph-matching problem.

Intuitively, we want to match the query pattern against the context document after having extended the requirement's tree in order to by-pass links and intermediate elements which are not relevant from the current user's point of view.

In order to perform the extension in a sensible way, we first evaluate XML elements of each context relying on fuzzy weights to express their relative importance (Bosc, Dubois, Pivert and Prade, 1997). Low values will correspond to the element carrying a negligible amount of information, while a value of 1 means that the information provided by the element (including its position in the document graph) is extremely important according to the context author.

Other than that, the semantics of our weights is only defined in relation to other weights in the same document/query. The computation of such weights should be carried out automatically, or at least to require limited manual effort.

Our method computes weights based upon (normalized, inverse-of) distance from the root, relying on the hypothesis that generality (and thus importance) grows when getting closer to the root.

We must nevertheless take into account the fact that information' text is concentrated inside terminal elements, possibly at the maximum depth. This means that, in general, a weighting technique should not allow for pruning edges leading to content-filled elements. Our content-insensitive, automatic arc weighting method relies on the following factors:

- *Depth* The closenesses to the root, which shows the generality of the concepts tied by the arc.
- *Content* The amount of content to indicate the arc leads to context text. For the sake of simplicity, here the amount of content is computed by simply evaluating the length of CDATA string content; however, multimedia -oriented metrics like the ones introduced elsewhere in this book are also applicable.
- *Tag name* Though content-insensitive, the technique could take into account the presence of particular tag names (possibly by using application or domain-specific Thesauri (Damiani and Fugini, 1995), and increase weights of arcs incoming to nodes whose names are considered as ``content bearers".

Our automatic weighting technique takes separately into account the aspects listed above, generating a value for each of them, and then aggregates these values within a single arc-weight.

Depth

It is quite intuitive that the containment relationship between XML elements causes generality to decrease as depth grows, and so we define a standard decreasing hyperbolic function that gives the lowest weights to the deepest nodes. If $a=(n_1,n_2)$ is an arc then

$$w_d(a) = \frac{\alpha}{\alpha + depth(n_1)}$$

where α is a parameter that can be easily tuned. Let us suppose, as an example, to have a tree with maximum depth 10. It is easy to see that, with $\alpha=1$ the weights go from 1 to 1/11, and with $\alpha=10$ the weights go from 1 to 1/2. The choice of α can also depend on the value of the maximum depth D. It is easy to show that, in this case, if $\alpha=D/k$ then the minimum weight is 1/(k+1).

Content

The techniques just described tend to give to leaf nodes less weight than they deserve, because they often are deep inside the document. This is a problem because in many applications information leaf nodes are the main information bearers, and indiscriminately pruning them would eliminate potentially useful content. For these reasons, we also weight nodes based on the amount of content. Since our weighting technique is content-insensitive, the only way we have to quantify the amount of information in a text node is to calculate the length of the PCDATA string. This approach is very reasonable when the considered documents contain substantial text blobs while, in more structured, schematic documents, more importance should be attached to the previous two factors. This means that, given an arc $a=(n_1,n_2)$ its weight (with respect to its content) should be proportional to the length of the text contained in n_2. If $C(a)$ is the text content of the destination node of a, then we have

$$w_c(a) = \frac{|C(a)|}{|C(a)| + \gamma}$$

where $|C(a)|$ is the length of $C(a)$, that can be expressed either in tokens (words) or in bytes (characters). As usual, a parameter γ can be used to tune the slope. Actually, γ represents the content length for which w_c=0.5.

8.4.1 Fuzzy Closure Computation

Once the weighting is completed, the context XML information can be regarded as a fuzzy tree. At this point, the fuzzy closure C of the fuzzy labeled tree representing the context is computed. Intuitively, computing graph-theoretical closure entails inserting a new arc between two nodes if they are connected via a path of any length in the original graph. The complexity of graph closure computation is well known to be polynomial with respect to the number of nodes of the graph. In our model, the weight of each closure arc in *C-G* is computed aggregating via a t-norm *T* the weights of the arcs belonging to the path it corresponds to in the original graph. Namely, for each arc (n_1,n_2) in the closure graph *C* we write:

$$w_{arc(n_i,n_j)} = T(w_{arc(n_i,n_r)}, w_{arc(n_r,n_s)},\ldots, w_{arc(n_t,n_j)})$$

where $\{(n_i,n_r)(n_r,n_s),\ldots,(n_t,n_j)\}$ is the set of arcs comprising the shortest paths from n_i to n_j in *G* and, again, *T* is a standard t-norm (Klir and Folger 1988)

Intuitively, the closure computation step gives an extended structure to the document, providing a looser view of the containment relation. Selecting the type of t-norm to be used for combining weights means deciding if and how a low weight on an intermediate element should affect the importance of a nested high-weight element. This can be a very difficult problem, as the right choice may depend on the dataset or even on the single data instance at hand. There are some cases in which the t-norm of the minimum best fits the context, other cases in which it is more reasonable to use the product or the Lukasiewicz t-norms (Klir and Folger 1988).

Often, it is convenient to use a family of t-norms indexed by a tunable parameter. In general, however, it is guessing the right context, or better the knowledge associated to it from some background of preliminary knowledge, that leads to the right t-norm for a given application.

For instance, suppose a node n_j is connected to the root via a single path of length 2, namely (n_{root},n_i) (n_i,n_j). Suppose now that

$$w_{arc(n_{root},n_i)} << w_{arc(n_i,n_j)}$$

Then, the weight of the closure arc (n_{root},n_j) will depend on how the t-norm *T* combines the two weights. In other words, how much should the high weight of (n_1,n_2) be depreciated by the fact that the arc is preceded by (comparatively) low-weight one (n_{root},n_i) ? While this may look like an abstract mathematical question, it can be readily translated in terms of context. How much less does an information item e.g., one enclosed in a XML tag pair like <offer></offer>) count if it is provided in a specific context? It is easy to see that we always have a conservative choice, namely $T = min$. However, this conservative choice does not always agree with human-centered intuition, because the *min* operator gives a value that depends only on one of the operands without considering the other (for instance, we have the *absorption property*: $T(x,0)=0$). Moreover, min does not provide the *strict-monotonicity* property:

$$\forall y,x \quad x' > x \rightarrow T(x',y) > T(x,y)$$

In other words, an increase in one of the operands does not ensure the result to increase if the other operand does not increase as well. To understand the effect of the *min*'s single operand dependency on human intuition in our case, consider the two arc pairs shown below:

1. (<product><version> 0.2)(<version><serialcode> 0.9)
2. (<product><version> 0.3)(<version><serialcode> 0.4)

when the *min* operation is used for conjunction, arc pair (1) is ranked above arc (2), while most people would probably decide that arc pair (2), whose second element has much higher importance, should be ranked first. The other t-operators somewhat alleviate the single operand dependency problem of the min for arc pairs (using the product, for instance, the outcome of the previous example would be reversed), they may introduce other problems for longer paths. Let's consider the following example, where we add a versioncode attribute to the <versionname> element:

(<product><version> 0.1)(<version><versionname> 0.9)(<versionname><versioncode> 0.1)

(<product><version> 0.2)(<version><modelname> 0.5)(<versionname><versioncode> 0.2)

In this case using the product we get $T(x,y,z)=T(x,T(y,z))=0.009$ for the first path, while the second gets 0.02; again this estimate of importance that ranks path (2) above path (1) may not fully agree with users' intuition. As we shall see, our environment allows the user to manually adjust the desired aggregation operator as a part of context initialization.

8.4.2 Query Execution

The extraction technique relies on the following procedure:

1. Weight the target context tree G and the query pattern Q according to the techniques described above.
2. Weights on target documents can be computed once for all (in most cases, at the cost of a visit to the document tree). Though weighting the queries must be done on-line, their limited cardinality is likely to keep the computational load negligible in most cases.
3. Compute the closure graph C of G using a T-norm or a suitable fuzzy aggregation of the weights. This operation is dominated by matrix multiplication, and its complexity lies in between $O(n^2)$ and $O(n^3)$ where n is the cardinality of the node-set V of the target document graph. Again, graph closure can be pre-computed once for all and cached for future requests. Perform a cut operation on C using a threshold (this operation gives a new, tailored target graph TG). The cut operation simply deletes the closure arcs whose weight is below a user-provided threshold α, and is linear in the cardinality of the edge-set of C-G.
4. Compute a fuzzy similarity matching between the sub graphs TG of the tailored context document and the query graph Q, according to selected type of matching. This operation coincides with the usual query execution procedure of pattern-based query languages, and its complexity can be exponential or polynomial with respect to the cardinality of the node-set V of the target document graph (Comai, Damiani, Posenato and Tanca, 1998)

The first steps of the above procedure are reasonably fast (as document weights and closure can be pre-computed, required on-line operation consists in a sequence of single-step lookups) and does not depend on the formal definition of weights. The last step coincides with standard pattern matching in the query execution of XML query languages (Ceri et al., 1999), and its complexity clearly dominates the other steps.

8.5 Sample Interaction

We are now ready to describe a sample interaction with the query and searching facility of our environment. Our tool maps context representations (company-wide, or organized on a per-project basis) into *virtual directories* that can be populated by XML information[6].

Figure 8.18 shows the selection of a virtual directory containing a set of information using our environment.

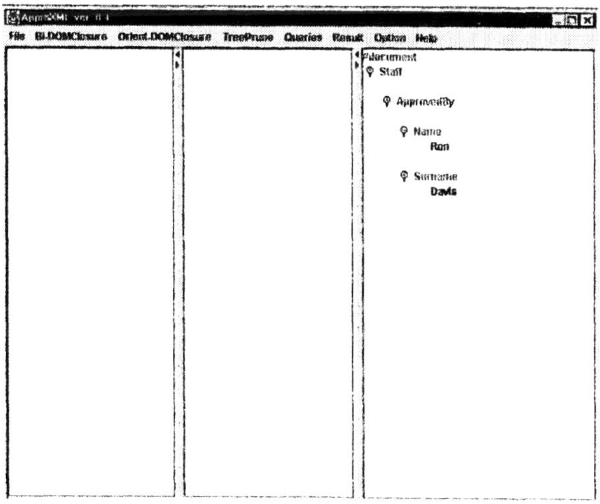

Figure 8.18 Selecting a Virtual Directory

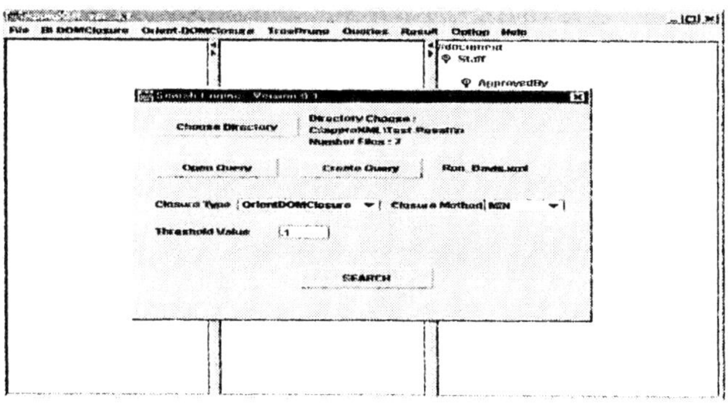

Figure 8.19: Setting the Context Search Parameters

[6] In our current prototype we use a relational database for physically storing all context information.

Figure 8.19 shows the window allowing for setting the search parameters, including the fuzzy closure type and the specific t-norm to be used for weight aggregation. Finally, Figures 8.20 and 8.21 show the query results in the form of fragments of XML information in the query environment's main window.

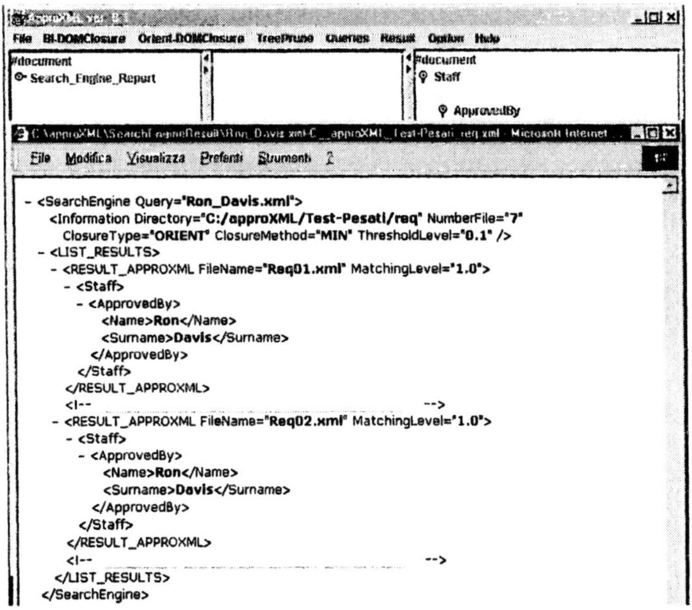

Figure 8.20 Retrieved Context Information in XML format

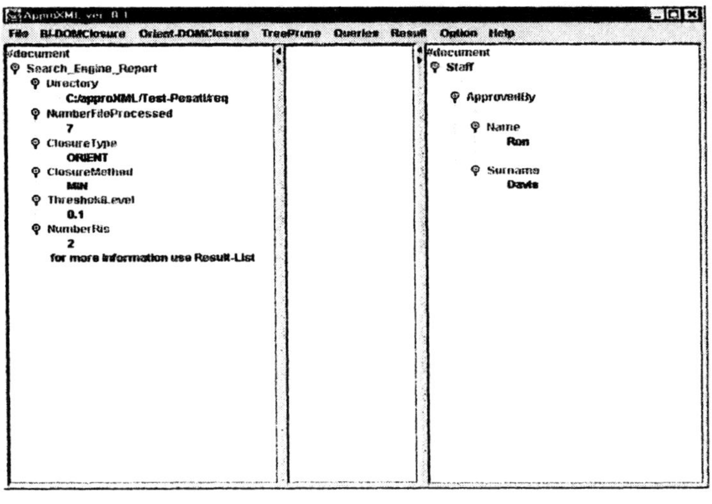

Figure 8.21 Retrieved Context Information in Tree Format

8.6. Summary

In this chapter we have shown how the problem solving agent layer of the HCVM can be used for developing the context model of the user in a e-business transaction. We have also shown how the XML distributed processing agent layer and the XML document layer can be seamlessly integrated with the supplier or server side XML schema. The five layers of HCVM as described in this chapter provide an agent based context management and decision support environment While domain decomposition can be flexibly partitioned into client-side and server side context, the former to be stored together with client requests, this solution is by no means mandatory. Fully server-side representation of context may well be employed in corporate settings, leaving to the client the lighter burden of authentication only.
We are currently exploring a number of applications of the HCVM-based approach in the framework of e-commerce and e-business.

Acknowledgements
The authors wish to thank David Rine for his precious assistance and valuable comments on information engineering. Thanks are also due to Mauro Madravio for his competent work on the software prototype.

References

Adler S. (1998), "Initial Proposal for XSL", available from: http://www.w3.org/TR/NOTE-XSL.html. Later superseded by the XSL Transformations (XSLT) Version 1.0 W3C Recommendation, 16 November 1999 http://www.w3.org/TR/xsl

Almeida V., Ribeiro V. and Ziviani N. (1999), "Efficiency Analysis of Brokers in the Electronic Marketplace", *Proceedings of the WWW8 Intl. Conference*, Toronto, Canada, pp.1-12

Data Interchange Standards Assoc. (1996) "Electronic Data Interchange X12 Standards, *Rel. 3070,* Alexandria,VA, 1996

Bailin S. C., "An Object-oriented Information Specifications Method", Communications of the ACM, 32(5), pp.608-623, May 1989

Barna A. and Porat L. (1976) *Introduction to Microcomputers and Microprocessors,* Wiley Interscience

Bellettini C., Damiani E. and Fugini M.G. (1999) "User Opinions and Rewards in a Reuse-Based Development System" *Proceedings of the International Symposium on Software Reuse (SSR '99)* Los Angeles, CA (US), pp.98-110

Berners-Lee, T., Hendler, J., and Lassila, O. The Semantic Web. Scientific American 284, 5 (2001), 34–43.

Blair B. and Boyer J. (1999), "XFDL: Creating Electronic Commerce Transaction Records Using XML", *Proceedings of the WWW8 Intl. Conference,* Toronto, Canada, pp. 533-544

Bosc P., Dubois D., Pivert O. and Prade H. (1997), "Flexible Queries In Relational Databases-The Example of The Operator", *Theoretical Computer Science*, vol.171, pp.45-57

Box D., Lam A. and Skonnard D., "XML: Beyond Markup", Addison-Wesley, 2001

Bray T. et al. (ed.) (1998), "Extensible Markup Language (XML) 1.0", available at http://www.w3.org/TR/1998/REC-xml-19980210. Later superseded by Extensible Markup Language (XML) 1.0. W3C Reccomendation. Feb. 1998. http://www.w3C.org/TR/REC-xml/

Bryan M., Marchal, B., Mikula, N., Peat, B. and Webber, D. "Guidelines for using XML for Electronic Data Interchange", available from: http://www.xmledi.net/

Buschmann F., Meurier R., Rohnert H., Sommerlad P. and Stal M. (1996) *A System of Patterns*, J. Wiley

Ceri S., Comai S., Damiani E., Fraternali P., Paraboschi S. and Tanca L. (1999) "XML-GL: A Graphical Query Language for XML, *Proceedings of the WWW8 Intl. Conference*, Toronto, Canada, pp.93-110

Comai S., Damiani E., Posenato R., Tanca L., "A Schema-Based Approach to Modeling and Querying WWW Data", in H.~Cristiansen, ed., Proceedings of Flexible Query Answering Systems (FQAS '98), Roskilde (Denmark), Lecture Notes in Artificial Intelligence 1495, Springer (1998).

Connolly D. (1995), "An Evaluation of the WWW as a Platform for Electronic commerce, *Proceedings of the Sixth Computer, Coordination and Collaboration Conference*, Austin, TX (US), pp. 55-70

Crocker D., "MIME Incapsulation of EDI Objects", RFC 1767 2/3/1995 http://www.ietf.org

Damiani E. and Fugini M.G. "Automatic Thesaurus Construction Supporting Fuzzy Retrieval of Reusable Components", Proceedings of ACM SIG-APP Conference on Applied Computing (SAC'95), Nashville, February 1995.

Damiani E. and Fugini M.G. (1997) "Fuzzy Identification Of Distributed Components, *Proceedings of the 5th Intl. Conference On Computational Intelligence*, Dortmund, Lecture Notes in Computer Science 1226, pp.95-98

Damiani E. and Khosla R. (1999) "A Human Centered Approach to Electronic Brokerage, *Proceedings. of the ACM Symposium. on Applied Computing* (SAC '99) San Antonio, TX, February 1999, pp.243-249

Damiani, E. De Capitani S., Paraboschi S. and Samarati P. (2000),"Securing XML Documents" *Proceedings of the Seventh International Conference on Extending Database Technology*, Kostanza, Germany, LNCS 1777 pp. 121-135

Deutsch A., Fernandez M., Florescu D., Levy A. and Suciu D. (1999) "A query language for XML" *Proceedings of the WWW8 Intl. Conference*, Toronto, Canada pp.77-92

Fernandez, M., Gomez-Perez, A., and Juristo, N. (1997) "Meta-ontology: From ontological art toward ontological engineering". Spring Symposium Series, Stanford University. Stanford, CA., 1997

Finin T., Fritzson R., MacKay D. and MacEntire R. (1994), "KQML as an Agent Communication Language, *Proceedings of the Third International Conference on Information and Knowledge Management*, pp.112-124

Fromkin, A.M., (1995) *The Essential Role of Trusted Third Parties in Electronic Commerce*, in Kalakota R., Whinston A. (eds.) *Readings in Electronic Commerce*, Addison-Wesley

Garfinkel S. (1995), *Pretty Good Privacy*, O'Reilly

Glushko R., Tenenbaum J. and Meltzer B. (1999) An XML-framework for Agent-Based Electronic commerce, *Communications of the ACM*, vol. 42 no. 3

Hands J., Patel A., Bessonov M. and Smith R. (1998), An Inclusive and Extensible Architecture for Electronic Brokerage", Proc. of the Hawai Intl. Conf. on System Sciences, Minitrack on Electronic Commerce, pp.332-339

Hamilton S. (1997), Electronic Commerce for the 21st Century, *IEEE Computer*, vol. 30, no. 5 pp. 37-41

Klir G., Folger J..(1988) ``Fuzzy Sets, Uncertainty, and Information". Prentice-Hall.

Lange D. and Oshima M. (1998), *Programming and Deploying Java Mobile Agents With Aglets*, Addison-Wesley

Lynch D., Lundquist L (1996), *Digital Money: The New Era of Electronic Commerce*, John Wiley

Maes, P., Guttman, R., and Moukas, A.G. Agents that Buy and Sell", *Communications of the ACM*, Vol. 42, n. 3, pp. 81-85

Neches R., "Electronic Commerce on the Internet, *white chapter to the Federal Electronic Commerce Action Team*, http://www.isi.edu/dasher/Internet-Commerce.html

Orfali, R. and Harkey, D., *Client/Server Programming with Java and COBRA*, John Wiley Computer Publishing

Osgood E., Suci G. and Tannenbaum P. (1957) *The Measurement of Meaning*, Oxford University Press

Patterson D. and Hennessy J. (1994), *Computer Organization and Design*,Morgan-Kaufmann,

Powley C., Benjamin D. and Grossman D. (1997) "DASHER: A Prototype for Federated Electronic commerce Services, *IEEE Internet Computing*, vol. 1, no. 6

Prescod P., "An Introduction to DSSL", available from http://cito.uwaterloo.ca/~papresco/dsssl/tutorial.html

Rutgers Security Team, "WWW Security. A Survey", available from http://www-ns.rutgers.edu/www-security/

Suzuki, J., Yamamoto, Y., "Making UML Models Exchangeable ovre the Internet with XML: the UXF Approach", *Proceedings of the UML'98 Conference*, S. Antonio, TX US, pp. 134-143.

Tenenbaum J., Chowdhry T. and Hughes K. "eCo System: CommerceNet's Architectural Framework for Internet Commerce", http://www.commercenet.org

Vuorimaa P., Rupponen T., von KnorringN. and. Honkala E.M. "A Java Based XML Browser for Consumer Device". Proceedings of the ACM Symposium on Applied Computing, Madrid, 2002

9 HUMAN-CENTERED KNOWLEDGE MANAGEMENT

9.1. Introduction

It is widely acknowledged that the main barrier to e-business lies in the need for applications to meaningfully share information. The negative impact on e-business of the inherent limitations of traditional approaches to knowledge sharing has been comparable to the Internet's initial lack of reliability or security. In the past, knowledge sharing and organization efforts nearly always produced *document-based Knowledge Management Systems* (KMS), i.e. collections of documents internally maintained by organizations and focused on particular domains.

Recent experience has shown that, useful as they may be, such systems are often rigid and very awkward to extend across organizational boundaries.

Also it is a widely shared opinion that document-based knowledge management systems turn out to be not scalable and ultimately worthless from the point of view of e-business, unless new and valuable content is continuously selected and added to them (Gruniger and Lee, 2002).

This *knowledge maintenance* problem becomes acute whenever some or most of the knowledge sources contributing to the are web sites whose content is not directly under control of the organization setting up the knowledge management system.

The role of shared knowledge in e-business is less certain. Shared document definitions certainly provide an intuitive framework for specifying the business logic and computations that must take place on each end of a business transaction. On the other hand, some companies still wonder that sharing reference concepts may turn out to be a disadvantage for sellers, making it too easy for buyers or competitors to compare products or prices. For this reason many buyers and sellers, especially in business-to-business markets, delayed dealing with concept sharing until other problems like availability, post-sales service had been solved. Therefore, many applications of knowledge sharing have been proposed at internal or at a pre-competitive level.

A promising technique is the one based on ontology-based organization and management of knowledge. Business ontologies, seen as ""the explicit specification of an abstract, simplified view of a world we desire to represent" (Grueber 1995). Ontologies are considered to be crucial toward semantics-aware organization of, and access to, WWW sources. They are also a key agent of the World Wide Web Council (W3C) Semantic Web Initiative (Berners-Lee, Hendler and Lassila, 2001).

In this chapter we outline human-centered multi-agent architecture for developing knowledge management systems with knowledge storing, knowledge indexing, knowledge sharing and decision support capabilities. The human-centered multi-agent architecture is based on the HCVM. We particularly focus on the ontology of the data layer of the HCVM for developing knowledge sharing and decision support capabilities. The ontology of the data layer is expressed using standard, XML-based *Resource Definition Format Schema* (RDFS) metadata syntax (Brickley and Guha, 2000). Our final goal is to create and maintain a complex knowledge management system for knowledge sharing and decision support which is aimed at a community of entrepreneurs, businessmen and government officials, enabling *Regional Innovation Leadership* (RIL) (Corallo, Damiani and Elia, 2002)

The chapter is organized around two aspects. Firstly, we outline the HCVM approach to knowledge sharing and decision support in knowledge management systems. We follow it up with the description of the ontology of data layer of HCVM. We then describe the virtual infrastructure of a knowledge management supporting RIL.

9.2. HCVM approach to Knowledge Sharing and Decision Support in Knowledge Management Systems:

The EU funded European networks of Excellence support the collaboration of international expert teams from academia business and industry. The EU funded project "Data Mining and Decision Support for Business Competitiveness: A European Virtual Enterprise" (IST-1999-11495 project Sol-Eu-Net, http://soleunet.ijs.si) aims at forming a dynamic network of expert teams with long term experience in data mining and decision support whose functionalities are complementary and oriented towards solving some difficult practical problems. The e-business model of this partnership is a virtual community model in which the participating partners join their efforts and expertise in solving developing methods, problem-solving protocols and practical DM and DS solutions, aimed at increasing their visibility and success in the market. The virtually community model involves a flexible association of academic institutions. and business entities which (although have different motivations for this partnership) share the main objective of promoting and selling advanced services offered by a pool of partners. The virtual enterprise model has to solve the problem of efficiently storing, updating, sharing, promoting and transferring knowledge In addition to technological solutions, organizational, economic, legislative, psychological and cultural issues have to be addressed as well. Appropriate knowledge management leads to a quick recognition of a business opportunity and timely response (e.g., a business offer). So that geographic dispersion of client and expert teams need not necessarily be a limit to successful business operations.

In Figure 9.1 we outline the HCVM approach for constructing knowledge management systems. The data layer is the lowest layer of the HCVM. It is shown as the RDF Description layer. The ontology of the data layer is aimed at exploiting modular business ontologies for knowledge sharing and decision support. Following

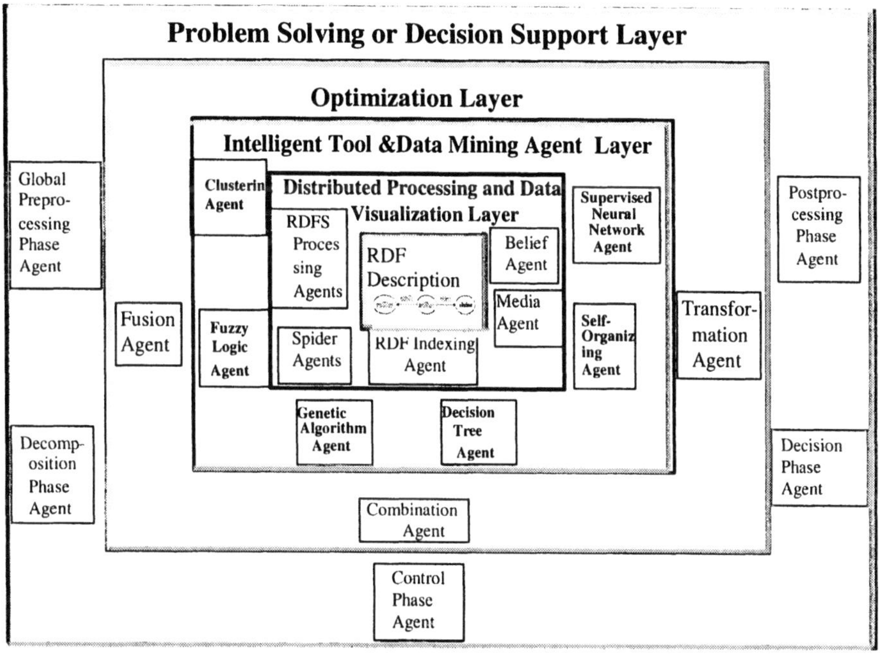

Figure 9.1 Human-Centered Knowledge Sharing Based on HCVM

the approach used in the last chapter, ontology of the data layer of the HCVM is expressed using standard, XML-based *Resource Definition Format Schema* (RDFS) metadata syntax (Brickley and Guha, 2000). Also data classification and navigation according to such an ontology will be consistent with our human-centered design principles. Our final goal is to create and maintain a complex knowledge management system for knowledge sharing and decision support which is aimed at a community of entrepreneurs, businessmen and government officials, enabling Regional Innovative Leadership (RIL) described in the next section.

The multi-layered structure of the HCVM for knowledge management systems is shown in Figure 9.1. This will be used to develop the knowledge sharing and decision support components of the knowledge management system based on , XML-based *Resource Definition Format Schema* (RDFS) data layer definition.

The information stored in our knowledge management system will be semi-automatically updated and organized from multiple WWW sources by means of ontology-based indexing tool.

The HCVM overall architecture is instantiated using a RDFS indexing agent to represent the common ontology (i.e., the shared hierarchy of concepts) underlying shared knowledge .

9.3. Resource Description Format (RDF) for Knowledge Representation

The Resource Description Framework (RDF) is a special-purpose XML Schema, specifically oriented to knowledge representation (Lassila and Swick, 1999). The RDF specification defines the concepts of *resources*, *properties* and *statements*. A statement represents a named relation between two resources, or between a resource and a value. The name of the relation is called a *property*.

RDF offers a flexible, standardized way to write down generic metadata. For example, you can define that the resource myURI.com is about "e-business" and that it is related to yourURI.com. An easy way to represent this data is by drawing a graph of it as shown in Figure 9.2.

Figure 9.2. A RDF Statement Represented as a Graph

For RDF metadata to be exchangeable, we need to define common names for it. The RDF data model provides neither a mechanism for describing properties, nor a technique for describing relationships between these properties and concepts. So RDF is not, in itself, a language for ontology design.

Rather, that is the role of the RDF Schema (RDFS) language (Brickley and Guha, 2000). RDFS language allows for defining classes and properties, which can then be used in RDF assertions about resources or about other classes. With RDF Schema, we can create a schema (corresponding to a business ontology) that defines a language to use in our RDF metadata. In the business ontology we can define the properties that we need for the particular domain that we're working on. In our case, properties are concepts needed in describing web pages that contain useful information for corporations and individuals taking decisions involving business innovation.

In other words, RDF Schema offers us the ability to define specific classes of resources (e.g. 'documents') and subclasses of these classes (e.g. 'web pages'). Furthermore, we can add domain constraints and range-constraints on properties,

demanding that the resource to which the property is applied and the value of the property must be of a specific class.

9.4. The Regional Innovation Leadership (RIL) Cycle

The *Regional Innovation Leadership* (RIL) cycle has been chosen as the background environment for this chapter because it synthesizes the main scientific contributions related to innovation and territorial business development based on the strategic role that is played by knowledge (Passiante,. Elia, and Massari, 2000). These contributions highlight the importance of knowledge as enabling factor for building sustainable competitive advantage at territorial level.

According to region-enterprise metaphor, RIL represents "the collective capacity of a regional community to initiate and sustain significant changes to work effectively with forces that shape change".

RIL cycle is supported by a number of methodologies and tools for promoting territorial cluster-based development, fostering interactive learning and innovation processes, assisting and sustaining local institutions and policy makers in their planning activities.

The organizational form we want to support for feeding the RIL cycle is the *community of practice* (CoP). "Communities of Practice" is a term coined by researchers who studied the ways in which people naturally work and cooperate together. In essence, communities of practice are groups of people who share similar goals and interests. In pursuit of these goals and interests, they employ work with the same tools and express themselves in a common language.

Through such common activity, people belonging to communities come to hold similar beliefs and value systems. Communities of practices are therefore characterized by a high capacity to create organizational knowledge, to develop informal learning processes, to build intra- and inter-organizational relationships based on common motivations and interests.

Besides adopting a human-centered decision support approach to community of practices, in this chapter we will rely on the well-known region-enterprise metaphor, namely, Knowledge Hub (KH) in order to create a favorable environment for developing regional community of practices. Our Knowledge Hub (KH) is a knowledge management system enabling RIL, through developing, supporting and growing of community of practices.

9.5. Knowledge Hub for RIL

In this section, we describe the architectural model that embodies and refines the tool agent and distributed processing layers of Figure 9.1. The Knowledge Hub's full architectural model is structured in five layers as shown in Figure 9.3

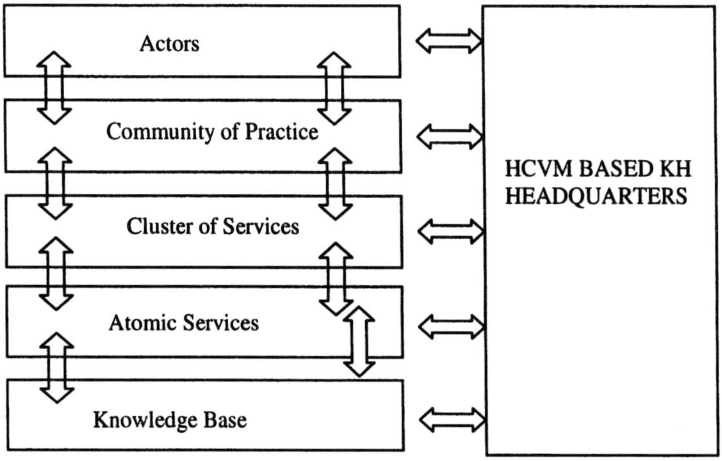

Figure 9.3. Knowledge Hub Architectural Model Structured in Five Layers

The HCVM based Knowledge Hub (KH) Headquarters can be seen as a sixth cross-functional layer (Passiante, Elia, and Massari, 2000), made up of all individuals, organizations and institutions that are responsible for co-ordination of the Knowledge Hub.

The headquarters main task is to configure and monitor dynamically the five layers' structure. The aim of our logical architecture is stimulating and supporting all actors involved in the local/regional innovation strategy, helping them to self-organize in a community of practice.

9.5.1. Knowledge Hub's Actors

The actors that interact with the Knowledge Hub belong to the following communities:

- Local and regional institutions, directly involved in planning and carrying out territorial growth and innovation projects;
- Local entrepreneurs and trade associations, representing the economical resource of a territory;
- Citizens and government officials, directly or indirectly involved in the local growth;
- Corporate headquarters and enterprises, attracted by new favorable environmental conditions and potentially interested in investing in the territory;

- Public and private research centers, representing the main source of innovation.

9.5.2. Cluster of Services

The Knowledge Hub is aimed at empowering all above categories of users and amplifying the network of existing relations among the typologies of actors listed in section 9.5.1. This purpose is achieved by increasing the frequency and effectiveness of their learning and knowledge sharing processes, through the organization of a *front office* area composed by dynamically configurable clusters of services. In this way, the Knowledge Hub is able to present a different, tailored set of atomic services to each community of practice, satisfying their needs and enhancing their potentialities.

The cluster of services for each community of practice is defined according to three fundamental guidelines: the objectives of each Community of practices, its needs and the perspectives and the results expected by the Knowledge Hub Headquarters. All Knowledge Hub services feed into and are fed by the contents of the knowledge base.

9.6. HCVM and Technological Architecture of the Knowledge Hub

We outline in this section how the HCVM methodology has been applied to define the technological architecture of the Knowledge Hub. The technological architecture shown in 9.4 is structured in two main areas, namely the front-office and back-office areas.

The front-office area is organized as a Web-based portal and functionally corresponds to the *Belief Agent* in the distributed processing layer of the HCVM in Figure 9.1. It represents the interface to the system through which the Knowledge Hub actors' beliefs are checked, imported into the system and converted into knowledge to be semi-automatically associated with concepts maintained by the RDF agents in the distributed processing layer of the HCVM. The decision support, optimization and intelligent tool and data mining agent layers of HCVM also provide added functionality to the user in the front-office area.

The main services offered through the portal include a discussion forum, mailing list, chat and teleconference facilities, e-learning support, on-line questionnaires, a document management system and a publishing system (for news and editorial content) and intelligent decision support.

The Knowledge Hub back office is centered on the content management system that is the heart of the whole system and exploits the network of concepts maintained by the RDF agents in Figure 9.2 .

Each of the services composing the Knowledge Hub continuously generates new knowledge, both directly (as the forum, the chat and the publishing system do) and indirectly.

The latter type of knowledge generation may occur is several ways, e.g. suggesting to the Knowledge Hub Headquarters new knowledge sources useful to solve specific problems or new discussion topics inside the different communities of practices.

Contents are organized according to a semantics-aware approach and are made available on the portal. The next section presents the main characteristics of our content management system.

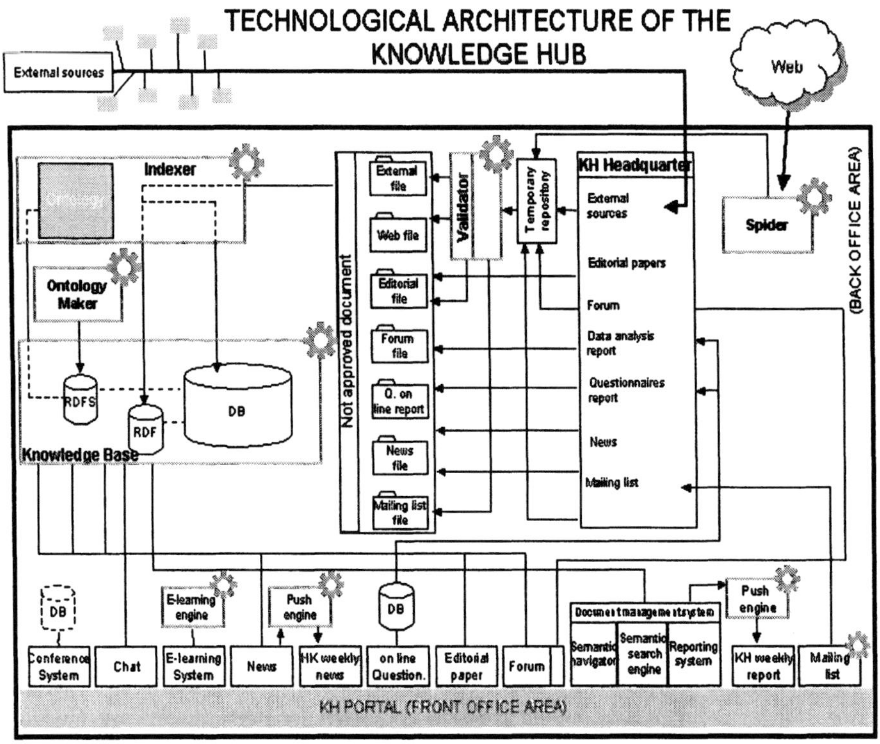

Figure 9.4: Technological Architecture of the Knowledge Hub

9.7. Knowledge Hub's Content Management System

The architecture of the Knowledge Hub's content management system is composed of a knowledge base and a set of HCVM based agents that implement the distributed processing layer of Figure 9.1. Such agents are employed for knowledge processing, i.e. for gathering, selecting, annotating and indexing documents (e.g., indexing agent shown in Figure 9.1), according to a chosen ontology. Moreover, there are a navigator for searching and retrieving documents (e.g., the RDFS processing agents in Figure 9.1 can be used as mobile agents for retrieving and fetching information), and an onto-maker module for codifying ontology domains into a machine-readable language.

Now, we briefly illustrate the main characteristics of the knowledge hub's processing agents and, in particular, of the indexing engine.

9.7.1. Spider and Validator Agents

The spider agent shown in Figures 9.4 and 9.1 respectively monitors the web, in order to find new knowledge items to be inserted in the knowledge base. The Knowledge Hub Headquarters members configure the spider using a web-configuration facility.

The validator agent allows adding notes and comments, keeping them separate from the rest of the document. In this way, each member of a community of practice can visualize both the notes and their authors, individuating immediately the core part of a document.

9.7.2. Indexing Agent

The indexing agent shown in Figures 9.4 and 9.1 respectively creates the link between documents and knowledge base. It allows associating to a document some concepts or semantic assertions, structured as subject-predicate-object sentences. In order to index a Web document, first it is necessary to open its XML or XHTML version. The indexing agent will show its XPath structure, on the right side of the screen. Then, it is necessary to open the ontology by which the document will be indexed. The indexing agent is able to interpret the syntax used to express the ontology (in our case, the RDFS language), representing it as a tree-structure, according to the selected browsing relation.

Browsing the ontology by concepts and changing the relations, the user can easily individuate the concepts related to the document. After selecting a XPath inside the document to be indexed, it is possible to associate to it one of the following typologies of semantic assertion: simple, complex or direct.

Simple semantic assertions associate single concepts of the ontology to a document (or part of document, i.e. a XPath). To obtain this, it is necessary to select the XPath and, then, to choose from the contextual menu the option related to simple assertion.

Then, it is necessary to individuate the concept of the ontology related to it, always using a fixed relation (conventionally called speak_about). For example, referring to the semantic assertion "Current document/Xpath speaks about an enterprise", the system will generate the following RDF statement:

1. <[xpath], indi:speak_about, onto: enterprise>

It is important to remark that speak_about is a relation defined in an autonomous XML namespace called indi. This generic XML namespace is HCVM-wide and extends with human-centered properties the standard set of classes and properties used in the process of creation and management of RDF assertions.

On the other hand, enterprise is a domain-specific concept belonging to the ontology defined (using RDFS) in the namespace onto, an application-specific XML namespace internal to Knowledge Hub containing classes and relations of the domain ontology used for the indexing process. Figure 9.5 shows the indexing agent user interface.

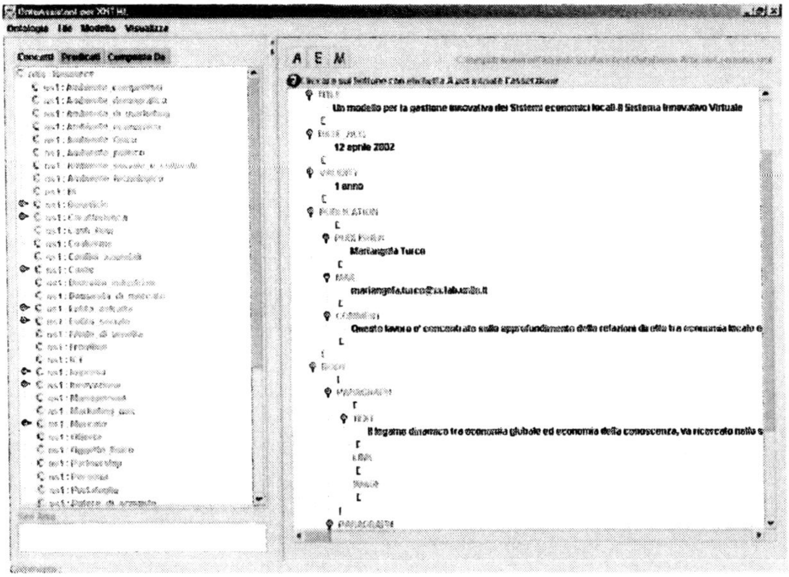

Figure 9.5: Indexing Agent Creating Semantic Assertions.

The indexing agent allows for specifying not only a set of concepts, but also their instances. Using the same encapsulation technique introduced before, instances are maintained using a separate XML namespace. For example, referring to the semantic assertion "Current document/Xpath speaks about the enterprise ACME", the indexing agent will generate the following set of RDF statements:

1. <[xpath], indi:speak_about, doc:ID_01>
2. < doc:ID_01, rdf:type, onto: enterprise>
3. < doc:ID_01, indi:name, "ACME">

Once again, Speak_about is a relation defined in the namespace indi; ID_01 represents the URI of the instance present in the namespace doc, containing all the instances and enterprise is a concept belonging to the ontology defined in the namespace onto.

Finally, ACME is the name of the enterprise and it is defined through the property name of the namespace indi.

In this way, it is possible to link a document (or part of it) to a two-levels metadata structure. Both levels are founded on the domain ontology. The former represents the concepts of the ontology, the latter represents instances of the concepts. Complex semantic assertion consists in associating to a document (or to a part of it, i.e., a

XPath) not only single concepts of the ontology but whole logic assertions, structured according to the model subject-predicate-object.

To obtain this, it is necessary to select the XPath to be indexed and, then, to choose from the contextual menu the option related to complex assertion. Then, it is necessary to individuate the subject of the assertion, selecting a concept from the ontology (or specifying an instance). After that, it is necessary to specify the predicate, choosing it among all the possible predicates suitable to the subject (considering also the inheritance among the concepts), according to the structure of the chosen ontology. As each predicate has only one end-concept, the object of the assertion is automatically defined. If needed, it is also possible to specify its instance.

Therefore, the number of RDF statements related to a complex semantic assertion goes from 5 to 9, depending on the presence of instances.

The following two examples illustrate the case of specification of concepts with and without instances.

Example 1: Encoding the complex semantic assertion "Current document/Xpath speaks about enterprise that invests in technology", the system will generate the following set of RDF statements:

1. <[xpath], indi:assert, doc_st_01>
2. <doc_st_01, rdf:type, rdf:statement>
3. <doc_st_01, rdf:subject, onto:enterprise>
4. <doc_st_01, rdf:predicate, onto:invest>
5. <doc_st_01, rdf:object, onto:technology>

Note that, in this semantic assertion, both subject and object are represented by concepts and not instances.

Assertions 1 and 2 say that the current Document/XPath asserts a statement. This statement has a subject-predicate-object structure, specified in the assertions 3, 4 and 5. In this example 3 namespaces are used: "indi", "onto" and "rdf". The first two have been already illustrated, while "rdf" is the default XML namespace defined by the World Wide Web Council (W3C), containing classes and properties needed for building the standard RDF assertions.

It is very important to realize that the sets of assertions encoding "subject-predicate-object" sentences carry a semantics which is much richer than the usual concept-instance association that we expressed above using the speak_about concept. Here we are not limited to saying that a resource is an instance of a concept; rather we can make virtually any comment about it. This will be further clarified in the following example.

Example 2: Referring to the complex semantic assertion "Current document/Xpath speaks about the enterprise ACME that invests in technology ORACLE", our system will generate the following set of RDF statements:

1. <[xpath], indi:assert, doc_st_01>

2. <doc_st_01, rdf:type, rdf:statement>
3. <doc_st_01, rdf:subject, doc:ID_01>
4. <doc_st_01, rdf:predicate, onto:invest>
5. <doc_st_01, rdf:object, doc:ID_02>
6. <doc:ID_01, rdf:type, onto:enterprise>
7. <doc:ID_01, indi:name, "ACME">
8. <doc:ID_02, rdf:type, onto:technology>
4. <doc:ID_02, indi:name, "ORACLE">

Note that in this semantic assertion both subject and object are represented by instances of ontology concepts. Assertions 1 and 2 say that the selected Document/XPath asserts a statement. This statement has a structure subject-predicate-object, specified in the assertions 3, 4 and 5. Assertion 3 states that the subject of the semantic assertion is the instance ID_01, belonging to doc namespace. Assertion 5 states that the object of the semantic assertion is the instance ID_02, again belonging to doc namespace. Assertion 4 specifies the relation of the ontology, defined in the namespace onto. Assertions 6 and 7 respectively specify the subject, while assertions 8 and 9 specify the object.

In this example, four namespaces are used: "indi", "rdf", "onto" and "doc". Direct semantic assertions are different from previous ones. They are usually employed together with the ontology for attaching a data type to the current XPath or document. Its structure is given according to the subject-predicate-object model and the phases of the process are the same described above (selection of Xpath/document, specification of subject, predicate and object).

There are two typologies of direct semantic assertion: simple and complex.Referring to the simple direct semantic assertion "Document/Xpath is an image", the system will generate the following RDF statement:

<[xpath], rdf:type, onto:immagine>

Referring to the complex semantic direct assertion "Document/Xpath is an image with a white background", the system will generate the following set of RDF statements:

1. <[xpath], rdf:type, onto:image>
2. <[xpath], onto:has_background, doc:ID_01>
3. <doc:ID_01, rdf:type, onto:colour >
4. <doc:ID_01, indi:name, "white">

After the generation of RDF statements, the indexing agent processes them and stores the relative semantic assertion into the database. In this way, the document becomes part of the knowledge base, together with a set of metadata and a set of semantic assertions.

A further functionality available for the three typology of semantic assertion is related to the specification of the instances. In fact, the indexing agent allows to users to recall the latest ones or to extract from the database the existing ones.

Moreover, the indexing agent allows seeing automatically generated RDF assertions, in order to verify their structure and correctness. Then there is also a text editor for creation of ad hoc RDF statements, integrating them with statements created automatically.

9.8. Decision Support and Navigation Agents

In the previous sections we discussed how our indexing agent can be used for creating an set of metadata and inserting them into our knowledge base, relying on a HCVM-wide ontology and on a set of domain-specific ones. Now we will see how knowledge can be exploited for semantics-aware navigation and decision support.

In order to set up our knowledge base, we have first built the structure of the concepts through a semantic network approach using the traditional KL-ONE model (Brachman and Schmolze, 1985).

Our second step has been the choice of a machine-readable language: RDFS (Resource Description Framework Schema) for formalizing the ontology and RDF (Resource Description Framework) for structuring the semantic assertions. This choice is justified from the arising importance of these two languages in the semantic web community (for web content definition), and for the role they play in structuring other languages (such as OIL).

In the definition process of our ontologies, we use 4 namespaces: the standard namespaces defined by W3C (rdf and rdfs) and two other namespaces built for the specific application context (indi and onto). The whole knowledge base (composed by the ontologies and the semantic assertions) is stored in a relational database. This choice was supported by the following considerations:

- Enhanced efficiency in searching documents;
- Improved maintenance of the knowledge base (in fact, it is possible to correct concepts and their instances without modifying the source code of RDF and RDFS files).

The decision support agent embodies HCVM decision support agents (shown in Figure 9.1) acting as a semantic-aware datawarehouse, extracting knowledge following conceptual links (namely, the speaks-about link) and in the application-specific ones (including the standard is-a and part-of ones).

Finally, the navigator represents the navigational interface of the knowledge base with the end-users. It allows selecting the documents not only through usual text retrieval techniques, but also through semantic search and semantic navigation. Figure 9.6 shows the Web-based interface of the semantic navigator. The navigation ontology is displayed on the left-hand side.

9.9. Summary

This chapter outlines the application of different layers of the HCVM to front and back office areas of the technological architecture of a Knowledge management system. The application of the HCVM and the human-centered approach to knowledge management described in this chapter, raises issues related to the encoding process of tacit knowledge.

The support for human centered techniques maximizes benefits coming from knowledge sharing process. For this reason human centered knowledge management system can be enriched by a wealth of new agents:, working at the distributed processing layer of HCVM. An interesting example related to the knowledge hub

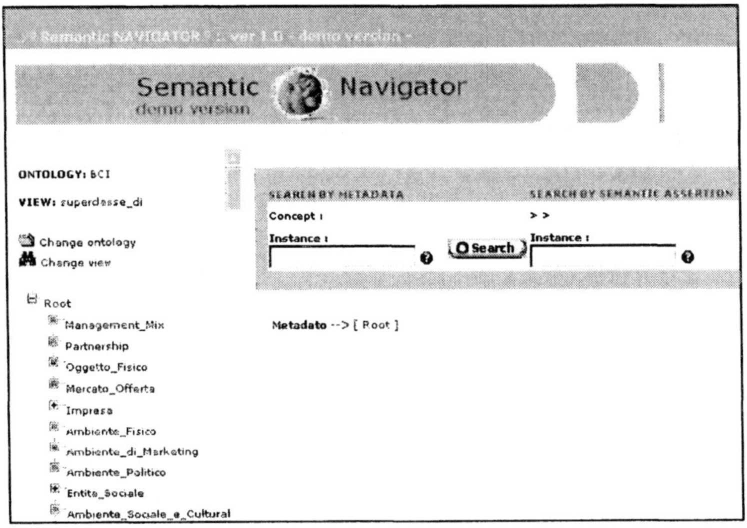

Figure 9.6: The Semantic Navigator interface

described in this chapter is an interactive viewer devoted to end users, allowing inserting notes and, at the same time, visualizing comments specified by other users.

Acknowledgements

Authors would like to thank Aldo Romano and his team at the E-business Management School at the University of Lecce, Italy for precious suggestions and joint work on knowledge management systems. Mario Marinazzo and Giusy Passiante. Angelo Corallo and Gianluca Elia (with the help of Mino Franza and Gianluca Lorenzo) worked hard to apply HCVM to the knowledge hub design. Finally, Serena Nichetti, Giuliana Severgnini, Marco Degli Angeli and Mirco Polini (M. Sc. candidates, University of Milan, Italy) gave important contributions to the implementation of the primary agents of the Knowledge Hub platform (in particular the spider, the indexing agent and the semantic navigator).

References

Berners-Lee, T., Hendler, J. and Lassila, O., (2001): “The Semantic Web,” Scientific American 284(5), pp.34-43

Brachman, R., Schmolze, J., (1985): "An Overview of the KL-ONE Knowledge Representation System", Cognitive Science 9(2), pp.171-216

Brickley, D., and Guha, R.V. (2000): “Resource Description Framework (RDF) Schema Specification 1.0” W3C Candidate Recommendation 27 March 2000.

Corallo, A., Damiani, E. and Elia, G. (2002) "A Knowledge Management System Enabling Regional Innovation", Proceedings of KES 2002, Crema, Italy

Grueber, T.G., (1995), Toward Principles for the Design of Ontologies Used for Knowledge sharing. Int. J. Hum. Comput. Stud 43, 5/6 907–9289

Gruniger, M. and Lee, J., (2002): "Ontology Applications and Design", Comm. of the ACM, 45(2), pp.39-41

Lassila, O., and Swick, R. R., (1999): “Resource Description Framework (RDF) – Model and Syntax” W3C Candidate Recommendation 22 February 1999.

Romano, A., Passiante, G. and Elia. V. (2001): “Creating Business Innovation Leadership – An ongoing experiment: the e-Business Management School at ISUFI”, Edizione Scientifiche Italiane

Passiante, G., Elia, V. and Massari, T., (2000): *Net Economy – Approcci interpretativi e modelli di sviluppo regionale*, Cacucci Editore.

Fensel, D. (2001): *Ontologies: A Silver Bullet for Knowledge Management and Electronic Commerce*, Springer, .

10 HYPERMEDIA INFORMATION SYSTEMS

10.1. Introduction

In the last four chapters we have described applications of HCVM in e-sales recruitment, e-banking, e-business data organization and knowledge management. In chapter 5 we also described the multimedia component of the HCVM. In all these chapters multimedia has been looked at in terms of how it can be used for improving the representational efficiency, effectiveness and interpretation of computer-based artifacts and also to some extent how it can be used for perceptual problem solving. In fact, multimedia data (e.g., text, image, video and audio) today is an inherent part of Internet and web-based applications. In that respect, there are interesting research issues and problems associated with management and retrieval of multimedia data from multimedia databases. Queries and operations based on classical approaches (e.g., relational database structures) just won't do for multimedia data, where browsing is an important paradigm. The importance of this paradigm is illustrated by the fact that multimedia databases are sometimes referred to as *hypermedia databases*. Standard indexing approaches won't work for annotation independent, content-based queries over multimedia data. The problem is further compounded by the fact that metadata of different media artifacts cannot be effectively used for modeling user queries involving text, image, video and audio data. Incorporating user semantics is an effective way of dealing with multimedia data indexing and retrieval.

In this chapter, we discuss several ways of modeling user semantics including relevance feedback, latent semantic indexing and defining media and domain independent human-centered ontological constructs. In the next chapter, we describe a web based multimedia application involving intelligent agents and relevance feedback. We start this chapter by outlining the background to multimedia data retrieval. We then discuss the basics of hypermedia information management, examine the nature of multimedia data and the area of multimedia data modeling, followed by a discussion of content-based retrieval. We end the chapter by outlining some commercial hypermedia systems.

10.2. Background

In the past fifteen years, the database field has been quite active, whether in discovering more efficient methods for managing classical alphanumeric data, in bringing application dependent concepts, such as rules, into the database environment (Widom et. al. 1996), or in managing such new types of data as images and video (Grosky 1994). When new types of data are first brought into a database environment, it is quite natural that this data is transformed so as to be representable in the existing database architectures. Thus, when images were first managed in a database, researchers developed numerous techniques concerned with how to represent them, first in a relational architecture (Tamura et. al 1984) and then in an object-oriented architecture (Gupta et. al. 1991).

If this representation is done in a way compatible with the types of queries and operations that are to be supported, then the various modules that comprise a database system ostensibly don't have to be changed to work with this new type of data. After all, if an image or its contents can be represented as a set of tuples over several relations, then why shouldn't the classical relational techniques developed for indexing, query optimization, buffer management, concurrency control, security, and recovery work equally well in this new environment? Historically, this is what indeed occurred. It is only after some experience working with new types of data transformed in such a way as to be part of existing database systems that one comes to the conclusion that there is an inherent weakness with this approach. There is a mismatch between the nature of the data being represented and the way one is forced to query and operate on it.

Queries and operations based on classical approaches just won't do for multimedia data, where browsing is an important paradigm. The importance of this paradigm is illustrated by the fact that multimedia databases are sometimes referred to as *hypermedia databases*. Standard indexing approaches won't work for annotation independent, content-based queries over multimedia data. Other modules of a database system likewise have to be changed in order to manage multimedia data efficiently. At the present time, we realize that this must be done, but there is no agreement on how to proceed. Commercially, the object-relational database systems (Stonebraker 1996) are at the state-of-the-art for implementing hypermedia database systems, but even these systems leave much to be desired.

The process of managing multimedia data in a database environment has gone through the following historical sequence:

1. Multimedia data was first transformed into relations in a very ad-hoc fashion (Tamura et. al. 1984). Depending on how this was done, certain types of queries and operations were more efficiently supported than others. At the beginning of this process, a query such as *Find all images containing the person shown dancing in this video* was extremely difficult, if not impossible, to answer in an efficient manner.
2. When the weaknesses of the above approach became apparent, researchers finally asked themselves what type of information should be extracted from images and videos and how this information should be represented so as to support content-based queries most efficiently. The

result of this effort was a large body of articles on multimedia data models (Grosky 1984).

3. Since these data models specified what type of information was extracted from multimedia data, the nature of a multimedia query was also discussed. Previous work on feature matching from the field of image interpretation was brought into a database environment and the field of multimedia indexing was initiated (Mehrotra et. al. 1988). This, in turn, started the ball rolling in multimedia query optimization techniques (Rabitti et. al. 1992).
4. A multimedia query was realized to be quite different than a standard database query, and close to queries in an information retrieval setting (Santini et. al. 1996). The implications of this important concept have still not played themselves out.
5. It was only after the preceding events that improvements in other database system modules were considered. These fields of research are still in their infancy.

10.3. Character of Multimedia Data

Multimedia data is quite different from standard alphanumeric data, both from a presentation as well as from a semantics point of view. From a presentation viewpoint, multimedia data is quite huge and has time dependent characteristics that must be adhered to for a coherent viewing. Whether a multimedia object is pre-existing or constructed on-the-fly, its presentation and subsequent user interaction push the boundaries of standard database systems. From a semantics viewpoint, metadata and information extracted from the contents of a multimedia object is quite complex and affects both the capabilities and the efficiency of a multimedia database system. How this is accomplished is still an active area of research.

Multimedia data consists of alphanumeric, graphics, image, animation, video, and audio objects. Alphanumeric, graphics, and image objects are time-independent, while animation, video, and audio objects are time-dependent. Video objects, being a structured combination of image and audio objects, also have an internal temporal structure which forces various synchronization conditions. A single frame of an NTSC quality video requires (512×480) pixels $\times$ 8 bits/pixel = 246 KB, while a single frame of an HDTV quality video requires $(1024 \times 2000) \times 24$ bits/pixel = 6.1 MB. Thus, at a 100:1 compression ratio, an hour of HDTV quality video would take 6.6 GB of storage, not even considering the audio portion. Utilizing a database system for presentation of a video object is quite complex, if the audio and image portions are to be synchronized and presented in a smooth fashion.

Besides its complex structure, multimedia data requires complex processing in order to extract semantics from its contents. Real-world objects shown in images, video, animations, or graphics, and being discussed in audio are participating in meaningful events whose nature is often the subject of queries. Utilizing state-of-the-art approaches from the fields of image interpretation and speech recognition, it is often possible to extract information from multimedia objects which is less complex and voluminous than the multimedia objects themselves and which can give some clues as to the semantics of the events being represented by these objects. This information consists of objects called *features,* which are used to recognize similar real-world objects and events across multiple multimedia objects.

How the logical and physical representation of multimedia objects are defined and relate to each other, as well as what features are extracted from these objects and how this is accomplished are in the domain of multimedia data modeling.

10.4. Hypermedia Data Modeling

In a standard database system, a data model is a collection of abstract concepts that can be used to represent real-world objects, their properties, their relationships to each other, and operations defined over them. These abstract concepts are capable of being physically implemented in the given database system. Through the mediation of this data model, queries and other operations over real-world objects are transformed into operations over abstract representations of these objects, which are, in turn, transformed into operations over the physical implementations of these abstract representations. In particular, in a hypermedia data model, the structure and behavior of multimedia objects must be represented. What makes this type of data model different from a standard data model is that multimedia objects are completely defined in the database and that they contain references to other real-world objects that should also be represented by the data model. For example, the person *Bill* is a real-world object that should be represented in a data model. The video *Bill's Vacation* is a multimedia object whose structure as a temporal sequence of image frames should also be represented in the same data model. However, when *Bill* is implemented in a database by a given sequence of bits, this sequence is not actually *Bill,* who is a person. On the other hand, the sequence of bits that implements the video *Bill's Vacation* in the database *is* the actual video, or can be considered to be such. In addition, the fact that *Bill* appears in various frames of the video *Bill's Vacation* doing certain actions should also be represented in the same data model.

Thus, the types of information that should be captured in a hypermedia data model include the following:

1. The detailed structure of the various multimedia objects.
2. Structure dependent operations on multimedia objects.
3. Multimedia object properties.
4. Relationships between multimedia objects and real-world objects.
5. Portions of multimedia objects that have representation relationships with real-world objects, the representation relationships themselves, and the methods used to determine them.
6. Properties, relationships, and operations on real-world objects.

For images, the structure would include such things as the image format, the image resolution, the number of bits/pixel, and any compression information, while for a video object, items such as duration, frame resolution, number of bits/pixel, color model, and compression information would be included. Modeling the structure of a multimedia object is important for many reasons, not the least of which is that operations are defined on these objects which are dependent on its structure. These operations are used to create derived multimedia objects for similarity matching (e.g., image edge maps), as well as various composite multimedia objects from individual component multimedia objects (e.g., multimedia presentations). A good discussion of these aspects of a multimedia data model is found in (Gibbs et. al. 1997).

An example of a multimedia object property is the name of the object; for example, *'Bill's Vacation'* is the name of a particular video object. A relationship between a multimedia object and a real-world object would be the *stars-in* relationship between the actor *Bill* and the video *Bill's Vacation.*

Suppose that *Golden Gate Bridge* is a real-world object being represented in the database and that a particular region of frame six of the video *Bill's Vacation* is known to show this object. This small portion of the byte span of the entire video is also considered to be a first-class database object, called a *semcon* (Grosky et. al. 1997), for i*con*ic data with *sem*antics, and both the *represents* relationship between this semcon and the *Golden Gate Bridge* object and the *appearing-in* relationship between the *Golden Gate Bridge* object and the video *Bill's Vacation* should be captured by the data model. Attributes of this semcon are the various features extracted from it that can be used for similarity matching over other multimedia objects. Semcons can be time-independent, as above, or time-dependent, in which case they correspond to events (Gupta et. al. 1991). See Figure 10.1 for an illustration of some image semcons.

10.5. Content-Based Retrieval Indexing

In this section a number of techniques for content-based retrieval and indexing. We start with intelligent browsing and then follow it with semcon matching and other techniques.

10.5.1. Intelligent Browsing

A multimedia database with the addition of an intelligent browsing capability is known as a hypermedia database. How to accomplish intelligent browsing in a multimedia collection can best be understood through the definition of a *browsing-schema,* which is nothing more than an object-oriented schema over non-media objects, which has undergone a transformation that will shortly be explained.

In the ensuing discussion, let us restrict ourselves to images; similar operations would apply to objects of other modalities. To transform our original object-oriented schema into a browsing-schema, we first add a class of images. Each image is actually a complex object, comprising various regions having semantic content (semcons). Similarly, each such region itself may be decomposed into various subregions, each having some semantic content. This decomposition follows the complex object structure of the non-media objects represented by the given regions. That is, if non-media object o_2 is a part of non-media object o_1, and o_1 has a representation r_1 appearing in some image (as a particular region), then, cases exist where r_1 would have a component r_2 that is a representation of object o_2. (This would not be the case where r_2 is occluded in the scene.) For example, a window is part of a building. Thus, the region of an image corresponding to a building may have various subregions, each of which corresponds to a window.

To the resulting schema, we now add a class of semcons. Attributes of this class are based on various extracted features such as shape, texture, and color, which are used for determining when one semcon is similar to another, and thus represents the same non-media object. We note that semcons as well as their attributes are considered as metadata.

To each non-media class, we then add a set-valued attribute *appearing-in,* which leads from each instantiation of that class to the set of images-locations where its corresponding semcon appears. We also add an attribute *represents* to the class of semcons, which leads from each semcon to the non-media object, which that semcon represents. The resultant schema is then defined as the browsing schema corresponding to the original object-oriented schema. It is now possible to view an image, specify a particular semcon within this media object, and determine information concerning the non-media object corresponding to this particular image region. For example, viewing an image of Professor Smith, it is now possible to navigate to a set of images containing representations of the students of Professor Smith.

Whenever viewing a particular image, the user can choose a particular semcon, *r,* for further examination. One of the actions the user can carry out is to view the value of any attribute, *a,* defined over the non-media object which *r* represents. This is accomplished in the browsing schema by calculating *represents(r).a.*. If the value of this attribute is of a simple data type (e.g., integer, real, or string), it is textually presented to the user. If, however, this attribute's value is another (non-media) object, the user is allowed to browse through a set of images, each of which contains a representation of this latter non-media object. This approach easily generalizes to set-valued attributes. In a similar fashion, the user can follow an association (relationship). For example, if semcon, *r,* is chosen by the user and the non-media object *represents(r)* participates in a binary relationship with a collection, *S,* of other non-media objects, then the user is allowed to browse through a set of images consisting of images which contain a representation of a non-media object from the collection *S.*

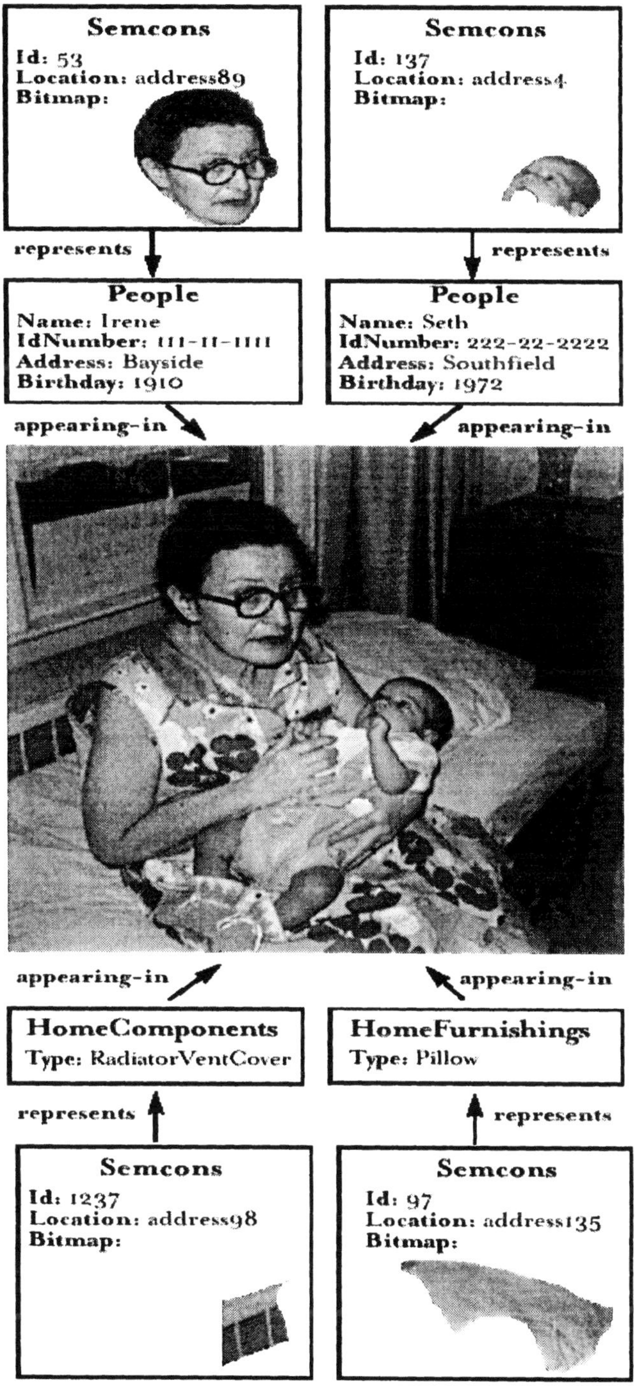

Figure 10.1: Some Image Semcons

When a particular semcon is chosen, the user can view a scrolling menu of choices, which includes each attribute and relationship in which the non-media object represented by the particular semcon participates. Through the use of filtering commands, the user will be able to navigate through paths composed of many relationships and attributes and restrict the collection of media objects at the final destination. For example, choosing a particular semcon which is an image of a particular Mayan artifact, a filtering command of the form **self.type.artifacts, where self.type.artifacts.discovered =`1923'**, will take the user to a collection of images which represent artifacts of the same type as the given Mayan artifact which were discovered in 1923.

A very important use of this approach is to navigate along a *similarity path*. Such a path proceeds from a given semcon to the set of images containing semcons similar to the given semcon. An illustration of this sort of navigation would be to proceed from an image containing some flowers to the set of all images in the database that also contain such flowers. This browsing path is not, however, mediated by the relationships *represents* and *appearing-in*, but by content-based retrieval techniques. After this is done, the user can choose to update the relations *represents* and *appearing-in*, so that future browsing can be done more efficiently. As different users view the resultant output of a content-based query in different ways, what is acceptable for one user may not be acceptable for another user. Thus, rather than globally update these two relations for all users, each user will have his own version of these relationships.

An important problem arises as to how the initial state of the browsing schema is constructed. At present, this must be done manually. Given a particular image collection, we assume the existence of a pre-existing database schema that captures the various entities and their relationships. Then, for each image, semcons and their corresponding database entities must be identified. We note that some images may also be inserted into the system without manual labeling and rely on similarity path browsing to identify the semcons appearing in them.

10.5.2. Image and Semcon Matching

Most existing techniques match entire images against one another. An alternative technique is to extract semcons from the query and database images and perform matching at the semcon level. This latter methodology is much more difficult, however, as finding semcons automatically is a difficult task. As mentioned later on in this section, a way around these difficulties is to decompose the image into using various fixed partitioning strategies.

Historically, image and semcon matching has consisted of developing representations for the image features of shape, color, and texture, along with appropriate distance measures. Throughout the years, different approaches have been developed for these features. This section illustrates existing techniques, while in the next section, we will present a generic approach that we have developed that captures the spatial relationships of an image's point feature map.

Shape retrieval can be categorized into exact match searching and similarity-based searching. For either type of retrieval, the dynamic aspects of shape information require expensive computations and sophisticated methodologies in the areas of image processing and database systems. So far, similarity-based shape retrieval is the most popular searching type. Extraction and representation of object shape are relatively difficult tasks and have been approached in a variety of ways. In Mehtre et. al. (1997), shape representation techniques are broadly divided into two categories: *boundary-based* and *region-based*. To be specific, boundary-based methods concern the border or contour of the shape without considering its interior information; region-based methods concern both the border and interior of the shape. However, one drawback of this categorization is that they put shape attributes such as *area*, *elongation*, and *compactness* into both categories. We view shape representation techniques as being in two distinct categories: *measurement-based methods,* ranging from simple, primitive measures such as *area* and *circularity* (Niblack et. al. 1993) to the more sophisticated measures of various *moment invariants* (Niblack et. al. 1993, Mehtre et. al. 1997); and *transformation-based methods,* ranging from functional transformations such as *Fourier descriptors* (Mehtre et. al. 1997) to structural transformations such as *chain codes* (Lu 1997) and *curvature scale space feature vectors* (Mokhtarian et. al. 1996). An attempt to compare the various shape representation schemes is made in (Mehtre et. al. 1997).

In Jagadish (1991), the notion of a rectangular cover of a shape was introduced. Since this is restricted to rectilinear shapes in two dimensions such that all of the shape angles are right angles, each shape in the database comprises an ordered set of rectangles. These rectangles are normalized, and then described by means of their relative positions and sizes. The proposed shape representation scheme supports any multi-dimensional point indexing method such as the grid-file (Nievergelt et. al. 1984) and K-D-B trees (Robinson 1981). This technique can be naturally extended to multiple dimensions. In addition to the limitations mentioned previously, the process of obtaining good shape descriptions of rectangular covers is not straightforward.

One of the first image retrieval projects was QBIC (Niblack et. al. 1993). Provided with a visual query interface, a user can draw a sketch to find images with similar sketches in terms of color, texture, and shape. A union of heuristic shape features such as area, circularity, eccentricity, major axis orientation and some algebraic moment invariants are computed for content-based image retrieval. Since similar moments do not guarantee similar shapes, the query results sometimes contain perceptually different matches.

In Mehrotra et. al. (1995), a general and flexible shape similarity-based approach to enable the retrieval of both rigid and articulated shapes was presented. In their scheme, each shape is coded as an ordered sequence of interest points such as the maximum local curvature boundary points or vertices of the shape boundary's polygonal approximation, with the indexed feature vectors representing the shape boundary. To answer a shape retrieval query, the query shape representation is extracted and the index structure is searched for the stored shapes that are possibly similar to the query shape, and the set of possible similar shapes is further examined to formulate the final solution to the query. In Lu (1997), assuming that each shape boundary is approximated by directed straight line segments, a unique chain coding method was introduced for shape representation by eliminating the inherent non-invariance of chain code. He also discusses the shape distance and similarity measures based on the derived shape indexes. One of the limitations of this approach is that the mirror image factor is not taken into account. Additionally, if the flattest segment of the boundaries does not happen to be along the major axis, this method may not work well.. In Ahmad et. al. (1999), a recursive decomposition of an image into a spatial arrangement of feature points was proposed. This decomposition preserved the spatial relationships among its various components. In their scheme, quadtrees are used to manage the decomposition hierarchy and help in quantifying the measure of similarity. This scheme is incremental in nature and can be adopted to find a match at various levels of details, from coarse to fine. This technique can also be naturally extended to higher dimensional space. One drawback of this approach is that the set of feature points characterizing shape and spatial information in the image has to be normalized before being indexed.

One of the earliest image retrieval projects utilizing spatial color indexing methods was QBIC (Niblack et. al. 1993), also mentioned above. Provided with a visual query interface, the user can manually outline an image object to facilitate image analysis in order to acquire an object boundary, and then request images containing objects whose color is similar to the color of the object in the query image. In the QBIC system, each image object is indexed by a union of area, circularity, eccentricity, major axis orientation and some algebraic moment invariants as its shape descriptors, along with color moments such as the average (R, G, B), (Y, i, q), (L, a, b) and MTM (Mathematical Transform to Munsell) coordinates, as well as a k element color histogram. Other research groups have also tried to combine color and shape features for improving the performance of image retrieval. In Jain and Vailaya (1996), the color in an image is represented by three 1-D color histograms in (R, G, B) space, while a histogram of the directions of the edge points is used to represent the general shape information. A composite feature descriptor is proposed in Mehtre et. al. (1998) based on a clustering technique, and it combines the information of both the shape and color clusters, which are characterized by seven invariant moments and color cluster means, respectively. In Belongie et. al. (1998), a system which uses a so-called *blobworld* representation to retrieve images is described, and it attempts to recognize the nature of images as combinations of objects so as to make both query and learning in the blobworld more meaningful to the user. In this scheme, each blob (region) in the image is described by the two dominant colors, the centroid for its location and a scatter matrix for its basic shape representation.

Though it is more meaningful to represent the spatial distribution of color information based on image objects or regions, various fixed image partitioning techniques have also been proposed because of their simplicity and acceptable performance. In Stricker et. al. (1996), an image is divided into five partially overlapped, fuzzy regions, with each region indexed by its three moments of the color distribution. In Dimai (1997), the inter-hierarchical distance (IHD) is defined as the color variance between two different hierarchical levels (i.e., an image region and its subregions). Based on a fixed partition of the image, an image is indexed by the color of the whole image and a set of IHD's which encode the spatial color information. The system Color-WISE is described in Sethi et. al. (1998). This approach partitions an image into 8*8 blocks with each block indexed by its dominant hue and saturation values.

Instead of partitioning an image into regions, there are other approaches for the representation of spatial color distribution. A histogram refinement technique is described in Pass et. al. (1996) by partitioning histogram bins based on the spatial coherence of pixels. A pixel is coherent if it is a part of some *sizable* similar-colored region, and incoherent otherwise. In Huang et. al. (1997), a statistical method is proposed to index an image by color correlograms which is actually a table containing color pairs, where the *k*-th entry for <*i*, *j*> specifies the probability of locating a pixel of color *j* at a distance k from a pixel of color *i* in the image.

We note that both the histogram refinement and correlogram approaches do not recognize the nature of images as combinations of objects. As for meaningful region-based image representations, two image objects are usually considered similar only if the corresponding regions they occupy overlap. Along with the position dependence of similar image objects, the fixed image partition strategy does not allow image objects to be rotated within an image. In addition, in order to check whether these image objects are in the requisite spatial relationships, even 2D-strings and its variants suffer from exponential time complexity in terms of the number of concerned image objects. Our *anglogram-based* approach to feature-matching, described in the next section, is, a quite generic approach. We have already used it for shape matching and color matching.

10.5.3. Generic Image Model

Humans are much better than computers at extracting semantic information from images. We believe that complete image understanding should start from interpreting image objects and their relationships. Therefore, it is necessary to move from image-level to object-level interpretation in order to deal with the rich semantics of images and image sequences. An *image object* is either an entire image or some other meaningful portion of an image that could be a union of one or more disjoint regions. Typically, an image object would be a *semcon* (iconic data with semantics) (Grosky et. al. 1998). For example, consider an image of a seashore scene shown in Figure 10. 2, consisting of some seagulls on the coast, with the sky overhead and a sea area in the center. Examples of image objects for this image would include the entire scene (with textual descriptor *Life on the Seashore*), the seagull region(s), the sand regions(s), the water region(s), the sky region(s), and the bird regions (the union of all the seagull regions). Now, each image object in an image database contains a set of unique and characterizing features $F = \{f_1, \ldots, f_k\}$. We believe that the nature as well as the spatial relationships of these various features can be used to characterize the corresponding image objects (Ahmad et. al. 1999, Hsu et. al. 1995, Belongie et. al. 1998, Smith et. al. 1999).

Figure 10.2: An Image of a Seashore Scene

In 2-D space, many features can be represented as a set of points. These points can be tagged with labels to capture any necessary semantics. Each of the individual points representing some feature of an image object we call a *feature point*. The entire image object is represented by a set of labeled feature points $\{p_1, \ldots, p_k\}$. For example, a corner point of an image region has a precise location and can be labeled with the descriptor *corner point*, some numerical information concerning the nature of the corner in question, as well as the region's identifier. A color histogram of an image region can be represented by a point placed at the center-of-mass of the given region and labeled with the descriptor *color histogram*, the histogram itself, as well as the region's identifier. We note that the various spatial relationships among these points are an important aspect of our work.

Effective semantic representation and retrieval requires labeling the feature points of each database image object. The introduction of such feature points and associated labels effectively converts an image object into an equivalent symbolic representation, called its *point feature map*. We have devised an indexing mechanism to retrieve all those images from a given image database which contain image objects whose point feature map is similar to the point feature map of a particular query image object (Ahmad et. al. 1999). An important aspect of our approach is that it is rotation, translation, and scale invariant when matching images containing multiple semcons.

10.5.4. Shape Matching

The methodology of our proposed shape representation for image object indexing is quite simple. Within a given image, we first identify particular image objects to be indexed. For each image object, we construct a corresponding point feature map. In this study, we assume that each feature is represented by a single feature point and that a point feature map consists of a set of distinct feature points having the same label descriptor, such as *Corner Point*. After constructing a Delaunay triangulation of these feature points of the point feature map, we then compute a histogram that is obtained by discretizing the angles produced by this triangulation and counting the number of times each discrete angle occurs in the image object of interest, given the selection criteria of what bin size will be, and of which angles will contribute to the final angle histogram. As the nature of our computational geometry-based shape representation consists of angle histograms, we call the shape index a *shape anglogram*. For example, the shape anglogram can be built by counting the two largest angles, the two smallest angles, or all three angles of each individual Delaunay triangle with some bin size between 0° and 90°. An $O(max(N, \#bins))$ algorithm is necessary to compute the shape anglogram corresponding to the Delaunay triangulation of a set of N points.

Our idea of using an anglogram to represent the shape of an image object originates from the fact that if two image objects are similar in shape, then both of them should have the same set of feature points. Thus, each pair of corresponding Delaunay triangles in the two resulting Delaunay triangulations must be *similar* to each other, independent of the image object's position, scale, and rotation. In this study, corner points, which are generally high-curvature points located along the crossings of an image object's edges or boundaries, will serve as the feature points for our various experiments. We have previously argued for representing an image by the collection of its corner points in (Ahmad et. al. 1999), which proposed an interesting technique for indexing such collections provided that the image object has been normalized. In our present approach, which is histogram-based, the image object does not have to be normalized. This technique also supports an incremental approach to image object matching, from coarse to fine, by varying the bin sizes.

Figure 10.3a shows the resulting Delaunay triangulation produced from the point feature map characterizing the shape of the image object, *leaf*, in which corner points serve as the feature points. Figure 10.3b shows the resulting shape anglogram built by counting all three angles of each individual Delaunay triangle, with a bin size of 10°.

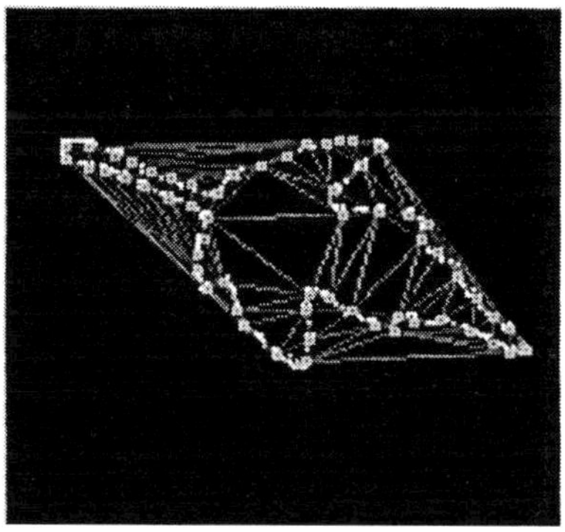

Figure 10.3a: Delauney Triangulation of a Leaf

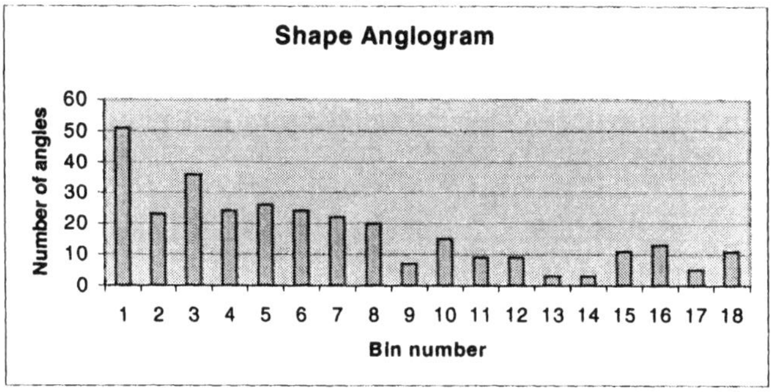

10.3b: Resulting Shape Anglogram

10.5.5. Color Matching

Digital images can be represented in different color spaces such as RGB, HSI, YIQ, or Munsell. Since a very large resolution of millions of colors is unwanted for image retrieval, the color space is usually quantized to a much coarser resolution. For example, HSI (Hue-Saturation-Intensity) color space is designed to resemble the human perception of color in which hue reflects the dominant spectral wavelength of a color, saturation reflects the purity of a color, and intensity reflects the brightness of a color. It is noted in (Wan et. al. 1996) that humans are less sensitive to differences in either saturation or intensity than to differences in the hue component, so that, in general, hue is quantized more finely than the saturation or intensity component for image retrieval when HSI is used for image representation. As the process of grouping low-level image features into meaningful image objects and then automatically attaching semantic descriptions to these image objects is still an unsolved problem in image understanding, our work intends to combine both the simplicity of fixed image partition and the nature of images as combinations of objects into spatial color indexing so as to facilitate image retrieval. Based on the assumption that salient image constituents generally tend to occupy relative homogeneous regions within an image, we expect that one or more meaningful image constituents may be composed of some image blocks with a particular color. Regardless of whether these image blocks are connected or not, they approximate the composition of the nature of images as combinations of objects. In our spatial color-indexing scheme, an image is first divided evenly into a number of $M*N$ non-overlapping blocks. Then each individual block is abstracted as a unique feature point labeled with its spatial location and dominant colors. After we adjust all two neighboring feature points to a fixed distance, all the normalized feature points form a *point feature map* of the original image for further analysis.

By representing an image as a point feature map, we capture not only the color information of the image, but also the spatial information about color. We can flexibly manipulate sets of feature points instead of dealing with image blocks. In order to compute our spatial color index of an image, we construct a Delaunay triangulation for each set of feature points in the point feature map labeled with the identical color, and then compute the feature point histogram by discretizing and counting the angles produced by this triangulation. An O(*max(N, #bins)*) algorithm is necessary to compute the feature point histogram corresponding to the Delaunay triangulation of a set of N points. The final image index is obtained by concatenating all the feature point histograms together. We note that in our spatial color indexing scheme, feature point histograms are not normalized, as a drawback of normalized histograms is its inability to match parts of image objects. For example, if region A is a part of region B, then, in general, the normalized histogram H_A is no longer a subset of the normalized histogram H_B.

An example is shown in Figures 10.4a to 10.4h respectively. Figure 10.4a shows a pyramid image of size 192*128; by dividing the image evenly into 16*16 blocks, Figure 10.4b and Figure 10.4c show the image approximation using dominant hue and saturation values to represent each block, respectively. Figure 10.4d shows the corresponding point feature map perceptually, and we note that the distance between any two neighboring feature points is fixed, as images of different sizes undergo normalization. Figure 10.4e highlights the set of feature points labeled with hue 2, and Figure10.4f shows the resulting Delaunay triangulation. Figure 10.4g shows the resulting Delaunay triangulation of a set of feature points labeled with saturation 5, and Figure10.4h shows the corresponding feature point histogram obtained by counting only the two largest angles out of each individual Delaunay triangle with bin size of 10°. Our work in (Tao and Grosky 1999a) has concluded that such a feature point histogram provides a sufficient and effective way for image object discrimination.

Figure 10.4a: A Pyramid Image

Figure 10.4b: Hue Component

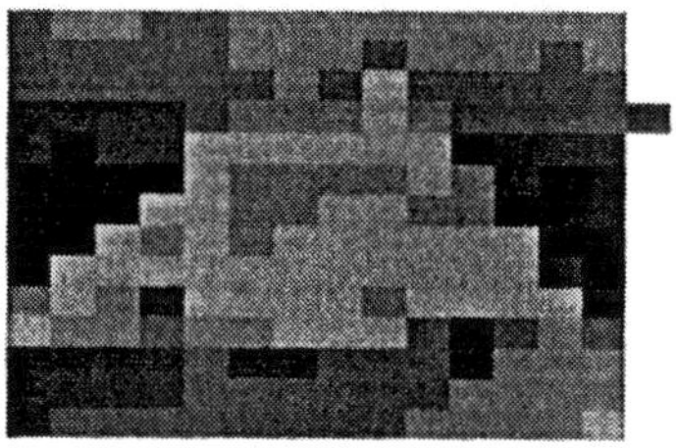

Figure 10.4c: Saturation Component

Figure 10.4d: Point Feature Map

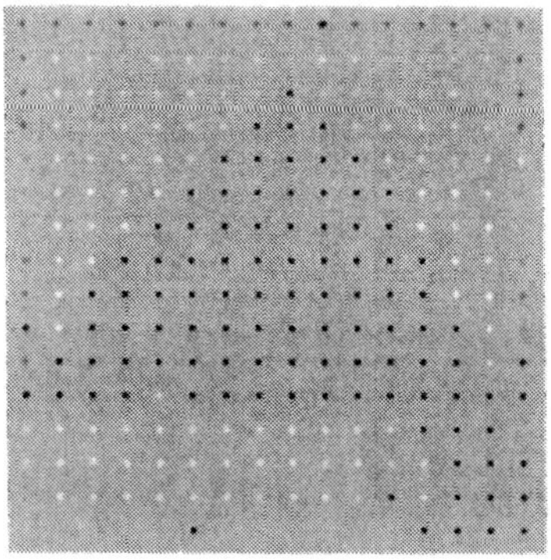

Figure 10.4e: Feature points of Hue 2

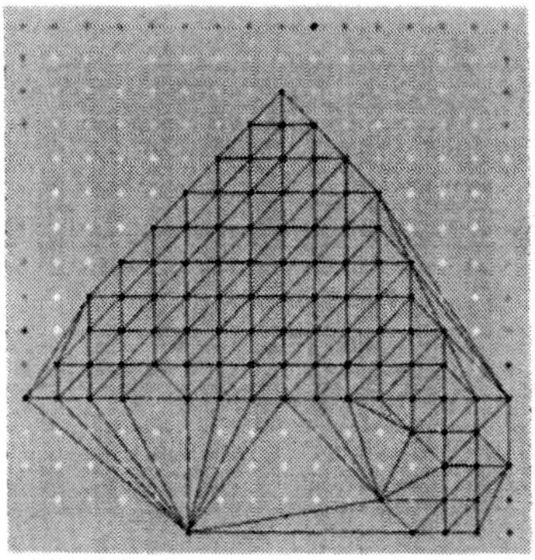

Figure 10.4f: Delauney Triangulation of Hue 2

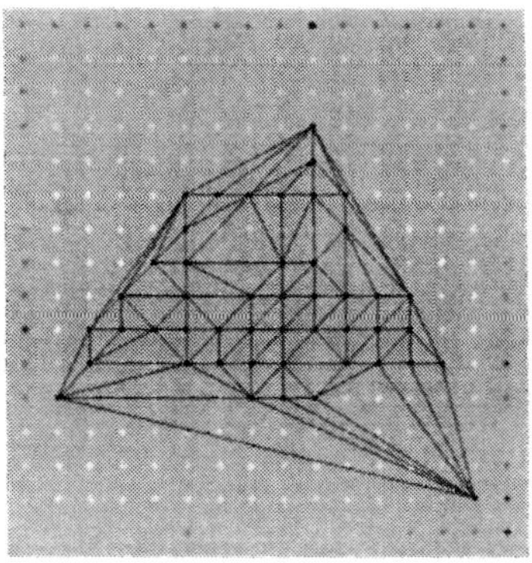

Figure 10.4g: Delauney Triangulation of Saturation 5

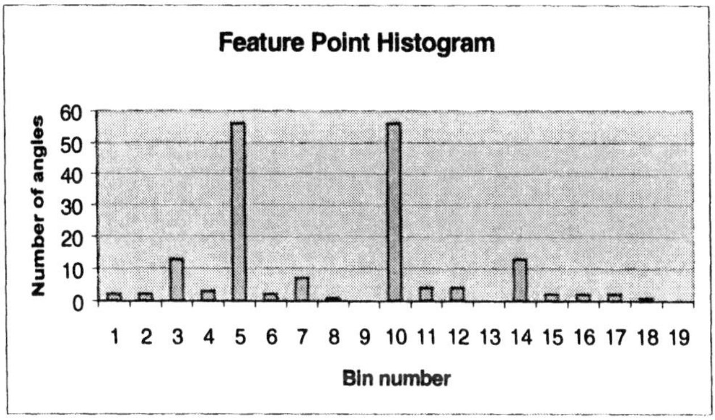

Figure 10.4h: Resulting Feature Point Histogram of Saturation 5

Histogram intersection was originally proposed in (Swain et. al. 1991) for comparing color histograms of query and database images. It was shown that histogram intersection is especially suited to comparing histograms for recognition. Additionally, histogram intersection is an efficient way of matching histograms, and its complexity is linear in the number of elements in the histograms. The intersection of the histograms I_{query} and $M_{database}$, each of n bins, is defined as follows.

$$D\left(I_{query}, M_{database}\right) = \frac{\sum_{j=1}^{n} \min\left(I_j, M_j\right)}{\sum_{j=1}^{n} I_j}$$

Suppose that Q is the query image index consisting of m color-related feature point histograms, Q_1, Q_2, ..., Q_m, DB is the database image index with corresponding m color-related feature point histograms DB_1, DB_2, ..., DB_m and w_i is the jth of m of variables which define the relative importance of color-related feature point histograms in our similarity calculation. For example, if HSI is used for image representation, hue-related feature point histograms are often assigned a larger weight value than saturation-related ones, as humans are more sensitive to hue variation. The similarity measure function used in this study is histogram intersection-based; it is given below.

Each $D(Q_i, DB_i)$ uses histogram intersection to obtain a fractional value between 0 and 1. Before being normalized by the number of angles in the query image, the result of histogram intersection is the number of angles from the database image that have the same corresponding angles in the query image. Therefore, we can meaningfully think about the spatial color index of an image. Any non-zero feature point histogram represents some image objects of a particular color, while any all-zero feature point histogram, called an *empty* histogram, means that there are no image objects of that color. Based on the histogram intersection-based similarity function, the comparison of query and database images using spatial color indices can be taken as a query-by-objects-appearing (Tao et. al. 1999b).

10.6 Bridging the Semantic Gap

In this section we discuss three ways of bridging the semantic gap, namely, relevance feedback, latent semantic indexing and user-centered multimedia search retrieval architecture.

10.6.1 Relevance Feedback and Latent Semmantic Indexing

Existing management systems for image collections and their users are typically at cross-purposes. While these systems normally retrieve images based on low-level features, users usually have a more abstract notion of what will satisfy them. Using low-level features to correspond to high-level abstractions is one aspect of the *semantic gap* (Gudivada et. al. 1995) between content-based system organization and the concept-based user. Sometimes, the user has in mind a concept so abstract that he himself doesn't know what he wants until he sees it. At that point, he may want images similar to what he has just seen or can envision. Again, however, the notion of similarity is typically based on high-level abstractions, such as activities taking place in the image or evoked emotions. Standard definitions of similarity using low-level features generally will not produce good results.

For all users, but especially for the user who doesn't know what he wants until he sees it, the efficiency of the system will likely be improved if it supports intelligent browsing so that the user will be satisfied in the shortest amount of time. It is our belief that intelligent browsing should be mediated by the paradigm of image similarity as well as by an appropriate organization of metadata, including annotations and self-describing image regions.

We characterize content-based retrieval systems that try to capture user semantics into two classes: *system-based* and *user-based*. System-based approaches either try to define various semantics globally, based on formal theories or consensus among domain experts, or use other techniques, not based on user-interaction, to get from low-level features to high-level semantics. User-based approaches, on the other hand, are adaptive to user behavior and try to construct individual profiles. An important component of most user-based approaches is the technique of relevance feedback.

Examples of system-based approaches are (Colombo et. al. 1999, La Cascia et. al. 1998, Rabitti et. al. 1989, Sethi et. al. 1998). Rabitti et. al. (1989) is the first paper that concerns retrieving images, in this case, graphic objects, based on user semantics. A methodology for composing features which evoke certain emotions is discussed in Colombo et. al. (1999), whereas La Cascia et al. (1998) uses textual information close to an image on a web page to derive information regarding the image's contents. Sethi et. al. (1998) explore a heterogeneous clustering methodology that overcomes the single-feature matching drawback of having images that are similar have different semantics.

Approaches that depend on some form of user interaction are (Chang et. al. 1998, Minka et. al. 1997, Santini et. al 2000). Mediated by user interaction, the system discussed in (Chang et. al. 1998) defines a set of queries that correspond to a user concept. (Minka et. al. 1997) is a system that learns how to combine various features in the overall retrieval process through user feedback. Their computationally efficient learning algorithm is based on AQ, a classical inductive learning technique. (Santini et. al. 2000) introduces an exploration paradigm based on an advanced user interface simulating 3-D space. In this space, thumbnail images having the same user semantics are displayed close to each other, and thumbnails that are far from the user's semantic view are smaller in size than thumbnails that are closer to the user's semantic view. The user can also convert images that are close to each other into a concept and replace the given set of thumbnails by a concept icon.

Some very interesting work appears in (Duygulu et. al. 2002), which explores linguistic-based techniques for textually annotating image regions.

There have been many papers that generalize the classical textually-based approach to relevance feedback to the image environment (Benitez et. al. 1998). Using the vector-space model for documents and queries, textually-based relevance feedback transforms the n-dimensional point corresponding to a query based on user feedback as to which of the documents returned as the query result are relevant and which are non-relevant. While the query is changed, the similarity measure used remains the same.

A similar approach can be implemented for content-based image retrieval using several techniques. These approaches differ in the way the query vector is changed. In one approach, positions in the vector representation of an image correspond to visual keywords. This approach is similar to that used for text. In another approach, the query vector changes, either because different feature extraction algorithms are being used for the same features, or different features are being used altogether. For example, color features can be extracted using many different approaches, such as global color histograms, local color histograms, and anglograms. Based on user feedback, the system can discover that one approach is better than the others. It may also discover that texture features are better for a particular query than color features. Then, there is a completely different approach, where the matching function is changed to give different weights to the given features (Bhanu et. al. 1998, Taycher et. al. 1997). For example, through user feedback, the system may decide to give more weight to color than to texture. The MARS project (Rui et. al. 1998) has examined many of these approaches throughout the last few years.

In addition, there are approaches probabilistic in nature (Cos, Miller and Minka 1998; Meilhac and Naster 1999) that use Bayesian inference to estimate the relevance of documents based on user interaction. In Zhou et. al. (2002), a method for integrating both image and textual features into the process of relevance feedback is discussed.

For textual information, the technique of latent semantic analysis has often been applied for improved semantic retrieval. This technique reduces the dimensionality of the document vectors by restructuring them. Each new attribute is a linear combination of some of the old attributes. Based on the co-occurrence of keywords in documents, this technique forms *concepts* from the collections of the old attributes. The result is that when a keyword, *kw*, is included in a query, documents which have the keywords from the same concept as *kw* may also be retrieved, whether *kw* is mentioned in the query or not. The original paper on this topic is (Deerwester et. al. 1990), while a good survey can be found in (Berry et. al. 1998).

Various techniques for latent feature discovery have been developed for text collections. These include latent semantic indexing and principal component analysis. There has not been much work on using these techniques for image collections (Ang et. al. 1995, Bigun 1993, Huang et. al. 1998, La Cascia et. al. 1998, Pecenovic 1997, Pentland et. al. 1996, Zhao et. al. 2002a, Zhao et al. 2002b). The only work previous to ours that intentionally uses such dimensional reduction techniques for images and text (La Cascia et. al. 1998) does so to solve a completely different problem. The environment of this work is that of web pages containing images and text. Instead of a term-document matrix, they define a term-image matrix, where the terms are taken from the text that appears close to the given image. Terms that appear closer to the given image are weighted higher than terms appearing further away. It is this term-image matrix that is used to discover latent features. An image feature vector is then comprised of components, one component representing various image features and another component representing the column vector corresponding to the given image from the transformed term-image matrix. This does not, however, solve the problem of trying to find different image features that co-occur with the same abstract concept, which would be of tremendous help in discovering the underlying semantics of images. The experiments in Pecenovic (1997) also combine associated text and image features, but this is presented as merely an aside to his main point, which is to study the efficiency (dimensional reduction) of latent semantic indexing in an image retrieval environment.

In Zhao et. al. (2002b) there is a discussion of various techniques which incorporate latent semantic indexing to improve retrieval results, including some experiments which rely on finding which image features co-occur with similar textual image annotations. They show the utility of textual information for pure image retrieval tasks. Zhao et. al. (2002a) continues this work by showing the utility of image information for pure text retrieval tasks.

10.6.2 User Semantics and HCVM

In chapter 3 we discussed about the need for developing an ontological level above the metadata level of multimedia databases. The domain and media independent ontological level will enable semantic correlation for queries dealing with single as well as multiple media artifacts. Figure 10.5 shows a HCVM based layered approach towards multimedia document search and retrieval. As can be seen in Figure10.5 the ontological layer corresponds to the problem solving agent layer. In the next chapter we show how genetic algorithm agent employs relevance feedback as means for guiding the search process in a web based multimedia application.

The belief agent in Figure 10.5 stores information related to the context of the user in a browsing environment. The media agent in Figure 10.5 is used for presentation and visualization of multimedia data.

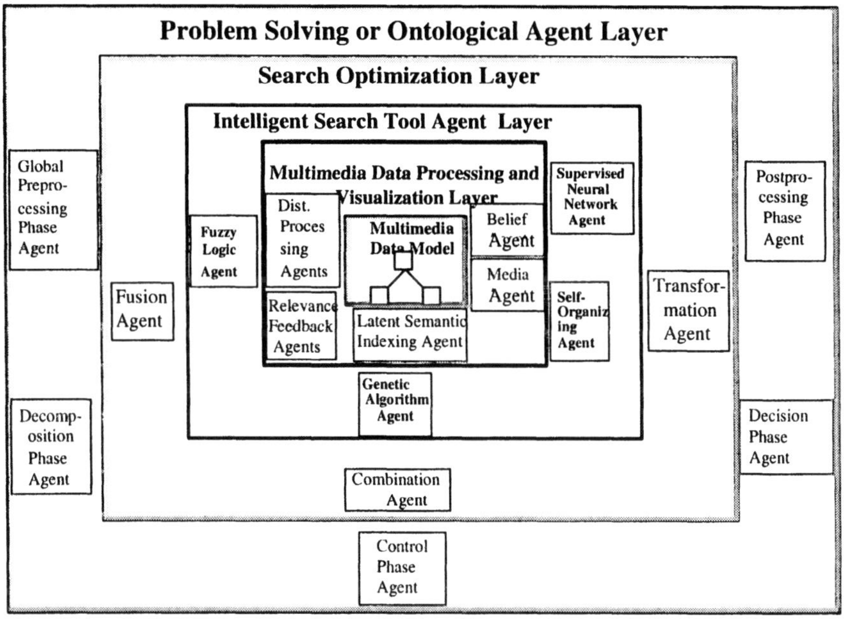

Figure 10.5 :User-Centered Multimedia Search and Retrieval Architecture

10.7. Commercial Systems for Hypermedia Information Systems

In the past, there were some heated discussions among researchers in the multimedia computing and database communities as to whether the then current database systems were sufficient to manage multimedia information (Jain 1993). On balance, people in multimedia computing were of the opinion that advances needed to be made in the database arena in order to manage this new type of data, whereas people in databases seemed to feel that the newer database architectures were sufficient to the task. Database architectures have surely changed from then to now, but there should be no argument that no existing database system contains all of the advanced options discussed in this article. Be that as it may, currently, there are at least three commercial systems for visual information retrieval (Excalibur Technologies: www.excalib.com; IBM: www.ibm.com; Virage: www.virage.com) and several commercial database systems at various levels on the object-relational scale (DB2 Universal Database: www.ibm.com; Oracle: www.oracle.com) that can manage multimedia information at an acceptable level. However, what is acceptable by today's standards will surely not be acceptable by tomorrow's.

In order for database systems to handle multimedia information efficiently in a production environment, some standardization has to occur. Relational systems are efficient because they have relatively few standard operations, which have been studied by many database researchers for many decades. This has resulted in numerous efficient implementations of these operations. Blades, cartridges, and extenders for multimedia information are at present designed in a completely ad-hoc manner. They work, but no one is paying much attention to their efficiency. Operations on multimedia must become standardized and extensible. If the base operations become standardized, researchers can devote their efforts to making them efficient. If they are extensible, complex operations can be defined in terms of simpler ones and still preserve efficiency. Hopefully, the efforts being devoted to MPEG-7 will address this concern.

10.8. Summary

Multimedia data (e.g., text, image, video and audio) today is an inherent part of Internet and web-based applications. This chapter outlines the inability of the traditional database techniques to handle multimedia retrieval and indexing. It outlines the need for developing new techniques for hypermedia data modeling and describes several techniques for content-based retrieval and indexing. Importantly it discusses the need for bridging the semantic gap between the user and multimedia applications. In this context the chapter discusses relevance feedback, latent semantic indexing and user-centered multimedia search and retrieval architecture among other techniques for bridging the semantic gap.

References

Ahmad, I. and Grosky, W.I. (1999). "Spatial Similarity-based Retrievals in Image Databases" in *Journal of Computer Science and Information Management,* 2, 1-10.

Ang, Y.H., Li, Z. and Ong, S.H. (1995). "Image Retrieval Based on Multidimensional Feature Properties" in *Storage and Retrieval for Image and Video Databases III,* 2420, 47-57.

Belongie, S., Carson, C., Greenspan, H. and Malik, J. (1998). "Color- and Texture-Based Image Segmentation Using EM and Its Application to Content-Based Image Retrieval" in *Proceedings of the International Conference on Computer Vision,* 675-682.

Benitez, A.B., Beigi, M. and Chang, S.-F. (1998). "Using Relevance Feedback in Content-Based Image Metasearch" in *IEEE Internet Computing,* 2, 59-69.

Berry, M.W., Drmac, Z. and Jessup, E.R. (1998). "Matrices, Vector Spaces, and Information Retrieval"in *SIAM Review,* 2, 335-362.

Bhanu, B., Peng, J. and Qing, S. (1998). "Learning Feature Relevance and Similarity Metrics in Image Databases" in *Proceedings of the IEEE Workshop on Content-Based Access of Image and Video Libraries,* 14-18.

Bigun, J. (1993). "Unsupervised Feature Reduction in Image Segmentation by Local Transforms" in *Pattern Recognition Letters,* 14, 573-583.

Chang, S.-F., Chen, W. and Sundaram, H. (1998). "Semantic Visual Templates: Linking Visual Features to Semantics" in *Proceedings of the IEEE International Conference on Image Processing*, 531-535.

Colombo, C., Del Bimbo, A. and Pala, P. (1999). "Semantics in Visual Information Retrieval" in *IEEE Multimedia*, 6, 38-53.

Cox, I.J., Miller, M.L., Minka, T.P. and Yianilos, P.N. (1998). "An Optimized Interaction Strategy for Bayesian Relevance Feedback" in *Proceedings of the IEEE Computer Society Conference on Computer Vision and Pattern Recognition*, 553-558.

Deerwester, S., Dumais, S.T. et. al. (1990). "Indexing by Latent Semantic Analysis" in *Journal of the American Society for Information Science*, 41, 391-407.

Dimai, A. (1997). "Spatial Encoding Using Differences of Global Features" in *Proceedings of SPIE Storage and Retrieval for Image and Video Databases*, 352-360.

Duygulu, P., Barnard, K., et. al. (2002). "Object Recognition as Machine Translation: Learning a Lexicon for a Fixed Image Vocabulary" in *Seventh European Conference on Computer Vision*, 97-112.

Gibbs, S., Breiteneder, C. and Tsichritzis, D. (1997). "Modeling Time-Based Media" in *The Handbook of Multimedia Information Management*, W.I. Grosky, R. Jain, and R. Mehrotra (Eds.), Prentice Hall PTR, 13-38.

Grosky, W.I. (1984). "Toward a Logical Data Model for Integrated Pictorial Databases" in *Computer Vision, Graphics and Image Processing*, 25, 371-382.

Grosky, W.I. (1994). "Multimedia Information Systems" in *IEEE Multimedia*, 1, 12-24.

Grosky, W.I., Fotouhi, F. and Jiang, Z. (1998). "Using Metadata for the Intelligent Browsing of Structured Media Objects" in *Managing Multimedia Data – Using Metadata to Integrate and Apply Digital Media*, A. Sheth and W. Klas (Eds.), McGraw-Hill Publishing Company, 67-92.

Gudivada V. and Raghavan, V.V. (1995). "Content-Based Image Retrieval Systems" in *IEEE Computer*, 28, 18-22.

Gupta, A., Weymouth, T. and Jain, R. (1991). "Semantic Queries with Pictures: The VIMSYS Model" in *Proceedings of the 17th International Conference on Very Large Databases,'* 69-79.

Hsu, W., Chua, T.S. and Pung, H.K. (1995). "An Integrated Color-Spatial Approach to Content-based Image Retrieval" in *Proceedings of ACM Multimedia*, 305-313.

Huang, J., Kumar, S.R., Mitra, M., Zhu, W.-J. and Zabih, R. (1997). "Image Indexing Using Color Correlograms" in *Proceedings of the IEEE Conference on Computer Vision and Pattern Recognition*, 762-768.

Huang, J., Kumar, S.R. and Zabih, R. (1998). "An Automatic Hierarchical Image Classification Scheme" in *Proceedings of the Sixth ACM International Conference on Multimedia*, 219-228.

Jain, R. (1993). "NSF Workshop on Visual Information Management Systems" in *Sigmod Record* 23, 57-75.

Jagadish, H.V. (1991) "A Retrieval Technique for Similar Shapes" in *Proceedings of the 1991 ACM SIGMOD Conference*, Denver, 208-217.

Jain A.K. and Vailaya, A. (1996). "Image Retrieval Using Color and Shape" in *Pattern Recognition*, 29, 1233-1244.

La Cascia, M., Sethi, S. and Sclaroff, S. (1998). "Combining Textual and Visual Cues for Content-Based Image Retrieval on the World Wide Web" in *Proceedings of the IEEE Workshop on Content-Based Access of Image and Video Libraries*, 24-28.

Lu, G.-J. (1997). "An Approach to Image Retrieval Based on Shape" in *Journal of Information Science*, 23, 119-127.

Mokhtarian, F, Abbasi, S. and Kitter, J. (1996). "Efficient and Robust Retrieval by Shape Content through Curvature Scale Space" in *Proceedings of International Workshop on Image Database and Multimedia Search*, 35-42.

Mehrotra, R. and Grosky, W.I. (1988). "SMITH: An Efficient Model-Based Two-Dimensional Shape Matching Technique" in *Syntactic and Structural Pattern Recognition,* G. Ferrate, T. Pavlidis, A. Sanfeliu, and H. Bunke (Eds.), Springer-Verlag, 233-248.

Mehrotra, R. and Gary, J.E. (1995). "Similar-Shape Retrieval in Shape Data Management" in *IEEE Computer*, 28, 57-62.

Meilhac, C. and Nastar, C. (1999). "Relevance Feedback and category Search in Image Databases" in *Proceedings of the IEEE International Conference on Multimedia Computing and Systems,* 512-517.

Minka, T.P. and Picard, R.W. (1997). "Interactive Learning with a Society of Models" in *Pattern Recognition,* 30, 565-581.

Mehtre, B.M., Kankanhalli, M.S., and Lee, W.-F. (1997). "Shape Measures for Content Based Image Retrieval: A Comparison" in *Information Processing & Management*, 33, 319-337.

Mehtre, B.M., Kankanhalli, M.S., and Lee, W.-F. (1998). "Content-Based Image Retrieval Using A Composite Color-Shape Approach" in *Information Processing & Management*, 34, 109-120.

Niblack, W., Barder, R. et. al. (1993). "The QBIC Project: Querying Images by Content Using Color, Texture, and Shape" in *Proceedings of SPIE Storage and Retrieval for Image and Video Databases*, 1908, 173-181.

Nievergelt, J., Hinterberger, H., and Sevcik, K.C. (1984). "The Grid File: An Adaptable Symmetric Multikey File Structure" in *ACM Transaction on Database Systems*, 9, 1984.

Pass, G. and Zabih, R. (1996). "Histogram Refinement for Content-Based Image Retrieval" in *IEEE Workshop on Applications of Computer Vision*, 96-102.

Pecenovic, Z. (1997). *Image Retrieval Using Latent Semantic Indexing,* Graduate Thesis, Department of Electrical Engineering, Swiss Federal Institute of Technology, Lausanne, Switzerland, June 1997.

Pentland, A., Piccard, R.W., and Sclaroff, S. (1996). "Photobook: Content-Based manipulation of Image Databases" in *International Journal of Computer Vision,* 18, 233-254.

Rabitti F. and Stanchev, P. (1989). "GRIM_DBMS: A Graphical Image DataBase System" in In *Visual Database Systems,* T. Kunii (Ed.), North-Holland Publishing Company, Amsterdam, The Netherlands, 415-430.

Rabitti, F. and Savino, P. (1992). "Query Processing on Image Databases" in *Visual Database Systems II,* E. Knuth and L.M. Wegner (Eds.), North Holland Publishing Company, Amsterdam, 169-183.

Rui, Y., Huang, T.S., Ortega, M., and Mehrotra, S. (1998). "Relevance Feedback: A Power Tool in Interactive Content-Based Image Retrieval" in *IEEE Transactions on Circuits and Systems for Video Technology,* 8, 644-655.

Robinson, J.T. (1981). "K-D-B tree: A Search Structure for Large Multidimensional Dynamic Indices" in *Proceedings of ACM SIGMOD Conference on the Management of Data*, 1981.

Santini, S. and Jain, R. (1996). "The Graphical Specification of Similarity Queries" in *Journal of Visual Languages & Computing,* 7, 403-421.

Santini, S. and Jain, R. (2000). "Integrated Browsing and Querying for Image Databases" in *IEEE Multimedia,* 7, 26-39.

Sethi, I.K., Coman, I., et. al. (1998). "'Color-WISE: A System for Image Similarity Retrieval Using Color" in *Proceedings of SPIE Storage and Retrieval for Image and Video Databases*, 3312, 140-149.

Smith, J.R. and Chang, S.-F. (1999). "Integrated Spatial and Point Feature Map Query," in *ACM Multimedia Systems Journal*, 7, 129-140.

Sheikholeslami G., Chang, W., and Zhang, A. (1998). "Semantic Clustering and Querying on Heterogeneous Features for Visual Data" in *Proceedings of the Sixth ACM International Conference on Multimedia,* 3-12.

Stricker, M. and Dimai, A. (1996). "Color Indexing with Weak Spatial Constraints" in Proceedings *of SPIE Storage and Retrieval for Image and Video Databases,* 2670, 29-39.

Stonebraker, M. (1996). *Object-Relational DBMSs – The Next Great Wave,* Morgan-Kaufmann Publishers, San Francisco, 1996.

Swain, M.J. and Ballard, D.H. (1991), "Color Indexing" in *International Journal of Computer Vision,* 7, 11-32.

Tao, Y. and Grosky, W.I. (1999a). "Delaunay Triangulation for Image Object Indexing: A Novel Method for Shape Representation" in *Proceedings of IS&T/SPIE's Symposium on Storage and Retrieval for Image and Video Databases VII,* pp. 631-642.

Tao, Y. and Grosky, W.I. (1999b). "Object-Based Image Retrieval Using Point Feature Maps" in *Proceedings of the 8th IFIP 2.6 Working Conference on Database Semantics,* 59-73.

Tamura, H. and Yokoya, N. (1984). "Image Database Systems: A Survey" in *Pattern Recognition,* 17, 29-43.

Taycher, L., La Cascia, M., and Sclaroff, S. (1997). "Image Digestion and Relevance Feedback in the ImageRover WWW Search Engine" in *Proceedings of the International Conference on Visual Information,* 85-92.

Wan, X. and Kuo, C.-J. (1996). "Color Distribution Analysis and Quantization for Image Retrieval" in *Proceedings of SPIE Storage and Retrieval for Image and Video Databases,* 2670, 8-16.

Widom, J. and Ceri, S. (1996). *Active Database Systems – Triggers and Rules for Advanced Database Processing,* Morgan Kaufmann Publishers, Inc., 1996.

Zhao, R. and Grosky, W.I. (2002a). "Narrowing the Semantic Gap – Improved Text-Based Web Document Retrieval Using Visual Features" in *IEEE Transactions on Multimedia,* 4, 189-200.

Zhao, R. and Grosky, W.I. (2002b). "Negotiating the Semantic Gap: From Feature Maps to Semantic Landscapes" in *Pattern Recognition,* 35, 51-58.

Zhou, X.S. and Huang, T.S. (2002). "Unifying Keywords and Visual Contents in Image Retrieval" in *IEEE Multimedia,* 9, 23-33.

11 HUMAN-CENTERED INTELLIGENT WEB BASED MISSING PERSON CLOTHING IDENTIFICATION SYSTEM

11.1. Introduction

In the last chapter we outlined relevance feedback as one of the methods for developing user-centered multimedia applications. On the other hand, researchers in the computational intelligence or soft computing community have been recently trying to develop intelligent applications which humanize computational intelligence technologies (Takagi 2001, 2002). In this chapter we describe an intelligent web multimedia system which employs relevance feedback as a means of assisting an Internet user (relative or friend of a missing person) to interactively identify the clothing of a missing person. The system can be used by the law enforcement authorities, like the police to identify the type, color and design of the shirt worn by a missing person.

We illustrate the humanization of computational intelligence by involving the user in interactively determining the objective function for searching the type, color and design of the shirt worn by a missing person. Genetic algorithms (one of the components of the tool agent layer of HCVM) use the objective function to optimize the search for the right combination of type, color and design of the shirt on line.

The chapter is organized as follows. In the next section we introduce some aspects related to identification of missing persons on the web. We then describe the design of the clothing identification using genetic algorithms. This is followed by a description of the implementation and results of the clothing identification system. The results illustrate the interactive and user-centered design of the web based system.

11.2. Relevance Feedback

Efficient and effective techniques to retrieve images are being developed due to the vast amount of images present. Users can search for images by using a query. A user's query provides a description of the desired image. This description can take many forms: it can be a set of keywords, a sketch of the desired image (Bimbo, Pala and Santini, 1994) an example image, or a set of low level features (i.e. color, brightness). For retrieval, an image can have a vast amount of possible attributes. The occurrence of a specific color, texture or shape (e.g. green grass) is one such possible type of attribute.

A query only approximates an information need. Users often start with short queries that tend to be poor approximations. A better query can be created automatically by analyzing relevant and non-relevant objects. Relevance feedback has been used and researched as a method to aid query modification since the mid 1960s. The method is used in traditional text based information retrieval systems. It is known as 'relevance feedback' because it automatically adjusts an existing query based on the relevance assessment fed back by the user for previously retrieved objects. The goal is to construct new queries that provide a better approximation to the user's information needs (Buckley and Salton 1995; Salton and McGill 1983). The new query is expected to show a greater degree of similarity with the retrieved relevant objects, and be less similar to the retrieved non-relevant objects (Buckley and Salton 1995).

An advantage of this approach is that the specification of weights is no longer the responsibility of the user (specification of weights requires the user to have a comprehensive knowledge of the low-level representations used in the retrieval environment and collection makeup). All the user has to do is indicate the relevance of the objects to their query. The weights are updated dynamically; hence the user is shielded from the details of the query formulation process. Also the wanted subject area is approached gradually due to the break down of the search process into a sequence of small steps (Salton and McGill 1988).

J.J.Rocchio depicted an approach that consisted of using vector addition and subtraction using feedback of relevant and non-relevant documents in order to obtain the optimal vector space query (vector space model) (Rocchio 1971). Robertson and Sparck Jones (1976) proposed the probabilistic model years later. Based on the distribution of individual terms in relevant and non-relevant documents that were retrieved in response to queries, the model proposed a way of adjusting these term weights (Robertson and Jones 1976).

11.2.1. Vector Space Model

The documents D and the queries Q can be represented as t-dimensional vectors of the form $D = (d_1,d_2,\ldots,d_t)$ and $Q = (q_1,q_2,\ldots,q_t)$. The weight of term i in D is represented by d_i and the weight of term i in Q is represented by q_I (Salton and McGill 1983).

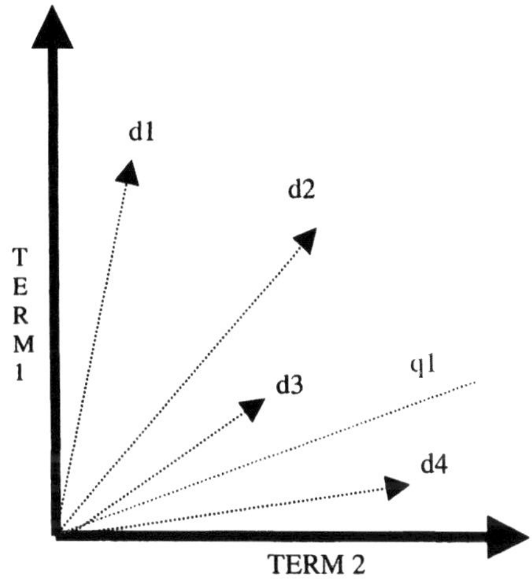

Figure 11.1a: Documents and Query on Term or Concept Dimensions

Each document and query is represented as a point in the space (Figure 11.1a). Their centroid point represents groups of documents.

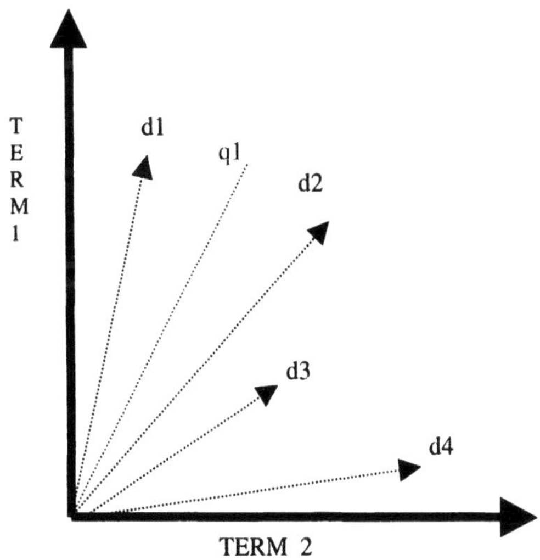

Figure 11.1b :Resulting Reformulated Query.

Figure 11.1b shows the resulting reformulated query if d1 and d2 are deemed relevant, d3 and d4 are non-relevant.

The goal is to move the query closer to relevant documents. A vector merging operation based on addition and subtraction expands queries. All terms that are in the retrieved documents are firstly added to the query, and then weighted according to their document relevance.

A query-document similarity measure can be computed as the inner product between corresponding vectors, that is:

The new query is a weighted average of the original query and relevant and non-relevant document vectors.

α and β are constants that define the relative importance of positive and negative feedback.

$$Sim(D,Q) = \sum_{k=1}^{t} d_i \cdot q_i$$

$$Q' = Q + \alpha \frac{1}{|R|} \sum_{R} D_i - \beta \frac{1}{|NR|} \sum_{NR} D_j$$

11.2.3. Evaluating Relevance Feedback

In order to evaluate the effectiveness of relevance feedback it is necessary to compare the performance of the first iteration feedback search with the results of the initial search performed with the initial query statements. [45]. The two measures used are Recall and Precision.

Recall (R): proportion of relevant items that are retrieved from the collection. That is, proportion of all documents in the collection that are relevant to a query and that are actually retrieved.

Precision (P): proportion of retrieved items that are relevant. That is, proportion of the retrieved set of documents that is relevant to the query.

11.3. Genetic Algorithms and Other Search Techniques

Biological systems in general are robust and flexible. Genetic algorithms have been proven to be robust, flexible and efficient in vast complex spaces (Holland 1975). The evolution process performed by GA's corresponds to a search through a space of potential solutions. This type of search requires a balance between exploiting the best solutions and exploring the search space (Michalewicz 1992).

One such strategy that exploits the best solution for possible improvement is Hill climbing. Hill climbing methods (also known as gradient methods) find an optimum by following the local gradient of a function. Since they generate successive results based exclusively on the previous results, they are deemed deterministic. A problem with hill climbing is that it neglects exploration of the search space due to the fact that they only find the local optimum in the neighborhood of the current point. Although parallel methods of hill climbing (using a large number of random starting points) can be used it can still be very difficult to reach an optimum solution, especially in very noisy spaces with a huge number of local maxima or minima. One of the most powerful features of genetic algorithms is that they are parallel. The GA implicitly processes successfully, in parallel, a large number of points (strings) simultaneously

Random search is a typical example of a strategy, which explores the search space yet, ignores exploiting the regions of the search space that are most promising. These random search algorithms do not use any knowledge gained from previous results thus they merely perform inefficient random walks. GA's are different from these random algorithms as they combine elements of directed and stochastic search.

The probabilistic nature of GA's set them apart from hill climbing techniques. Every individual, regardless of how poor its fitness is, still has a chance of being involved in the evolutionary process. This has parallels with simulated annealing where individuals that are known to be inferior are occasionally selected.

Another important aspect of the GA is that they use populations of individuals, rather than a single point on the problem space. This gives it the ability to search noisy spaces by looking at several different areas of the problem space at once. It does not rely on a single point as other search techniques do.

Other techniques require a range of information to guide the search. Derivatives of a function are used by hill climbing techniques for example. A GA only needs the fitness value of a point in the space to guide its search. The GA will always perform the same simple operations regardless of the particular domain.

11.4 Design Components Of Clothing Identification System

The skeleton design outline of the web-based missing person clothing identification system is shown in Figure 11.2. The interactive web-based system is used for identifying type, color and design of a missing person's shirt. There are three main design component categories of the system, namely, the Shirt component, Genetic Algorithm component and. the Interactive component

The Start, Continue and Process, and the Convert Population to Images are web-based interactive components which are used to interact with the user to initiate the clothing identification system, take relevance feedback from the user and display optimized shirt designs to the user.

We now briefly outline parts of the Shirt and GA and Interactive components respectively.

11.4.1: Shirt Component

As shown in Figure 11.3 the clothing or shirt component consists of tasks like draw shirt, display all shirts, record user details and show filenames. These tasks are described next.

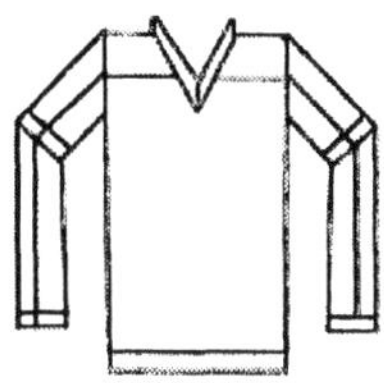

Figure 11.2: Shirt Object and Shirt Parts

11.4.1.1. Draw Shirt

This task facilitates the drawing of each individual part of the shirt to make up a complete shirt as a whole. The shirt object is shown in Figure 11.4. Each bit in a GA string refers to a particular shirt part. The definition of each bit is outlined below.

0 – existence of long or short sleeves

1 – torso of the shirt

2 - long sleeves
3 – long sleeve stripe
4 - long sleeve cuffs
5 – short sleeves
6 – short sleeve stripe
7 – short sleeve cuffs
8 – waist band stripe
9 – collar
10 – existence of vertical or horizontal stripes
11 – horizontal stripes
12 – vertical stripes
13 – shoulder stripes

In Figure 11.3 we show the representation of different parts as a GA string array index. The value of each bit in Figure 11.3 refers to the specific color of the shirt part.

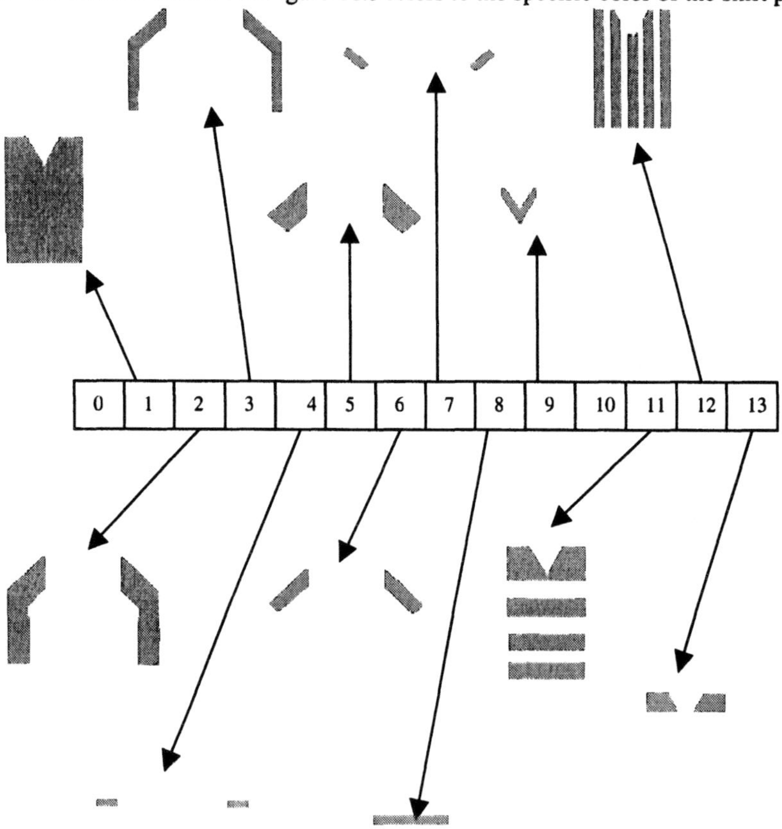

Figure 11.3 Shirt Parts and Corresponding GA String Array Index

Figure 11.4 illustrates the bit value and its corresponding color. The shoulder stripe shirt part (13th bit in Figure 11.3) is used for this example.

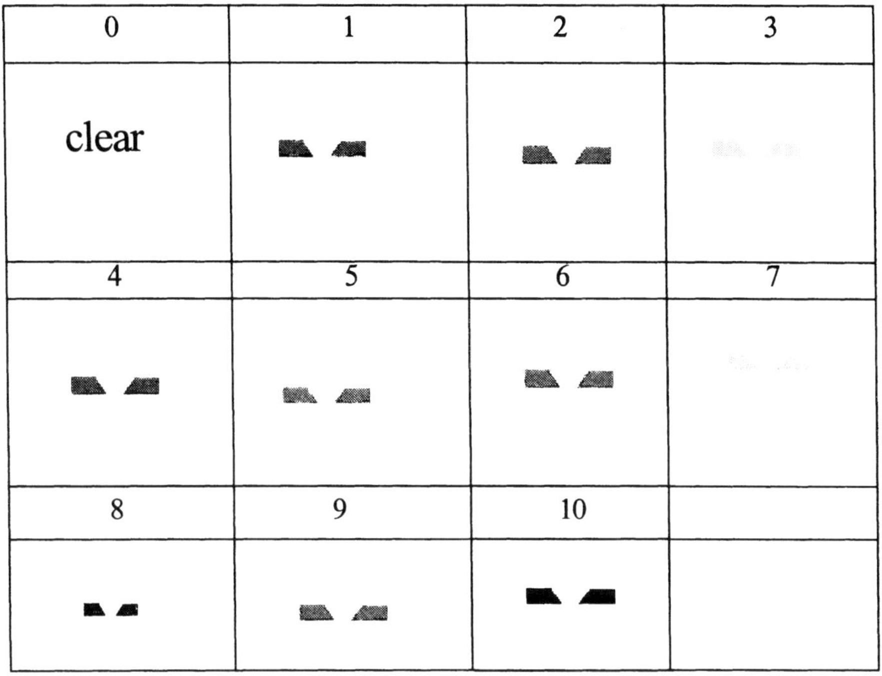

Figure 11.4: Bit Values and Corresponding Colors for Shoulder Stripes

Each shirt part has been drawn using Adobe Photoshop 5.0. All shirt parts are drawn on a 4.23 x 5.64 cm canvas. In relation to pixels, the shirt parts are 120 (width) x 160 (height) pixels. They have a resolution of 72 pixels/inch.

The shirts have been drawn by using Figure 11.3 as a template. Each part has been individually cut out and saved. The next step in drawing the shirts is to color each part. After each part is colored, it is then saved.

Some shirt parts have had a filter applied to them (e.g., the torso of the shirt, the long and short sleeves, and the horizontal and vertical stripes). The filter used is a texturizer using a canvas texture, 50% scaling, relief = 2, and light direction = left.

A major difficulty encountered was the positioning of each shirt part on the screen in order to provide a whole shirt that did not look fragmented. Neither JavaScript nor HTML provided a facility that could allow the placement of images (each shirt part) at a specific area or co-ordinates on the screen. Other methods had to be explored.

The chosen method was that of using transparent images placed on top of each other. By using the template image, coloring the required part and making the rest of the image transparent, the shirt could be drawn effectively. Placing each part at a specific set of co-ordinates was no longer required since each part was located at a set position on the template image (refer Figure 11.5).

In order to have the images as transparent, they had to be converted to the GIF format. When an indexed-color image is exported to GIF, the background

The chosen method was that of using transparent images placed on top of each other. By using the template image, coloring the required part and making the rest of the image transparent, the shirt could be drawn effectively. Placing each part at a specific set of co-ordinates was no longer required since each part was located at a set position on the template image (refer Figure 11.5).

In order to have the images as transparent, they had to be converted to the GIF format. When an indexed-color image is exported to GIF, the background transparency can be assigned to areas in the image. All areas containing the colors that are specified are recognized as transparency by Web browsers.

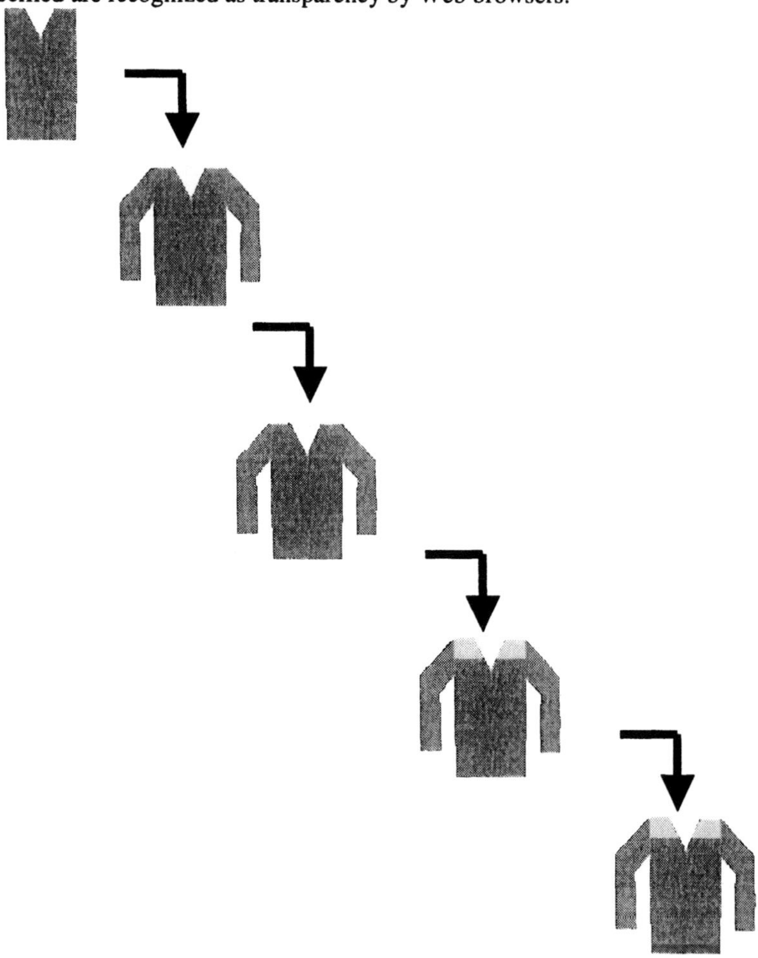

Figure 11.5 Shirt Drawing Process

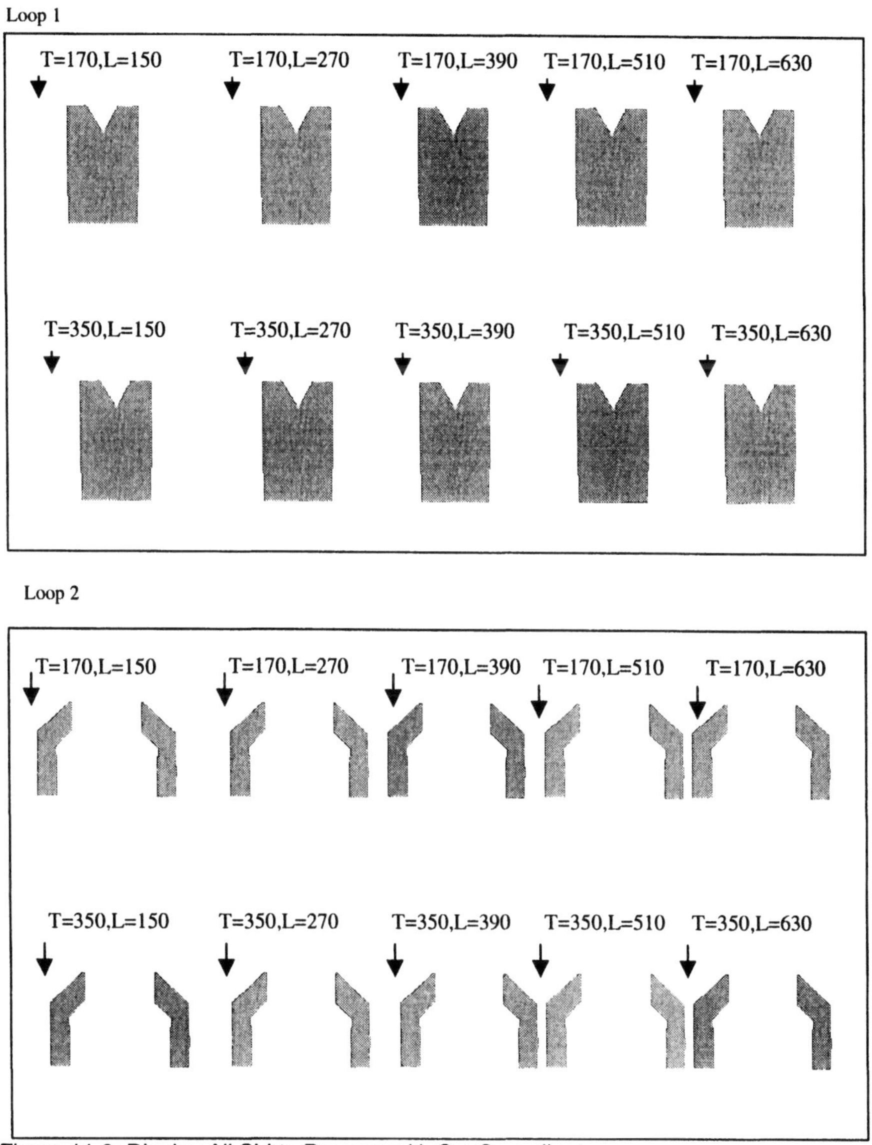

Figure 11.6: Display All Shirts Process with Set Co-ordinates

11.4.1.2. Display All Shirt

The aim of this task is to display every shirt on the screen in a way that is straightforward and simple for the viewer. Once a shirt has been drawn, the next task is to display all shirts in the population on the same screen. They must be positioned so that they are easily seen and identifiable by the user. As discussed previously, there is no provision in the coding languages for images to be directly placed at specific co-ordinates on a screen. This can be overcome by incorporating HTML layers. HTML layers position blocks off HTML content. Attributes for the layer such as ID, TOP, LEFT, BGCOLOR, WIDTH, and HEIGHT can be specified. The TOP and LEFT attributes are used to specify the position of the shirt on the screen. The idea of a layer is to act as a single entity of content. For this program it is required that the layers contain more than one element, thus a layer style is applied to a containing element such as DIV, that contains all the content.

The two functions in the program that perform this component are draw_image and *show_image*. *Show_image* opens a new window and sets the starting co-ordinates. It then proceeds to loop through the filenames array. Draw image is a recursive function that draws each part of the shirt at different co-ordinates. It loops through all the parts until all the shirt parts have been drawn. A count is kept to ensure that there are two rows of five shirts drawn on the screen. Figure 11.6 shows this process.

11.4.1.3. User Details and Relevance Feedback

This component handles the various forms that are employed in order to record the different user details and feedback. The user relevance feedback rankings are acquired via the use of radio buttons. Three categories of rankings were chosen:

Non relevant (Non Rel.)
Undecided (Unde.)
Relevant (Rel)

The three categories are each given a different weighting factor. The relevance feedback is primarily implemented using HTML. The weighting factor is used to compute the quality of user feedback and store the value in the *rel_feedback[ ]* array.

11.4.1.4. Show Filenames

The various parts that make up the final shirt ,that is chosen by the user must, in some manner, be sent to the web master of the website that has this program incorporated into it. This is required so that the web master can re-create the actual shirt that was selected at the end of the search process. Each part of the shirt is represented by a filename.

11.4.2. GA Component

The GA agent definition is shown in Table 11.1. Some of the tasks associated with the GA agent are now outlined.

11.4.2.1. Initial Population

This task involves initializing the GA with a totally random population. It is essential that the initial population is random thus ensuring that there is a minimal likelihood of premature convergence.

Table 11.1: GA Agent Definition

Name :	Genetic Algorithm Agent
Goals:	Optimization
Some Tasks:	Reproduction Crossover Mutation
Task Constraints:	Computing Resources
Precondition:	Fitness function defined
Postcondition:	Optimized search results
Communicates with:	Media Agent, Shirt Agent, User
Communication Constructs:	Request: search parameters Inform: search results
Linguistic/non-linguistic features:	Gene (e.g., shirt parts), search parameters, population size, fitness function
External Tools:	Software: Graphic object Domain: Shirt objects
Internal Tools:	Search algorithm, distributed processing
Actions:	Math_floor Selection Randomly mutate gene Return fittest chromosomes

It fills each bit of a string in the population array with a random number. The random number generator is seeded automatically when the script is first loaded. This number is then multiplied by a value from the boundaries array. The boundaries array stores the maximum value that a bit may have. Finally, *Math_floor* function is used to return the greatest integer less than or equal to the calculated random number.

11.4.2.2. Reproduction

The reproduction component models the reproduction/selection operation carried out during a G.A search, with the emphasis on giving preference to the 'fitter' string. The function *selection* simulates the reproduction component of a G.A search. The reproduction scheme followed is that of the 'roulette wheel'. Each shirt is given a relevance feedback ranking by the user. This is stored in the *rel_feedback* array. The selection function uses this *rel_feedback* array to calculate a cumulative sum of the rankings (*cumulative[ ]* array). Each shirt is assigned a range of values. A random number is generated and the shirt string that corresponds to this random value is copied into the mating pool array. This process loops until the mating pool is filled. For example, if there were only four shirts in the population, we can use Table 11.2.

Table 11.2: Four Shirt Population Based Search

0Shirt #	*1String*	*2Fitness Value*	*3Probability*
1	3456	2	2/10 = 0.20
2	5464	5	5/10 = 0.50
3	4643	1	1/10 = 0.10
4	3563	2	2/10 = 0.20

The following values are then assigned to each shirt:

Shirt #	Range of values
1	0,1
2	2,3,4,5,6
3	7
4	8,9

The cumulative array would look like this:

2	7	8	10

Then the random number between 0 and 9 inclusive is generated. If the number were 5 then shirt #2 would be chosen and copied into the mating pool. If the random number were 0 then shirt #1 would be chosen and copied into the mating pool.

11.4.2.3. Crossover

As described in chapter 2, crossover models the swapping of values of two strings about a pre-defined crossover point. The crossover functions simulate a single point crossover operation. Two parents are randomly chosen from the mating pool. Each string in the mating pool has an equal probability of being selected. Once the two parents are selected they are copied into two temporary arrays (*parent1[ ]* and *parent2 [ ]*). Another random number is generated and if this falls below the probability of crossover (*CROSSOVER_PROB*) then crossover occurs. The values of the two parents are swapped about the crossover point and copied into the new population (In this case the new string is copied over the old string in the population array). The crossover is achieved by using the temporary arrays, *parent1[ ]* and *parent2[ ]* as an intermediate when copying from the *mating_pool[ ]* to the *population[ ]*. If crossover does not occur then the two strings are simply copied into the new population.

11.4.2.4. Mutation

Mutation to a string is simulated in order to overcome the problem of a sub optimum solution dominating the population. The *check_same* function is designed to overcome a member of the population dominating the population thus disrupting the search process. The goal of this function is to check if identical strings exist. If the number of identical strings is greater than a predefined value (in this case the value is two), then mutation is to be performed (i.e., the third identical string will be mutated).

The *mutation* function mutates three random bits in the given string. This results in a minimal alteration to the original string and introduces slightly new genetic material into the search.

The Start and Continue process component shown in Figure 11.2 enables the G.A search process to begin, continue or go back a step via user interaction. The Convert Population to Images component in Figure 11.3 takes the population of strings from the GA component and converts them into a format that is easily readable by the Graphical Representation component shown in Figure 11.2. This component will be covered in some more detail in the implementation section 11.4.

11.4.3 Interactive Component

The broad flow of interaction diagram of the interactive missing person clothing identification system is shown in Figure 11.7. The various steps are briefly outlined in this section

1 – Population Initialized.
The initial population has been filled with a random set of strings.
2 – Shirt Drawn.
The individual parts of a shirt have all been drawn to produce a shirt as a whole.
3 – Shirts Displayed.
All shirts, with each shirt corresponding to a member of the population, have been displayed on the screen to the user.
4 – Relevance Feedback Received.
The user has completed inputting the relevance rankings for each shirt according to how closely they resemble the goal state.
5 – Current Generation Completed
6 – Mating Pool Filled.
The mating pool, used in the Genetic Algorithm search process, has been filled with the fittest strings after the reproduction operation. The Relevance feedback rankings are used as a fitness function.

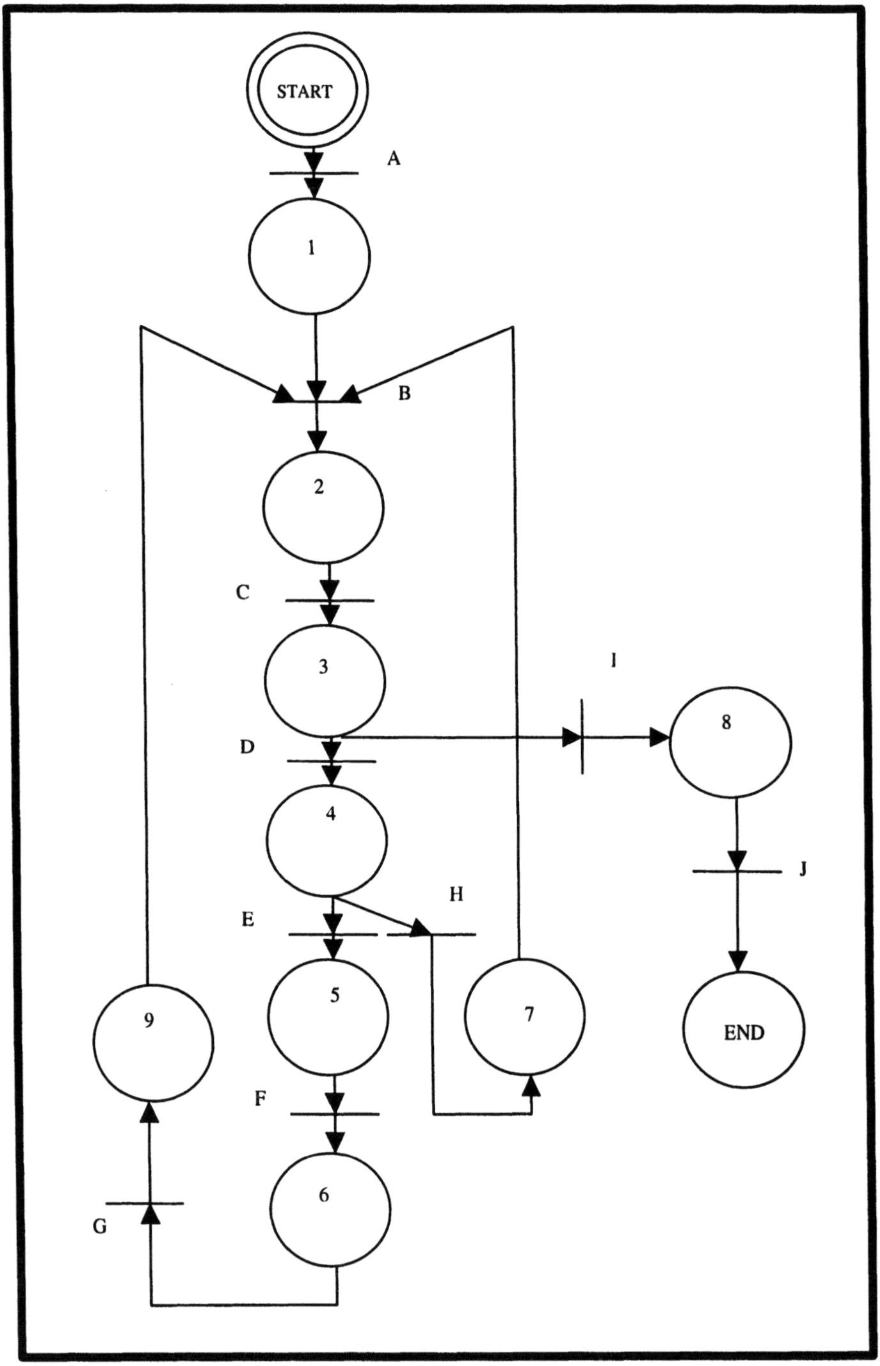

Figure 11.7: Broad Flow of Interaction

7 – Previous Population Restored.
The previous population has been restored due to the user request to 'go back a step'. The search process now uses this population as the current population.
8 – Details Screen.
The screen that includes the facilities that allow the user to input his/her details is displayed.
9 – Next Generation Completed
The next generation of strings have been completed after the crossover operation has been applied to strings in the mating pool.

The letters 'A' to 'J' in Figure 11.8 represent different user events. These are enumerated below.

A – User presses 'Start' button.
B – Draw Shirt.
C – Display Shirts.
D – Relevance Feedback.
E – User presses 'Continue' button.
F – Perform Reproduction
G – Perform Crossover
H - User presses 'Back' button.
I – Shirt Selected.
J – User Details.

11.5. Implementation and Results

This section discusses some parts of the implementation and the data structures used for developing the program. It is followed by a visual depiction of some of the implementation results of the system A sample missing report form and a typical missing person's report is shown in Figure 11.8 and 11.9 respectively.

11.5.1. Programming Languages Used

The two programming languages used are JavaScript and HyperText Mark up Language (HTML). The system was implemented on Internet Explorer Ver. 5.0 and is designed to work for any Internet Explorer browsers that incorporate the JavaScript (or the Microsoft version of JavaScript, JScript) language version 1.3 or above.

Post a missing person report

1. Downloading a text file (PDF or Word)

2. Writing out the report and sending it via email

3. Directly filling out a form on the web page and submitting the form

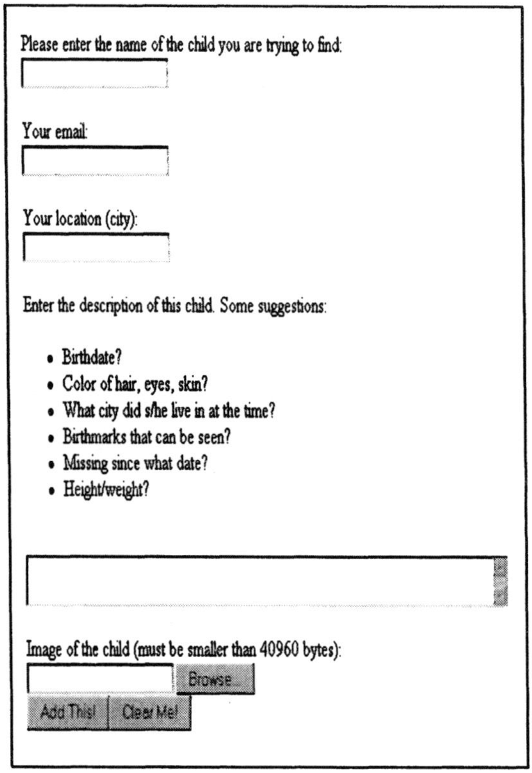

Figure 11.8: Missing Report Form (www.missingreport.com)

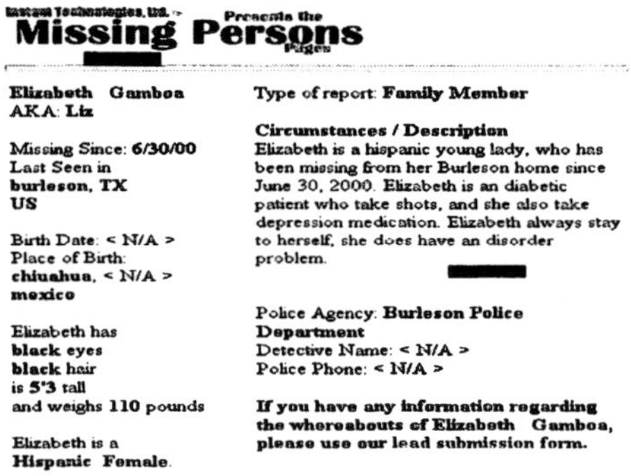

Presents the
Missing Persons
Pages

Elizabeth Gamboa
AKA: **Liz**

Missing Since: **6/30/00**
Last Seen in
burleson, TX
US

Birth Date: < N/A >
Place of Birth:
chiuahua, < N/A >
mexico

Elizabeth has
black eyes
black hair
is **5'3** tall
and weighs **110** pounds

Elizabeth is a
Hispanic Female.

Type of report: **Family Member**

Circumstances / Description
Elizabeth is a hispanic young lady, who has been missing from her Burleson home since June 30, 2000. Elizabeth is an diabetic patient who take shots, and she also take depression medication. Elizabeth always stay to herself, she does have an disorder problem.

Police Agency: **Burleson Police Department**
Detective Name: < N/A >
Police Phone: < N/A >

If you have any information regarding the whereabouts of Elizabeth Gamboa, please use our lead submission form.

Figure 11.9: Typical Missing Person's Report (www.missingreport.com)

11.5.2 Data Structures

The data structures of most importance are those that are concerned with the storage of the population of strings. The population of strings and the mating pool are stored as multi-dimensional arrays. Each index in the array (i.e. each bit in the string) refers to a unique part of the shirt. For example *population [9][2]* in the population array refers to the collar of shirt number 3 (remembering that counting begins at 0), and *population [12][0]* refers to the vertical stripes of shirt number 1.

A multi-dimensional array is also used to store a copy of the population (used when going back a step), and to store the filename associated with each image used in the make up of the shirt (see discussion on 'converting population to images' below).

The following Global Constants are used to set the dimensions of the arrays during initialization as well as store variables required during the search process: POP_SIZE (number of strings in the population, integer), STRING_LENGTH (length of the string, integer), MP_SIZE (number of strings in the mating pool, integer), CROSSOVER_POINT (index value for the crossover point, integer) and CROSSOVER_PROB (probability of crossover, double). Figure 11.10 illustrates these structures.

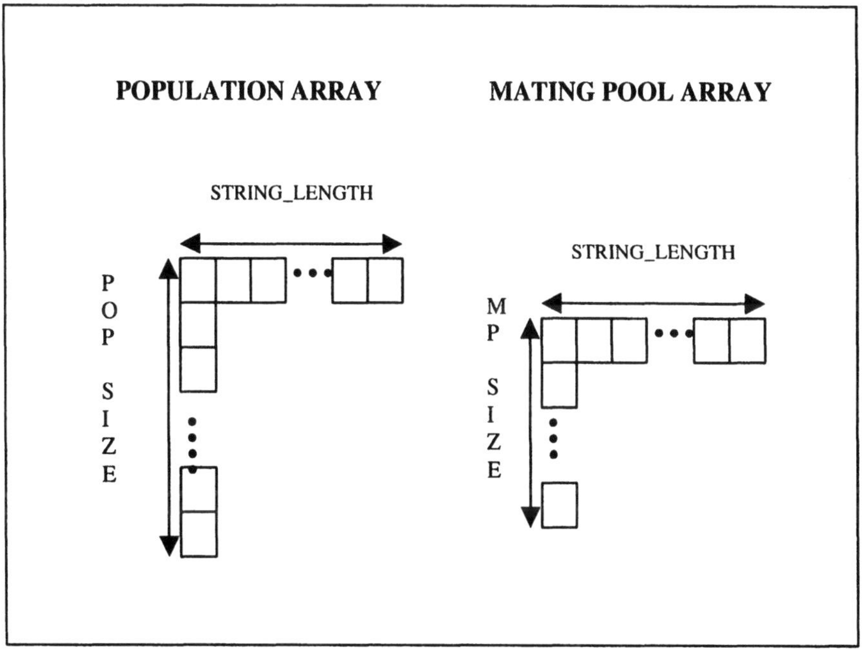

Figure 11.10: Program Structures

11.5.3. Relevance Feedback

The relevance feedback is primarily implemented using HTML. The code in Figure 11.11 corresponds to relevance feedback form for a single shirt (shirt #10).

```
<FORM NAME="myform">
<B>#10</B>
<INPUT TYPE="radio" NAME="rel" onCLick="if (this.checked) {gf(0,9)}" >NON REL.
<INPUT TYPE="radio" NAME="rel" onCLick="if (this.checked) {gf(1,9)}" >UNDEC.
<INPUT TYPE="radio" NAME="rel" onCLick="if (this.checked) {gf(2,9)}" >REL.
<IMG SRC='selectbuttonup.jpg' onMouseOver="src='selectbutton.jpg'"
onMouseOut="src='selectbuttonup.jpg'"onCLick="selectg(9)">
</FORM>
```

Figure 11.11: Sample Code for Modeling Relevance feedback

When the user checks a radio box, the *gf* function is called with two arguments. The first argument relates to the weight given to the shirt, and the second argument relates to the index corresponding to that shirt. For the example above, if the user chose shirt #10 to be relevant, then *gf (2,9)* would be called. The *gf* function simply multiplies the weight by 2 and stores this vale in the *rel_feedback[ ]* array.

11.5.3. Converting Population to Images

The population is stored in a multi-dimensional array. The first index of this array corresponds to a shirt part. *Population[B][A]* would refer to part B of shirt #A. The actual value of *population[B][A]* refers to the color of part B of shirt #A. The index B and the value of *population[B][A]* are used to form the filename for the image file that matches the required shirt part and color. Consequently the filenames for each image take the form "*picB_[B][A].GIF*".

Hence the filename for the following image:

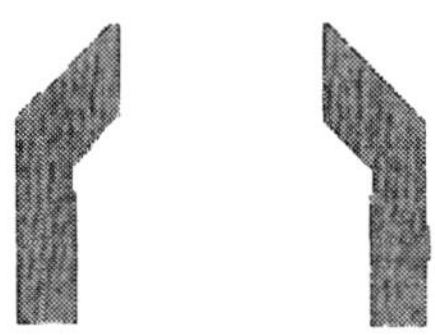

is *pic2_3.gif* where '2' refers to the index for long sleeves and '3' refers to the color blue. The function *imagefilename* performs this conversion and stores the filenames as strings in the *file_names[ ]* array.

Although *population[0][ ]* denotes whether long or short sleeves are used, the filenames for both short and long sleeve images are still copied into the *file_names[ ]* array (this is also the case for *population[10][ ]* which denotes the existence of vertical or horizontal stripes.) To overcome this problem a series of if statements have been used to clear the non required shirt part from being displayed. The *imagefilename* function checks to see which shirt part is not supposed to be shown and copies a clear image in its place (the file name for this clear image *is 'clear3.GIF'*).

11.5.4. Starting the Process

Figure 11.12 represents the main interface of the clothing identification (composite) system. The process begins by the user clicking the 'start' button shown in Figure 11.12. This user action calls the *startd* function, which in turn initializes the population (*initialize_population*), converts the population to images (*imagefilename*), and draws the initial random population (*show_image*).

11.5.5. Continuing the Process

When the 'CONT.' button is clicked (not shown in Figure 11.12), the process is continued via the *cont* function. This function begins by declaring an array *pop_copy[ ]*. *Pop_copy[ ]* stores an identical copy of the population. This is used when the user requires the process to 'go back a step'. The function then proceeds to call *selection* (to perform reproduction), *exchange* (to perform crossover), *check_same*, *imagefilename*, and finally *show_image* functions respectively.

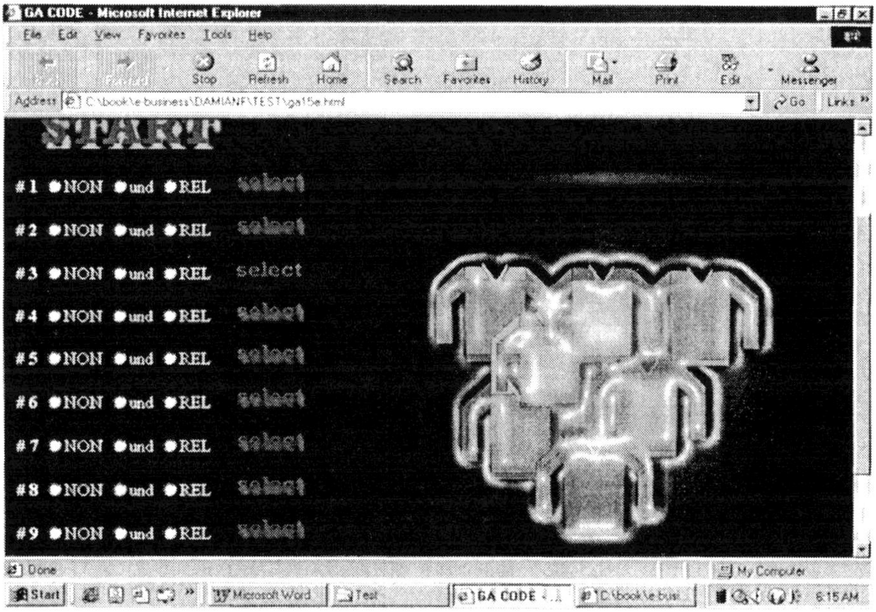

Figure 11.12: Opening Page of Clothing Identification System

11.5.6. Go 'Back One Step' in the Search Process

This option is enabled when the user clicks on the 'BACK' button located at the bottom of the page of Figure 11.12 (as opposed to the 'back' button located on the browsers tool bar).

The *back* function, when called, copies the previous population (stored in *pop_copy[ ]*) back into the *population[ ]* array. It then proceeds to convert the population to images using the imagefilename function, and draw the images using *show_image* function. At this stage the search can go back only one step.

11.5.7. User Feedback and Show Filenames

The *selectg* function is invoked when the user clicks on the 'select' button. The function contains HTML code to write the various forms required to receive the user's details. The file names that make up the user selected shirt are also output to one of the forms, making it possible for the webmaster to re-create the shirt. The user details screen includes the facility for the user to upload two photos of the missing person.

As this program is intended to be incorporated into the many missing person web pages, the user details screen may require additional forms, depending on each individual 'missing persons' web site. The code has been designed so that the page is easily modifiable and any additional fields can be simply added. Although they are included, the web master of the missing person site may discard these forms and use any existing pages that are already implemented on their system. The most important aspect of the user details component is its ability to provide a means by which the web master can receive the filenames that make up the shirt chosen by the user, hence this particular form is vital and must not be removed.

11.6. Relevance Feedback Results

Figures 11.13, 11.14 and 11.15 show results of relevance feedback in the web based interactive clothing composite system. Figure 11.14 displays a range of 10 shirts after user initiates the system by selecting the START button. Please note the design of shirts 3 and 5 in Figure 11.13. Figure 11.14 shows that the user selects shirts 5 and 3 as related by selecting the REL radio buttons. All other shirts are selected as non-related as can be seen in Figure 11.14. After select the related shirt designs, the user selects the CONT button shown in Figure 11.14. The feedback is used by the GA agent to optimize search and display revised shirt designs as shown in Figure 11.15. It may be noted that shirt3 and 5 shown in Figure 11.15 are quite similar. The user can also select the BACK button shown in Figure 11.14 and go back one step in the search process.

11.7. Summary

This chapter describes a web based missing person clothing identification application for law enforcement agencies. It employs relevance feedback as a means of involving the user in identifying the type, color and design of the shirt worn by a missing persons. It further allows the user to define the objective function for optimizing the search using a Genetic Algorithm agent. It thus illustrates human-centeredness from two perspectives. Firstly, from a multimedia information system perspective, in order to capture the user semantics it employs the relevance feedback method. Secondly, from a computational intelligence perspective the user is involved in defining objective function for optimizing search.

The on line web based missing person clothing identification system primarily consists of three component categories. These are the shirt component, GA component and the interactive component. The shirt component defines a GA string based on 13 different parts of a shirt. It uses the 13 parts to draw and display different types of shirts with different designs to the user. The GA component performs initialization, reproduction, crossover and mutation to create the shirt design and color which matches with the user's perception of the shirt worn by the missing person. Finally, the interactive component is used to initialize the system, take relevance feedback from the user and display shirts for user to select from till one finally matches the user's perception.

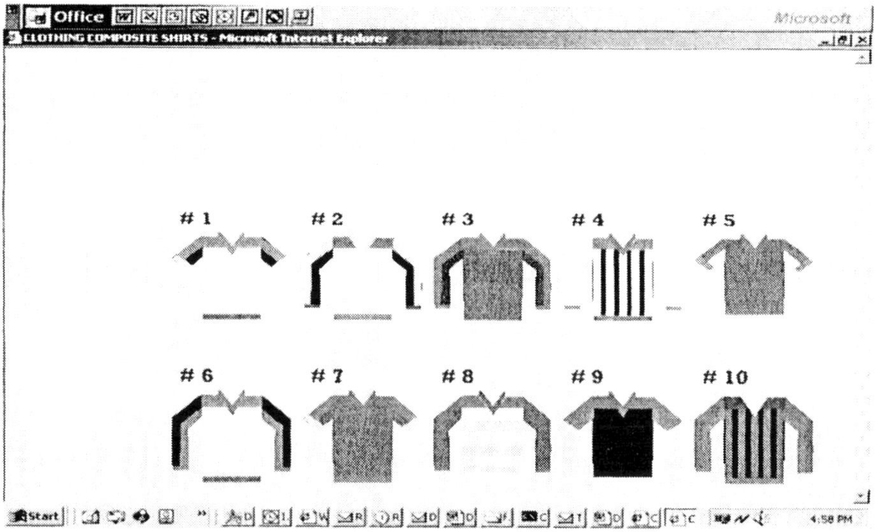

Figure 11.13: Original Shirt Designs Without Relevance Feedback

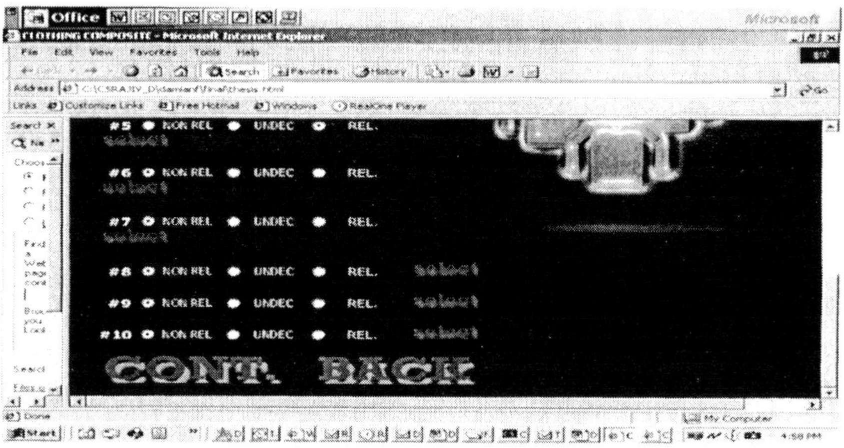

Figure 11.14: Relevance Feedback on 10 Shirts Using Radio Buttons

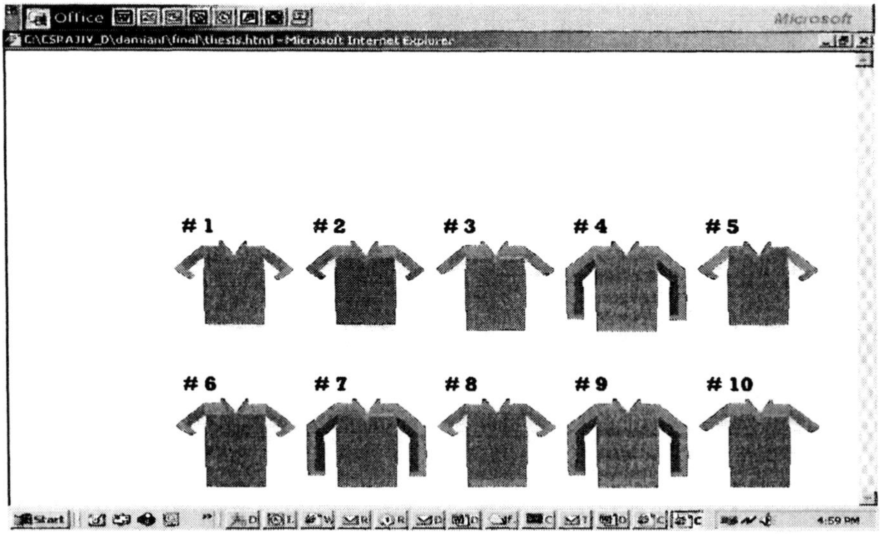

Figure 11.15: Revised Shirt Designs (Note 3 and 5 are Similar)

References

Bimbo, A.D., Pala, P., and Santini, S. (1994) "Visual Image Retrieval by Elastic Deformation of Object Sketches," in *Proceedings of IEEE Symposium on Visual Languages*, pp. 216-23.

Buckley, C. and Salton, G. (1995) "Optimization of Relevance feedback Weights," *in Proceedings SIGIR'95.*

Holland, J. (1975) *Adaptation in natural and Artificial Systems,* University of Michigan Press, Ann Arbor, MI, USA.

Michalewicz, Z. (1992) *Genetic Algorithms + Data Structures = Evolution Programs*, Springer-Verlag, Berlin.

Rocchio, J.J. (1971) "Relevance Feedback in Information Retrieval," *SMART Retrieval System*, Prentice Hall, pp. 313-23.

Salton, G. and McGill, M.J.(1983) *Introduction to Modern Information Retrieval*, New York: McGraw-Hill

Salton, G. and McGill, M.J.(1988) *Improving Retrieval Performance by Relevance Feedback*, New York: McGraw-Hill

Takagi, H.K.(2002) "Humanization of Computational Intelligence," Plenary Speech in IEEE world Congress On Computational Intelligence, Hawaii, May 2002.

Takagi, H.K. (2001) "Interactive Evolutionary Computation: Fusion of the Capabilities of EC Optimization and Human Evaluation," *Proceedings of the IEEE*, vol. 89, No. 9, September

Index

A

C

D

E

H

I

K

M

O

P

X